Critical Acclaim for *Habits of the Heart*

"Brilliant analysis . . . Easily the richest and most readable study of American society since David Riesman's '50s classic *The Lonely Crowd.*"

—*Newsweek*

"*Habits of the Heart* holds up a mirror to American values, makes us examine ourselves and dares us to question where our society is going. [It] will make you question your own habits and look into your own heart. Not many books possess that ability."

— George Keller, *Baltimore Sun*

"Beautifully written . . . a set of acute observations on the American national character. This book states quite unequivocally that the United States is good, and could be a lot better."

—David Martin, *Times Literary Supplement*

"Penetrating . . . remarkable . . . well written and absolutely free of jargon, [it] conveys a powerful moral urgency."

—Peter Steinfels, (front page) *New York Times Book Review*

"The contemporary benchmark from which to look back and look forward in the continuing inquiry about American character."

—Daniel Bell

INDIVIDUALISM & COMMITMENT in American Life

Readings on the Themes of

HABITS OF THE HEART

EDITORS

ROBERT N. BELLAH

RICHARD MADSEN

WILLIAM M. SULLIVAN

ANN SWIDLER

STEVEN M. TIPTON

Harper & Row, Publishers, New York

Cambridge, Philadelphia, San Francisco, Washington

London, Mexico City, São Paulo, Singapore, Sydney

Copyright acknowledgments appear on pages 473–475.

Also available: Study Guide to *Individulaism and Commitment in American Life*
A free study guide designed to direct discussion with the context of a varitey of courses and study groups is available. Please order #TG/13. Requests should be sent to: Department #361, Harper & Row, Publishers, 10 East 53 Street, New York, NY 10022

INDIVIDUALISM AND COMMITMENT IN AMERICAN LIFE. Copyright © 1987 by Robert N. Bellah, Richard Madsen, William M. Sullivan, Ann Swidler, Steven M. Tipton. All rights reserved. Printed in the United States of America. No part of this book may be used or reproduced in any manner whatsoever without written permission except in the case of brief quotations embodied in critical articles and reviews. For information address Harper & Row, Publishers, Inc., 10 East 53rd Street, New York, N.Y. 10022. Published simultaneously in Canada by Fitzhenry & Whiteside Limited, Toronto.

FIRST EDITION

Designer: Ruth Bornschlegel

Copy editor: Rick Hermann

Library of Congress Cataloging-in-Publication Data
Individualism and commitment in American life.

1. United States—Civilization—1945– .
2. National characteristics, American. 3. Individualism.
4. Civics. 5. Habits of the heart. I. Bellah,
Robert Neelly, 1927–
E169.12I47. 1987 306′.0973 86-46213
ISBN 0-06-096191-0 (pbk.)

87 88 89 90 91 MPC 10 9 8 7 6 5 4 3 2 1

CONTENTS

76335-

PREFACE

This reader is a sourcebook and companion volume to *Habits of the Heart,* and it stands in its own right as an interdisciplinary guide to exploring the moral meaning of American institutions and culture. The book focuses inquiry on themes of individualism and commitment in our lives together. It also reaches across the contrasting traditions of our culture and the varied structures of our society to provide a contemporary vision of America that unifies humanistic and social-scientific points of view.

The anthology is organized into eleven parts so that it can be read in parallel sequence with the chapters of *Habits of the Heart.* The readings are also thematically arranged to accompany varied approaches to the study of American society and thought. "America's Cultural Conversation," the essay by Robert Bellah in Part One, takes Tocqueville's "Of Individualism in Democracies" as a point of departure and introduces the volume as a whole. Each of the ten sections of readings that follow begins with a brief introduction that outlines the central themes uniting the articles in the section; the introduction also summarizes the content and significance of each selection.

The readings in Part Two trace the roots of America's major cultural traditions by juxtaposing representative excerpts from John Winthrop, Thomas Jefferson, Ben Franklin, and Walt Whitman. Parts Three through Six deal in turn with the elements of conventional "private life": selfhood; love, marriage, and the family; friendship and interpersonal relations. These concentric circles of everyday life and interaction lead into "public life" in Parts Seven through Ten. These selections pursue the dimensions of local community, the callings of work and citizenship, religion, and the national society. Part Eleven concludes with visions of America's future that are at once analytical and moral.

The selected readings range from seminal works of America's founders through studies of its social and historical growth to current criticism of our culture and institutions. The breadth and binocularity of vision that results is especially important on subjects where gender, race, class, and generation make for deep differences in our experience of the life we share and our efforts to make moral sense of it.

The readings seek to outline a broadly inclusive, socially representative angle of vision, although they cannot fill in the whole of it. They do not fully represent all our founding mothers and fathers, for example. Rather than achieving comprehensive social coverage, our aim is to reveal the underlying cultural drama played out among the key experiential and moral viewpoints represented in the texts, and to clarify the moral argument they sustain. Thus, Part Three provides examples of *social* selfhood and asks what it means to be Negro or black, female or male, hipster or square. Part Four probes the interrelation of gender, race, and class in shaping the meaning of love and marriage. Part Seven looks at both the Chicago ghetto and the embattled white lower middle class in Canarsie, and it exposes the underlying structure and origins of our society's segmentation.

These readings suggest how differences in experience and attitude are not simply a function of different locations in social space and historical time, but are formed by diverse cultural modes of understanding. These find expression in characteristic patterns of language which define our life together even as they reflect it. The brief literary selections that set off many sections of the readings give eloquent voice to the distinctive understanding and discourse of one generation or the next, of women or men, black or white, middle class or poor. These narrative and lyrical voices intersect with other sorts of evidence and interpretation—historical, ethnographic, philosophical, and sociological. Such differences both inform and are formed by modes of discourse and understanding voiced by various social groups bound together in their very disagreement.

Thus, Carol Gilligan distinguishes in Part Three between women's primary moral syntax of caring and responsible relationship in contrast to men's stress on the equality of individuals' rights and rules of fair play. So, too, we hear the conflicting sermons of Jerry Falwell and Jesse Jackson in Part Nine; and the political addresses of Dwight Eisenhower, Ronald Reagan, and Mario Cuomo in Part Ten. In Part Eleven, Helen Vendler reflects on teaching others how to love the classic stories that we have loved and lived by, while Wendell Berry reveals the moral truth of both biblical and classical insight into America's "unsettling."

These voices and visions bring to life this book's thesis that the meaning of America is not a monolith or a monologue but a living argument. We experience and engage this argument in forms that vary with gender, race, class, and age. These forms also vary with the traditions of our culture, the institutional spheres of our society, and the epochs of our history. Yet through the binding continuity of this argument that forms the heart of our cultural conversation, we can criticize and transform our institutions, not only defend them. We can judge ourselves for betraying our ideals and renew ourselves by trying to live up to them.

The editors wish to thank Judith Rosseli for her help in gathering the source materials for this reader, and Gary Hauk for his bibliographic and administrative assistance in compiling it. We are grateful to Harry Boyte, Elizabeth Fox-Genovese, Brooks Holifield, and David Minter for their suggestions in selecting the readings. Our thanks also go to Janet Goldstein at Harper & Row for her help in planning and editing the book.

Robert Bellah wrote the selection in Part One that introduces the volume. Richard Madsen, William Sullivan, and Steven Tipton shared in writing the sections that introduce each subsequent part of the readings. Tipton conceived this book and joined Madsen in its initial organization, with Swidler's counsel, while Sullivan bore chief responsibility for its final editing.

PART ONE

INTRODUCTION

AMERICA'S CULTURAL CONVERSATION

$\blacklozenge$ $\blacksquare$ $\blacklozenge$

The short chapter from *Democracy in America* entitled "Of Individualism in Democracies" (which follows this essay) states in condensed form the question which *Habits of the Heart* set out to answer, namely, have we so "withdrawn into the circle of family and friends" that we have finally become "shut up in the solitude of [our] own heart[s]?" In other words, has the individualism that Tocqueville observed with anxiety become so all-pervasive that we are no longer citizens?

In this brief chapter and elsewhere in *Democracy in America* Tocqueville contrasts the tendencies of an egalitarian democratic society with those of a hierarchical, aristocratic one. He sees virtues and defects in both and in the end favors a way of combining the advantages of each rather than a pure form of either. At one point (in a footnote to chapter 21, part III, volume II) he indicates that it is the chaotic but creative moment of transition from aristocracy to democracy that makes the best form of society possible. At that moment the repressive and conservative features of the old society are broken through so that new ideas can come forth, but there is still enough social solidarity left that initiative from popular leaders can mobilize support for significant reform. What Tocqueville is saying is that critical discussion, the production of new ideas, experiment, and reform can occur most easily at that moment. When traditional, hierarchical relationships are too strong, there is little room for discussion and experiment. But when people are reduced to isolated individuals, there, too, public discussion and popular initiative will languish and decisions will be made by administrative bureaucrats in the interest of maintaining their own power. Tocqueville's practical suggestions for maintaining freedom in a democratic society all have to do with ways by which the creative moment might be prolonged by cultivating the right mores and building the right institutions.

Habits of the Heart is an effort to look at the mores and institutions today to see whether or not they have the vitality to produce discussion, vision, and innovation. This reader is an effort to amplify the discussion by bringing in material from past and contemporary writers that has influenced the authors of *Habits* or supplements our argument. This book can be seen as an attempt to widen the circle of discussion beyond *Habits,* both to find out where we are and to assess the chances for strengthening the life of active citizenship in America today.

The authors of *Habits of the Heart,* following Tocqueville and others, have argued that the citizens of a democracy can effectively govern themselves only if they face their common problems in light of who they are as defined by their past. Truthfulness about memory and about current reality, tested by critical argument and discussion in the public arena, is the precondition for democratic self-rule. But there are many barriers to such truthfulness in public discussion. Individualism narrows our concern to our own immediate problems, often cutting us off from our own past as well as the history of our society. The languages of individualism—utilitarian and expressive, as we discuss them in *Habits*—are impoverished vehicles for public discussion because they focus on immediate payoff or inner feelings. They do not help us think about the traditions that have formed us or about the larger problems of our society, including the problems of those in situations quite different from our own. The monoculture of the mass media is couched largely in utilitarian and expressive form. It is oriented to our immediate wants, desires, and emotions. Television, for example, is much more effective in transmitting powerful images and emotional reactions than in stimulating careful and rational discussion, though perhaps when consciously and carefully combined with reading and discussion it could have an educational role to play in the life of a democratic society.

The selections included in this reader are intended to increase the competence of the person who has read *Habits of the Heart,* or is currently reading it, to understand where American culture came from and what its current problems are. Both *Habits* and this book are also intended to serve as the basis for the kind of discussion essential in a free society. It is therefore important to say something about the focus of this book and its limitations as well as its strengths.

Habits of the Heart explicitly concentrated on the white middle class, and this reader, staying close to the book, maintains that focus, though it significantly broadens the circle by including selections dealing with working-class and black Americans. The focus on the white middle class was determined by the limited resources of a small research group and even more by a sense that the white middle class is a strategic point of entry into the study of American culture because that culture has been so oriented to this group from the beginning. The white middle class has been the model held up for all other groups in America. If its success is partial, or hollow, or seriously flawed, then the whole of society is in trouble. If this group has difficulty holding on to a sense of its own past, is losing a sense of its own historic identity, then by understanding why this is the case we may begin to understand the forces that erode all communities of memory in America. In any case, to say that one group is socially powerful and culturally central is not to say that other groups, racial minorities in particular, are not important. Indeed, the response to *Habits* from blacks, Chicanos, Asian-Americans, and American Indians has suggested that the problems of the white middle class are endemic to all groups in our society whenever significant numbers of them enter the middle class, however differently their experience may be nuanced. We hope and expect that research and discussion stimulated by *Habits* will continue to widen the circle of discussion so that the genuine pluralism of American society will be represented more adequately than we have been able to do so far in *Habits* or even in this reader.

One advantage of our approach is that it may help us distinguish genuine from spurious pluralism. Indeed, *pluralism* is one of those overworked words whose meaning bears examination. *Pluralism* seems to imply that our society is made up of individuals and groups that are distinctly, even radically, different. But when we realize that belief in pluralism is almost mandatory in our society, our suspicions might begin to be aroused. A belief that we are all unique (and unique in exactly the same way) is a basic tenet of American individualism. The assertion of pluralism therefore can be merely an expression of our basic individualism rather than the recognition of genuine cultural differences, concerning, among other things, individualism itself. Differences arising from gender, skin color, national origin, religion, or language cannot automatically be assumed to correlate with a tangible pluralism. If persons different in these respects share the attitudes and practices of the white middle class, then no genuine pluralism is involved. The study of the white middle class is exemplary if it can show us, as we believe it can, that even the white middle class was not always dominated by the culture of utilitarian and expressive individualism, that even this group carries traditions and conceptions of community that are not easily reconciled with the presently dominant culture. Once we see that even in the mainstream of American culture, among its most dominant and favored groups, there are communities of memory (see *Habits* Glossary) that carry a richer range of options than modern individualism has allowed, that there survive in a variety of forms of what in *Habits* we call the traditions of biblical religion and civic republicanism (as discussed in parts II, VII, VIII, IX, and XI of this reader), then we are in a position to draw on the many other communities of memory that the dominant culture has even more effectively submerged. The strategy is one of progressively widening cultural recovery, and we hope this reader can significantly contribute to that process.

Though the focus both in *Habits* and in this reader is on culture, we do not imagine that the issues with which we deal are matters merely of competing ideas. Rather, cultural ideas and symbols are closely related to the structure of society and its existing institutions. Structural features, such as the economy and the state, are repeatedly referred to in both books. The story we tell is one of an essentially agrarian and small-town society transformed by the growth of the market economy, the bureaucratic state, and modern technology. It is in terms of these three critical developments within modern society that modern individualism makes sense, as is discussed particularly in chapters 5 and 6 of *Habits* and in parts V, VI, and VIII of this reader.

Yet together these three elements (economy, bureaucracy, technology) cannot make a viable society and do not account for the fullness of our present common life. In particular, the family, the local community, religion, and democratic politics require beliefs and practices rooted in communities of memory. Though these elements of the "lifeworld" are eroded, even "colonized," by the modern economic, bureaucratic, and technological "systems," to use the language of Jürgen Habermas, they nonetheless survive and provide the possible bases for recovering social coherence and solidarity. Indeed, the only hope for a free, self-governing society is in the revitalization of these lifeworld structures and their effective control of the modern systems. Many of the selections in parts V through VIII of this reader are concerned with the structures and institutions that impinge on our lives and how we use our cultural traditions to think about them. Active, critical discussion of these issues is an important aspect strengthening the lifeworld institutions—family, local community, religion, and democratic politics—but such discussion must eventuate in decisions that effectively change structures, for merely changing consciousness will not be enough. We never imagined that "a change of heart" would solve all our problems. For example, if corporate decisions about plant closings seriously endanger the viability of families and whole local communities, then effective action to change the decision-making process and mitigate its consequences will have to be taken—action that will almost certainly involve local, regional, and national politics as well as efforts to influence corporations themselves. On the whole both *Habits* and this reader are more concerned with the cultural bases of social policy than about policy itself, though a more systematic analysis of policy alternatives is the next major work that the *Habits of the Heart* group plans to undertake. But the Catholic Bishops' "Pastoral Letter on Catholic Social Teaching and the U.S. Economy," which is excerpted in part XI of this reader, could well be read in its entirety as an example of how cultural concerns can lead to policy recommendations.

Both in *Habits of the Heart* and in this reader we contrast the first language of modern individualism, with its amalgam of the utilitarian and expressive strands, to our second languages of biblical religion and civic republicanism, and suggest that the priorities should be reversed. Some of our critics have objected to that suggestion as returning to a pattern that would merely substitute an older form of domination for a newer one. Taking that criticism seriously, we can suggest the metaphor of multilingualism instead of the metaphor of first and second languages. Utilitarian and expressive individualism are useful in their particular spheres, such as the calculation of economic decisions or the handling of some aspects of interpersonal relations. They only become destructive when they become general languages of moral and political discussion and crowd out considerations better expressed by biblical religion and civic republicanism. In such a situation we would still argue that our most urgent task is to recover the endangered languages by understanding better the traditions that lie behind them and the vital institutions in our current society that depend upon them. Such an effort would involve not abandoning the languages of utilitarian and expressive individualism, but learning the limits of their usefulness and recovering the other languages that we have half forgotten: in other words, becoming genuinely multilingual. It might be a useful exercise to go over the selections in this reader, classifying them in terms of which language they are primarily using, criticizing them when they push particular languages beyond their appropriate limits (which would involve some hard thinking about what those limits are), and choosing those selections for special consideration that are of most help to us in recovering the endangered languages, perhaps following leads from this reader to the originals for a fuller discussion.

One of the many aspects of American life that did not receive the attention it deserves in *Habits* or in this reader is education in general and university education in particular (though there are some comments about higher education in chapter 11 of *Habits* and in the selection by Helen Vendler in part XI of this reader). Both because of the intrinsic importance of education, and especially because this reader will probably be used mostly by college undergraduates, it is appropriate to conclude this introduction with some comments about the relationship between the argument of *Habits of the Heart* and education.

Education is an institution that relates closely both to what we have called the lifeworld—those institutions where we live our lives in an effort to fulfill the good life for human beings; that is, family, community, religion, and democratic politics—and to what we have called the systems—those institutions that provide the means (wealth, power, technological conveniences) for living the good life, but which always threaten to become ends in themselves; that is, the economy, bureaucracy, and technology. Education has traditionally, as in the Greek idea of *paideia,* been a means of forming character and preparing people to become good citizens in the lifeworld. But education is also central for the acquisition of skills that make one effective in the systems.

Today we can see a conflict at every level between these two functions of education. There are those who see education as essentially in the service of the systems, and who emphasize things such as math scores and computer literacy almost exclusively. This conception of education fits in nicely with Alasdair MacIntyre's notion of "bureaucratic individualism" as described in the selection from his book *After Virtue* in part VI of this reader. Acquisition of skills useful to the systems will be rewarded in the form of good jobs and high pay that benefit the individual privately but neither improve his character nor necessarily contribute to the common good. Indeed, education as a means to purely private advancement has almost crowded out the idea of education for character and citizenship. And even though these older ideas receive lip service in primary and secondary education, they have few defenders in the university, which is dedicated to the advance of specialized (technical) knowledge on the one hand and the preparation of students for higher-echelon jobs in the systems on the other.

Yet there are still those who argue, and we hope that our work will strengthen them in their arguments, that university education is concerned with reflection upon and critical appropriation of those aspects of the tradition that help us define who we are as persons and what kind of society we ought to live in. That process of critical appropriation should, of course, take place in the context of an informed sense of our present reality and problems, also a significant subject for study and reflection in a university education. As a result of this process, students become genuinely educated persons who understand their future careers not simply as means to the acquisition of private rewards but as forms of public service, whose rewards are as much the satisfaction that comes from forwarding the common good as from any personal enrichment or prestige.

From this point of view the university is not only a place for specialized research and the acquisition of skills. It is also a "community of interpreters," to borrow a phrase from the American philosopher Josiah Royce, including both teachers and students as they attempt to understand the past that defines them and engage that past in a critical dialogue about our present problems. Indeed, it is our hope that a course in which *Habits of the Heart* and this reader are assigned might become in microcosm just such a community of interpreters engaged in the study, transmission, and reinterpretation of our various traditions as they impinge on our common life in our efforts to become better persons and build a better society. Learning in such a community is not a matter of acquiring skills or accumulating objective knowledge alone. It is also a process of critical self-reflection, about both ourselves and our world, that calls upon our hearts as well as our minds, and that has the capacity to change both ourselves and the society in which we live. In such a community, above all, we do not merely learn what the authors we read say (though that is in itself a demanding task). We struggle with the authors, seek to understand their weaknesses and oversights as well as what they have to contribute, so that we may come up with our own contributions to the ongoing community of interpreters. In so doing we do not stand apart from those we study but rather participate with them in a common enterprise that links us with all other human beings past, present, and future.*

Robert N. Bellah
May 1987

*For a fuller explication of this conception of the intellectual life, see the Appendix to *Habits of the Heart.*

Democracy In America

OF INDIVIDUALISM IN DEMOCRACIES

I have shown how, in ages of equality, every man finds his beliefs within himself, and I shall now go on to show that all his feelings are turned in on himself.

"Individualism" is a word recently coined to express a new idea. Our fathers only knew about egoism.

Egoism is a passionate and exaggerated love of self which leads a man to think of all things in terms of himself and to prefer himself to all.

Individualism is a calm and considered feeling which disposes each citizen to isolate himself from the mass of his fellows and withdraw into the circle of family and friends; with this little society formed to his taste, he gladly leaves the greater society to look after itself.

Egoism springs from a blind instinct; individualism is based on misguided judgment rather than depraved feeling. It is due more to inadequate understanding than to perversity of heart.

Egoism sterilizes the seeds of every virtue; individualism at first only dams the spring of public virtues, but in the long run it attacks and destroys all the others too and finally merges in egoism.

Egoism is a vice as old as the world. It is not peculiar to one form of society more than another.

Individualism is of democratic origin and threatens to grow as conditions get more equal.

Among aristocratic nations families maintain the same station for centuries and often live in the same place. So there is a sense

Alexis de Tocqueville, "Of Individualism in Democracies," from *Democracy in America*, vol. 2, trans. George Lawrence, ed. J. P. Mayer (New York: Doubleday, Anchor Books, 1969), pp. 506–8.

in which all the generations are contemporaneous. A man almost always knows about his ancestors and respects them; his imagination extends to his great-grandchildren, and he loves them. He freely does his duty by both ancestors and descendants and often sacrifices personal pleasures for the sake of beings who are no longer alive or are not yet born.

Moreover, aristocratic institutions have the effect of linking each man closely with several of his fellows.

Each class in an aristocratic society, being clearly and permanently limited, forms, in a sense, a little fatherland for all its members, to which they are attached by more obvious and more precious ties than those linking them to the fatherland itself.

Each citizen of an aristocratic society has his fixed station, one above another, so that there is always someone above him whose protection he needs and someone below him whose help he may require.

So people living in an aristocratic age are almost always closely involved with something outside themselves, and they are often inclined to forget about themselves. It is true that in these ages the general conception of *human fellowship* is dim and that men hardly ever think of devoting themselves to the cause of humanity, but men do often make sacrifices for the sake of certain other men.

In democratic ages, on the contrary, the duties of each to all are much clearer but devoted service to any individual much rarer. The bonds of human affection are wider but more relaxed.

Among democratic peoples new families continually rise from nothing while others fall, and nobody's position is quite stable. The woof of time is ever being broken and the track of past generations lost. Those who have gone before are easily forgotten, and no one gives a thought to those who will follow. All a man's interests are limited to those near himself.

As each class catches up with the next and gets mixed with it, its members do not care about one another and treat one another as strangers. Aristocracy links everybody, from peasant to king, in one long chain. Democracy breaks the chain and frees each link.

As social equality spreads there are more and more people who, though neither rich nor powerful enough to have much hold over others, have gained or kept enough wealth and enough understanding to look after their own needs. Such folk owe no man anything and hardly expect anything from anybody. They form the habit of thinking of themselves in isolation and imagine that their whole destiny is in their own hands.

Thus, not only does democracy make men forget their ancestors, but also clouds their view of their descendants and isolates them from their contemporaries. Each man is forever thrown back on himself alone, and there is danger that he may be shut up in the solitude of his own heart.

PART TWO

THE ROOTS OF TRADITION

It is hard to realize that one is speaking a particular language until one hears someone speaking in a different one. So intimate and pervasive is the relation between our most immediate thoughts and the language we speak. In a similar way, it has often been visitors and newcomers to the United States who have pointed out to Americans that they were in fact speaking, and thinking and acting as well, in distinctive ways. So, for example, the French visitor of the 1830s Alexis de Tocqueville, heard the Americans of his time speaking about their lives in an idiom he characterized as "individualism," as we have seen in part one.

Habits of the Heart takes up Tocqueville's theme by asking the question, What distinctive moral languages shape American life today? Chapter 2 of *Habits* identifies the kind of individualistic idiom Tocqueville found so distinctive as still alive and prominent in America, giving it the name "utilitarian individualism." The chapter locates this moral language by describing the historical development of the social conditions of a commercial, market society. But for *Habits of the Heart* utilitarian individualism is only one of four distinct linguistic patterns or moral languages. The others are expressive individualism, biblical religious language, and civic republicanism. (All are briefly defined in the Glossary to *Habits*.)

These are moral "languages" in the sense that each is a mode of moral discourse that includes a distinct vocabulary and characteristic patterns of moral reasoning. For example, utilitarian individualism tends to speak about "rights" and "interests" of the individual, and reasons largely in terms of the costs and benefits that any situation or course of action is likely to bring for the individual and his or her efforts to claim his rights or achieve her interests. Moral reasoning in this language means, for the most part, calculating the consequences of one's actions with reference to their probable effects on one's well-being, particularly material well-being, as in the common use of the phrase "self-interest."

As a moral language, utilitarian individualism enables Americans to interpret situations and evaluate them, and do this in a way that is so familiar that at first it may be hard to see that this is a particular way of interpreting life at all, as opposed to being simply the "natural" way to think, the way things really are. However, Americans also speak quite often about the duties and obligations which come from relationships, as well those attendant on membership in communities, religious bodies, and the claims of citizenship. In these contexts the language of utilitarian individualism is likely to give way to others, rooted in different traditions.

A culture is built up over time of the interactions among patterns of understanding and evaluation, and American culture is no exception. These patterns of understanding, or traditions, always have moral languages at their core, and individuals become the persons they are as they learn to give form to their lives out of the resources of tradition. There is nothing automatic about this process, and it is important to realize that human beings shape the traditions they share as well as receive much of their formation from their traditions. A tradition develops as an "argument" through the conflict among its constitutive moral languages. But this argument takes place as individuals attempt, in and through the languages available to them, to make coherent sense of themselves and their lives.

In the American context, the argument among the four moral languages has been over questions fundamental for both individual and social life. The questions of identity and value—Who am I? and, What is worth striving for and safeguarding?—have always been asked in America, and as public rather than merely private issues. The four moral languages, together with the practices of life they describe and interpret, each provide a different answer to these questions. Each strand of the American tradition carries a distinctive notion of the self and of the world. At the center of each of these visions there is always, in turn, a moral ideal of how the various parts of life as it is lived in American society are meant to fit together.

The readings in this section present the biblical, civic republican, utilitarian individualist, and expressive individualist conceptions of identity and value through figures and texts that have served as important (classic) reference points for later American discussion. The ordering of the selections, like the argument of *Habits of the Heart,* is designed to keep raising the basic philosophical issue of how adequately each language can provide a vision of a morally coherent life. Without such a vision neither a stable self nor enduring cooperation and commitment with others—and thus no "good life"—is possible.

In the first selection, "A Modell of Christian Charity," John Winthrop, the Puritan magistrate, applies the tradition of biblical religion he had inherited to the challenging experiment of establishing a model society in the New World. Winthrop's sermon sets out in short compass virtually the entire religious vision of Calvinist Christianity as it pertains to the practical life of individuals in community. For Winthrop, everything that is, including human beings and the whole of nature, exists to show forth the infinite richness of the divine creative will. This will is a benevolent one, and though frustrated by the selfish rebellion of the first humans, God's purpose continues in the world, even after the Fall, through the grace that has called first Israel, and then all who trust in Christ, into a Covenant of reconciliation.

This Covenant, as set forth in the Bible, defines the meaning of nature and the purpose of human life. For Winthrop's tradition, nature is a unified whole that contains an organized ranking of kinds of creatures, "ordering all these differences for the preservation and good of the whole." In a similar way, the social order is made up of unequal ranks or estates, bound to each other in moral relations of mutual obligation as defined by a natural moral order knowable by human reason. To this natural order, the Covenant instituted by God in history has added a law of grace, a relationship of reciprocal duties and rights based on divine command to love first God, and then one's neighbor or oneself.

For Winthrop, the self is always understood as existing in relationship, a relation to the natural and social worlds ordered by the "lawe of nature" or the "modelle law," and a relationship to God and neighbor, particularly fellow members of the Covenant, ordered by the "lawe of grace" or "the lawe of the gospell." Winthrop defines the Covenant as a call to building a "City Upon a Hill," an exemplary community whose hallmark will be its members' willingness to be "knitt together in this worke as one man," even to be willing "to abridge our selves of our superfluities, for the supply of others necessities." Finally, this great work is going forward under divine judgment: If this new people of the Covenant is unfaithful, and turns to "other Gods, our pleasures and profits, and serve them; . . . wee shall surely perishe out of this good Land."

By contrast with Winthrop's biblical understanding, Thomas Jefferson's republican humanism distinguished sharply between the rationally knowable natural moral law and the claims of revealed religion. Jefferson counted among his proudest accomplishments his authorship of the Virginia Statute of Religious Liberty, which aimed to ensure that nothing like Winthrop's integration of church and state could ever appear again in America. And yet, there are profound continuities and compatibilities between the biblical vision of the New England Calvinists and the civic ideals of the American founders. For Jefferson, too, the self receives its identity from the relationships it has within a larger order governed by divinely given laws, particularly the moral law of justice and equity.

Jefferson's First Inaugural Address of 1801 is a remarkable compendium of classic republican ideals. In the republican tradition, the best human community is the civic body of a republic governed by laws grounded in human reason. For this tradition, the ancient republics of Greece and Rome have played an exemplary— and admonitory—role somewhat comparable to the way Winthrop used ancient Israel as both example and warning. Jefferson's great hope for himself and his nation rests on the "resources of wisdom, of virtue and of zeal" present in his fellow citizens as they seek their mutual fulfillment through the shared practices of citizenship in pursuit of the common good. Yet, his ideal of a just republic is not guided by a blind faith in the will of the majority, recognizing that "that will, to be rightful, must be reasonable" and that "the minority possess their equal rights."

The optimism of the Enlightenment's faith in reason was strong in Jefferson's brand of republicanism. In the First Inaugural Address he asked: "Can he [man] be trusted with the government of others? Or have we found angels in the form of kings to govern him?" He answered: "Let history answer this question!" In "Aristocracy and Liberty," a letter to John Adams a decade later, on October 28, 1813, Jefferson explained more fully the basis for this confidence in popular government, which was in his day just coming to be described with favorable connotation as democracy. Then Jefferson argued that the form of government is best, and will ultimately best succeed, which "provides most effectually for a pure selection of these natural aristoi [literally, the "best"] into the offices of government," pointing out that this "natural" aristocracy of talent is often inhibited by the development in a nation of an "artificial aristocracy" of birth or wealth. The key to successful republican government, then, was to have citizens sufficiently educated and economically secure to be able to judge wisely among candidates for office.

For another Founder of the American Republic, Benjamin Franklin, reason has another connotation. In the selection from his *Autobiography* he speaks of reason as the faculty for calculating one's interests. While granting the "mere speculative conviction that it was our interest to be completely virtuous," when Franklin sought actually to become virtuous he turned neither to the disciplines of the Calvinist Christianity in which he had been reared nor to the practices of citizenship, but to a "method" of entirely self-oriented effort. In Franklin's account, a person achieves virtue in much the way he or she attains wealth, position, or learning—by ceaseless productive activity. Franklin's end-in-view is virtue, and by the term he includes much of the content of Christian morality and classical civic concern. But the framework within which he places these goods is no longer inspired by faith or enlightened by an objective moral reason. Rather, the self with its desires and ends has become the focal point of a new calculus of success and failure. The familiar perspective of utilitarian individualism has been established.

The fourth representative author is Walt Whitman. His poetry, novel in form as well as content, startled the America of the mid–nineteenth century. Whitman was the poet of a new sensibility, and simultaneously the definer of a new moral language. In "One's-Self I Sing," from *Leaves of Grass,* Whitman sets out his new perspective on the individual self as at once "a simple separate person" and at the same time called by "the word Democratic, the word En-Masse." This is a self that unlike Franklin's can enjoy time to be at ease and "loafe," as in "Song of Myself," yet feel itself a part of the pulse of all life around and outside. This sense that "I need no assurances,

I am a man who is pre-occupied of his own soul," is the keynote of Whitman's expressive individualism.

The self is defined by inner feelings and empathic experiences, and persons are good because they are sensitive to themselves and to the situation at the moment. Yet, the meaning of life is finally realized in a rapturous communion with another, as described in "To a Stranger." This is a meeting whose power and significance transcends all limitations of sex and gender, all moral bonds and strictures, whether of revealed command, natural reason, or the prudent calculation of interest. This mystical, romantic, and highly physical sense of connection is Whitman's replacement for Winthrop's biblical Covenant, Jefferson's bonds of rational law, and Franklin's careful prudence. In Whitman's vision of expressive individualism, the possibility of such communion among free selves is the supreme good, as it is also his great hope for a democratic America.

JOHN WINTHROP

A Modell of Christian Charity

Written on Boarde the Arbella,
On the Attlantick Ocean. Anno 1630

A MODELL HEREOF

God Almightie in his most holy and wise providence hath soe disposed of the Condicion of mankinde, as in all times some must be rich, some poore, some highe and eminent in power and dignitie; others meane and in subjeccion.

THE REASON HEREOF

1. Reason: *First,* to hold conformity with the rest of his workes, being delighted to shewe forthe the glory of his wisdome in the variety and differance of the Creatures and the glory of his power, in ordering all these differences for the preservacion and good of the whole; and the glory of his greatnes that as it is the glory of princes to have many officers, soe this great King will have many Stewards, counting himselfe more honoured in dispenceing his guifts to man by man, than if hee did it by his owne immediate hand.

2. Reason: *Secondly,* That he might have the more occasion to manifest the worke of his Spirit: first, upon the wicked in moderateing and restraineing them: soe that the riche and mighty should not eate upp the poore, nor the poore and dispised rise upp against their superiours and shake off thiere yoake; secondly in the regenerate in exerciseing his graces in them, as in the greate ones, their

---

John Winthrop, "A Modell of Christian Charity," from *Winthrop Papers*, vol. 2 (Boston: The Massachusetts Historical Society, 1931), pp. 40–43.

love, mercy, gentlenes, temperance, etc., in the poore and inferiour sorte, theire faithe, patience, obedience, etc.

3. Reason: *Thirdly,* That every man might have need of other, and from hence they might be all knitt more nearly together in the Bond of brotherly affeccion: from hence it appeares plainely that noe man is made more honourable than another or more wealthy etc., out of any perticuler and singuler respect to himselfe but for the glory of his Creator and the Common good of the Creature, Man; Therefore God still reserves the propperty of these guifts to himselfe as Ezek: 16.17. he there calls wealthe his gold and his silver, etc. Prov: 3.9 he claimes theire service as his due, honour the Lord with thy riches, etc. All men being thus (by divine providence) rancked into two sortes, riche and poore; under the first, are comprehended all such as are able to live comfortably by theire owne meanes duely improved; and all others are poore according to the former distribution. There are two rules whereby wee are to walke one towards another: JUSTICE and MERCY. These are allwayes distinquished in theire Act and in theire object, yet may they both concurre in the same Subject in eache respect; as sometimes there may be an occasion of shewing mercy to a rich man, in some sudden danger of distresse, and allsoe doeing of meere Justice to a poor man in regard of some perticuler contract, etc. There is likewise a double Lawe by which wee are regulated in our conversacion one towardes another: in both the former respects, the lawe of nature and the lawe of grace, or the morrall lawe or the lawe of the gospell, to omitt the rule of Justice as not propperly belonging to this purpose otherwise than it may fall into consideraction in some perticuler Cases: By the first of these lawes man as he was enabled soe withall [is] commaunded to love his neighbour as himselfe. Upon this ground stands all the precepts of the morrall lawe, which concernes our dealings with men. To apply this to the works of mercy this lawe requires two things: first, that every man afford his help to another in every want or distress. Secondly, That hee performe this out of the same affeccion which makes him carefull of his owne good according to that of our Saviour, Math: [7.12] Whatsoever ye would that men should doe to you. This was practised by Abraham and Lott in entertaineing the Angells and the old man of Gibea.

The Lawe of Grace or the Gospell hath some differance from

the former as in these respects: first, the lawe of nature was given to man in the estate of innocency; this of the gospell in the estate of regeneracy. Secondly, the former propounds one man to another, as the same fleshe and Image of god; this as a brother in Christ allsoe, and in the Communion of the same spirit and soe teacheth us to put a difference betweene Christians and others. Doe good to all, especially to the household of faith; upon this ground the Israelites were to putt a difference betweene the brethren of such as were strangers though not of the Canaanites. Thirdly, the Lawe of nature could give noe rules for dealeing with enemies, for all are to be considered as friends in the estate of innocency, but the Gospell commands love to an enemy. Proofe: If thine Enemie hunger feede him; Love your Enemies, doe good to them that hate you, Math: 5.44.

This Lawe of the Gospell propoundes likewise a difference of seasons and occasions. There is a tyme when a Christian must sell all and give to the poore, as they did in the Apostles times. There is a tyme allsoe when a Christian (though they give not all yet) must give beyond theire ability, as they of Macedonia. Cor: 2.6. Likewise community of perills calls for extraordinary liberallity and soe doth Community in some speciall service for the Churche. Lastly, when there is noe other meanes whereby our Christian brother may be relieved in this distresse, wee must help him beyond our ability, rather than tempt God, in putting him upon help by miraculous or extraordinary meanes.

It rests now to make some application of this discourse by the present designe which gave the occasion of writeing of it. Herein are four things to be propounded: first, the persons; secondly, the worke; thirdly, the end; fourthly, the meanes.

1 For the persons, wee are a Company professing our selves fellow members of Christ, in which respect onely though wee were absent from eache other many miles, and had our imploymentes as farre distant, yet wee ought to account our selves knitt together by this bond of love, and live in the exercise of it, if wee would have comforte of our being in Christ. This was notorious in the practise of the Christians in former times, as is testified of the Waldenses from the mouth of one of the adversaries Aeneas Sylvius, mutuo [solent amare] penè antequam norint. They use to

love any of theire own religion even before they were acquainted with them.

2. For the worke wee have in hand, it is by a mutuall consent through a speciall overruleing providence, and a more than an ordinary approbation of the Churches of Christ to seeke out a place of Cohabitation and Consorteshipp under a due forme of Government both civill and ecclesiasticall. In such cases as this the care of the publique must oversway all private respects, by which not onely conscience, but meare Civill pollicy doth binde us; for it is a true rule that perticuler estates cannott subsist in the ruine of the publique.

3. The end is to improve our lives, to doe more service to the Lord, the comforte and encrease of the body of Christ whereof wee are members, that our selves and posterity may be the better preserved from the Common corrupcions of this evill world, to serve the Lord and worke out our Salvacion under the power and purity of his holy Ordinances.

4. For the meanes whereby this must bee effected, they are twofold, a Conformity with the worke and end wee aime at; these wee see are extraordinary, therefore wee must not content our selves with usuall ordinary meanes. Whatsoever wee did or ought to have done when wee lived in England, the same must wee doe and more allsoe where we goe: That which the most in theire Churches mainteine as a truthe in profession onely, wee must bring into familiar and constant practice, as in this duty of love wee must love brotherly without dissimulation, wee must love one another with a pure hearte fervently, wee must beare one anothers burthens, wee must not looke onely on our owne things but allsoe on the things of our brethren, neither must wee think that the lord will beare with such faileings at our hands as hee dothe from those among whome wee have lived.

Thus stands the cause betweene God and us. Wee are entered into Covenant with him for this worke, wee have taken out a Commission, the Lord hath given us leave to draw our owne Articles, wee have professed to enterprise these Accions upon these and these ends, wee have hereupon besought him of favour and blessing: Now if the Lord shall please to heare us, and bring us in peace to the place wee desire, then hath hee ratified this Covenant and sealed our Commission [and] will expect a strickt performance of the Articles contained in it, but if wee shall neglect the observacion of these Articles which are the ends wee have propounded, and dissembling with our God, shall fall to embrace this present world and prosecute our carnall intencions seekeing great things for our selves and our posterity, the Lord will surely breake out in wrathe against us, be revenged of such a perjured people and make us knowe the price of the breache of such a Covenant.

Now the onely way to avoyde this shipwracke and to provide for our posterity is to followe the Counsell of Micah, to doe Justly, to love mercy, to walke humbly with our God. For this end, wee must be knitt together in this worke as one man, wee must entertaine each other in brotherly Affeccion, wee must be willing to abridge our selves of our superfluities, for the supply of others necessities, wee must uphold a familiar Commerce together in all meeknes, gentlenes, patience and liberallity, wee must delight in each other, make others Condicions our owne, rejoyce together, mourne together, labour and suffer together, allwayes haveing before our eyes our Commission and Community in the worke, our Community as members of the same body, soe shall wee keepe the unitie of the spirit in the bond of peace, the Lord will be our God and delight to dwell among us as his owne people and will commaund a blessing upon us in all our wayes, soe that wee shall see much more of his wisdome, power, goodnes and truthe than formerly wee have beene acquainted with. Wee shall finde that the God of Israell is among us, when tenn of us shall be able to resist a thousand of our enemies, when hee shall make us a prayse and glory, that men shall say of succeeding plantacions: the lord make it like that of New England: for wee must Consider that wee shall be as a Citty upon a Hill, the eies of all people are uppon us; soe that if wee shall deale falsely with our god in this worke wee have undertaken and soe cause him to withdrawe his present help from us, wee shall shame the faces of many of gods worthy servants, and cause theire prayers to be turned into Cursses upon us till wee be consumed out of the good land whither wee are goeing: And to shutt upp this discourse with that exhortacion of Moses, that faithfull servant of the Lord in his last farewell to Israell, Deut. 30. Beloved there is now sett before us life, and good, deathe and evill in that wee are Commaunded this day to love the Lord our God, and to love one another, to walke in his wayes and to keepe his Commaundements and his Ordinance, and his lawes, and the Articles of our Covenant with him that wee may live and be multiplied, and that the Lord our God may blesse us in the land whither we goe to possesse it/ But if our heartes shall turne away soe that wee will not obey, but shall be seduced and worship . . . other Gods, our pleasures, and proffitts, and serve them; it is propounded unto us this day, wee shall surely perishe out of the good Land whither wee passe over this vast Sea to possesse it;

⌐Therefore lett us choose life,
that wee, and our Seede,
may live; by obeyeing his
voyce, and cleaveing to him,
for hee is our life, and
our prosperity.⌐

THOMAS JEFFERSON

First Inaugural Address

Friends and fellow citizens: Called upon to undertake the duties of the first executive office of our country, I avail myself of the presence of that portion of my fellow citizens which is here assembled, to express my grateful thanks for the favor with which they have been pleased to look toward me, to declare a sincere consciousness that the task is above my talents, and that I approach it with those anxious and awful presentiments which the greatness of the charge and the weakness of my powers so justly inspire. A rising nation, spread over a wide and fruitful land, traversing all the seas with the rich productions of their industry, engaged in commerce with nations who feel power and forget right, advancing rapidly to destinies beyond the reach of mortal eye—when I contemplate these tran-

Thomas Jefferson, "First Inaugural Address," March 4, 1801, and "Aristocracy and Liberty," from *The Complete Jefferson,* ed. Saul K. Padover (Freeport, New York: Books for Libraries Press, 1943), pp. 384–87, 282–87.

scendent objects, and see the honor, the happiness, and the hopes of this beloved country committed to the issue and the auspices of this day, I shrink from the contemplation, and humble myself before the magnitude of the undertaking. Utterly indeed, should I despair, did not the presence of many whom I here see remind me, that in the other high authorities provided by our constitution, I shall find resources of wisdom, of virtue, and of zeal, on which to rely under all difficulties. To you, then, gentlemen, who are charged with the sovereign functions of legislation, and to those associated with you, I look with encouragement for that guidance and support which may enable us to steer with safety the vessel in which we are all embarked amid the conflicting elements of a troubled world.

During the contest of opinion through which we have passed, the animation of discussion and of exertions has sometimes worn an aspect which might impose on strangers unused to think freely and to speak and to write what they think; but this being now decided by the voice of the nation, announced according to the rules of the constitution, all will, of course, arrange themselves under the will of the law, and unite in common efforts for the common good. All, too, will bear in mind this sacred principle, that though the will of the majority is in all cases to prevail, that will, to be rightful, must be reasonable; that the minority possess their equal rights, which equal laws must protect, and to violate which would be oppression. Let us, then, fellow-citizens, unite with one heart and one mind. Let us restore to social intercourse that harmony and affection without which liberty and even life itself are but dreary things. And let us reflect that having banished from our land that religious intolerance under which mankind so long bled and suffered, we have yet gained little if we countenance a political intolerance as despotic, as wicked, and capable of as bitter and bloody persecutions. During the throes and convulsions of the ancient world, during the agonizing spasms of infuriated man, seeking through blood and slaughter his long-lost liberty, it was not wonderful that the agitation of the billows should reach even this distant and peaceful shore; that this should be more felt and feared by some and less by others; that this should divide opinions as to measures of safety. But every difference of opinion is not a difference of principle. We have called by different names brethren of the same principle. We are all republicans—we are federalists. If there be any among us who would wish to dissolve this Union or to change its republican form, let them stand undisturbed as monuments of the safety with which error of opinion may be tolerated where reason is left free to combat it. I know, indeed, that some honest men fear that a republican government cannot be strong; that this government is not strong enough. But would the honest patriot, in the full tide of successful experiment, abandon a government which has so far kept us free and firm, on the theoretic and visionary fear that this government, the world's best hope, may by possibility want energy to preserve itself? I trust not. I believe this, on the contrary, the strongest government on earth. I believe it is the only one where every man, at the call of the laws, would fly to the standard of the law, and would meet invasions of the public order as his own personal concern. Sometimes it is said that man cannot be trusted with the government of himself. Can he, then, be trusted with the government of others? Or have we found angels in the forms of kings to govern him? Let history answer this question.

Let us, then, with courage and confidence pursue our own federal and republican principles, our attachment to our union and representative government. Kindly separated by nature and a wide ocean from the exterminating havoc of one quarter of the globe; too high-minded to endure the degradations of the others; possessing a chosen country, with room enough for our descendants to the hundredth and thousandth generation; entertaining a due sense of our equal right to the use of our own faculties, to the acquisitions of our industry, to honor and confidence from our fellow citizens, resulting not from birth but from our actions and their sense of them; enlightened by a benign religion, professed, indeed, and practiced in various forms, yet all of them including honesty, truth, temperance, gratitude, and the love of man; acknowledging and adoring an overruling Providence, which by all its dispensations proves that it delights in the happiness of man here and his greater happiness hereafter; with all these blessings, what more is necessary to make us a happy and prosperous people? Still one thing more, fellow citizens—a wise and frugal government, which shall restrain men from injuring one another, which shall leave them otherwise free to regulate their own pursuits of industry and improvement, and shall not take from the mouth of labor the bread it has earned.

This is the sum of good government, and this is necessary to close the circle of our felicities.

About to enter, fellow citizens, on the exercise of duties which comprehend everything dear and valuable to you, it is proper that you should understand what I deem the essential principles of our government, and consequently those which ought to shape its administration. I will compress them within the narrowest compass they will bear, stating the general principle, but not all its limitations. Equal and exact justice to all men, of whatever state or persuasion, religious or political; peace, commerce, and honest friendship with all nations—entangling alliances with none; the support of the State governments in all their rights, as the most competent administrations for our domestic concerns and the surest bulwarks against anti-republican tendencies; the preservation of the general government in its whole constitutional vigor, as the sheet anchor of our peace at home and safety abroad; a jealous care of the right of election by the people—a mild and safe corrective of abuses which are lopped by the sword of the revolution where peaceable remedies are unprovided; absolute acquiescence in the decisions of the majority—the vital principle of republics, from which there is no appeal but to force, the vital principle and immediate parent of despotism; a well-disciplined militia—our best reliance in peace and for the first moments of war, till regulars may relieve them; the supremacy of the civil over the military authority; economy in the public expense, that labor may be lightly burdened; the honest payment of our debts and sacred preservation of the public faith; encouragement of agriculture, and of commerce as its handmaid; the diffusion of information and the arraignment of all abuses at the bar of public reason; freedom of religion; freedom of the press; freedom of person under the protection of the *habeas corpus;* and trial by juries impartially selected—these principles form the bright constellation which has gone before us, and guided our steps through an age of revolution and reformation. The wisdom of our sages and the blood of our heroes have been devoted to their attainment. They should be the creed of our political faith—the text of civil instruction—the touchstone by which to try the services of those we trust; and should we wander from them in moments of error or alarm, let us hasten to retrace our steps and to regain the road which alone leads to peace, liberty, and safety.

I repair, then, fellow citizens, to the post you have assigned me. With experience enough in subordinate offices to have seen the difficulties of this, the greatest of all, I have learned to expect that it will rarely fall to the lot of imperfect man to retire from this station with the reputation and the favor which bring him into it. Without pretensions to that high confidence reposed in our first and great revolutionary character, whose preeminent services had entitled him to the first place in his country's love, and destined for him the fairest page in the volume of faithful history, I ask so much confidence only as may give firmness and effect to the legal administration of your affairs. I shall often go wrong through defect of judgment. When right, I shall often be thought wrong by those whose positions will not command a view of the whole ground. I ask your indulgence for my own errors, which will never be intentional; and your support against the errors of others, who may condemn what they would not if seen in all its parts. The approbation implied by your suffrage is a consolation to me for the past; and my future solicitude will be to retain the good opinion of those who have bestowed it in advance, to conciliate that of others by doing them all the good in my power, and to be instrumental to the happiness and freedom of all.

Relying, then, on the patronage of your good will, I advance with obedience to the work, ready to retire from it whenever you become sensible how much better choice it is in your power to make. And may that Infinite Power which rules the destinies of the universe, lead our councils to what is best, and give them a favorable issue for your peace and prosperity.

Thomas Jefferson

Aristocracy and Liberty[1]

The passage you quote from Theognis, I think has an ethical rather than a political object.[2] The whole piece is a moral *exhortation*, παραινεςις, and this passage particularly seems to be a reproof to man, who, while with his domestic animals he is curious to improve the race, by employing always the finest male, pays no attention to the improvement of his own race, but intermarries with the vicious, the ugly, or the old, for considerations of wealth or ambition. It is in conformity with the principle adopted afterwards by the Pythagoreans, and expressed by Ocellus in another form; "πεφι δε τ³ς ε₉χ των αλληλων ανθφωπων γενεσεως, etc.—ουχ ηδουησενεχα η μιξις" which, as literally as intelligibility will admit, may be thus translated: "concerning the interprocreation of men, how, and of whom it shall be, in a perfect manner, and according to the laws of modesty and sanctity, conjointly, this is what I think right. First to lay it down that we do not commix for the sake of pleasure, but of the procreation of children. For the powers, the organs and desires for coition have not been given by God to man for the sake of pleasure, but for the procreation of the race. For as it were incon-

1. Letter to John Adams.
2. On July 9, 1813, Adams wrote to Jefferson, mentioning a book of moral sentences from the ancient Greek poets: "In one of the oldest of them, I read in Greek, that I cannot repeat, a couplet, the sense of which was: 'Nobility in men is worth as much as it is in horses, asses, or rams; but the meanest blooded puppy in the world, if he gets a little money, is as good a man as the best of them.' Yet birth and wealth together have prevailed over virtue and talents in all ages. The many will acknowledge no other αριςτοι."
On September 15, 1813, Adams wrote him again: "I asked you in a former letter how far advanced we were in the science of aristocracy since Theognis' Stallions, Jacks and Rams' Have not Chancellor Livingston and Major General Humphreys introduced an hereditary aristocracy of Merino Sheep? How shall we get rid of this aristocracy? It is entailed upon us forever. And an aristocracy of land jobbers and stock jobbers is equally and irremediably entailed upon us, to endless generations." Jefferson's reply is given above.

gruous, for a mortal born to partake of divine life, the immortality of the race being taken away, God fulfilled the purpose by making the generations uninterrupted and continuous. This, therefore, we are especially to lay down as a principle, that coition is not for the sake of pleasure." But nature, not trusting to this moral and abstract motive, seems to have provided more securely for the perpetuation of the species, by making it the effect of the *oestrum* implanted in the constitution of both sexes. And not only has the commerce of love been indulged on this unhallowed impulse, but made subservient also to wealth and ambition by marriage, without regard to the beauty, the healthiness, the understanding, or virtue of the subject from which we are to breed. The selecting the best male for a Harem of well chosen females also, which Theognis seems to recommend from the example of our sheep and asses, would doubtless improve the human, as it does the brute animal, and produce a race of veritable αφιςτος. For experience proves, that the moral and physical qualities of man, whether good or evil, are transmissible in a certain degree from father to son. But I suspect that the equal rights of men will rise up against this privileged Solomon and his Harem, and oblige us to continue acquiescence under the "Αμανφωςις γενεος αςτων" which Theognis complains of, and to content ourselves with the accidental aristoi produced by the fortuitous concourse of breeders. For I agree with you that there is a natural aristocracy among men. The grounds of this are virtue and talents. Formerly, bodily powers gave place among the aristoi. But since the invention of gunpowder has armed the weak as well as the strong with missile death, bodily strength, like beauty, good humor, politeness and other accomplishments, has become but an auxiliary ground of distinction. There is also an artificial aristocracy, founded on wealth and birth, without either virtue or talents; for with these it would belong to the first class. The natural aristocracy I consider as the most precious gift of nature, for the instruction, the trusts, and government of society. And indeed, it would have been inconsistent in creation to have formed man for the social state, and not to have provided virtue and wisdom enough to manage the concerns of the society. May we not even say, that that form of government is the best, which provides the most effectually for a pure selection of these natural aristoi into the offices of government? The artificial aristocracy is a mischievous ingredient in government, and provision should be made to prevent its ascendency. On the question, what is the best provision, you and I differ; but we differ as rational friends, using the free exercise of our own reason, and mutually indulging its errors. You think it best to put the pseudo-aristoi into a separate chamber of legislation, where they may be hindered from doing mischief by their co-ordinate branches, and where, also, they may be a protection to wealth against the Agrarian and plundering enterprises of the majority of the people. I think that to give them power in order to prevent them from doing mischief, is arming them for it, and increasing instead of remedying the evil. For if the co-ordinate branches can arrest their action, so may they that of the co-ordinates. Mischief may be done negatively as well as positively. Of this, a cabal in the Senate of the United States has furnished many proofs. Nor do I believe them necessary to protect the wealthy; because enough of these will find their way into every branch of the legislation, to protect themselves. From fifteen to twenty legislatures of our own, in action for thirty years past, have proved that no fears of an equalization of property are to be apprehended from them. I think the best remedy is exactly that provided by all our constitutions, to leave to the citizens the free election and separation of the aristoi from the pseudo-aristoi, of the wheat from the chaff. In general they will elect the really good and wise. In some instances, wealth may corrupt, and birth blind them; but not in sufficient degree to endanger the society.

It is probable that our difference of opinion may, in some measure, be produced by a difference of character in those among whom we live. From what I have seen of Massachusetts and Connecticut myself, and still more from what I have heard, and the character given of the former by yourself (vol. i, page iii), who know them so much better, there seems to be in those two States a traditionary reverence for certain families, which has rendered the offices of the government nearly hereditary in those families. I presume that from an early period of your history, members of those families happening to possess virtue and talents, have honestly exercised them for the good of the people, and by their services have endeared their names to them. In coupling Connecticut with you, I mean it politically only, not morally. For having made the Bible the common law of their land, they seem to have modeled their morality on the story of Jacob and Laban. But although this hereditary succession to office with you, may, in some degree, be founded in real family merit, yet in a much higher degree, it has proceeded from your strict alliance of Church and State. These families are canonised in the eyes of the people on common principles, "you tickle me, and I will tickle you." In Virginia we have nothing of this. Our clergy, before the revolution, having been secured against rivalship by fixed salaries, did not give themselves the trouble of acquiring influence over the people. Of wealth, there were great accumulations in particular families, handed down from generation to generation, under the English law of entails. But the only object of ambition for the wealthy was a seat in the King's Council. All their court then was paid to the crown and its creatures; and they Philipised in all collisions between the King and the people. Hence they were unpopular; and that unpopularity continues attached to their names. A Randolph, a Carter, or a Burwell must have great personal superiority over a common competitor to be elected by the people even at this day. At the first session of our legislature after the Declaration of Independence, we passed a law abolishing entails. And this was followed by one abolishing the privilege of primogeniture, and dividing the lands of intestates equally among all their children, or other representatives. These laws, drawn by myself, laid the axe to the foot of pseudo-aristocracy. And had another which I prepared been adopted by the legislature, our work would have been complete. It was a bill for the more general diffusion of learning. This proposed to divide every county into wards of five or six miles square, like your townships; to establish in each ward a free school for reading, writing and common arithmetic; to provide for the annual selection of the best subjects from these schools, who might receive, at the public expense, a higher degree of education at a district school; and from these district schools to select a certain number of the most promising subjects, to be completed at an University, where all the useful sciences should be taught. Worth and genius would thus have been sought out from every condition of life, and completely prepared by education for defeating the competition of wealth and birth for public trusts. My proposition had, for a further object, to impart to these wards those portions of self-government for which they are best qualified, by confiding to them the care of their poor, their roads, police, elections, the nomination of jurors, administration of justice in small cases, elementary exercises of militia; in short, to have made them little republics, with a warden at the head of each, for all those concerns which, being under their eye, they would better manage than the larger republics of the county or State. A general call of ward meetings by their wardens on the same day through the State, would at any time produce the genuine sense of the people on any required point, and would enable the State to act in mass, as your people have so often done, and with so much effect by their town meetings. The law for religious freedom, which made a part of this system, having put down the aristocracy of the clergy, and restored to the citizen the freedom of the mind, and those of entails and descents nurturing an equality of condition among them, this on education would have raised the mass of the people to the high ground of moral respectability necessary to their own safety, and to orderly government; and would have completed the great object of qualifying them to select the veritable aristoi, for the trusts of government, to the exclusion of the pseudalists; and the same Theognis who has furnished the epigraphs of your two letters, assures us that "Ουδεμιαν πω, Κυφν', αγαθοι πολιν ωλεςαν ανδφες." Although this law has not yet been acted on but in a small and inefficient degree, it is still considered as before the legislature, with other bills of the revised code, not yet taken up, and I have great hope that some patriotic spirit will, at a favorable moment, call it up, and make it the key-stone of the arch of our government.

With respect to aristocracy, we should further consider, that before the establishment of the American States, nothing was known to history but the man of the old world, crowded within limits either small or overcharged, and steeped in the vices which that situation generates. A government adapted to such men would be one thing; but a very different one, that for the man of these States. Here everyone may have land to labor for himself, if he chooses; or, preferring the exercise of any other industry, may exact for it such compensation as not only to afford a comfortable subsistence, but wherewith to provide for a cessation from labor in old age. Everyone, by his property, or by his satisfactory situation, is interested in the support of law and order. And such men may safely and advantageously reserve to themselves a wholesome control over their public affairs, and a degree of freedom, which, in the hands of the *canaille* of the cities of Europe, would be instantly perverted to the demolition and destruction of everything public and private. The history of the last twenty-five years of France, and of the last forty years in America, nay of its last two hundred years, proves the truth of both parts of this observation.

But even in Europe a change has sensibly taken place in the mind of man. Science had liberated the ideas of those who read and reflect, and the American example had kindled feelings of right in the people. An insurrection has consequently begun, of science, talents, and courage, against rank and birth, which have fallen into contempt. It has failed in its first effort, because the mobs of the cities, the instrument used for its accomplishment, debased by ignorance, poverty, and vice, could not be restrained to rational action. But the world will recover from the panic of this first catastrophe. Science is progressive, and talents and enterprise on the alert. Resort may be had to the people of the country, a more governable power from their principles and subordination; and rank, and birth, and tinsel-aristocracy will finally shrink into insignificance, even there. This, however, we have no right to meddle with. It suffices for us, if the moral and physical condition of our own citizens qualifies them to select the able and good for the direction of their government, with a recurrence of elections at such short periods as will enable them to displace an unfaithful servant, before the mischief he meditates may be irremediable.

I have thus stated my opinion on a point on which we differ, not with a view to controversy, for we are both too old to change opinions which are the result of a long life of inquiry and reflection; but on the suggestions of a former letter of yours, that we ought not to die before we have explained ourselves to each other. We acted in perfect harmony, through a long and perilous contest for our liberty and independence. A constitution has been acquired, which, though neither of us thinks perfect, yet both consider as competent to render our fellow citizens the happiest and the securest on whom the sun has ever shone. If we do not think exactly alike as to its imperfections, it matters little to our country, which, after devoting to it long lives of disinterested labor, we have delivered over to our successors in life, who will be able to take care of it and of themselves.

Of the pamphlet on aristocracy which has been sent to you, or who may be its author, I have heard nothing but through your letter.

If the person you suspect, it may be known from the quaint, mystical, and hyperbolical ideas, involved in affected, new-tangled and pedantic terms which stamp his writings. Whatever it be, I hope your quiet is not to be affected at this day by the rudeness or intemperance of scribblers; but that you may continue in tranquillity to live and to rejoice in the prosperity of our country, until it shall be your own wish to take your seat among the aristoi who have gone before you. Ever and affectionately yours.

BENJAMIN FRANKLIN

Autobiography

It was about this time I conceiv'd the bold and arduous project of arriving at moral perfection. I wish'd to live without committing any fault at any time; I would conquer all that either natural inclination, custom, or company might lead me into. As I knew, or thought I knew, what was right and wrong, I did not see why I might not always do the one and avoid the other. But I soon found I had undertaken a task of more difficulty than I had imagined. While my care was employ'd in guarding against one fault, I was often surprised by another; habit took the advantage of inattention; inclination was sometimes too strong for reason. I concluded, at length, that the mere speculative conviction that it was our interest to be completely virtuous, was not sufficient to prevent our slipping; and that the contrary habits must be broken, and good ones acquired and established, before we can have any dependence on a steady, uniform rectitude of conduct. For this purpose I therefore contrived the following method.

In the various enumerations of the moral virtues I had met with in my reading, I found the catalogue more or less numerous, as different writers included more or fewer ideas under the same

Benjamin Franklin, excerpts from his *Autobiography*, in *The Works of Benjamin Franklin, 1731–1757*, vol. 1 (New York: Putnam's, 1904), pp. 188–95, 199–200.

name. Temperance, for example, was by some confined to eating and drinking, while by others it was extended to mean the moderating every other pleasure, appetite, inclination, or passion, bodily or mental, even to our avarice and ambition. I propos'd to myself, for the sake of clearness, to use rather more names, with fewer ideas annex'd to each, than a few names with more ideas; and I included under thirteen names of virtues all that at that time occurr'd to me as necessary or desirable, and annexed to each a short precept, which fully express'd the extent I gave to its meaning.

These names of virtues, with their precepts, were:

1. TEMPERANCE
Eat not to dullness; drink not to elevation.

2. SILENCE
Speak not but what may benefit others or yourself; avoid trifling conversation.

3. ORDER
Let all your things have their places; let each part of your business have its time.

4. RESOLUTION
Resolve to perform what you ought; perform without fail what you resolve.

5. FRUGALITY
Make no expense but to do good to others or yourself; *i.e.*, waste nothing.

6. INDUSTRY
Lose no time; be always employ'd in something useful; cut off all unnecessary actions.

7. SINCERITY
Use no hurtful deceit; think innocently and justly; and, if you speak, speak accordingly.

8. JUSTICE
Wrong none by doing injuries, or omitting the benefits that are your duty.

9. Moderation

Avoid extreams; forbear resenting injuries so much as you think they deserve.

10. Cleanliness

Tolerate no uncleanliness in body, cloaths, or habitation.

11. Tranquillity

Be not disturbed at trifles, or at accidents common or unavoidable.

12. Chastity

Rarely use venery but for health or offspring, never to dullness, weakness, or the injury of your own or another's peace or reputation.

13. Humility

Imitate Jesus and Socrates.

My intention being to acquire the *habitude* of all these virtues, I judg'd it would be well not to distract my attention by attempting the whole at once, but to fix it on one of them at a time; and, when I should be master of that, then proceed to another, and so on till I had gone thro' the thirteen; and, as the previous acquisition of some might facilitate the acquisition of certain others, I arrang'd them with that view, as they stand above. Temperance first, as it tends to procure that coolness and clearness of head, which is so necessary where constant vigilance was to be kept up, and guard maintained against the unremitting attraction of ancient habits, and the force of perpetual temptations. This being acquir'd and establish'd, Silence would be more easy; and my desire being to gain knowledge at the same time that I improv'd in virtue, and considering that in conversation it was obtain'd rather by the use of the ears than of the tongue, and therefore wishing to break a habit I was getting into of prattling, punning, and joking, which only made me acceptable to trifling company, I gave *Silence* the second place. This and the next, *Order,* I expected would allow me more time for attending to my project and my studies. *Resolution,* once become habitual, would keep me firm in my endeavors to obtain all the subsequent virtues; *Frugality* and Industry freeing me from my remaining debt, and producing affluence and independence, would make more easy the practice of Sincerity and Justice, etc., etc. Conceiving, then, that, agreeably to the advice of Pythagoras in his *Golden Verses,* [1] daily examination would be necessary, I contrived the following method for conducting that examination.

I made a little book, in which I allotted a page for each of the

1. The verses here referred to are thus given as Englished from the version of Hierocles:

"In this place you should collect together the sense of all the foregoing precepts, that so giving heed to them as to the laws of God in the inward judicature of the soul, you may make a just examination of what you have done well or ill. For how will our remembrance reprehend us for doing ill, or praise us for doing well, unless the preceding meditation receive some laws, according to which the whole tenor of our life should be ordered, and to which we should conform the very private recesses of conscience all our lives long? He requires also that this examination be daily repeated, that by continual returns of recollection we may not be deceived in our judgment. The time which he recommends for this work is about even or bed-time, that we may conclude the action of the day with the judgment of conscience, making the examination of our conversation an evening song to God. Wherein have I transgressed? What have I done? What duty have I omitted? So shall we measure our lives by the rules above mentioned, if to the law of the mind we join the judgment of reason.

"What then does the law of the mind say? That we should honor the more excellent natures according to their essential order, that we should have our parents and relations in high esteem, love and embrace good men, raise ourselves above corporal affections, everywhere stand in awe of ourselves, carefully observe justice, consider the frailty of riches and momentary life, embrace the lot which falls to us by divine judgment, delight in a divine frame of spirit, convert our mind to what is most excellent, love good discourses, not lie open to impostures, not be servilely affected in the possession of virtue, advise before action to prevent repentance, free ourselves from uncertain opinions, live with knowledge, and lastly, that we should adapt our bodies and the things without to the exercise of virtue. These are the things which the law-giving mind has implanted in the souls of men, which when reason admits, it becomes a most vigilant judge of itself, in this manner, Wherein have I transgressed? what have I done? and if afterwards she finds herself to have spent the whole day agreeably to the foregoing rules, she is rewarded with a divine complacency. And if she find any thing done amiss, she corrects herself by the restorative of an after admonition.

"Wherefore he would have us keep off sleep by the readiness and alacrity of reason. And this body will easily endure, if temperately dieted it has not contracted a necessity of sleeping. By which means even our most natural appetites are subjected to the empire of reason.

"Do not admit sleep (says he) till you have examin'd every action of the day. And what is the form of examination? Wherein have I transgress'd? what have I done? what duty have I omitted? For we sin two ways. By doing what we should not, virtues.[2] I rul'd each page with red ink, so as to have seven columns, one for each day of the week, marking each column with a letter for the day. I cross'd these columns with thirteen red lines, marking the beginning of each line with the first letter of one of the virtues, on which line, and in its proper column, I might mark, by a little black spot, every fault I found upon examination to have been committed respecting that virtue upon that day.

I determined to give a week's strict attention to each of the virtues successively. Thus, in the first week, my great guard was to avoid every the least offence against *Temperance,* leaving the other virtues to their ordinary chance, only marking every evening the faults of the day. Thus, if in the first week I could keep my first line, marked T, clear of spots, I suppos'd the habit of that virtue so much strengthen'd, and its opposite weaken'd, that I might venture ex-

---

and by not doing what we should. For 't is one thing not to do well, and another thing to commit evil. One is a sin of omission, and the other of commission.

"For instance, 't is our duty to pray, but not to blaspheme; to nourish our parents, but not to revile them. He that does the former of these, does what he ought; he that does the latter, what he ought not. Though there is as much guilt in a sin of omission as in a sin of commission.

"He exhorts also that we proceed methodically in our examination from the beginning to the end, leaving nothing out in the middle, which is implied by the word, runover. For oftentimes change of order deceives the judgment, and makes us favorable to our ill actions through disorder of memory. Besides, a daily recollection of our actions begets care and studiousness of conversation, and a sense of our immortality. And this is worth our admiration, that when he bid us recollect everything, yet he added not, Wherein have I done well? or what duty have I perform'd? But he turn'd the memory to what was a less occasion of pride, requiring a scrutiny only of our sins. And as for the judge, he has constituted that which is most just and impartial, and most intimate and domestick, the conscience, right reason, or a man's self, which he had before caution'd us to stand in awe of above all things. For who can so admonish another as every man can himself? For he that is at his own liberty will use the freedom of nature, and shake off the admonition of others, when he is not minded to follow them. But reason, which is within us, cannot chuse but hear itself. God has set this over us as a guardian, instructor, and schoolmaster. And this the verse makes the judge of the day's action, acquiesces in its determination whether it condemns or approves itself. For when it reads over what is done in the register of memory, then, looking into the exemplar of the law, it pronounces itself worthy of honor or dishonor. This course, if daily follow'd, perfects the divine image in them that use it, leading them by additions and subtractions to the beauty of virtue, and all attainable perfection. For here end the instructions about civil virtue."

2. This "little book" is dated 1st of July, 1733.

ending my attention to include the next, and for the following week
eep both lines clear of spots. Proceeding thus to the last, I could
;o thro' a course compleat in thirteen weeks, and four courses in
a year. And like him who, having a garden to weed, does not attempt
o eradicate all the bad herbs at once, which would exceed his reach
and his strength, but works on one of the beds at a time, and, having
accomplish'd the first, proceeds to a second, so I should have, I
hoped, the encouraging pleasure of seeing on my pages the prog-
ess I made in virtue, by clearing successively my lines of their spots,
till in the end, by a number of courses, I should be happy in viewing
a clean book, after a thirteen weeks' daily examination.

In truth, I found myself incorrigible with respect to Order; and
now I am grown old and my memory bad, I feel very sensibly the
want of it. But, on the whole, tho' I never arrived at the perfection
I had been so ambitious of obtaining, but fell far short of it, yet I
was, by the endeavour, a better and a happier man than I otherwise
should have been if I had not attempted it; as those who aim at
perfect writing by imitating the engraved copies, tho' they never
reach the wish'd-for excellence of those copies, their hand is
mended by the endeavour, and is tolerable while it continues fair
and legible.

It may be well my posterity should be informed that to this little
artifice, with the blessing of God, their ancestor ow'd the constant
felicity of his life, down to his 79th year, in which this is written.
What reverses may attend the remainder is in the hand of Providence; but, if they arrive, the reflection on past happiness enjoy'd
ought to help his bearing them with more resignation. To Temperance he ascribes his long-continued health, and what is still left to
him of a good constitution; to Industry and Frugality, the early
easiness of his circumstances and acquisition of his fortune, with all
that knowledge that enabled him to be a useful citizen, and obtained
for him some degree of reputation among the learned; to Sincerity
and Justice, the confidence of his country, and the honorable employs it conferred upon him; and to the joint influence of the whole
mass of virtues, even in the imperfect state he was able to acquire
them, all that evenness of temper, and that cheerfulness in conversation, which makes his company still sought for and agreeable even
to his younger acquaintances. I hope, therefore, that some of my
descendants may follow the example and reap the benefit.

WALT WHITMAN

Leaves of Grass

ONE'S-SELF I SING

One's-self I sing, a simple separate person,
Yet utter the word Democratic, the word En-Masse.

Of physiology from top to toe I sing,
Not physiognomy alone nor brain alone is worthy
    for the Muse, I say the Form complete is
    worthier far,
The Female equally with the Male I sing.

Of Life immense in passion, pulse, and power,
Cheerful, for freest action form'd under
    the laws divine,
The Modern Man I sing.

SONG OF MYSELF

1

I CELEBRATE myself, and sing myself,
And what I assume you shall assume,
For every atom belonging to me as good
    belongs to you.

I loafe and invite my soul,
I lean and loafe at my ease observing a
    spear of summer grass.

My tongue, every atom of my blood, form'd
    from this soil, this air,

Walt Whitman, "One's-Self I Sing," "Song of Myself," "For You O Democracy,"
"Assurances," "A Noiseless Patient Spider," "To a Stranger," "This Moment Yearning and Thoughtful," "I Hear It Was Charged Against Me," "When I Peruse the
Conquer'd Fame," in *Leaves of Grass* (Boston: Small, Maynard and Co., 1897), pp. 9,
29, 99, 106, 107, 342, 343.

Born here of parents born here from parents
    the same, and their parents the same,
I, now thirty-seven years old in perfect health
    begin,
Hoping to cease not till death.

Creeds and schools in abeyance,
Retiring back a while sufficed at what they are, but
    never forgotten,
I harbor for good or bad, I permit to speak at
    every hazard,
Nature without check with original energy.

2

Houses and rooms are full of perfumes, the shelves
    are crowded with perfumes,
I breathe the fragrance myself and know it and
    like it,
The distillation would intoxicate me also, but I
    shall not let it.

The atmosphere is not a perfume, it has no taste
    of the distillation, it is odorless,
It is for my mouth forever, I am in love with it,
I will go to the bank by the wood and become
    undisguised and naked,
I am mad for it to be in contact with me.

FOR YOU O DEMOCRACY.

COME, I will make the continent indissoluble,
I will make the most splendid race the sun ever
    shone upon,
I will make divine magnetic lands,
With the love of comrades,
With the life-long love of comrades.

I will plant companionship thick as trees along all
    the rivers of
America, and along the shores of the great lakes,
    and all
over the prairies,

I will make inseparable cities with their arms about
    each other's necks,
By the love of comrades,
By the manly love of comrades.

For you these from me, O Democracy, to serve you
    ma femme!
For you, for you I am trilling these songs.

ASSURANCES

I NEED no assurances, I am a man who is
    pre-occupied of his own soul;
I do not doubt that from under the feet and
    beside the hands and face I am not cognizant
    of, are now looking faces I am not
    cognizant of, calm and actual faces,
I do not doubt but the majesty and beauty of the
    world are latent in any iota of the world,
I do not doubt I am limitless, and that the
    universes are limitless, in vain I try to think
    how limitless,
I do not doubt that the orbs and the systems of
    orbs play their swift sports through the air
    on purpose, and that I shall one day be eligible
    to do as much as they, and more than they,
I do not doubt that temporary affairs keep on and
    on millions of years,
I do not doubt interiors have their interiors,
    and exteriors have their exteriors, and that the
    eyesight has another eyesight, and the hearing
    another hearing, and the voice another voice,
I do not doubt that the passionately-wept deaths of
    young men are provided for, and that the
    deaths of young women and the deaths of little
    children are provided for,
(Did you think Life was so well provided for, and
    Death, the purport of all Life, is not well
    provided for?)

I do not doubt that wrecks at sea, no matter what
    the horrors of them, no matter whose wife,
    child, husband, father, lover, has gone down,
    are provided for, to the minutest points,
I do not doubt that whatever can possibly happen
    anywhere at any time, is provided for in the
    inherences of things,
I do not think Life provides for all and for Time
    and Space, but I believe Heavenly Death
    provides for all.

A NOISELESS PATIENT SPIDER

A NOISELESS patient spider,
I mark'd where on a little promontory it stood
    isolated,
Mark'd how to explore the vacant vast
    surrounding,
It launch'd forth filament, filament, filament,
    out of itself,
Ever unreeling them, ever tirelessly speeding them.

And you O my soul where you stand,
Surrounded, detached, in measureless oceans of
    space,
Ceaselessly musing, venturing, throwing, seeking
    the spheres to connect them,
Till the bridge you will need be form'd, till the
    ductile anchor hold,
Till the gossamer thread you fling catch
    somewhere, O my soul.
And I broke off a twig with a certain number of
    leaves upon it, and twined around it a little
    moss,
And brought it away, and I have placed it in sight
    in my room,
It is not needed to remind me as of my own dear
    friends,

(For I believe lately I think of little else than of
    them.)
Yet it remains to me a curious token, it makes me
    think of manly love;
For all that, and though the live-oak glistens
    there in Louisiana solitary in a wide flat space,
Uttering joyous leaves all its life without a friend a
    lover near,
I know very well I could not.

TO A STRANGER

PASSING stranger! you do not know how longingly
    I look upon you,
You must be he I was seeking, or she I
    was seeking, (it comes to me as
    of a dream,)
I have somewhere surely lived a life of joy
    with you,
All is recall'd as we flit by each other, fluid,
    affectionate, chaste, matured,
You grew up with me, were a boy with me or a girl
    with me,
I ate with you and slept with you, your body
    has become not yours only nor left my body
    mine only,
You give me the pleasure of your eyes, face, flesh,
    as we pass, you take of my beard, breast,
    hands, in return,
I am not to speak to you, I am to think of you
    when I sit alone or wake at night alone,
I am to wait, I do not doubt I am to meet
    you again,
I am to see to it that I do not lose you.

THIS MOMENT YEARNING AND THOUGHTFUL

THIS moment yearning and thoughtful sitting
    alone,
It seems to me there are other men in other lands
    yearning and thoughtful,

It seems to me I can look over and behold them in
   Germany, Italy, France, Spain,
Or far, far away, in China, or in Russia or Japan,
   talking other dialects,
And it seems to me if I could know those men I
   should become attached to them as I do to
   men in my own lands,
O I know we should be brethren and lovers,
I know I should be happy with them.

I HEAR IT WAS CHARGED AGAINST ME

I HEAR it was charged against me that I sought to
   destroy institutions,
But really I am neither for nor against institutions,
(What indeed have I in common with them?
   or what with the destruction of them?)
Only I will establish in the Mannahatta and in
   every city of these States inland and seaboard,
And in the fields and woods, and above every keel
   little or large that dents the water,
Without edifices or rules or trustees or any
   argument,
The institution of the dear love of comrades.

PART THREE

SELFHOOD AND SOCIETY

"Just be yourself." Whether it is spoken as reassurance or crit
cism, the phrase implies you should know who you are, even
acting that way is not always easy. Selfhood is not only the creatio
of personal experience within the relationships, social settings, an
historical moments that shape our awareness. Selfhood is also
cultural conception. More than one such cultural conception of th
self has grown up in America. For each of the moral tradition
sketched in part II of this reader, and in *Habits of the Heart,* the
question of what sort of self one should become is bound togethe
with the matter of what sort of society we should embrace and build

In the revealed tradition of biblical religion, the self is God':
creation, fulfilled through a Covenant with God. For the Puritans
life was a pilgrimage of the soul to God. The self was a *microchristus,*
the virtuous application of Christ's example in this world, like "the
image of the Seal in the Wax." Human community is essentially
religious, binding persons together by love as members of the same
body, the church as the body of Christ.

In the tradition of classical republican humanism, by contrast,
human community is essentially the civic body of a republic governed by principled laws grounded in nature and known by human
reason. The self is part of nature conceived as a cosmos, as having
an ultimate regularity and purpose to its order. The self is a *microcos-
mos,* then, not a *microchristus;* and so, too, is a lawful society.

In the modern city anticipated by Ben Franklin's Philadelphia,
by contrast to Athens and Jerusalem, we find the self defined by its
progress, not as a pilgrim on the way to God or a philosopher-
citizen on the ascent to truth, but as an entrepreneur on the way to
wealth. A good society, then, is more like a thriving market, a pro-

ductive machine, or a fair contract than the corporate body of a church or a republic.

The romantic and expressive tradition scorns the city's marketplace and offices for its colorful streets or the grassy countryside of poets like Walt Whitman and therapists like Fritz Perls. It begins with the individual not as an actor efficiently pursuing her own self-interest but as a personality which experiences, feels, and simply is, at one with herself and with others. As an intimate circle of friends and lovers, expressive community resembles a commune or club more than a church, a republic, or a marketplace.

The self that philosopher and pundit Ralph Waldo Emerson extols in "Self-Reliance" emerges from these two traditions of individualism, especially the latter, and it seeks to transform its biblical and classical predecessors. Sentiment outweighs thought, and genius sets aside tradition to make "what is true for you in your private heart" into a universal truth. "Trust thyself: every heart vibrates to that iron string," Emerson advises, and so do divine providence and human reason. Each person possesses a power "new in nature" whose entrepreneurial outworking bears fruit only through his own toil on his own plot of ground. Society, by contrast, preaches conformity instead of self-reliance. It is a "joint-stock company," which bribes its members to surrender their liberty to better secure their bread. For Emerson individual integrity of mind and heart makes up the only measure of morality, and spiritual affinity between like-minded individuals lays down the only basis for social responsibility or charity. A genuine self does its own work and speaks its own word apart from social roles, institutions, and "communities of opinion." Conformity disguises us in "the prison-uniform of the party" and "the forced smile" of unchosen company. Unmasked, we know ourselves through no other's eyes but our own, in no other time but the present moment. Unfettered by social position or property, our "aboriginal Self" is spontaneously and mystically one with the whole of existence.

In sociologist David Riesman's seminal criticism of postwar American society in *The Lonely Crowd* we hear echoes of Emerson's call to cast off falsely personalized overconformity for genuine autonomy and freedom. But Riesman traces the necessary conjunction of character and society through distinctive modes of conformity

across Western history. "Tradition-directed" types of characte
prevail in premodern societies with populations stabilized by higl
birth and death rates and "primary" economies based on subsist
ence agriculture, hunting, and mining. Customary forms of kinship
political hierarchy, routine labor, and religious rites minutely con
trol personal behavior and uniformly fix personal destiny. With the
Industrial Revolution, Reformation, and early modern politica
revolutions, populations rapidly increase in tandem with "secondary" economies built on continually expanding manufacturing production, capital accumulation, and free labor. "Inner-directed"
types of character arise in response to the greater choices this less
rigidly organized sort of society offers, and the greater initiative it
demands. More individuated and self-conscious, these modern pioneers shape their own destiny and careers guided by a kind of moral
"gyroscope" that revolves around highly general yet inescapably
compelling goals, for example, the ascetic ideals of systematic work
and creditworthiness prescribed by the "Protestant ethic" and
secularized by Ben Franklin. In the twentieth century, as economies
shift from agricultural and industrial labor to the "tertiary" sector
of services and expertise, birth rates decline and societies grow
more bureaucratically centralized. Other people become more of a
problem than the material environment. Gyroscopic self-control for
the sake of entrepreneurial production and savings gives way to the
interpersonal "radar" of "other-directed" types of character more
attuned to bureaucratic cooperation and consumption. Guided by
others' responses and the images of new mass media that personal-
ize events instead of moralizing them, members of the urban, educated "new" middle class shift their goals and attitudes in conformity with the shifting wishes and actions of those around them in
white-collar offices and smaller, more permissive families. Anxiety
over losing others' approval replaces a traditional sense of shame
or inner guilt.

The social constitution of selfhood has long been a central
theme of social science. Developmental psychologists such as Piaget, Erikson, and Kohlberg have built on insights pioneered by
Sigmund Freud and sociologist Emile Durkheim to show how this
process unfolds over the course of a person's life and across varied
social institutions. In Lawrence Kohlberg's sequence of moral
stages, an outlook that stresses relationship to others and responsi-

bility for them as interdependent members of a community, is localized within the home and equated with conformity to convention. The "higher" stages of moral consciousness subordinate relationships to rules and rules to universal principles of justice that serve autonomous selfhood, grounded in a liberal logic of equality and reciprocity. This view of morality favors men and ignores the peculiar sense of selfhood and morality women represent, argues psychologist Carol Gilligan. The social experience of women within the family as mothers and homemakers supports a relational ethic of nurturant care, interdependence, and recognition of unequal needs as relevant to moral desert. Women emphasize this outlook over ethics of equal rights, even exchange, and procedural justice, which guide the marketplace and bureaucracy, which are disproportionately filled and controlled by men. Gilligan clarifies the distinctive moral character of women and men, and the character of the different social institutions in which they develop. Her work underscores the need for an integration of rights and responsibilities in the self-understanding of both sexes, and in our shared understanding of both "private" and "public" institutions.

As readings in parts Four to Seven suggest, social class shapes selfhood through different forms of work and education as well as marriage and family life. In works such as Melvin Kohn's *Class and Conformity,* social psychologists show how class-specific socialization in the family transmits work-related differences in moral character and outlook from one generation to the next. Conformity to act-specific commands stands out in the laborer's home, for example, while self-directive, empathic communication about attitudes and consequences comes to the fore in the manager's family.

From literature and social science alike have come socially sensitive inquiries into the conjunction of character and culture within racial and ethnic communities in America, especially Black communities faced with racial injustice and economic inequality. The juxtaposition of Norman Mailer's breathless celebration of "The White Negro" with Gwendolyn Brooks' probing autobiographical meditation on Negro and black identity dramatizes the deep impact of race on selfhood in America, and its cultural complexity. Mailer turns the Negro into a servant of bohemian protest against the boring security of bourgeois life and the demanding conformity of its "totalitarian" society. Refracted through the prism of the white male "hipster" of the 1950s, the Negro is a victim turned anti-bourgeois rebel. Denied a stable home and secure work, this bohemian, masculine figure balances between humiliation and violent danger—a romantic primitive who forgoes the future and shuts the mind's eye to live only for ecstatic feeling in "the enormous present."

Gwendolyn Brooks opens our eyes to how powerfully the common human nature of all races is obscured by our cultural bias in defining color and justifying caste. "Black" is the opposite of white; it is dirty, evil, and sad. "White" is the color of snow and milk, purity and innocence. To be a person is to be a member of a people. To be black is to belong to a community of memory suffused with the suffering of "bitter birth and intrinsic sorrow." Yet it also breathes with a faith in its own integrity that can sustain demands for justice, promises of love, and hope for their social fulfillment. A sense of selfhood unfolds through history and across generations, not only through the seasons of a person's life, and so selfhood can be transformed. So it was transformed during the 1960s for Brooks, already a distinguished woman of letters yet reborn at the age of fifty from "a 'Negro' fraction" to a whole black person, "an essential African." A truly interracial society first requires the enlargement of black fellow-feeling. To this end Brooks concludes with a call for practices of commitment that will bind and celebrate black community, and with a warning that we cannot continue to live at racial odds and come to know ourselves as truly human.

Ralph Waldo Emerson

Self-Reliance

I read the other day some verses written by an eminent painter which were original and not conventional. The soul always hears an admonition in such lines, let the subject be what it may. The sentiment they instil is of more value than any thought they may contain. To believe your own thought, to believe that what is true for you in your private heart is true for all men,—that is genius. Speak your latent conviction, and it shall be the universal sense; for the inmost in due time becomes the outmost, and our first thought is rendered back to us by the trumpets of the Last Judgment. Familiar as the voice of the mind is to each, the highest merit we ascribe to Moses, Plato and Milton is that they set at naught books and traditions, and spoke not what men, but what *they* thought. A man should learn to detect and watch that gleam of light which flashes across his mind from within, more than the lustre of the firmament of bards and sages. Yet he dismisses without notice his thought, because it is his. In every work of genius we recognize our own rejected thoughts; they come back to us with a certain alienated majesty. Great works of art have no more affecting lesson for us than this. They teach us to abide by our spontaneous impression with good-humored inflexbility then most when the whole cry of voices is on the other side. Else to-morrow a stranger will say with masterly good sense precisely what we have thought and felt all the time, and we shall be forced to take with shame our own opinion from another.

There is a time in every man's education when he arrives at the conviction that envy is ignorance; that imitation is suicide; that he must take himself for better or worse as his portion; that though the

Ralph Waldo Emerson, excerpted from "Self-Reliance," in *The Complete Writings of Ralph Waldo Emerson*, vol. 1 (New York: Wm. H. Wise & Co., 1929), pp. 138–44.

wide universe is full of good, no kernel of nourishing corn can come to him but through his toil bestowed on that plot of ground which is given to him to till. The power which resides in him is new in nature, and none but he knows what that is which he can do, nor does he know until he has tried. Not for nothing one face, one character, one fact, makes much impression on him, and another none. This sculpture in the memory is not without preëstablished harmony. The eye was placed where one ray should fall, that it might testify of that particular ray. We but half express ourselves, and are ashamed of that divine idea which each of us represents. It may be safely trusted as proportionate and of good issues, so it be faithfully imparted, but God will not have his work made manifest by cowards. A man is relieved and gay when he has put his heart into his work and done his best; but what he has said or done otherwise shall give him no peace. It is a deliverance which does not deliver. In the attempt his genius deserts him; no muse befriends; no invention, no hope.

Trust thyself: every heart vibrates to that iron string. Accept the place the divine providence has found for you, the society of your contemporaries, the connection of events. Great men have always done so, and confided themselves childlike to the genius of their age, betraying their perception that the absolutely trustworthy was seated at their heart, working through their hands, predominating in all their being.

* * *

These are the voices which we hear in solitude, but they grow faint and inaudible as we enter into the world. Society everywhere is in conspiracy against the manhood of every one of its members. Society is a joint-stock company, in which the members agree, for the better securing of his bread to each shareholder, to surrender the liberty and culture of the eater. The virtue in most request is conformity. Self-reliance is its aversion. It loves not realities and creators, but names and customs.

Whoso would be a man, must be a nonconformist. He who would gather immortal palms must not be hindered by the name of goodness, but must explore if it be goodness. Nothing is at last sacred but the integrity of your own mind. Absolve you to yourself, and you shall have the suffrage of the world. I remember an answer which when quite young I was prompted to make to a valued adviser who was wont to importune me with the dear old doctrines of the church. On my saying, "What have I to do with the sacredness of traditions, if I live wholly from within?" my friend suggested,—"But these impulses may be from below, not from above." I replied, "They do not seem to me to be such; but if I am the Devil's child, I will live then from the Devil." No law can be sacred to me but that of my nature. Good and bad are but names very readily transferable to that or this; the only right is what is after my constitution; the only wrong what is against it. A man is to carry himself in the presence of all opposition as if every thing were titular and ephemeral but he. I am ashamed to think how easily we capitulate to badges and names, to large societies and dead institutions. I shun father and mother and wife and brother when my genius calls me. I would write on the lintels of the door-post, *Whim.* I hope it is somewhat better than whim at last, but we cannot spend the day in explanation. Expect me not to show cause why I seek or why I exclude company. Then again, do not tell me, as a good man did to-day, of my obligation to put all poor men in good situations. Are they *my* poor? I tell thee, thou foolish philanthropist, that I grudge the dollar, the dime, the cent I give to such men as do not belong to me and to whom I do not belong. There is a class of persons to whom by all spiritual affinity I am bought and sold; for them I will go to prison if need be; but your miscellaneous popular charities; the education at college of fools; the building of meeting-houses to the vain end to which many now stand; alms to sots, and the thousand-fold Relief Societies;—though I confess with shame I sometimes succumb and give the dollar, it is a wicked dollar, which by and by I shall have the manhood to withhold.

* * *

The objection to conforming to usages that have become dead to you is that it scatters your force. It loses your time and blurs the impression of your character. If you maintain a dead church, contribute to a dead Bible-society, vote with a great party either for the government or against it, spread your table like base housekeepers,—under all these screens I have difficulty to detect the precise man you are: and of course so much force is withdrawn from your proper life. But do your work, and I shall know you. Do your work, and you shall reinforce yourself. A man must consider what a blind-man's-buff is this game of conformity. Well, most men have bound their eyes with one or another handkerchief, and attached themselves to some one of these communities of opinion. This conformity makes them not false in a few particulars, authors of a few lies, but false in all particulars. Their every truth is not quite true. Their two is not the real two, their four not the real four; so that every word they say chagrins us and we know not where to begin to set them right. Meantime nature is not slow to equip us in the prison-uniform of the party to which we adhere. We come to wear one cut of face and figure, and acquire by degrees the gentlest asinine expression. There is a mortifying experience in particular, which does not fail to wreak itself also in the general history: I mean "the foolish face of praise," the forced smile which we put on in company where we do not feel at ease, in answer to conversation which does not interest us. The muscles, not spontaneously moved but moved by a low usurping wilfulness, grow tight about the outline of the face, with the most disagreeable sensation.

* * *

The other terror that scares us from self-trust is our consistency; a reverence for our past act or word because the eyes of others have no other data for computing our orbit than our past acts, and we are loth to disappoint them.

But why should you keep your head over your shoulder? Why drag about this corpse of your memory, lest you contradict somewhat you have stated in this or that public place? Suppose you should contradict yourself; what then? It seems to be a rule of wisdom never to rely on your memory alone, scarcely even in acts of pure memory, but to bring the past for judgment into the thousand-eyed present, and live ever in a new day. In your metaphysics you have denied personality to the Deity, yet when the devout motions of the soul come, yield to them heart and life, though they should clothe God with shape and color. Leave your theory, as Joseph his coat in the hand of the harlot, and flee.

A foolish consistency is the hobgoblin of little minds, adored by little statesmen and philosophers and divines. With consistency a great soul has simply nothing to do. He may as well concern himself with his shadow on the wall. Speak what you think now in hard words and to-morrow speak what to-morrow thinks in hard words again, though it contradict every thing you said to-day.—"Ah, so you shall be sure to be misunderstood."—Is it so bad then to be misunderstood? Pythagoras was misunderstood, and Socrates, and Jesus, and Luther, and Copernicus, and Galileo, and Newton, and every pure and wise spirit that ever took flesh. To be great is to be misunderstood.

The magnetism which all original action exerts is explained when we inquire the reason of self-trust. Who is the Trustee? What is the aboriginal Self, on which a universal reliance may be grounded? What is the nature and power of that science-baffling star, without parallax, without calculable elements, which shoots a ray of beauty even into trivial and impure actions, if the least mark of independence appear? The inquiry leads us to that source, at once the essence of genius, of virtue, and of life, which we call Spontaneity or Instinct. We denote this primary wisdom as Intuition, whilst all later teachings are tuitions. In that deep force, the last fact behind which analysis cannot go, all things find their common origin. For the sense of being which in calm hours rises, we know not how, in the soul, is not diverse from things, from space, from light, from time, from man, but one with them and proceeds obviously from the same source whence their life and being also proceed. We first share the life by which things exist and afterwards see them as appearances in nature and forget that we have shared their cause. Here is the fountain of action and of thought.

DAVID RIESMAN

The Lonely Crowd

CHARACTER AND SOCIETY

What is the relation between social character and society? How is it that every society seems to get, more or less, the social character it "needs"? The link between character and society is to be found

David Riesman with Nathan Glazer and Reuel Denney, excerpted and abridged from *The Lonely Crowd: A Study of the Changing American Character* (New Haven, Conn.: Yale University Press, 1950, 1961), pp. 5–25, 249–50, 307.

in the way in which society ensures some degree of conformity from the individuals who make it up. In each society, such a mode of ensuring conformity is built into the child, and then either encouraged or frustrated in later adult experience.

My concern is with two revolutions and their relation to the "mode of conformity" or "social character" of Western man since the Middle Ages. The first of these revolutions has in the last four hundred years cut us off pretty decisively from the family- and clan-oriented traditional ways of life in which mankind has existed throughout most of history; this revolution includes the Renaissance, the Reformation, the Counter-Reformation, the Industrial Revolution, and the political revolutions of the seventeenth, eighteenth, and nineteenth centuries. This revolution is, of course, still in process, but in the most advanced countries of the world, and particularly in America, it is giving way to another sort of revolution—a whole range of social developments associated with a shift from an age of production to an age of consumption. I tentatively seek to link certain social and characterological developments, as cause and effect, with certain population shifts in Western society since the Middle Ages.

It seems reasonably well established, despite the absence of reliable figures for earlier centuries, that during this period the curve of population growth in the Western countries has shown an S-shape of a particular type (as other countries are drawn more closely into the net of Western civilization, their populations also show a tendency to develop along the lines of this S-shaped curve). The bottom horizontal line of the S represents a situation where the total population does not increase or does so very slowly, for the number of births equals roughly the number of deaths, and both are very high. In societies of this type, a high proportion of the population is young, life expectancy is low, and the turnover of generations is extremely rapid. Such societies are said to be in the phase of "high growth potential"; for should something happen to decrease the very high death rate (greater production of food, new sanitary measures, new knowledge of the causes of disease, and so on), a "population explosion" would result, and the population would increase very rapidly. This in effect is what happened in the West, starting with the seventeenth century. This spurt in population was most marked in Europe, and the countries settled by Europeans, in the nineteenth century. It is represented by the vertical bar of the S. Demographers call this the stage of "transitional growth," because the birth rate soon begins to follow the death rate in its decline. The rate of growth then slows down, and demographers begin to detect in the growing proportion of middle-aged and aged in the population the signs of a third stage, "incipient population decline." Societies in this stage are represented by the top horizontal bar of the S, again indicating, as in the first stage, that total population growth is small—but this time because births and deaths are low.

My thesis is, in fact, that each of these three different phases on the population curve appears to be occupied by a society that enforces conformity and molds social character in a definably different way.

The society of high growth potential develops in its typical members a social character whose conformity is insured by their tendency to follow tradition: these I shall term *tradition-directed* people and the society in which they live *a society dependent on tradition-direction*.

The society of transitional population growth develops in its typical members a social character whose conformity is insured by their tendency to acquire early in life an internalized set of goals. These I shall term *inner-directed* people and the society in which they live *a society dependent on inner-direction*.

Finally, the society of incipient population decline develops in its typical members a social character whose conformity is insured by their tendency to be sensitized to the expectations and preferences of others. These I shall term *other-directed* people and the society in which they live one *dependent on other-direction*.

My reference is as much to the complex of technological and institutional factors related—as cause or effect—to the development of population as to the demographic facts themselves. It would be almost as satisfactory, for my purposes, to divide societies according to the stage of economic development they have reached. Thus, Colin Clark's distinction between the "primary," "secondary," and "tertiary" spheres of the economy (the first refers to agriculture, hunting and fishing, and mining; the second to manufacturing; the third to trade, communications, and services) corresponds very closely to the division of societies on the basis of demographic characteristics. In those societies which are in the phase of "high growth potential," the "primary" sphere is dominant (for example, India); in those that are in the phase of "transitional" growth, the "secondary" sphere is dominant (for example, Russia); in those that are in the phase of "incipient decline," the "tertiary" sphere is dominant (for example, the United States). And of course, no nation is all of a piece, either in its population characteristics or its economy—different groups and different regions reflect different stages of development, and social character reflects these differences.

A definition of tradition-direction. Since the [pre-industrial] type of social order is relatively unchanging, the conformity of the individual tends to reflect his membership in a particular age-grade, clan, or caste; he learns to understand and appreciate patterns which have endured for centuries, and are modified but slightly as the generations succeed each other. The important relationships of life may be controlled by careful and rigid etiquette, learned by the young during the years of intensive socialization that end with initiation into full adult membership. Moreover, the culture, in addition to its economic tasks, or as part of them, provides ritual, routine, and religion to occupy and to orient everyone. Little energy is directed toward finding new solutions of the age-old problems, let us say, of agricultural technique or medicine, the problems to which people are acculturated.

The individual in some primitive societies is far more appreciated and respected than in some sectors of modern society. For the individual in a society dependent on tradition-direction has a well-defined functional relationship to other members of the group. If he is not killed off, he "belongs"—he is not "surplus," as the modern unemployed are surplus, nor is he expendable as the unskilled are expendable in modern society. But by very virtue of his "belonging," life goals that are *his* in terms of conscious choice appear to shape his destiny only to a very limited extent, just as only to a limited extent is there any concept of progress for the group.

A definition of inner-direction. In western history the society that emerged with the Renaissance and Reformation and that is only now vanishing serves to illustrate the type of society in which inner-direction is the principal mode of securing conformity. Such a society is characterized by increased personal mobility, by a rapid accumulation of capital (teamed with devastating technological shifts), and by an almost constant *expansion:* intensive expansion in the production of goods and people, and extensive expansion in exploration, colonization, and imperialism. The greater choices this society gives—and the greater initiatives it demands in order to cope with its novel problems—are handled by character types who can manage to live socially without strict and self-evident tradition-direction. These are the inner-directed types.

The source of direction for the individual is "inner" in the sense that it is implanted early in life by the elders and directed toward generalized but nonetheless inescapably destined goals.

We can see what this means when we realize that, in societies in which tradition-direction is the dominant mode of insuring conformity, attention is focused on securing strict conformity in generally observable words and actions, that is to say, behavior. While behavior is minutely prescribed, individuality of character need not be highly developed to meet prescriptions that are objectified in ritual and etiquette—though to be sure, a social character *capable* of such behavioral attention and obedience is requisite. By contrast, societies in which inner-direction becomes important, though they also are concerned with behavioral conformity, cannot be satisfied with behavioral conformity alone. Too many novel situations are presented, situations which a code cannot encompass in advance. Consequently the problem of personal choice, solved in the earlier period of high growth potential by channeling choice through rigid social organization, in the period of transitional growth is solved by channeling choice through a rigid though highly individualized character.

This rigidity is a complex matter. While any society dependent on inner-direction seems to present people with a wide choice of aims—such as money, possessions, power, knowledge, fame, goodness—these aims are ideologically interrelated, and the selection made by any one individual remains relatively unalterable throughout his life. Moreover, the means to those ends, though not fitted into as tight a frame of social reference as in the society dependent on tradition-direction, are nevertheless limited by the new voluntary associations—for instance, the Quakers, the Masons, the Mechanics' Associations—to which people tie themselves. Indeed, the term "tradition-direction" could be misleading if the reader were to conclude that the force of tradition has no weight for the inner-directed character. On the contrary, he is very considerably bound by traditions: they limit his ends and inhibit his choice of means. The point is rather that a splintering of tradition takes place, connected in part with the increasing division of labor and stratification of society. Even if the individual's choice of tradition is largely determined for him by his family, as it is in most cases, he cannot help becoming aware of the existence of competing traditions—hence of tradition as such. As a result he possesses a somewhat greater degree of flexibility in adapting himself to ever changing requirements and in return requires more from his environment.

As the control of the primary group is loosened—the group that both socializes the young and controls the adult in the earlier era—a new psychological mechanism appropriate to the more open society is "invented": it is what I like to describe as a psychological gyroscope.[1] This instrument, once it is set by the parents and other authorities, keeps the inner-directed person, as we shall see, "on course" even when tradition, as responded to by his character, no longer dictates his moves. The inner-directed person becomes capable of maintaining a delicate balance between the demands upon him of his life goal and the buffetings of his external environment.

This metaphor of the gyroscope, like any other, must not be taken literally. It would be a mistake to see the inner-directed man as incapable of learning from experience or as insensitive to public opinion in matters of external conformity. He can receive and utilize certain signals from outside, provided that they can be reconciled with the limited maneuverability that his gyroscope permits him. His pilot is not quite automatic.

Huizinga's *The Waning of the Middle Ages* gives a picture of the anguish and turmoil, the conflict of values, out of which the new forms slowly emerged. Already by the late Middle Ages people were forced to live under new conditions of awareness. As their self-consciousness and their individuality developed, they had to make themselves at home in the world in novel ways. They still have to.

---

1. Since writing the above I have discovered Gardner Murphy's use of the same metaphor in his volume *Personality* (New York, Harper, 1947).

INCIPIENT DECLINE OF POPULATION: OTHER-DIRECTED TYPES

The tradition-directed person, as has been said, hardly thinks of himself as an individual. Still less does it occur to him that he might shape his own destiny in terms of personal, lifelong goals or that the destiny of his children might be separate from that of the family group. He is not sufficiently separated psychologically from himself (or, therefore, sufficiently close to himself), his family, or group to think in these terms. In the phase of transitional growth, however, people of inner-directed character do gain a feeling of control over their own lives and see their children also as individuals with careers to make. At the same time, with the shift out of agriculture and, later, with the end of child labor, children no longer become an unequivocal economic asset. And with the growth of habits of scientific thought, religious and magical views of human fertility—views that in an earlier phase of the population curve made sense for the culture if it was to reproduce itself—give way to "rational," individualistic attitudes. Indeed, just as the rapid accumulation of productive capital requires that people be imbued with the "Protestant ethic" (as Max Weber characterized one manifestation of what is here termed inner-direction), so also the decreased number of progeny requires a profound change in values—a change so deep that, in all probability, it has to be rooted in character structure.

As the birth rate begins to follow the death rate downward, societies move toward the epoch of incipient decline of population. Fewer and fewer people work on the land or in the extractive industries or even in manufacturing. Hours are short. People may have material abundance and leisure besides. They pay for these changes however—here, as always, the solution of old problems gives rise to new ones—by finding themselves in a centralized and bureaucratized society and a world shrunken and agitated by the contact—accelerated by industrialization—of races, nations, and cultures.

The hard enduringness and enterprise of the inner-directed types are somewhat less necessary under these new conditions. Increasingly, *other people* are the problem, not the material environment. And as people mix more widely and become more sensitive to each other, the surviving traditions from the stage of high growth potential—much disrupted, in any case, during the violent spurt of industrialization—become still further attenuated. Gyroscopic control is no longer sufficiently flexible, and a new psychological mechanism is called for.

Furthermore, the "scarcity psychology" of many inner-directed people, which was socially adaptive during the period of heavy capital accumulation that accompanied transitional growth of population, needs to give way to an "abundance psychology" capable of "wasteful" luxury consumption of leisure and of the surplus product. Unless people want to destroy the surplus product in war, which still does require heavy capital equipment, they must learn to enjoy and engage in those services that are expensive in terms of man power but not of capital—poetry and philosophy, for instance.[2] Indeed, in the period of incipient decline, nonproductive consumers, both the increasing number of old people and the diminishing number of as yet untrained young, form a high proportion of the population, and these need both the economic opportunity to be prodigal and the character structure that allows it.

Has this need for still another slate of character types actually been acknowledged to any degree? My observations lead me to believe that in America it has.

A definition of other-direction. The type of character I shall describe as other-directed seems to be emerging in very recent years in the upper middle class of our larger cities. Yet in some respects this type is strikingly similar to the American, whom Tocqueville and other curious and astonished visitors from Europe, even before the Revolution, thought to be a new kind of man. Indeed, travelers' reports on America impress us with their unanimity. The American is said to be shallower, freer with his money, friendlier, more uncertain of himself and his values, more demanding of approval than the European. It all adds up to a pattern which, without stretching matters too far, resembles the kind of character that a number of social scientists have seen as developing in contemporary, highly industri-

2. These examples are given by Allan G. B. Fisher, *The Clash of Progress and Security* (London, Macmillan, 1935).

alized, and bureaucratic America: Fromm's "marketer," Mills's "fixer," Arnold Green's "middle class male child."[3]

If we wanted to cast our social character types into social class molds, we could say that inner-direction is the typical character of the "old" middle class—the banker, the tradesman, the small entrepreneur, the technically oriented engineer, etc.—while other-direction is becoming the typical character of the "new" middle class—the bureaucrat, the salaried employee in business, etc. Many of the economic factors associated with the recent growth of the "new" middle class are well known. There is a decline in the numbers and in the proportion of the working population engaged in production and extraction—agriculture, heavy industry, heavy transport—and an increase in the numbers and the proportion engaged in white-collar work and the service trades. People who are literate, educated, and provided with the necessities of life by an ever more efficient machine industry and agriculture, turn increasingly to the "tertiary" economic realm. The service industries prosper among the people as a whole and no longer only in court circles.

Education, leisure, services, these go together with an increased consumption of words and images from the new mass media of communications. While societies in the phase of transitional growth step up the process of distributing words from urban centers, the flow becomes a torrent in the societies of incipient population decline. This process, while modulated by profound national and class differences, connected with differences in literacy and loquacity, takes place everywhere in the industrialized lands. Increasingly, relations with the outer world and with oneself are mediated by the flow of mass communication. For the other-directed types political events are likewise experienced through a screen of words by which the events are habitually atomized and personalized—or pseudo-personalized. For the inner-directed person who remains still extant in this period the tendency is rather to systematize and moralize this flow of words.

3. See Erich Fromm, *Man for Himself*; C. Wright Mills, "The Competitive Personality," *Partisan Review*, XIII (1946), p. 433; Arnold Green, "The Middle Class Male Child and Neurosis," *American Sociological Review*, XI (1946), p. 31. See also the work of Jurgen Ruesch, Martin B. Loeb, and co-workers on the "infantile personality."

These developments lead, for large numbers of people, to changes in paths to success and to the requirement of more "socialized" behavior both for success and for marital and personal adaptation. Connected with such changes are changes in the family and in child-rearing practices. In the smaller families of urban life, and with the spread of "permissive" child care to ever wider strata of the population, there is a relaxation of older patterns of discipline. Under these newer patterns the peer-group (the group of one's associates of the same age and class) becomes much more important to the child, while the parents make him feel guilty not so much about violation of inner standards as about failure to be popular or otherwise to manage his relations with these other children. Moreover, the pressures of the school and the peer-group are reinforced and continued—in a manner whose inner paradoxes I shall discuss later—by the mass media: movies, radio, comics, and popular culture media generally. Under these conditions types of character emerge that we shall here term other-directed. *What is common to all the other-directed people is that their contemporaries are the source of direction for the individual—either those known to him or those with whom he is indirectly acquainted, through friends and through the mass media. This source is of course "internalized" in the sense that dependence on it for guidance in life is implanted early. The goals toward which the other-directed person strives shift with that guidance: it is only the process of striving itself and the process of paying close attention to the signals from others that remain unaltered throughout life.* This mode of keeping in touch with others permits a close behavioral conformity, not through drill in behavior itself, as in the tradition-directed character, but rather through an exceptional sensitivity to the actions and wishes of others.

Of course, it matters very much who these "others" are: whether they are the individual's immediate circle or a "higher" circle or the anonymous voices of the mass media; whether the individual fears the hostility of chance acquaintances or only of those who "count." But his need for approval and direction from others—and contemporary others rather than ancestors—goes beyond the reasons that lead most people in any era to care very much what others think of them. While all people want and need to be liked by some of the people some of the time, it is only the modern other-directed types who make this their chief source of direction and chief area of sensitivity.[4]

The three types compared. One way to see the structural differences that mark the three types is to see the differences in the emotional sanction or control in each type.

The tradition-directed person feels the impact of his culture as a unit, but it is nevertheless mediated through the specific, small number of individuals with whom he is in daily contact. These expect of him not so much that he be a certain type of person but that he behave in the approved way. Consequently the sanction for behavior tends to be the fear of being *shamed.*

The inner-directed person has early incorporated a psychic gyroscope which is set going by his parents and can receive signals later on from other authorities who resemble his parents. He goes through life less independent than he seems, obeying this internal piloting. Getting off course, whether in response to inner impulses or to the fluctuating voices of contemporaries, may lead to the feeling of *guilt.*

Since the direction to be taken in life has been learned in the privacy of the home from a small number of guides, and since principles, rather than details of behavior, are internalized, the inner-directed person is capable of great stability. Especially so when it turns out that his fellows have gyroscopes too, spinning at the same speed and set in the same direction. But many inner-directed individuals can remain stable even when the reinforcement of social approval is not available—as in the upright life of the stock Englishman isolated in the tropics.

Contrasted with such a type as this, the other-directed person learns to respond to signals from a far wider circle than is constituted by his parents. The family is no longer a closely knit unit to which he belongs but merely part of a wider social environment to which he early becomes attentive. In these respects the other-

4. This picture of the other-directed person has been stimulated by, and developed from, Erich Fromm's discussion of the "marketing orientation" in *Man for Himself,* pp. 67–82. I have also drawn on my portrait of "The Cash Customer," *Common Sense,* XI (1942), p. 183.

directed person resembles the tradition-directed person: both live in a group milieu and lack the inner-directed person's capacity to go it alone. The nature of this group milieu, however, differs radically in the two cases. The other-directed person is cosmopolitan. For him the border between the familiar and the strange—a border clearly marked in the societies depending on tradition-direction—has broken down. As the family continuously absorbs the strange and reshapes itself, so the strange becomes familiar. While the inner-directed person could be "at home abroad" by virtue of his relative insensitivity to others, the other-directed person is, in a sense, at home everywhere and nowhere, capable of a rapid if sometimes superficial intimacy with and response to everyone.

The tradition-directed person takes his signals from others, but they come in a cultural monotone; he needs no complex receiving equipment to pick them up. The other-directed person must be able to receive signals from far and near; the sources are many, the changes rapid. What can be internalized, then, is not a code of behavior but the elaborate equipment needed to attend to such messages and occasionally to participate in their circulation. As against guilt-and-shame controls, though of course these survive, one prime psychological lever of the other-directed person is a diffuse *anxiety*. This control equipment, instead of being like a gyroscope, is like a radar.[5]

THE AUTONOMOUS AMONG THE
INNER-DIRECTED

The autonomous person, living like everyone else in a given cultural setting, employs the reserves of his character and station to move away from the adjusted mean of the same setting. For autonomy, like anomie, is a deviation from the adjusted patterns, though a deviation controlled in its range and meaning by the existence of those patterns.

The autonomous person in a society depending on inner-direction, like the adjusted person of the same society, possessed clearcut, internalized goals and was disciplined for stern encounters with a changing world. But whereas the adjusted person was driven

5. The "radar" metaphor was suggested by Karl Wittfogel.

toward his goals by a gyroscope over whose speed and direction he had hardly a modicum of control and of the existence of which he was sometimes unaware, his autonomous contemporary was capable of choosing his goals and modulating his pace. The goals, and the drive toward them, were rational, nonauthoritarian and noncompulsive for the autonomous; for the adjusted, they were merely given.

If the other-directed people should discover how much needless work they do, discover that their own thoughts and their own lives are quite as interesting as other people's, that, indeed, they no more assuage their loneliness in a crowd of peers than one can assuage one's thirst by drinking sea water, then we might expect them to become more attentive to their own feelings and aspirations.

The enormous potentialities for diversity in nature's bounty and men's capacity to differentiate their experience can become valued by the individual himself, so that he will not be tempted and coerced into adjustment or, failing adjustment, into anomie. The idea that men are created free and equal is both true and misleading: men are created different; they lose their social freedom and their individual autonomy in seeking to become like each other.

Carol Gilligan

In a Different Voice

The arc of developmental theory leads from infantile dependence to adult autonomy, tracing a path characterized by an increasing differentiation of self from other and a progressive freeing of thought from contextual constraints. The vision of Luther, journeying from the rejection of a self defined by others to the assertive

Carol Gilligan, abridged from "In a Different Voice: Women's Conceptions of Self and Morality," *Harvard Education Review*, Vol. 47, No. 4 (November 1977), pp. 481-517; material later included in the book *In a Different Voice: Psychological Theory and Women's Development* (Cambridge, Mass.: Harvard University Press, 1982).

boldness of "Here I stand" and the image of Plato's allegorical man in the cave, separating at last the shadows from the sun, have taken powerful hold on the psychological understanding of what constitutes development. Thus, the individual, meeting fully the developmental challenges of adolescence as set for him by Jean Piaget, Erik Erikson, and Lawrence Kohlberg, thinks formally, proceeding from theory to fact, and defines both the self and the moral autonomously, that is, apart from the identification and conventions that had comprised the particulars of his childhood world. So equipped, he is presumed ready to live as an adult, to love and work in a way that is both intimate and generative, to develop an ethical sense of caring and a genital mode of relating in which giving and taking fuse in the ultimate reconciliation of the tension between self and other.

Yet the men whose theories have largely informed this understanding of development have all been plagued by the same problem, the problem of women, whose sexuality remains more diffuse, whose perception of self is so much more tenaciously embedded in relationships with others and whose moral dilemmas hold them in a mode of judgment that is insistently contextual. The solution has been to consider women as either deviant or deficient in their development.

That there is a discrepancy between concepts of womanhood and adulthood is nowhere more clearly evident than in the series of studies on sex-role stereotypes reported by Broverman, Vogel, Broverman, Clarkson, and Rosenkrantz.[1] The repeated finding of these studies is that the qualities deemed necessary for adulthood—the capacity for autonomous thinking, clear decision making, and responsible action—are those associated with masculinity but considered undesirable as attributes of the feminine self. The stereotypes suggest a splitting of love and work that relegates the expressive capacities requisite for the former to women while the instrumental abilities necessary for the latter reside in the masculine domain. Yet, looked at from a different perspective, these stereotypes reflect a conception of adulthood that is itself out of balance, favoring the separateness of the individual self over its connection

1. I. Broverman, S. Vogel, D. Broverman, F. Clarkson, & P. Rosenkrantz, "Sex-role Stereotypes: A Current Appraisal. *Journal of Social Issues*, Vol. 28 (1972): 59-78.

to others and leaning more toward an autonomous life of work than toward the interdependence of love and care.

CHARACTERISTICS OF THE FEMININE VOICE

The revolutionary contribution of Piaget's work is the experimental confirmation and refinement of Kant's assertion that knowledge is actively constructed rather than passively received. Time, space, self, and other, as well as the categories of developmental theory, all arise out of the active interchange between the individual and the physical and social world in which he lives and of which he strives to make sense. The development of cognition is the process of reappropriating reality at progressively more complex levels of apprehension, as the structures of thinking expand to encompass the increasing richness and intricacy of experience.

Moral development, in the work of Piaget and Kohlberg, refers specifically to the expanding conception of the social world as it is reflected in the understanding and resolution of the inevitable conflicts that arise in the relations between self and others. The moral judgment is a statement of priority, an attempt at rational resolution in a situation where, from a different point of view, the choice itself seems to do violence to justice.

Kohlberg,[2] in his extension of the early work of Piaget, discovered six stages of moral judgment, which he claimed formed an invariant sequence, each successive stage representing a more adequate construction of the moral problem, which in turn provides the basis for its more just resolution. The stages divide into three levels, each of which denotes a significant expansion of the moral point of view from an egocentric through a societal to a universal ethical conception. With this expansion in perspective comes the capacity to free moral judgment from the individual needs and social conventions with which it had earlier been confused and anchor it instead in principles of justice that are universal in application. These principles provide criteria upon which both individual and societal claims can be impartially assessed. In Kohlberg's view, at

2. Lawrence Kohlberg & R. Kramer, "Continuities and Discontinuities in Childhood and Adult Moral Development, *Human Development*. Vol. 12 (1969) 93-120.

the highest stages of development morality is freed from both psychological and historical constraints, and the individual can judge independently of his own particular needs and of the values of those around him.

That the moral sensibility of women differs from that of men was noted by Sigmund Freud in the following by now well-quoted statement:

> I cannot evade the notion (though I hesitate to give it expression) that for women the level of what is ethically normal is different from what it is in man. Their super-ego is never so inexorable, so impersonal, so independent of its emotional origins as we require it to be in men. Character-traits which critics of every epoch have brought up against women—that they show less sense of justice than men, that they are less ready to submit to the great exigencies of life, that they are more often influenced in their judgments by feelings of affection or hostility—all these would be amply accounted for by the modification in the formation of their super-ego which we have inferred above.[3]

While Freud's explanation lies in the deviation of female from male development around the construction and resolution of the Oedipal problem, the same observations about the nature of morality in women emerge from the work of Piaget and Kohlberg. Piaget, in his study of the rules of children's games, observed that, in the games they played, girls were "less explicit about agreement [than boys] and less concerned with legal elaboration"[4]. In contrast to the boys' interest in the codification of rules, the girls adopted a more pragmatic attitude, regarding "a rule as good so long as the game repays it"[5]. As a result, in comparison to boys, girls were found to be "more tolerant and more easily reconciled to innovations"[6].

3. Sigmund Freud, "Some Psychical Consequences of the Anatomical Distinction between the Sexes," in J. Strachey, Ed., *The Standard Edition of the Complete Psychological Works of Sigmund Freud,* Vol. 19. (London: Hogarth Press 1961), pp. 257-258. (Originally published, 1925.)
4. Jean Piaget, *The Moral Judgment of the Child* (New York: The Free Press, 1965), p. 93. (Originally published, 1932.)
5. Piaget, *Child*, p. 83.
6. Piaget, *Child*, p. 52.

Kohlberg also identifies a strong interpersonal bias in the moral judgments of women, which leads them to be considered as typically at the third of his six-stage developmental sequence. At that stage, the good is identified with "what pleases or helps others and is approved of by them"[7]. This mode of judgment is conventional in its conformity to generally held notions of the good but also psychological in its concern with intention and consequence as the basis for judging the morality of action.

That women fall largely into this level of moral judgment is hardly surprising when we read from the Broverman et al. list that prominent among the twelve attributes considered to be desirable for women are tact, gentleness, awareness of the feelings of others, strong need for security, and easy expression of tender feelings. And yet, herein lies the paradox, for the very traits that have traditionally defined the "goodness" of women, their care for and sensitivity to the needs of others, are those that mark them as deficient in moral development. The infusion of feeling into their judgments keeps them from developing a more independent and abstract ethical conception in which concern for others derives from principles of justice rather than from compassion and care. Kohlberg, however, is less pessimistic than Freud in his assessment, for he sees the development of women as extending beyond the interpersonal level, following the same path toward independent, principled judgment that he discovered in the research on men from which his stages were derived. In Kohlberg's view, women's development will proceed beyond Stage Three when they are challenged to solve moral problems that require them to see beyond the relationships that have in the past generally bound their moral experience.

What then do women say when asked to construct the moral domain; how do we identify the characteristically "feminine" voice? What begins to emerge from interviews with women in and around a university community is a sense of vulnerability that impedes these women from taking a stand, what George Eliot regards

7. Kohlberg, From Is to Ought: How to Commit the Naturalistic Fallacy and Get Away with It in the Study of Moral Development. In T. Mischel, Ed., *Cognitive Development and Epistemology.* (New York: Academic Press, 1971), p. 164.

as the girl's "susceptibility" to adverse judgments of others, which stems from her lack of power and consequent inability to do something in the world.[8] While relativism in men, the unwillingness to make moral judgments that Kohlberg and Kramer[9] and Kohlberg and Gilligan[10] have associated with the adolescent crisis of identity and belief, takes the form of calling into question the concept of morality itself, the women's reluctance to judge stems rather from their uncertainty about their right to make moral statements or, perhaps, the price for them that such judgment seems to entail. This contrast echoes that made by Matina Horner (1972), who differentiated the ideological fear of success expressed by men from the personal conflicts about succeeding that riddled the women's responses to stories of competitive achievement.

> Most of the men who responded with the expectation of negative consequences because of success were not concerned about their masculinity but were instead likely to have expressed existential concerns about finding a "non-materialistic happiness and satisfaction in life." These concerns, which reflect changing attitudes toward traditional kinds of success or achievement in our society, played little, if any, part in the female stories. Most of the women who were high in fear of success imagery continued to be concerned about the discrepancy between success in the situation described and feminine identity.

When women feel excluded from direct participation in society, they see themselves as subject to a consensus or judgment made and enforced by the men on whose protection and support they depend and by whose names they are known. A divorced middle-aged woman, mother of adolescent daughters, resident of a sophisticated university community, tells the story as follows:

> As a woman, I feel I never understood that I was a person, that I can make decisions and I have a right to make decisions. I always felt that that belonged to my father or my husband in some way or

8. George Eliot, *The Mill on the Floss* (New York: New American Library, 1965). (Originally published, 1860.)

9. See note 2.

10. Kohlberg & Gilligan, "The Adolescent as a Philosopher: The Discovery of the Self in a Postconventional World, *Daedalus*, Vol. 100 (1971): 1051-1056.

church which was always represented by a male clergyman. They were the three men in my life: father, husband, and clergyman, and they had much more to say about what I should or shouldn't do. They were really authority figures which I accepted. I didn't rebel against that. It only has lately occurred to me that I never even rebelled against it, and my girls are much more conscious of this, not in the militant sense, but just in the recognizing sense. . . . I still let things happen to me rather than make them happen, than to make choices, although I know all about choices. I know the procedures and the steps and all. [Do you have any clues about why this might be true?] Well, I think in one sense, there is less responsibility involved. Because if you make a dumb decision, you have to take the rap. If it happens to you, well, you can complain about it. I think that if you don't grow up feeling that you ever had any choices, you don't either have the sense that you have emotional responsibility. With this sense of choice comes this sense of responsibility.

The essence of the moral decision is the exercise of choice and the willingness to accept responsibility for that choice. To the extent that women perceive themselves as having no choice, they correspondingly excuse themselves from the responsibility that decision entails. Childlike in the vulnerability of their dependence and consequent fear of abandonment, they claim to wish only to please but in return for their goodness they expect to be loved and cared for. This, then, is an "altruism" always at risk, for it presupposes an innocence constantly in danger of being compromised by an awareness of the trade-off that has been made. Asked to describe herself, a Radcliffe senior responds:

I have heard of the onion skin theory. I see myself as an onion, as a block of different layers, the external layers for people that I don't know that well, the agreeable, the social, and as you go inward there are more sides for people I know that I show. I am not sure about the innermost, whether there is a core, or whether I have just picked up everything as I was growing up, these different influences. I think I have a neutral attitude towards myself, but I do think in terms of good and bad. . . . Good—I try to be considerate and thoughtful of other people and I try to be fair in situations and be tolerant. I use the words but I try and work them out practically. . . . Bad things—I am not sure if they are bad, if they are altruistic or I am doing them basically for approval of other people. [Which things are these?] The values I have when I try to act them out. They deal mostly with interpersonal type relations. . . . If I were doing it for approval, it would be a very tenuous thing. If I didn't get the right feedback, there might go all my values.

Ibsen's play *A Doll House* (1879/1965) depicts the explosion of just such a world through the eruption of a moral dilemma that calls into question the notion of goodness that lies at its center. Nora, the "squirrel wife," living with her husband as she had lived with her father, puts into action this conception of goodness as sacrifice and, with the best of intentions, takes the law into her own hands. The crisis that ensues, most painfully for her in the repudiation of that goodness by the very person who was its recipient and beneficiary, causes her to reject the suicide that she had initially seen as its ultimate expression and chose instead to seek new and firmer answers to the adolescent questions of identity and belief.

The availability of choice and with it the onus of responsibility has now invaded the most private sector of the woman's domain and threatens a similar explosion. For centuries, women's sexuality anchored them in passivity, in a receptive rather than active stance, where the events of conception and childbirth could be controlled only by a withholding in which their own sexual needs were either denied or sacrificed. That such a sacrifice entailed a cost to their intelligence as well was seen by Freud when he tied the "undoubted intellectual inferiority of so many women" to "the inhibition of thought necessitated by sexual suppression."[11] The strategies of withholding and denial that women have employed in the politics of sexual relations appear similar to their evasion or withholding of judgment in the moral realm. The hesitance expressed in the previous examples to impose even a belief in the value of human life on others, like the reluctance to claim one's sexuality, bespeaks a self uncertain of its strength, unwilling to deal with consequence, and thus avoiding confrontation.

Thus women have traditionally deferred to the judgment of men, although often while intimating a sensibility of their own

11. Freud, " Civilized' Sexual Morality and Modern Nervous Illness," in J. Strachey, ed., *The Standard Edition of the Complete Psychological Works of Sigmund Freud,* Vol. 9 (London: Hogarth Press, 1959), p. 199. (Originally published, 1908.)

which is at variance with that judgment. Maggie Tulliver, in *The Mill on the Floss* responds to the accusations that ensue from the discovery of her secretly continued relationship with Phillip Wakeham by acceding to her brother's moral judgment while at the same time asserting a different set of standards by which she attests her own superiority:

> I don't want to defend myself. . . . I know I've been wrong—often continually. But yet, sometimes when I have done wrong, it has been because I have feelings that you would be the better for it if you had them. If *you* were in fault ever, if you had done anything very wrong, I should be sorry for the pain it brought you; I should not want punishment to be heaped on you.[12]

An eloquent defense, Kohlberg would argue, of a Stage Three moral position, an assertion of the age-old split between thinking and feeling, justice and mercy, that underlies many of the clichés and stereotypes concerning the difference between the sexes. But considered from another point of view, it is a moment of confrontation, replacing a former evasion, between two modes of judging, two differing constructions of the moral domain—one traditionally associated with masculinity and the public world of social power, the other with femininity and the privacy of domestic interchange. While the developmental ordering of these two points of view has been to consider the masculine as the more adequate and thus as replacing the feminine as the individual moves toward higher stages, their reconciliation remains unclear.

DEVELOPMENTAL THEORY RECONSIDERED

The developmental conception delineated at the outset, which has so consistently found the development of women to be either aberrant or incomplete, has been limited insofar as it has been predominantly a male conception, giving lip-service, a place on the chart, to the interdependence of intimacy and care but constantly stressing, at their expense, the importance and value of autonomous judgment and action. To admit to this conception the truth of the feminine perspective is to recognize for both sexes the central impor-

12. Eliot, p. 188.

tance in adult life of the connection between self and other, the universality of the need for compassion and care. The concept of the separate self and of the moral principle uncompromised by the constraints of reality is an adolescent ideal, the elaborately wrought philosophy of a Stephen Daedalus, whose flight we know to be in jeopardy. Erik Erikson, in contrasting the ideological morality of the adolescent with the ethics of adult care, attempts to grapple with this problem of integration, but is impeded by the limitations of his own previous developmental conception.[13] When his developmental stages chart a path where the sole precursor to the intimacy of adult relationships is the trust established in infancy and all intervening experience is marked only as steps toward greater independence, then separation itself becomes the model and the measure of growth. The observation that for women, identity has as much to do with connection as with separation led Erikson into trouble largely because of his failure to integrate this insight into the mainstream of his developmental theory.[14]

The morality of responsibility which women describe stands apart from the morality of rights which underlies Kohlberg's conception of the highest stages of moral judgment. Kohlberg sees the progression toward these stages as resulting from the generalization of the self-centered adolescent rejection of societal morality into a principled conception of individual natural rights.[15] To illustrate this progression, he cites as an example of integrated Stage Five judgment, "possibly moving to Stage Six," the following response of a twenty-five-year-old subject from his male longitudinal sample:

[What does the word morality mean to you?] Nobody in the world knows the answer. I think it is recognizing the right of the individual, the rights of other individuals, not interfering with those rights. Act as fairly as you would have them treat you. I think it is basically to preserve the human being's right to exis-

13. Erikson, *Insight and Responsibility* (New York: W. W. Norton, 1964).
14. Erikson, *Identity: Youth and Crisis* (New York: W. W. Norton, 1968).
15. Kohlberg, L. *Continuities and Discontinuities in Childhood and Adult Moral Development Revisited.* Unpublished paper, Harvard University, 1973.

tence. I think that is the most important. Secondly, the human being's right to do as he pleases, again without interfering with somebody else's rights.[16]

Another version of the same conception is evident in the following interview response of a male college senior whose moral judgment also was scored by Kohlberg[17] as at Stage Five or Six:

[Morality] is a prescription, it is a thing to follow, and the idea of having a concept of morality is to try to figure out what it is that people can do in order to make life with each other livable, make for a kind of balance, a kind of equilibrium, a harmony in which everybody feels he has a place and an equal share in things, and it's doing that—doing that is kind of contributing to a state of affairs that go beyond the individual, in the absence of which the individual has no chance for self-fulfillment of any kind. Fairness; morality is kind of essential, it seems to me, for creating the kind of environment, interaction between people, that is prerequisite to this fulfillment of most individual goals and so on. If you want other people to not interfere with your pursuit of whatever you are into, you have to play the game.

In contrast, a woman in her late twenties responds to a similar question by defining a morality not of rights but of responsibility:

[What makes something a moral issue?] Some sense of trying to uncover a right path in which to live, and always in my mind is that the world is full of real and recognizable trouble, and is it heading for some sort of doom and is it right to bring children into this world when we currently have an overpopulation problem, and is it right to spend money on a pair of shoes when I have a pair of shoes and other people are shoeless. . . . It is part of a self-critical view, part of saying, how am I spending my time and in what sense am I working? I think I have a real drive to, I have a real maternal drive to take care of someone. To take care of my mother, to take care of children, to take care of other people's children, to take care of my own children, to take care of the world. I think that goes back to your other question, and when I am dealing with moral issues,

16. Kohlberg, "Continuities," p. 29.
17. Kohlberg, Personal communication, August, 1976.

I am sort of saying to myself constantly, are you taking care of the things that you think are important and in what ways are y[ou] wasting yourself and wasting those issues?

While the postconventional nature of this woman's perspect[ive] seems clear, her judgments of Kohlberg's hypothetical moral dile[m]mas do not meet his criteria for scoring at the principled lev[el.] Kohlberg regards this as a disparity between normative and me[ta]ethical judgments which he sees as indicative of the transition b[e]tween conventional and principled thinking. From another perspe[c]tive, however, this judgment represents a different mo[ral] conception, disentangled from societal conventions and raised [to] the principled level. In this conception, moral judgment is orient[ed] toward issues of responsibility. The way in which the responsibil[ity] orientation guides moral decision at the postconventional level [is] described by the following woman in her thirties:

> [Is there a right way to make moral decisions?] The only way I kno[w] is to try to be as awake as possible, to try to know the range of wh[at] you feel, to try to consider all that's involved, to be as aware as yo[u] can be to what's going on, as conscious as you can of where you'[re] walking. [Are there principles that guide you?] The principle wou[ld] have something to do with responsibility, responsibility and carin[g] about yourself and others. . . . But it's not that on the one hand yo[u] choose to be responsible and on the other hand you choose to b[e] irresponsible—both ways you can be responsible. That's wh[y] there's not just a principle that once you take hold of you settle—the principle put into practice here is still going to leave you wit[h] conflict.

The moral imperative that emerges repeatedly in the women'[s] interviews is an injunction to care, a responsibility to discern an[d] alleviate the "real and recognizable trouble" of this world. For th[e] men Kohlberg studied, the moral imperative appeared rather as a[n] injunction to respect the rights of others and thus to protect from interference the right to life and self-fulfillment. Women's insis[-] tence on care is at first self-critical rather than self-protective, whil[e] men initially conceive obligation to others negatively in terms o[f] noninterference. Development for both sexes then would seem to entail an integration of rights and responsibilities through the dis-covery of the complementarity of these disparate views. For the women I have studied, this integration between rights and responsibilities appears to take place through a principled understanding of equity and reciprocity. This understanding tempers the self-destructive potential of a self-critical morality by asserting the equal rights of all persons to care. For the men in Kohlberg's sample as well as for those in a longitudinal study of Harvard undergraduates[18] it appears to be the recognition through experience of the need for a more active responsibility in taking care that corrects the potential indifference of a morality of noninterference and turns attention from the logic to the consequences of choice. In the development of a postconventional ethic understanding, women come to see the violence generated by inequitable relationships, while men come to realize the limitations of a conception of justice blinded to the real inequities of human life.

Kohlberg's dilemmas, in the hypothetical abstraction of their presentation, divest the moral actors from the history and psychology of their individual lives and separate the moral problem from the social contingencies of its possible occurrence. In doing so, the dilemmas are useful for the distillation and refinement of the "objective principles of justice" toward which Kohlberg's stages strive. However, the reconstruction of the dilemma in its contextual particularity allows the understanding of cause and consequence which engages the compassion and tolerance considered by previous theorists to qualify the feminine sense of justice. Only when substance is given to the skeletal lives of hypothetical people is it possible to consider the social injustices which their moral problems may reflect and to imagine the individual suffering their occurrence may signify or their resolution engender.

The proclivity of women to reconstruct hypothetical dilemmas in terms of the real, to request or supply the information missing about the nature of the people and the places where they live, shifts their judgment away from the hierarchical ordering of principles and the formal procedures of decision making that are critical for scoring at Kohlberg's highest stages. This insistence on the particular signifies an orientation to the dilemma and to moral problems

18. Gilligan & Murphy *The Philosopher and the "Dilemma of the Fact": Moral Development in Late Adolescence and Adulthood,* unpublished manuscript, Harvard University, 1977.

in general that differs from any of Kohlberg's stage descriptions. Given the constraints of Kohlberg's system and the biases in his research sample, this different orientation can only be construed as a failure in development. While several of the women in the research sample clearly articulated what Kohlberg regarded as a postconventional metaethical position, none of them were considered by Kohlberg to be principled in their normative moral judgments of his hypothetical moral dilemmas.[19] Instead, the women's judgments pointed toward an identification of the violence inherent in the dilemma itself which was seen to compromise the justice of any of its possible resolutions. This construction of the dilemma led the women to recast the moral judgment from a consideration of the good to a choice between evils. When women begin to make direct moral statements, the issues they repeatedly address are those of exploitation and hurt. In doing so, they raise the issue of nonviolence in precisely the same psychological context that brought Erikson (1969) to pause in his consideration of the truth of Gandhi's life.

In the pivotal letter, around which the judgment of his book turns, Erikson confronts the contradiction between the philosophy of nonviolence that informed Gandhi's dealing with the British and the psychology of violence that marred his relationships with his family and with the children of the ashram. It was this contradiction, Erikson confesses,

> which almost brought *me* to the point where I felt unable to continue writing *this* book because I seemed to sense the presence of a kind of untruth in the very protestation of truth; of something unclean when all the words spelled out an unreal purity; and, above all, of displaced violence where nonviolence was the professed issue.

In an effort to untangle the relationship between the spiritual truth of Satyagraha and the truth of his own psychoanalytic understanding, Erikson reminds Gandhi that "Truth, you once said, 'excludes the use of violence because man is not capable of knowing the absolute truth and therefore is not competent to punish' ". The affinity between Satyagraha and psychoanalysis lies in their shared

19. Kohlberg, L. Personal communication, August, 1976.

commitment to seeing life as an "experiment in truth," in their being

> somehow joined in a universal "therapeutics," committed to the Hippocratic principle that one can test truth (or the healing power inherent in a sick situation) only by action which avoids harm—or better, by action which maximizes mutuality and minimizes the violence caused by unilateral coercion or threat.

Erikson takes Gandhi to task for his failure to acknowledge the relativity of truth. This failure is manifest in the coercion of Gandhi's claim to exclusive possession of the truth, his "unwillingness to learn from *anybody anything* except what was approved by the 'inner voice' ". This claim led Gandhi, in the guise of love, to impose his truth on others without awareness or regard for the extent to which he thereby did violence to their integrity.

The moral dilemma, arising inevitably out of a conflict of truths, is by definition a "sick situation" in that its either/or formulation leaves no room for an outcome that does not do violence. The resolution of such dilemmas, however, lies not in the self-deception of rationalized violence—"I was," said Gandhi, "a cruelly kind husband. I regarded myself as her teacher and so harassed her out of my blind love for her"—but rather in the replacement of the underlying antagonism with a mutuality of respect and care.

Gandhi, whom Kohlberg has mentioned as exemplifying Stage Six moral judgment and whom Erikson sought as a model of an adult ethical sensibility, instead is criticized by a judgment that refuses to look away from or condone the infliction of harm. In denying the validity of his wife's reluctance to open her home to strangers and in his blindness to the different reality of adolescent sexuality and temptation, Gandhi compromised in his everyday life the ethic of nonviolence to which in principle and in public he was so steadfastly committed.

The blind willingness to sacrifice people to truth, however, has always been the danger of an ethics abstracted from life. This willingness links Gandhi to the biblical Abraham, who prepared to sacrifice the life of his son in order to demonstrate the integrity and supremacy of his faith. Both men, in the limitations of their fatherhood, stand in implicit contrast to the woman who comes before

Solomon and verifies her motherhood by relinquishing truth in order to save the life of her child. It is the ethics of an adulthood that has become principled at the expense of care that Erikson comes to criticize in his assessment of Gandhi's life.

This same criticism is dramatized explicitly as a contrast between the sexes in *The Merchant of Venice* (1598/1912), where Shakespeare goes through an extraordinary complication of sexual identity (dressing a male actor as a female character who in turn poses as a male judge) in order to bring into the masculine citadel of justice the feminine plea for mercy. The limitation of the contractual conception of justice is illustrated through the absurdity of its literal execution, while the "need to make exceptions all the time" is demonstrated contrapuntally in the matter of the rings. Portia, in calling for mercy, argues for that resolution in which no one is hurt, and as the men are forgiven for their failure to keep both their rings and their word, Antonio in turn foregoes his "right" to ruin Shylock.

The research findings that have been reported in this essay suggest that women impose a distinctive construction on moral problems, seeing moral dilemmas in terms of conflicting responsibilities. This construction was found to develop through a sequence of three levels and two transitions, each level representing a more complex understanding of the relationship between self and other and each transition involving a critical reinterpretation of the moral conflict between selfishness and responsibility. The development of women's moral judgment appears to proceed from an initial concern with survival, to a focus on goodness, and finally to a principled understanding of nonviolence as the most adequate guide to the just resolution of moral conflicts.

For the present, my aim has been to demonstrate the centrality of the concepts of responsibility and care in women's constructions of the moral domain, to indicate the close tie in women's thinking between conceptions of the self and conceptions of morality, and, finally, to argue the need for an expanded developmental theory that would include, rather than rule out from developmental consideration, the difference in the feminine voice. Such an inclusion seems essential, not only for explaining the development of women but also for understanding in both sexes the characteristics and precursors of an adult moral conception.

NORMAN MAILER

Advertisements for Myself

It is on this bleak scene that a phenomenon has appeared: the American existentialist—the hipster, the man who knows that if our collective condition is to live with instant death by atomic war, relatively quick death by the State as *l'univers concentrationnaire,* or with a slow death by conformity with every creative and rebellious instinct stifled (at what damage to the mind and the heart and the liver and the nerves no research foundation for cancer will discover in a hurry), if the fate of twentieth-century man is to live with death from adolescence to premature senescence, why then the only life-giving answer is to accept the terms of death, to live with death as immediate danger, to divorce oneself from society, to exist without roots, to set out on that uncharted journey into the rebellious imperatives of the self. In short, whether the life is criminal or not, the decision is to encourage the psychopath in oneself, to explore that domain of experience where security is boredom and therefore sickness, and one exists in the present, in that enormous present which is without past or future, memory or planned intention, the life where a man must go until he is beat, where he must gamble with his energies through all those small or large crises of courage and unforeseen situations which beset his day, where he must be with it or doomed not to swing. The unstated essence of Hip, its psychopathic brilliance, quivers with the knowledge that new kinds of victories increase one's power for new kinds of perception; and defeats, the wrong kind of defeats, attack the body and imprison

Norman Mailer, excerpted from "The White Negro," in his *Advertisements for Myself* (New York: Putnam's, 1959), pp. 339–441.

one's energy until one is jailed in the prison air of other people's habits, other people's defeats, boredom, quiet desperation, and muted icy self-destroying rage. One is Hip or one is Square (the alternative which each new generation coming into American life is beginning to feel), one is a rebel or one conforms, one is a frontiersman in the Wild West of American night life, or else a Square cell, trapped in the totalitarian tissues of American society, doomed willy-nilly to conform if one is to succeed.

A totalitarian society makes enormous demands on the courage of men, and a partially totalitarian society makes even greater demands, for the general anxiety is greater. Indeed if one is to be a man, almost any kind of unconventional action often takes disproportionate courage. So it is no accident that the source of Hip is the Negro for he has been living on the margin between totalitarianism and democracy for two centuries. But the presence of Hip as a working philosophy in the sub-worlds of American life is probably due to jazz, and its knifelike entrance into culture, its subtle but so penetrating influence on an avant-garde generation—that postwar generation of adventurers who (some consciously, some by osmosis) had absorbed the lessons of disillusionment and disgust of the twenties, the depression, and the war. Sharing a collective disbelief in the words of men who had too much money and controlled too many things, they knew almost as powerful a disbelief in the socially monolithic ideas of the single mate, the solid family and the respectable love life. If the intellectual antecedents of this generation can be traced to such separate influences as D. H. Lawrence, Henry Miller, and Wilhelm Reich, the viable philosophy of Hemingway fit most of their facts: in a bad world, as he was to say over and over again (while taking time out from his parvenu snobbery and dedicated gourmandize), in a bad world there is no love nor mercy nor charity nor justice unless a man can keep his courage, and this indeed fitted some of the facts. What fitted the need of the adventurer even more precisely was Hemingway's categorical imperative that what made him feel good became therefore The Good.

So no wonder that in certain cities of America, in New York of course, and New Orleans, in Chicago and San Francisco and Los Angeles, in such American cities as Paris and Mexico, D.F., this particular part of a generation was attracted to what the Negro had to offer. In such places as Greenwich Village, a ménage-à-trois was completed—the bohemian and the juvenile delinquent came face-to-face with the Negro, and the hipster was a fact in American life. If marijuana was the wedding ring, the child was the language of Hip for its argot gave expression to abstract states of feeling which all could share, at least all who were Hip. And in this wedding of the white and the black it was the Negro who brought the cultural dowry. Any Negro who wishes to live must live with danger from his first day, and no experience can ever be casual to him, no Negro can saunter down a street with any real certainty that violence will not visit him on his walk. The cameos of security for the average white: mother and the home, job and the family, are not even a mockery to millions of Negroes; they are impossible. The Negro has the simplest of alternatives: live a life of constant humility or ever-threatening danger. In such a pass where paranoia is as vital to survival as blood, the Negro had stayed alive and begun to grow by following the need of his body where he could. Knowing in the cells of his existence that life was war, nothing but war, the Negro (all exceptions admitted) could rarely afford the sophisticated inhibitions of civilization, and so he kept for his survival the art of the primitive, he lived in the enormous present, he subsisted for his Saturday night kicks, relinquishing the pleasures of the mind for the more obligatory pleasures of the body, and in his music he gave voice to the character and quality of his existence, to his rage and the infinite variations of joy, lust, languor, growl, cramp, pinch, scream and despair of his orgasm. For jazz is orgasm, it is the music of orgasm, good orgasm and bad, and so it spoke across a nation, it had the communication of art even where it was watered, perverted, corrupted, and almost killed, it spoke in no matter what laundered popular way of instantaneous existential states to which some whites could respond, it was indeed a communication by art because it said, "I feel this, and now you do too."

So there was a new breed of adventurers, urban adventurers who drifted out at night looking for action with a black man's code to fit their facts. The hipster had absorbed the existentialist synapses of the Negro, and for practical purposes could be considered a white Negro.

The Field of the Fever

> *Everybody has to go to the bathroom.*
> *That's* good.
> *That's* a great thing.

If by some quirk of fate Blacks had to go to the bathroom and whites didn't I shudder to think of the genocidal horrors that would be visited on the Blacks of the whole world. Here is what my little green *Webster's New World* has to say about a world-shaking word:

black (blak), adj. (A S *blaec*) 1. opposite to white: see color. 2. dark-complexioned. 3. Negro. 4. without light; dark. 5. dirty. 6. evil; wicked. 7. sad; dismal. 8. sullen. n. 1. black pigment; opposite of white. 2. dark clothing, as for mourning. 3. a Negro. v.t.&v.i., to blacken.—black-out, to lose consciousness.—blackly, adv:—blackness, n.

Interestingly enough, we do not find that "white" is "opposite of black." That would "lift" black to the importance-level of white.

white (hwit), adj. (A S hwit). 1. having the color of pure snow or milk. 2. of a light or pale color. 3. pale; wan. 4. pure; innocent. 5. having a light-colored skin. n. 1. the color of pure snow or milk. 2. a white or light-colored thing, as the albumen of an egg, the white part of the eyeball, etc. 3. a person with a light-colored skin; Caucasian.—whiteness, n.

Until 1967 my own Blackness did not confront me with a shrill spelling of itself. I knew that I was what most people were calling "a Negro"; I called myself that, although always the word fell awk-

Gwendolyn Brooks, excerpted from "The Field of the Fever, the Time of the Tall-Walkers," in *Report from Part One, An Autobiography,* (Detroit: Broadside Press, 1972), pp. 75–78.

wardly on a poet's ear; I had never liked the sound of it (Caucasian has an ugly sound, too, while the name Indian is beautiful to look at and to hear.) *And* I knew that people of my coloration and distinctive history had been bolted to trees and sliced or burned or shredded; knocked to the back of the line; provided with separate toilets, schools, neighborhoods; denied, when possible, voting rights; hounded, hooted at, or shunned, or patronizingly patted (often the patting hand was, I knew, surreptitiously wiped after the Kindness, so that unspeakable contamination might be avoided). America's social climate, it seemed, was trying to tell me something. It was trying to tell me something Websterian. Yet, although almost secretly, I had always felt that to be Black was good. Sometimes, there would be an approximate whisper around me: *others* felt, it seemed, that to be Black was good. The translation would have been something like "Hey—being Black is *fun.*" Or something like "Hey—our folks have got stuff to be proud of!" Or something like "Hey—since we are so good why aren't we treated like the other 'Americans'?"

❋   ❋   ❋

There is indeed a new Black today. He is different from any the world has known. He's a tall-walker. Almost firm. By many of his own *brothers* he is not understood. And he is understood by *no* white. Not the wise white; not the Schooled white; not the Kind white. Your *least* prerequisite toward an understanding of the new Black is an exceptional Doctorate which can be conferred only upon those with the proper properties of bitter birth and intrinsic sorrow. I know this is infuriating, especially to those professional Negro-understanders, some of them so *very* kind, with special portfolio, special savvy. But I cannot say anything other, because nothing other is the truth.

I—who have "gone the gamut" from an almost angry rejection of my dark skin by some of my brainwashed brothers and sisters to a surprised queenhood in the new Black sun—am qualified to enter at least the kindergarten of new consciousness now. New consciousness and trudge-toward-progress.

I have hopes for myself.

A capricious bunch of entries and responses has brought me to my present understanding of fertile facts. Know-nows: I know now that I am essentially an essential African, in occupancy here because of an indeed "peculiar" institution. I know now that the Indian is the authentic American, unless *he* did some forcible country-taking, too. I know that I am in that company of thousands now believing that Black tragedy is contrived. I know now that Black fellow-feeling must be the Black man's encyclopedic Primer. I know that the Black-and-white integration concept, which in the mind of some beaming early saint was a dainty spinning dream, has wound down to farce, to unsavory and mumbling farce, and that Don L. Lee, a major and muscular Black voice of this day, is correct in "The New Integrationist":

> I
> seek
> integration
> of
> negroes
> with
> black
> people.

I know that the Black emphasis must be not *against white* but *FOR Black*. I know that a substantial manner of communication and transaction with whites will be, eventually, arrived at, arranged—*if* Blacks remain in this country; but the old order shall not prevail; the day of head pats for nice little niggers, bummy kicks for bad bad Biggers, and apparent Black acceptance of both, is done. In the Conference-That-Counts, whose date may be 1980 or 2080 (woe betide the Fabric of Man if it is 2080), there will be no looking up nor looking down.

It frightens me to realize that if I had died before the age of fifty, I would have died a "Negro" fraction. . . .

Yes, needed is a holiday for Blacks everywhere, a Black World Day, with Black excitement and Black trimmings in honor of the astounding strength and achievement of Black people. A yearly Black People's Day—akin, perhaps, to the Black concept Kwanza, which, based on a traditional African holiday, is considered by many Black people an alternative to commercial Christmas; for the week beginning December twenty-sixth, homes are decorated in red and black and green, the black representing the blacknation, the red representing our shed blood, the green featured as a symbol of land for nation-establishment and a symbol, too, for live faith in our young.

I see, feel, and hear a potential celebration as Africa colors—thorough, direct. A thing of shout but of African quietness, too, because in Africa these tonals can almost coincide. A clean-throated singing. Drums; and perhaps guitars. Flags or a flag. Costumery, wholesomely gaudy; costumery which, for the African, is not affectation but merely a right richness that the body deserves. Foods; not pâté de foie gras or creamed lobster de bon bon, but figs and oranges, and vegetables. . . . AND the profound and frequent shaking of hands, which in Africa is so important. The shaking of hands in warmth and strength and union.

PART FOUR

LOVE, MARRIAGE, AND FAMILY

To live one's adult life in an enduring marriage "until death do us part" with someone one truly loves is an ideal still cherished by the vast majority of Americans. Yet when a national sample was asked in 1978 whether "most couples getting married today expect to remain married for the rest of their lives," 60 percent said no. The kind of commitment that we most desire is one that for many of us is becoming increasingly difficult to make. The readings in this chapter highlight this contradiction in our culture and trace out some of its causes and consequences.

Daniel Yankelovich, a social psychologist who is a well known specialist in survey research, documents a dramatic shift in Americans' ideas about family life within the last thirty years. In the 1950s most Americans took it for granted that almost all decent, "normal" people would get married and raise children. Now most Americans see such a way of life as but one valid option among many. Over the past generation the majority of Americans have come to accept sex outside of marriage as morally tolerable, at least under some circumstances. A majority also thinks it acceptable for couples to live together even if they are not married. Over 80 percent believe that it is morally acceptable to be married and not have children, while over 70 percent say it is morally acceptable to be single and have children. Marriage can no longer be taken for granted, accepted as an inevitable part of the life course. It has to be chosen, and those who do choose it have constantly to decide whether they will remain married.

These changes are intimately connected with transformations in several dimensions of our social life, in the repertoire of symbols, myths, and rituals that constitute American culture on the one hand and in the structure of American economy and society on the other.

The readings by the sociologist and *Habits of the Heart* co-author Ann Swidler, and the historian Nancy Cott both explore this complex of interconnected changes. Swidler focuses especially on the cultural dimension and Cott on the social-structural dimension, but both recognize that changes in one dimension cannot be fully understood in isolation from the other.

Ann Swidler's "Love and Adulthood in American Culture" puts recent changes in attitudes toward love and marriage in the perspective of historical shifts within American cultural traditions. In Western culture the idea of love—the "love myth"—combines a rich array of tensions: choice versus commitment, rebellion versus attachment, self-realization versus self-sacrifice, and libidinal expression versus restraint. "In the traditional love myth, individuals rebelled against society (family, convention, tradition), but in loving they simultaneously sought new commitments and found their own place in the social world." Because of its individualism, however, early modern American culture resisted thinking of love in terms of a balance between these tensions. The greatest heroes in nineteenth and early twentieth century American literature were not people who rebelled against society in order to seek new commitments and find a settled place in the social world. Heroic figures in the greatest American novels, from *The Last of the Mohicans, Huckleberry Finn,* and *Moby Dick* to the modern novels of Faulkner and Nathaniel West, were men who refused to settle down. To the extent that love implied getting trapped into domesticity, they had to be wary of it. The popular literature that did give a strong place to love—particularly "women's literature" such as romantic novels and Gothic romances—did indeed identify love in terms of becoming settled down—"All women were mothers, not mistresses or lovers, and all love implied being trapped into congealed domesticity." In popular American culture, love was thus shorn of the "sense of passionate choice and rebellious assertion of identity that gave depth and power to English and European forms of the love myth." It embodied a "conservative" set of meanings and was always on the defensive against the culture's dominant individualism.

In contemporary American culture, Swidler argues, the love myth is being restructured. However, this restructuring does not bring the classic tensions of the myth into better balance, it merely substitutes a predominant emphasis on the rebellious, free, individualistic side of love for a one-sided emphasis on the conservative, constrained, socially committed side. In modern literature and cinema, "love is not the emblem of a crystallized identity but the mandate for continuing self-exploration"; "the hidden message in modern treatments of love is not self-sacrifice but self-development." These changes are grounded in changing definitions of the self and they are linked to changes in the American social structure.

Nancy Cott analyzes the social structural circumstances that in early modern America supported an identification of love with domesticity and domesticity with a "women's sphere" of life separate from and ultimately subordinate to the heroic male sphere of individualistic self-assertion. The transition from preindustrial to modern work patterns in the late eighteenth and early nineteenth centuries separated the mainstream of economic life from the life of the household. Work outside the home in the emerging industrial organizations of modern society demanded calculating, disciplined striving after economic success, the kind of effort that *Habits of the Heart* associates with utilitarian individualism. Work inside the home—cooking meals, making clothes, caring for children—"retained the irregularity, the responsiveness to immediate and natural demands, and the admixture with social occasion common to preindustrial occupations."

The way of life associated with the "woman's sphere" of the household thus increasingly diverged from that of the masculine world of work. The virtues appropriate to women's sphere came to be seen as fundamentally separate from the characteristics that could enable men to succeed in their jobs and careers. The primary virtue of women's sphere was "disinterested" love, love as self-sacrificial caring. American culture idealized this kind of love but isolated its practice from the all-important realm of work and ultimately devaluated it. The cozy comforts of women's sphere were after all dependent on the wealth earned by calculating, competitive men in their modern forms of employment.

If the place of the love myth in early modern American culture was shaped by the split between work and family life characteristic of industrialization, what changes in the social structure have shaped the contemporary version of the love myth? Cott's analysis does not go beyond the nineteenth century, but Swidler suggests answers to this question. In our contemporary society, her article suggests, the relationship between work and family life has changed. Social life is dominated more fully by the terms of economic life than ever before. The isolation of women's sphere is thus breaking down. In the modern economy, most women have to work outside the home. Women cannot afford to live their lives so thoroughly around the ideal of home-centered disinterested love as they could in earlier history. And they have more options for defining the terms of their relationship with their spouses than before. Moreover, the modern world of work demands greater flexibility than ever before. "Only the person who is always ready with a new idea, who can move from one organization or role to another, can succeed." This demand for ceaseless flexibility affects many members of the middle class, encouraging them to find meaning only in relationships that do not tie them down, that allow them to keep "growing." The experience of living in such a world encourages the idea that what makes a love relationship good is not that it binds a couple into a permanent union, but that it allows each member to grow, even if that means growing apart.

The demands for flexibility imposed by a modern, dynamic economy do not necessarily feel like opportunities for growth to people at all levels of the economy, however. People who do not have the economic and educational resources to move continually upward in such an economy may feel helplessly pushed around by the pressures to make a living, their lives painfully bent into unchosen shapes. Such is the experience of the working-class narrator in "I Stand Here Ironing," a story by the feminist novelist Tillie Olsen. Her daughter, the narrator says, "was a child of anxious, not proud, love." The narrator was poor. She was nineteen years old and it was during the depression when she gave birth to her daughter. Her lover, the child's father, left her when her daughter was less than a year old, no longer able to "endure . . . sharing want with us." The need to find work meant that she couldn't "grow" as she would have liked, and—even more painful for her—she couldn't give her daughter the kind of love that would enable the child to grow properly. "Anxious, not proud love" is a love that includes the

76,335

desire for individual self-expression and feels the need to consummate such self-expression in commitment to spouse and children. But it is a love unsustained by the economic resources that would enable the lover to freely express herself and to live up to her felt responsibilities towards those whom she loves. American culture gives the narrator her hopes about what love can and should be, but the American economy often makes people of her status unable to fulfill those hopes.

DANIEL YANKELOVICH

New Rules: Searching for Self-Fulfillment in a World Turned Upside Down

When I asked young women in the 1950s why they cherished marriage, family, and children as their inevitable destiny, many were rendered tongue-tied. My question struck them as unanswerable, meaningless. Asked why she wanted to get married and have children, one woman replied, sarcastically, "Why do you put on your pants in the morning? Why do you walk with two feet instead of one?"

We all know that very little can be taken for granted any longer when it comes to Americans' attitudes toward sexual relations, marriage, family, and childrearing. Some of the changes that have taken place are so profound that we may not realize that they may yet be evolving into newer forms, forms that can now be only dimly discerned. However, to get a perspective on what may be happening, we need to appreciate the shifts of the past few decades.

A variety of surveys point to at least 20 major normative changes in American life in recent years. These 20 are not necessarily the most important changes, they simply are the ones that have been measured in surveys. But at least half of them have to do with domestic norms and portray the virtual abandonment of some of our most deeply entrenched beliefs about marriage and the family. In some instances we have trend data going back to the 1930s; in others, the comparisons go back only 10 or 20 years or even less; and, in a few instances, there are no previous measures, so we must infer from other evidence that a change has taken place.

The study I conducted in the late 1950s among single and

married women in their teens and early 20s demonstrated the strength of marriage norms. All the single women I interviewed assumed they would marry and have children. The married women who did not yet have children all stated that they planned to have them, most wanted three or four children or more. The mothers in the study were all married, and each pronounced herself thoroughly satisfied with being a mother. Although several of the young mothers admitted that they had become pregnant without intending to, none of them felt comfortable saying outright that she did not want to have a child.

These attitudes toward marriage and children were confirmed by a study conducted by the University of Michigan at about the same time. The study asked a national cross section of Americans what they thought of anyone, man or woman, who rejected the idea of marriage. An overwhelming majority—a full 80 percent— severely criticized those who preferred the single state, stigmatizing them as "sick" or "neurotic" or "immoral." The remaining 20 percent were neutral, neither condemnatory nor approving. Fewer than one percent had anything good to say about the unmarried state.

By the late 1970s the country's interpretation of the kind of person who would deliberately choose to remain unmarried had shifted strikingly. In another Michigan study, condemnatory attitudes shrunk from 80 percent to a mere 25 percent—from virtual consensus to minority standing. A three-fifths majority (61 percent) swung into the neutral column, and a significant number (14 percent) praised the choice of the unmarried state as a valid and positive way of life. In other words, in the late 1950s, 80 percent of all Americans held that being unmarried was an unnatural state for a man or woman: to be normal was to be married. By the late 1970s, a mere generation later, virtually the same proportion (75 percent) had changed their normative premise.

According to Elizabeth Douvan, a Michigan researcher associated with the study, "Norms about marriage and parenthood have changed dramatically over the past 20 years. Today marriage and parenthood are rarely viewed as necessary, and people who do not choose these roles are no longer considered social deviants."

Furthermore, and also in sharp contrast with the past, it has become normal to think of marriage as not being permanent. When an NBC Associated Press poll asked Americans in 1978 whether they thought "most couples getting married today expect to remain married for the rest of their lives," a 60 percent majority said no. As Sheila M. Rothman writes in *Woman's Proper Place:* "In the 1950s as in the 1920s, diamonds were 'forever.' In the 1970s diamonds were for 'now.' "

These shifts are not just a matter of our changing attitudes and values. Norms influence behavior. Single households (defined by the U.S. Census Bureau as men or women living alone or with an unrelated person) have had an explosive growth rate. Increasing 66 percent from 1960 to 1980. During this same period, single-parent families (mainly women, but now including more than one and a half million men) also grew rapidly—from 9 percent of all households in 1960 to 14 percent now. Together, these two categories constitute nearly four out of 10 households. Marriage and traditional family life are growing less universal all the time.

Between 1960 and 1977 it is estimated that the number of unmarried couples living together more than doubled—from 439,000 to 957,000. *Time* magazine quotes one woman, a 27-year-old graduate student living in Kansas, describing her parents' reaction to the news that she was living with a man: "When I first told my parents I had a new roommate, they immediately knew what was going on. My mother's first words were, 'Don't do all the cooking and cleaning.' " When Yankelovich, Skelly, and White asked in surveys for *Time* whether people thought it was "morally wrong for couples who are not married to live together," more than half (52 percent) answered no.

There has been a dramatic change in attitudes toward childbearing as well. From the once universally held norm that a childless woman was, by definition, barren and not a complete woman, we have moved to a widespread acceptance of childlessness without stigma. A study by my firm shows that virtually all Americans (83 percent) now believe it is acceptable to be married and not have children. A majority (59 percent) reject even the weaker version of that concept, that "people who do not have children are selfish." In the same tolerant spirit, three out of four Americans say it is now morally acceptable to be single and have children—an astonishing turnabout in mores when one recalls the scandal and disgrace formerly associated with having a child out of wedlock.

Here, too, changes in behavior parallel the shift in norms. In recent years the fertility of American women has followed a steady downward trend—from 118.3 births per 1,000 women of childbearing age in 1955, to 66.7 in 1975. In the period from 1955 to 1959, a woman in her childbearing years could expect to have 3.7 births; in 1965 to 1969, 2.6 births; in 1977, 1.8. In the 1950s married young women who did not want babies were reluctant to admit it. Now I often encounter the reverse situation in interviews: many young women deny any interest in having babies, they admit to harboring a "curiosity" about the experience of childbirth and mothering only if pressed.

So much has been written in recent years about changing sexual norms that we need not dwell on them at length. A few survey findings sum up the story. As recently as 1967, a Yankelovich, Skelly, and White survey for CBS News found that most parents of college-age youths (85 percent) condemned all premarital sex as morally wrong. Now, a majority (63 percent) condone it: "If two people love each other, there's nothing morally wrong with having sexual relations." Nearly the same majority (57 percent) reject the norm that a woman should be a virgin when she gets married. And most Americans now reject the old double standard: "If a husband plays around a little, that's excusable, but a wife never should."

In another form, the double standard lives on. Its existence can be documented in the mere 45 percent plurality of Americans who find male nudes in women's magazines acceptable, as compared with the nearly 60 percent who accept female nudes in men's periodicals. The divergence is merged again, however, in the nearly doubled acceptance of total nudity in films and plays in the last 10 years.

Another change: for the first time in American society, only minorities of adults report discomfort at "having friends who are homosexuals," and while slim majorities still feel that homosexual relations may be morally wrong, there is a declining willingness to restrict the sexual preferences of consenting adults by law; barely one-quarter of the population (21 percent) express a desire for a return to traditional standards in sexual relations.

ANN SWIDLER

Love and Adulthood in American Culture

Adulthood, which once seemed an uneventful, predictable time of life, has more recently come to seem problematic and mysterious. We find ourselves asking whether adulthood is a period of stability or of change, whether adults "develop" or only drift, whether there are patterned "stages" of adult development or only more and less successful responses to external pressures. The answers to these questions depend in large part on emerging shifts in the way our culture patterns adulthood. By examining the ideology of love, one of the central anchors of our culture's view of adult life, I will explore the changing structure of meaning that shapes the contemporary adult life course.

Love in our culture is both an experience and an ideal, richly arrayed in symbol and myth. These myths outline the shape of adulthood, and the rituals of love mark its moments of transition. Like religious experience, the culturally grounded experience of love links the lives of individuals—their private struggles and triumphs—to larger issues, framing the meaning of adult life. Thus Freud's statement that an adult must be able "to love and to work" is a moral as well as a psychological ideal. If this ideal is undermined, if love and work no longer seem to be significant achievements, the integrity and meaning of adult life are undermined as well.

As Erik Erikson's work has made us aware, ideological and religious images provide symbolic resources which structure individual developmental crises and make possible their resolution. Although love in real life is not like love in literature or in the movies, our culture's images of love provide a background, a language, and a set of symbols within which people enact their own

Ann Swidler, excerpted from "Love and Adulthood in American Culture," in *Themes of Work and Love in Adulthood,* ed. Neil Smelser and Erik Erikson (Cambridge, Mass.: Harvard University Press, 1980), pp. 120–46.

lives. In loving and being loved, people give themselves over, at least for brief periods, to intensely moving experiences through which they achieve new awareness of self and others. Love can make possible periods of crystallization or reformulation of the self and the self's relationship to the world. Beliefs about love permeate people's hopes for themselves, their evaluations of experience, and their sense of achievement in the world.[1]

While love is only one part of adulthood, its symbolic richness makes it an ideal place to examine the cultural dilemmas of contemproary adulthood. We may ask both what resources our culture provides for building a satisfactory adulthood, and what new models and images of adulthood are developing to give meaning to emerging challenges in adult life.

THE TRADITIONAL CULTURE OF LOVE

In the West the ideal of love became infused with moral meaning. While the heroes of most societies are great warriors, or leaders who dedicate themselves to their people, in our culture the drama of love embodies a struggle for moral perfection and social commitment. This symbolic link between love and moral life is the legacy of courtly love.[2]

1. Geertz (1965, p. 8) has said that religious symbols provide "models of" and "models for" reality. "Culture patterns . . . give meaning, i.e., objective conceptual form, to social and psychological reality both by shaping themselves to it and by shaping it to themselves." While for many people in modern society religious symbols and rituals have lost their vividness and their direct applicability to daily life, love is still an experience to which people give themselves, and which allows at least a partial experience of transcendence. Like religious experience, culturally grounded experiences of love do not dominate every moment of daily life. As Geertz (1968, p. 110) says, "The key to the question of how religion shapes social behavior, is that much of religion's practical effect, like much of dreaming's, comes in terms of a kind of pale, remembered reflection of religious experience proper, in the midst of everyday life." It is in part through moments of heightened experience and its "pale, remembered reflection" in everyday life that our culture's myths about love shape the experience of adulthood.

2. C. S. Lewis (1958, pp. 3–4) writes: "It seems to us natural that love should be the commonest theme of serious imaginative literature: but a glance at classical antiquity or at the Dark Ages at once shows us that what we took for 'nature' is really a special state of affairs, which will probably have an end, and which certainly had a beginning in eleventh-century Provence . . . [The French poets] effected a change

Courtly love, from which our modern love mythology derives, grew out of the crisis of feudal loyalty in twelfth- and thirteenth-century Europe (Lewis, 1958; Bloch, 1964). The moral ideal of the vassal's devotion to his lord came under strain as vassal warriors became hereditary aristocrats whose interests conflicted with those of the lords they served. Emergent states established wider principles of moral and legal order which competed with feudal traditions of personal loyalty and perpetual warfare (Bloch, 1977). In courtly love the feudal ideals of service and devotion were transferred from the noble lord to the lady, and the knightly virtue of courage in battle was transmuted into the display of heroism and moral worth in the quest for love. Courtly love articulated a new conception of individual moral autonomy, expressed in the conflicts of choices faced by the courtly lovers. Originating in southern France at the end of the eleventh century, courtly poetry and the games of courtly love spread rapidly throughout the courts of Europe, providing the central motifs of aristocratic culture for the next six-hundred years.

While courtly love and its associated code of chivalry remained the status ethic of a narrow class, they gave a distinctive orientation to Western ideals of love. Broadened and popularized, courtly love provided the images and symbols underlying the bourgeois love ethic that is ours today. Most important among these ideals is that love ennobles and transforms the lover. As Andreas Capellanus, the twelfth-century codifier of the "rules of love," wrote in *The Art of Courtly Love*: "Now it is the effect of love that a true lover cannot be degraded with any avarice. Love causes a rough and uncouth man to be distinguished for his handsomeness; it can endow a man even of the humblest birth with nobility of character; it blesses the proud with humility; and the man in love becomes accustomed to performing many services gracefully for everyone. O what a wonderful thing is love, which makes a man shine with so many virtues and teaches everyone, no matter who he is, so many good traits of character!" Through an elaborate code of sexual flirtation combined with sexual restraint, courtly love heightened self-control, so that passion

which has left no corner of our ethics, our imagination, or our daily life untouched, and they erected impassable barriers between us and the classical past or the Oriental present. Compared with this revolution, the Renaissance is a mere ripple on the surface of literature."

could inspire virtue, putting the power of sexual feeling behind the demands of self-perfection.

But courtly love had a second side—a side of treachery, suffering, and death. As Denis de Rougemont (1956) has emphasized, the great love stories, from Tristan and Iseult to Romeo and Juliet, are of forbidden love which ends in tragedy and death. The great chivalry romances, like the stories of Lancelot and Guinevere or Tristan and Iseult, are tales of adultery—of a terrible conflict between love of a lady and loyalty to the lord to whom she is married. Thus in the crisis of feudal loyalty, courtly love sustained the traditional virtues of devotion and courage, and added to them more refined qualities such as "courtesy," humility, and a willingness to protect the weak and helpless. But it was also a code of adulterous love, mythicizing a rebellion against social obligations. Love was both virtue and sin; while it ennobled, it also led to betrayal, and ultimately to tragedy and death. This duality of the courtly love, its fusion of moral striving and social rebellion, has deeply influenced our own love mythology.

Although courtly love provides the basic ingredients of our view of love, in courtly love these elements still lack their modern shape. Only in the eighteenth century did the emerging middle class, influenced by Protestant conceptions of individual destiny and faced with the dilemmas of social life in a market economy, reappropriate the aristocratic love myth, using it to formulate a new relationship between individual identity and social life and a new conception of the shape of the adult life course. Now the power of love would sustain and glorify the individual's attempt to forge his identity, to know himself, and to find his place in the social world.

The novel was the new literary form whose emergence in eighteenth-century England marked the triumph of a bourgeois conception of love and a new interpretation of society and the self. This literary evidence is important because the mythic themes of the novel still dominate popular culture, and because the basic structure of the novel—its description of life as a plot, with a beginning, middle, and end, linked by comprehensive unity of character and action—is such a perfect embodiment of our culture's view of the adult life course.

In *The Rise of the Novel,* Ian Watt (1957) argues that the novel's characteristic themes, structure, and formal properties reflected the needs of an emerging middle class—involved in market exchange, individualized, and anxious in a new way about achieving success. To crystallize the novel as a literary form (in contrast to loosely organized prose narratives such as the rogue biographies or dramatic genres with fewer claims to "realism"), a satisfactory ending was required—an ending that could believably bring dramatic closure to the lives of ordinary individuals. The event that could serve as a resolution for complex problems of character and action in a realistic social setting was marriage. As a symbolic turning point in the lives of individuals, marriage fused together important themes in middle-class life with the formal needs of the novel.

Especially for the women who predominated among the early novel-reading public, marriage concentrated into one critical event all the questions about livelihood, mobility, and achievement that were becoming critical for the middle class. The increasing separation of work and home in the seventeenth and eighteenth centuries denied women their traditional role in the domestic economy and made middle-class women who did not marry—the "maiden aunts" and "spinster" daughters or sisters—dependent on the charity of others. Women had to marry, and whom they married was the major determinant of their life chances. So Samuel Richardson's Pamela, the virtuous maidservant who became wife of the master, was the epitome of female success. Marriage, linking questions of class, mobility, and money to the most intimate aspects of private experience, could symbolize the new middle-class concern with individual merit and achievement (Watt, 1957). The Protestant view of the self as having a single, unified inner essence decisive for the individual's fate was, in the love myth, linked to a single moment in the adult life course when a person could find out who she (or he) was, and what her fate was to be.

AMERICAN CULTURE AS A FRAMEWORK FOR ADULTHOOD

The way adulthood is experienced is shaped by the way a culture organizes and frames adult life. In Western culture love has played a central symbolic role in integrating the issues of individual identity, moral choice, and social commitment. Courtly tradition made love a moral matter, ennobling and disciplining the self; bourgeois culture made love a central symbol of the individual quest for identity, integrity, and fulfillment.

In the traditional love myth, individuals rebelled against society (family, convention, tradition), but in loving they simultaneously sought new commitments and found their own place in the social world. The search for love and the search for a way to deal with society were inextricably linked. But American culture dealt differently with the symbolism of adulthood. What does the love myth tell us about the attitude of our culture toward adulthood, toward the nexus of individual identity with social commitment? How is this attitude changing? By examining the peculiar form the love myth has taken in American culture, and exploring contemporary changes in the ideology of love, we will see how adulthood itself is changing. In doing so we will better understand whether our culture can infuse the tasks of adulthood, achievement of fidelity, love, care, and wisdom with richness and meaning.

The traditional American attitude toward adulthood has been one of fear, and along with this fear has gone great uncertainty about love. The power of the love myth has always come from its ability to bind together contradictory elements—ennobling passion and adulterous betrayal in courtly love; individual rebellion and social commitment in bourgeois romantic love. These conflicting images embody the tension between individual and social demands, and the love myth promises their resolution. But in America the relation between the individual and society has been particularly problematic, and thus the attitude toward love peculiarly ambivalent.

While the traditional love myth has always had a strong place in American popular culture, particularly in "women's literature" (romantic novels, women's magazine fiction, and Gothic romances), Leslie Fiedler (1966) noted some time ago that the greatest American novels, from *The Last of the Mohicans, Huckleberry Finn,* and *Moby Dick* to the modern novels of Faulkner or Nathaniel West, avoid passionate love as a central theme, their male heroes seeking self definition against nature or Gothic terror and seeking intimacy in the companionship of other men. In the American myth, women and love represent the entangling bonds of social obligation, and the only real self-definition comes from a Faustian quest to face inner and outer evil alone (Fiedler, 1966). Even in popular culture, our traditional heroes are the cowboy and the private eye, men pursuing their own self-created image of freedom and justice outside the corrupting times of social life (Cawelti, 1976).[3]

Americans have also been criticized, by themselves and others, for a sort of premature closing-off of the self. Kenneth Keniston (1968) has written of an adolescence in which inner conflict is submerged in conformity to the peer group and an adult identity achieved by reluctant submission to the demands of work and marriage. The irony of American identity formation, as Erikson (1963) has written, is that it "seems to support an individual's ego identity as long as he can preserve a certain element of deliberate tentativeness of autonomous choice. The individual must be able to convince himself that the next step is up to him and that no matter where he is staying or going he always has the choice of leaving or turning in the opposite direction if he chooses to do." In fantasy Americans remain perpetual adolescents, while adult commitments represent the defeat rather than the fulfillment of the quest for identity. People are "trapped" into marriage;[4] work is a loss of freedom, a shameful "settling down."

3. While the mythic structure of American culture is not the exclusive property of either sex, the love myth is, at least symbolically, differently shaped for men and women. In women's literature the happy ending is still marriage, and love still allows people to find themselves as they find each other. High culture, on the whole, is dominated by men and by the male version of the myth, in which the man escapes both women and society in his lonely quest for selfhood. Of course there can be Faustian heroes who are women (Hester Prynne in *The Scarlet Letter*) and men can fight for love and commitment. But in general, the polarization of the sexes around the different sides of the love myth, while it accounts in large part for the tone of aggressive warfare in America's cultural treatment of the "battle of the sexes" (from Blondie and Dagwood or Little Abner and Daisy Mae to the head nurse in *One Flew over the Cuckoo's Nest*, women tie men down, curtailing their quest for freedom and self-definition), both men and women are caught by the conflict about social commitment expressed in America's treatment of love.

4. Lillian Rubin (1976) and Mirra Komarovsky (1962) have both pointed out how unwillingly many working-class men claim to marry. A high proportion of marriages are precipitated by a pregnancy, so that both men and women marry without having fully chosen to do so. The only way to develop social commitments is to be "trapped." This pattern corresponds to the fantasy Martha Wolfenstein and Nathan Leites (1950) found in their study of American movies. Men and women are thrown together on a train, or forced together by some accident, so that their involvement occurs in spite of or because of, their wishes in the matter.

Americans have, perhaps, a more passionately developed sense of individuality and selfhood than members of most other cultures, but this individuality remains forever locked in a sort of childish wish not to become adult, a cultural rejection of adulthood itself. The love myth has always had a place in American culture, but a degraded one. While it promised individuality, integrity, and independence, these were compromised by the danger of a confining, settled adulthood. What American culture could not do was to make the achievement of adult commitment, fidelity, intimacy, and care themselves seem heroic, meaningful achievements. In the current period the love myth is undergoing a change. The historic oppositions which traditionally gave the love myth its emotional appeal and cultural dynamism are being intensified, while the balance of elements in the myth is shifting. These changes have important consequences for the definition and meaning of adulthood.

The emerging love ethic reemphasizes the rebellious, free, individualistic side of the love myth. In some ways the values of permanence and commitment have been undermined even further, while the adolescent-fantasy core of American culture has strengthened its hold. On the other hand, the emerging love ideology, because it endorses flexibility and eschews permanence, also sees love more as a continuing process than as a once-and-for-all culmination of life, after which people need only live happily ever after. The central elements of the love myth remain; people still seek moral self-definition, fulfilling intimacy, and a meaningful identity. But the framework of expectations about what it means to achieve these things, and thus the cultural definition of adulthood itself, is changing.

Changes in the cultural meaning of love are grounded on the one hand in changing definitions of the self (and thus implicitly of adulthood as a whole) and on the other hand in changing social-structural demands on the life course. There are four distinguishable oppositions within our culture's love mythology, tensions which have given the myth its richness, its seeming power to reconcile divergent needs and opposing parts of the self. Each of these four oppositions links the lives of individuals to aspects of the social world and thus to specific changes in contemporary society. The tension between choice and commitment embodies the problem of moral self-definition and the achievement of identity. Choice of a marriage partner and its implication of permanent commitment have provided the structural foundation of this aspect of the love myth. The second important symbolic tension in the love myth is that between rebellion against social obligation versus attachment to the social world, particularly the world of work. The third opposition is that between self-realization and self-sacrifice. Love traditionally promised self-realization, yet required self-sacrifice, especially when love led to children and the full burdens of family life. Finally, libidinal expression through love is in tension with the libidinal restraint required by the traditional norm of fidelity and the related problem of the sources and grounds of intimacy.

CHOICE VERSUS COMMITMENT

The tension between choice and commitment involves the problem of identity. If identity is something that must be won only once, if the self is a stable achievement, remaining constant despite superficial flux, then the choice that symbolically consolidates identity forecloses further possibilities of or needs for choice. But when the fixity of the self cannot be taken for granted, the tensions implicit in the love myth's treatment of choice and commitment become more apparent.

The love myth describes the attempt to define one's self by the free choice of a love partner, fusing the problem of the search for one's true self with the quest for one's right mate. The correlate of such self-definition is identity and, in Erikson's terms, fidelity. Faithfulness to one's choice becomes faithfulness to oneself. The capacity to make a commitment and stick to it is the measure of successful identity formation. Yet the traditional model of choice and commitment implies a relatively static notion of both love and identity. While a process of liberating personal growth culminates in choice of the "right" partner, the choice consolidates that growth while prohibiting further change. One chooses only once, after which commitment closes off alternative choices and alternative identities.

Here we can see a profound shift in the ideology of love—an attempt to preserve its ennobling moral quality and its power of defining identity, while giving up the ideal of commitment which was traditionally the hallmark of both moral achievement and secure identity. Modern moral ideals for the self, in particular the emphasis on self-actualization and the demand for continuing growth and change in adulthood, clash head on with the traditional ideal of love as commitment.

New ideologies of love attempt to preserve the heroic myth of the struggle for identity by giving it a new content.

The search for self-knowledge and identity is still central, but that search can no longer be defined by a single decisive choice, a struggle against external obstacles to assert the self against the world. Now the obstacles to love are internal to the self and to the relationship (as, for example, in Ingmar Bergman's "Scenes from a Marriage"), and one can love most fully by deepening the honesty and communication in a relationship, even if the relationship ends as a consequence. True love is not a love to which one is committed, so much as a love in which one can have complete communication. And communication is difficult; it requires heroic struggle with the self and the lover. By the same token, a love relationship that does not require painful change no longer performs its function. The value of love, and its challenge, is that it must stimulate and absorb perpetual change.

New images of love do not reject the core elements of the traditional love myth—that love is a moral achievement, capable of defining and transforming the self. But what the self is, and how it is to be defined and enshrined, is differently conceived. Ralph Turner (1976) has argued that there are two fundamentally opposed ways of viewing the self, which he calls "institution" and "impulse." People who locate the "true self" institutionally define themselves by acts of choice and will, in the institutionalized roles to which they commit themselves. People who define their real selves by impulse see as true only what wells up outside institutional roles. "The outburst or desire is recognized—fearfully or enthusiastically—as an indication that the real self is breaking through a deceptive crust of institutional behavior. Institutional motivations are external, artificial constraints and superimpositions that bridle manifestations of the real self". What the traditional ideal of love accomplished was to fuse these two conceptions of self together into one overriding achievement. One could follow his deepest impulses to find his true self, and imbed that self in an institutional commitment. Will and desire could merge in the achievement of identity. In the shifting structure of the love myth, the impulsive sides of the self are given greater emphasis, and the ideal of permanence is undermined. What is good about a relationship is not the commitment it embodies, but how much a person learns about himself from the relationship. Love is not the emblem of a crystallized identity but the mandate for continuing self-exploration.

In the traditional view, a love that ended was a failure, a sign of some terrible mistake in the search for self and identity. But the new love imagery can claim great gains from failed relationships. Each person can grow and learn, even from loss and disappointment. In-deed permanence, which was the hallmark of success in the earlier model of identity formation, becomes almost a sign of failure. After all, is it likely that one can keep growing and changing with the same partner? Doesn't permanence in a relationship necessarily require some compromise of individual possibilities for growth? And even for those who value permanent commitment, its meaning is changed. Enduring relationships mean a deeper challenge and even more profound opportunities for growth than do short-term relationships. So both those who value long-term and short-term relationships increasingly justify relationships by the opportunities they offer for challenge and change. The greatest sin a lover can commit is not betrayal, renegging on a commitment, but obstruction, trying to thwart, hamper, or limit another's freedom to grow.

While the new mythology of love and the new ideal of the self have been criticized as examples of the "new narcissism" (Lasch, 1976), the new ideology is also a shift in the direction of adulthood. In keeping alive the image of love as a crucible for identity, but making the quest for identity and the quest for love continuing preoccupations, the emerging love mythology validates adulthood as a period of continuing crisis, challenge, and change. It rejects the notion that life's dilemmas are resolved at one crucial moment of choice and commitment, after which one must only live happily ever after.

Both Robert Lifton (1971) and Kenneth Keniston (1968) have argued that modern society changes the nature of identity, making it more flexible, less fixed, and less permanent than traditional models of personal development allowed. What we see in the contemporary culture of love is an attempt to give moral content, added meaning, to this new model of development. By drawing on the rich symbolic resources of the Western love mythology, contemporary culture redefines the morally significant elements of love, focuses attention on new frontiers of the quest for identity (communication and understanding rather than permanence and commitment), and enshrines a new image of the self. While in some ways it means abandonment of central aspects of the love myth in our culture, it also opens up new possibilities for exploring the meanings of adult life. By reappropriating elements of the love ideology, it offers the possibility of new cultural grounding for the adult life course.

SELF-REALIZATION VERSUS SELF-SACRIFICE

How much to give and what one will be allowed to take, the balance between satisfaction and sacrifice, has been a continuing theme in stories of love. In the traditional mythology the lover seeks his own happiness, fights for his own gratification, and yet the highest form of love is selfless giving. In the traditional imagery of love, the ecstasy of possessing another merges with the altruistic wish to sacrifice oneself for the other's well-being.

As long as we believe that a person can fulfill himself only through love of another, the tension between self-realization and self-sacrifice is minimized. One realizes himself *through* self-sacrifice. But with changes in the kinds of self-definition people expect from love goes a change in the norms and language of love. While these shifts may sound like simple cloaks for self-indulgence, they contain deeper meanings. The obligation to sacrifice oneself for another is replaced by the duty to respect the other person's separateness, to recognize the other's needs for growth and change, to give to the other in return for what one receives.

Marcia Millman (1972), in a study of experimental small groups, has written of two contrasting sets of metaphors with which group relationships are described, which she calls "exchange" and "tragic-mythic." Exchange imagery describes what people "get out of a relationship," how much they will "take" from one another, who will "dump" what onto the group. Tragic-mythic imagery, on the other hand, imbed the relationship in a dramatic structure: "The group member who uses 'tragic-mythic' imagery frequently describes his relationships in the group in terms of his search for identity, of recalling certain things from his past and rediscovering himself, and of his downfall in the group. He is concerned with the issues of free will and destiny, and his attention is on action. He understands the other characters in terms of their origins and culminations, and he views his present relationships as the reenactment of old stories". The traditional love myth is a "tragic-mythic" organization of self and experience, in which life can be given meaning by its "culmination," the climax of the novel's (or of life's) story. The emerging cultural view of love, on the other hand, emphasizes exchange. What is valuable about a relationship is "what one gets out of it." One values what one can learn from another person, what one can take away from the experience. One is valued in turn for what he gives in exchange. Rather than a relationship standing as the culmination of a drama of self-discovery, the partners in a relationship remain autonomous and separate, each concerned about what he will have gained, what he will take away, when the relationship is over.

Exchange metaphors, indeed, imply impermanence. In a successful exchange each person is enhanced so that each is more complete, more autonomous, and more self-aware than before. Rather than becoming part of a whole, a couple, whose meaning is complete only when both are together, each person becomes stronger; each gains the skills he was without and, thus strengthened, is more "whole." If we enter love relationships to complete the missing sides of ourselves, then in some sense when the exchange is successful we have learned to get along without the capacities the other person had supplied.

Exchange metaphors and the ideal of the autonomous individual are closely linked. We can see the image in changing ideals of male-female relations, for example, where the demand is for two people who can each be "whole people" with a balance of instrumental and affective capacities, rather than two people who are each specialized halves of a couple but inadequate as individual human beings. This imagery is used explicitly by Philip Slater (1970), and it underlies much of the rhetoric of the women's movement. The moral ideal is the person who is complete in himself or herself, who is able to stand alone, whether or not she chooses to do so.

The hidden message in modern treatments of love is, then, not self-sacrifice but self-development. A good relationship is one in which one has learned something and can leave it a stronger or better person. Most profoundly, the emphasis in love stories is on survival, on a person's need to be reassured that he can endure any loss, can get along without anyone. So in one of the most popular love stories of our recent history, *Love Story*, the essential drama was not that Oliver and Jenny won each other, but rather that Jenny gave Oliver a great lesson in survival. She helped him learn to love and to forgive his parents and to win greater control over himself before she died, leaving him unencumbered yet strong. In a similar way, the theme of movies such as *Alice Doesn't Live Here Anymore* or *An Unmarried Woman* is that people can learn to survive alone, and indeed to prefer their hard-won autonomy to renewed ties of dependence.

This anxiety about the wholeness and integrity of the self also shows up as a new concern with self-realization and a denunciation of self-sacrifice. Of course in social-structural terms, the most significant sacrifice to which one can be committed by loving is the sacrifice one makes for one's children. While one marries for love, for the fulfillment of one's own needs, marrying commits one to a life of serving others—one's spouse and especially one's children.

But in contemporary literature even the sacrifice of parents for their children has been brought into question. Several modern novels portray a conflict between sacrifice for anyone else, including children, and the necessary attention to the imperiled self. Novelists can now portray children as predators or enemies who demand without giving, who threaten the necessary self-nurture of their parents. Recent women's literature, of course, takes up this theme, though in most feminist literature the husband-lover is the enemy who robs women of the energy they need for themselves. But in novels such as *The War between the Tates* children are portrayed as sullen strangers, and in Joseph Heller's *Something Happened,* the demanding child is an enemy to be outsmarted, the retarded child a symbol of hopelessness, and the bright, good child an emblem of the father's guilt.

Self-sacrifice, which once seemed the ultimate proof of love, now seems suspect. For people to try to realize themselves through the sacrifices they make for others comes to seem not nobility but parasitism. We fear clinging wives and smothering mothers and we condemn the man or woman who cannot stand up for his or her own needs. The drama in many modern love stories is whether people will be able to resist the temptations of love and surrender in order to perform the more difficult task of finding themselves.

This cultural legitimation of "selfishness" is in many ways a claim on behalf of adulthood. We no longer believe that an adult's life can be meaningfully defined by the sacrifice he or she makes for spouse or children. Current ideologies of child-rearing emphasize that parents have rights also, that it is not enough to use up each adult life in nurturing the lives that come after it. Adulthood is viewed as a period with its own tasks and demands. Just as husbands and wives cannot submerge their own needs in those of their partners, so adults cannot sacrifice themselves completely to their children.

We can cite demographic changes that have intensified the problem of how to live as an adult, particularly for women: the reduced period of child-rearing and the prolonged period of the "empty nest" when parental roles no longer define the meaning of a couple's relationship; widowhood and divorce which force women, and men as well, to face the question of what to make of their own lives; and delayed marriage which allows adults to be more fully formed before they undertake marriage at all. But accompanying these demographic challenges to old models of adulthood are new cultural values—a new concern with the survival, wholeness, and autonomy of the self that makes self sacrifice seem weakness, and self-realization seem a moral duty. In this context the very meaning of love changes. In the attempt to legitimate a concern with adult life on its own terms, our culture also holds up a model of human relatedness that makes the sufficiently complete self a precondition for relations with others. Other people can be only a stimulus to our own growth and development, not a source of the meaning of our lives. We are mistrustful of those who seek to find themselves through love, rather than loving from a position of strength, fully in possession of themselves.

* * *

In Western culture the experience of love is imbedded in a matrix of moral ideas which have given shape, definition, and meaning to the individual life course. Rich in ritual, myth, and symbols, love has provided an element of broader meaning at the core of the life experience. But the love myth contains tensions between opposing elements, oppositions that account in part for the depth and resonance of the myth. By arousing contradictory impulses, by fusing together divergent aspects of individual experience, love acquires great power as an experience and as a symbolic consolidation of life.

Choice versus commitment, rebellion versus attachment, self-realization versus self-sacrifice and libidinal expression versus restraint—these are contradictions not in the sense that they present people with irreconcilable alternatives in their practical life arrangements, but in the sense that they permeate the cultural meaning of love with contradictory expectations. The great power of the love myth is that it promises to resolve those contradictions, to fulfill both sides of the duality at once: Love provides the opportunity for profound choice, the choice of a life-long commitment; love sanctions rebellion against social ties in the service of attaching oneself to society; love inspires self-realization through sacrifice of oneself for another; and love intensifies and deepens sexual expression by channeling it through sexual restraint. These paradoxical promises are not accidents or cultural "mistakes"—quite the opposite. The reason love can provide a crucible for identity formation, a symbol of achievement of a place in the social world, a capacity for dedication to something outside oneself, and a potent consolidation of one's deepest emotional urges is precisely because it can embody these dual meanings.

But in American culture the balance of these tensions has been unequal, and hence their power diminished, because of the central importance Americans give to individuality and the low value they place on social connectedness. While the romantic myth has upheld the ideals of attachment, commitment, and intimacy, it has been on the defensive against the culture's dominant individualism. Abandoned on the whole by high culture, the love myth was weakened, so that the "conservative" set of meanings it embodied—love as commitment, acceptance of social attachment, self-sacrifice, and libidinal restraint—predominated, no longer complemented by the sense of passionate choice and rebellious assertion of identity that gave depth and power to the English and European forms of the love myth. All women were mothers, not mistresses or lovers, and all love implied being trapped into congealed domesticity.

In the contemporary period, complex changes are occurring in our love ideology, with important implications for adulthood. The traditional oppositions in the love myth fused together aspirations of youth and adulthood; the myth sanctioned youthful rebellion in the service of finding adult commitments. But in this fusion one moment was given moral meaning—the moment of transition from youth to adulthood. The power of the myth came from glorifying and intensifying the period when identity was crystallized, attachment discovered, aspirations for fulfillment realized, and intimacy achieved. But this left the "adult" sides of the love myth without sustaining meaning. Identity, commitment, self-realization, and intimacy, once achieved, were simply supposed to last a lifetime. Moral meaning lay in being able to stick to what one had chosen, to continue to be animated by the commitments one had made. But in the contemporary period, the valence of the love myth is shifting—in ways which often seem regressive. These "youthful" aspirations for rebellion, choice, self-realization, and sexual expression are being idealized all over again. That is, our culture now seeks moral significance in acts of choice, in attempts to discover, clarify, or deepen the self, whether or not these choices lead to or remain within a commitment. The ideology of love is being partially reworked, so that elements of the love myth—that love transforms, that love allows one to know his true self, that love is a crucible for self-development—are being incorporated into a new structure.

The fate of these shifts in cultural emphasis is still obscure. What is clear, however, is that our culture's view of adulthood is changing. What once seemed a secure if difficult accomplishment, a once-and-for-all achievement, has come to seem much less secure. Pressures for flexibility in adult love and work have cut loose the anchors for many of the old definitions of successful, meaningful, morally integrated adulthood. It is hard for us to find metaphors to express the meaning of love that is not forever and work that is not a lifetime commitment. Much of our cultural response to the uncertainties of modern adulthood has been a kind of empty despair in high culture, abandoning hope for meaning, and in popular culture a shallow and somewhat hysterical emphasis on protecting a childish version of the self.

But there are also signs of hope. As moral emphasis shifts from life-long commitments to a lifetime of choices, there is the possibility of rejoining the fractured elements of the love myth, but on new terms. An identity developed through continuing choice may be a fuller and richer achievement than a single, climactic consolidation of the self. Social attachments may also be more gratifying and less terrifying if they do not mean stifling closure in work or love, but can continue to embody a rebellious streak, a search for new constellations in the relationship of self to the social world. Intimacy can certainly be deeper if there is openness to continuing mutual exploration. A commitment to another person may go beyond loyalty, to an understanding of shared responsibility for the quality of a continuing relationship. And even self-sacrifice, or the possibility of generative giving to others, can perhaps be made richer if it is matched by recognition of one's own incompleteness, one's own capacities for continuing growth and change.

In some ways the most crucial shift in our culture is a change in the symbolic and moral grounding of the self in modern society. If the self can no longer find definition in a single set of adult commitments, a set of roles which consolidate identity, what can the self be? If it must be defined, as seems implicit in the modern culture of love, by its ability to resist attachment, by its ability to go through changes without being fundamentally changed, then we have an ideal of the self cut off from meaningful connection to others, from any danger of commitment, attachment, sacrifice, or self-restraint. This is a model of human relationships in which people are not willing to take the risks of disappointment and defeat that inevitably accompany meaningful love or work.

And yet, there is strength in the recognition that "the capacity to love and to work" is not a one-time accomplishment that settles the adult life course once and for all. Further risks, further choices, further efforts are demanded, and further opportunities for self-knowledge, intimacy, and joy await us. In the past our love ideology has dealt largely with the problems of becoming an adult, as if after the adult course was set there was nothing left to worry about— people did not have to keep living together after they won each other, work did not continue to be problematic after one had settled on an identity. Now we have a cultural attempt to deal with adulthood, to develop a set of myths and images that can give moral meaning and purpose to a life that has no fixed end, no dramatic conclusion. In some ways the reaction to this challenge seems to be a culture of narcissism, in which the self and its perpetuation become all, in which the trick is to remain alive and whole without risking attachments or making binding choices. But the other side of these cultural explorations is a search for models of self and models of love that are compatible with continuing growth and change, that permeate with moral significance the ups and downs of daily life, the struggle to live well, rather than giving moral meaning only to the dramatic moment of the shift from youth to adulthood.

NANCY COTT

The Bonds of Womanhood

By the nineteenth century, married women's work at home distinguished itself most visibly from men's work, especially as the latter began to depart from the household/farm/craftshop to separate shops, offices, and factories. The rhythms of adult men's and women's work diverged even as did their places of work. During the eighteenth century, in agricultural towns, men and women had largely shared similar work patterns; their work, tied to the land, was seasonal and discontinuous. It was conditioned by tradition, family position, and legal obligation as well as by economic incentive.[1] E. P. Thompson has called the dominant characteristic of work in such an agricultural/artisanal economy its "task-orientation," in contrast to the "time-discipline" required under industrial capitalism. Task-orientation implies that the worker's own sense of customary need and order dictates the performance of work. Intensification or delay occurs as a response to perceived necessity: in farming, for instance, the former occurs in harvest time, or the latter during stormy weather. Irregular work patterns typically result. "Social inter-

1. See Keith Thomas, "Work and Leisure in Pre-Industrial Society," *Past and Present* 29 (1964):pp. 50–66.

Nancy Cott, excerpted from *The Bonds of Womanhood: "Woman's Sphere" in New England, 1780–1835* (New Haven, Conn.: Yale University Press, 1977), pp. 58–71.

course and labour are intermingled," Thompson also has pointed out, "the working-day lengthens or contracts according to the task—and there is no great sense of conflict between labour and 'passing the time of day.' " Persons accustomed to time-discipline, however, may consider task oriented patterns "wasteful and lacking in urgency." analysis derived from his study of eighteenth-century English farmers, artisans, and laborers but can be applied to their contemporaries in New England. Even eighteenth-century colonial merchants, who, as risk taking capitalists, might be expected to initiate disciplined work habits, structured their work lives in what Thompson would denote "preindustrial" ways; intermingling their work with recreation and with the conduct of their households. "The Founding Fathers, after all, lived in a preindustrial, but simply an 'agrarian' society," as Herbert Gutman has remarked, "and the prevalence of premodern work habits among their contemporaries was natural."[2]

The social transformation from 1780 to 1835 signalled a transition from preindustrial to modern industrial work patterns.[3] The replacement of family production for direct use with wage earning, the institution of time-discipline and machine regularity in place of natural rhythms, the separation of workplaces from the home, and the division of "work" from "life" were overlapping layers of the same phenomenon. Richard D. Brown, who has described a "modernization" of personal outlook taking place among white Americans in the post-Revolutionary generation, uses evidence that individuals then adopted occupational ambition, planned ahead systematically, took risks for economic ends, and attuned them-

2. E.P. Thompson, "Time, Work-Discipline, and Industrial Capitalism," *Past and Present* 38 (1967):pp. 56–59, 60 (quotation), pp. 70–79; Arthur Cole, "The Tempo of Mercantile Life in Colonial America," *Business History Review*, 33 (1959):pp. 277–99; Herbert G. Gutman, "Work, Culture, and Society in Industrializing America, 1815–1919," *AHR* 78 (1973):pp. 532.
3. In "Time, Work-Discipline, and Industrial Capitalism," pp. 80–90, Thompson cites division and supervision of laborers, punitive use of bells, clocks, and fines, money incentives, preaching and schooling, and suppression of irregularities such as holidays or sports as the immediate means used to impose time-discipline and form new labor habits in industry.

selves to time-discipline. "Americans organized their use of time on an unprecedented scale," he points out:

> Almanacs, which plotted the weather in relation to the calendar, had first been published in the mid-1700's but now they were printed by the thousands, becoming every farmer's companion. One English traveler observed that wherever he had been, ". . . in every cabin where there was not a chair to sit on, there was sure to be a Connecticut clock." The same man also remarked that the phrase "I calculate" had become the American synonym for "I believe" or "I think."[4]

Were Americans—or primarily *male* Americans—moving toward calculated, time-disciplined work habits? Household work, still the chief work of adult women, retained the irregularity, the responsiveness to immediate and natural demands, and the intermixture with social occasion common to preindustrial occupations. Even when domestic employments diminished in scope they were task-oriented. Not the clock, but human need, regulated preparation of meals, sewing of garments, and tending of children. Care of children is "the most task-oriented of all," as E. P. Thompson has acknowledged.[5] Habits such as the alternation between intense work and leisure, and the use of social occasions for work or work for social occasions (as in quilting bees), persisted in women's lives. Even their work for pay, when it was performed intermittently and in the household, conformed to the traditional rhythms, although given-out industry imposed on them the demands of entrepreneurs and distant marketplaces rather than familiar needs. Female mill operatives and other industrial workers outside the household, on the contrary, were subject to time-discipline. The repeated difficulties New England mill owners had in making operatives conform to clock-time and machine regularity testified to the rootedness among them of a different, longer-standing approach to work.[6] Because

4. Richard D. Brown, "Modernization and the Modern Personality in Early America, 1600–1865: A Sketch of a Synthesis," *JIII* 2 (1972):pp. 219–20. See also his *Modernization: The Transformation of American Life, 1600–1865* (New York: Hill and Wang, 1976), esp. pp. 95, 134–35. The English traveler made his remarks in 1844.

5. "Time, Work-Discipline, and Industrial Capitalism," p. 79.

6. See Gutman, "Work, Culture, and Society," pp. 544–45.

young women's employment outside the household was sporadic, it did not easily or quickly convert them to time-discipline. The turnover rate among mill operatives was notably high.[7] Most women who were employed away from home periodically returned to family and to household work. The vast majority eventually married. Recurrent opportunities or requirements to help in family-related tasks—such as Lucy Larcom's stint with her married sister—reaffirmed accustomed domestic patterns of work for them.

Despite the changes in its social context adult women's work, for the most part, kept the traditional mode and location which both sexes had earlier shared. Men who had to accept time-discipline and specialized occupations may have begun to observe differences between their own work and that of their wives. Perhaps they focused on the remaining "premodern" aspects of women's household work: it was reassuringly comprehensible, because it responded to immediate needs; it represented not strictly "work" but "life," a way of being; and it also looked unsystematized, inefficient, nonurgent. Increasingly men did distinguish women's work from their own, in the early nineteenth century, by calling it women's "sphere," a "separate" sphere.

Women's sphere was "separate" not only because it was at home but also because it seemed to elude rationalization and the cash nexus, and to integrate labor with life. The home and occupations in it represented an alternative to the emerging pace and division of labor. Symbol and remnant of preindustrial work, perhaps the home commanded men's deepest loyalties, but these were loyalties that conflicted with "modern" forms of employment. To be idealized, yet rejected by men—the object of yearning, and yet of scorn—was the fate of the home-as-workplace. Women's work (indeed women's very character, viewed as essentially conditioned by the home) shared in that simultaneous glorification and devaluation.

DOMESTICITY

In 1833, when Esther Grout returned to Hawley, Massachusetts, from her travels in search of employment, and wrote in her diary

---

7. See Gitelman, "The Waltham System," and Dublin, "Women at Work," p. 68.

"Home is sweet"—"there is no place like home"—those phrases were freshly minted clichés.[8] A host of New Englanders were using the printed word to confirm and advance her sentiments. Essays, sermons, novels, poems and manuals offering advice and philosophy on family life, child rearing and women's role began to flood the literary market in the 1820s and 1830s, with a tide that has not yet ceased.

The central convention of domesticity was the contrast between the home and the world. Home was an "oasis in the desert," a "sanctuary" where "sympathy, honor, virtue are assembled," where "disinterested love is ready to sacrifice everything at the altar of affection." In his 1827 address on female education a New Hampshire pastor proclaimed that "It is at home, where man . . . seeks a refuge from the vexations and embarrassments of business, an enchanting repose from exertion, a relaxation from care by the interchange of affection: where some of his finest sympathies, tastes, and moral and religious feelings are formed and nourished;—where is the treasury of pure disinterested love, such as is seldom found in the busy walks of a selfish and calculating world." The ways of the world, in contrast, subjected the individual to "a desolation of feeling," in the words of the Ladies' Magazine; there "we behold every principle of justice and honor, and even the dictates of common honesty disregarded, and the delicacy of our moral sense is wounded; we see the general good, sacrificed to the advancement of personal interest, and we turn from such scenes, with a painful sensation. . . ."[9]

The contradistinction of home to world had roots in religious motives and rhetoric. Christians for centuries had depreciated "the world" of earthly delights and material possessions in comparison to Heaven, the eternal blessings of true faith. In the 1780s and 1790s British Evangelicals doubled the pejorative connotation of "the world," by preferring bourgeois respectability above the "gay

8. Diary of Esther Grout, Aug. 4, 1833, Pocumtuck Valley Memorial Association Library Collections, HD.
9. "Home," by I. E., Ladies' Magazine 3 (May 1830): pp. 217–18; Charles Burroughs, An Address on Female Education, Delivered in Portsmouth, N.H., Oct. 26, 1827 (Portsmouth, 1827), pp. 18–19.

world" of aristocratic fashion. Living in an era of eroding public orthodoxy, they considered family transmission of piety more essential than ever to the maintenance of religion; consequently they conflated the contrasts of Heaven versus "the world" and bourgeois virtue versus the "gay world" with the contrast between the domestic fireside and the world outside.[10] In that tradition, when Esther Grout wrote in her diary, "oh how sweet is retirement. The pleasantest & I think some of the most profitable moments of my life have been spent in retirement," she was referring to her withdrawal from the world in solitary religious devotion and *also* to her repose *at home.*[11]

The rhetorical origins of the contrast between home and world demand less interpretation than the canon of domesticity built upon it. That contrast infused the new literature became in simplest terms, it seemed to explain and justify material change in individual's lives. Between the Revolution and the 1830s New England's population became more dense and more mobile, its political system more representative and demanding of citizens, its social structure more differentiated and its economic structure more complex than in earlier years when the business of "the world" had mostly taken place in households. Economic growth and rationalization and the entry of the market mechanism into virtually all relations of production fostered specialized and standardized work and a commercial ethic. Because of regional division of production and marketing, agricultural production itself became more specialized and more speculative. The farmer's success was not in his own hands when he produced for distant markets. In handicrafts the functional differentiation of wholesale merchant, retail merchant, contractor

10. For examples of Evangelical writings see Thomas Gisborne, *An Enquiry into the Duties of the Female Sex* (London, reprinted Philadelphia, 1798), and Hannah More, *Strictures on the Modern System of Female Education,* vol. 1, 9th ed. (London, 1801); see also M. G. Jones, *Hannah More* (Cambridge, 1952); Gordon Rattray Taylor, *The Angel-Makers: A Study in the Psychological Origins of Historical Change 1750–1850* (London: Heinemann, 1958) esp. pp. 12–36; Christopher Hill, "Clarissa Harlowe and her Times," *Essays in Criticism* 5 (1955): pp. 320; Keith Thomas, "The Double Standard," *Journal of the History of Ideas* 20 (1959): pp. 204–5; and Ian Watt, "The New Woman, Samuel Richardson's Pamela," R. L. Coser, ed., *The Family: Its Structure and Functions* (New York: St. Martin's, 1964), pp. 286–88.

11. Esther Grout diary, Sept. 13, 1830.

or "boss," and pieceworker replaced the unified eighteenth-century pattern in which an artisan made and sold his wares from his residence. Masters (now employers) and their journeymen or apprentices no longer assumed a patriarchal relationship; wages and prices defined their relationship to one another and to the merchants above them. Trends such as the decline of traditional determinants of deference, the assertion of an individualist ethos, increasing extremes of wealth and poverty, and replacement of unitary association networks by pluralistic ones, indicated deep change in social relations.[12] Differentiation and specialization characterized this transformation of society. These were portrayed and symbolized most powerfully in the separation of production and exchange from the domestic arena—the division between "world" and "home."

The canon of domesticity encouraged people to assimilate such change by linking it to a specific set of sex-roles. In the canon of domesticity, the home contrasted to the restless and competitive world because its "presiding spirit" was woman, who was "removed from the arena of pecuniary excitement and ambitious competition." Women inhabited the "shady green lanes of domestic life," where she found "pure enjoyment and hallowed sympathies" in her "peaceful offices." If man was the "fiercest warrior, or the most unrelenting votary of stern ambition," "toil-worn" by "troubled scenes of life," woman would "scatter roses among the thorns of his appointed track." In the "chaste, disinterested circle of the fireside" only—that is, in the hearts and minds of sisters, wives, and mothers—could men find "reciprocated humanity . . . unmixed with hate or the cunning of deceit."[13] The spirit of business and public life

12. See David Montgomery, "The Working Classes of the Pre-Industrial American City," *Labor History* 9 (1968): pp. 3–22; John R. Commons, "American Shoemakers, 1648–1895," *Quarterly Journal of Economics* 24 (1909):pp. 39–84; and David Hackett Fischer, "America: A Social History, Vol. 1, The Main Lines of the Subject 1650–1975," unpublished MS draft, 1974, esp. chap. 4, pp. 42–43, chap. 12, pp. 20–22.

13. Quotations from "Woman," probably by S. J. Hale, *Ladies' Magazine* 3 (Oct. 1830): pp. 441, 444; "Influence of Woman—Past and Present," *Ladies' Companion* 13 (Sept. 1840): pp. 245; Virginia Cary, *Letters on Female Character* (2d ed., Philadelphia, 1830), p. 47; *The Discussion: or the Character, Education, Prerogatives, and Moral Influence of Woman* (Boston, 1837), pp. 225–26.

thus appeared to diverge from that of the home chiefly because the two spheres were the separate domains of the two sexes.

In accentuating the split between "work" and "home" and proposing the latter as a place of salvation, the canon of domesticity tacitly acknowledged the capacity of modern work to desecrate the human spirit. Authors of domestic literature, especially the female authors, denigrated business and politics as arenas of selfishness, exertion, embarrassment, and degradation of soul. These rhetoricians suggested what Marx's analysis of alienated labor in the 1840s would assert, that "the worker . . . feels at ease only outside work, and during work he is outside himself. He is at home when he is not working and when he is working he is not at home."[14] The canon of domesticity embodied a protest against that advance of exploitation and pecuniary values. Nancy Sproat, a pious wife and mother who published her own family lectures in 1819, warned that "the air of the world is poisonous. You must carry an antidote with you, or the infection will prove fatal." (A latter-day Calvinist, she clearly gave "the world" dual meaning, opposing it to both "home" and "Heaven." Her antidote, likewise, was a compound, of domestic affection and religious faith.) No writer more consistently emphasized the anti-pecuniary bias of the domestic rhetoric than Sarah Josepha Hale, influential editor of the Boston *Ladies' Magazine* from 1828 to 1836 and subsequently of *Godey's Baby's Book* in Philadelphia. "Our men are sufficiently money-making," Hale said. "Let us keep our women and children from the contagion as long as possible. To do good and to communicate, should be the motto of Christians and republicans." She wished "to remind the dwellers in this 'bank-note world' that there are objects more elevated, more worthy of pursuit than wealth." "Time is money" was a maxim she rejected, and she urged mothers to teach their children the relative merits of money and of good works.

Yet the canon of domesticity did not directly challenge the modern organization of work and pursuit of wealth. Rather, it accommodated and promised to temper them. The values of domesticity undercut opposition to exploitative pecuniary standards in the

14. Karl Marx, "Alienated Labor" (1844), in *Writings of the Young Marx on Philosophy and Society,* ed. and trans. Loyd D. Easton and Kurt II. Guddat (Garden City, N.Y.: Anchor Books, 1967), pp. 292–93.

work world, by upholding a "separate sphere" of comfort and compensation, instilling a morality that would encourage self-control, and fostering the idea that preservation of home and family sentiment was an ultimate goal. Family affection, especially maternal affection, was portrayed as the "spirit indefatigable, delighting in its task," which could pervade and "regenerate" society. Furthermore, women, through their reign in the home, were to sustain the "essential elements of moral government" to allow men to negotiate safely amid the cunning, treachery, and competition of the marketplace.[15] If a man had to enter the heartless and debasing world, his wife at home supplied motive and reward for him, to defuse his resentment:

> O! what a hallowed place home is when lit by the smile of such a being; and enviably happy the man who is the lord of such a paradise. . . . When he struggles on in the path of duty, the thought that it is for *her* in part he toils will sweeten his labors. . . . Should he meet dark clouds and storms abroad, yet sunshine and peace await him at home; and when his proud heart would resent the language of petty tyrants, "dressed in a little brief authority," from whom he receives the scanty remuneration for his daily labors, the thought that she perhaps may suffer thereby, will calm the tumult of his passions, and bid him struggle on, and find his reward in her sweet tones, and soothing kindness, and that the bliss of home is thereby made more apparent.[16]

The literature of domesticity thus enlisted women in their domestic roles to absorb, palliate, and even to redeem the strain of social and

15. *Woman's Mission* (New York, 1840), pp. 20–21; *The Discussion,* p. 225. Cf. Mary Ryan's conclusion, in "American Society and the Cult of Domesticity, 1830–1860" (Ph.D. diss., University of California, Santa Barbara, 1971), esp. pp. 70–71, 337, that the literature of domesticity of the 1840s included a complete theory of the psychologically specialized and socially integrative functions of the family in industrial society. Ryan observes that women in the home instilled in their husbands and children national values and an ethic of social control; "by sustaining their husbands through the discomforts of modern work situations, and gently restraining them from antisocial behavior, American women facilitated the smooth operation of the industrial system." The nineteenth-century definition of "social integration" was "the moral power of woman" (pp. 70, 337).

16. "Essay on Marriage," *Universalist and Ladies' Repository* 2 (April 19, 1834):pp. 371.

economic transformation. In the home, women symbolized and were expected to sustain traditional values and practices of work and family organization. The very shrillness of the *cri de coeur* against modern work relations, in the canon of domesticity, meant that women's role in the home would be inflexibly defined.

Recoiling from the spirit of self-interest and self-aggrandizement they saw in the marketplace, rhetoricians of domesticity looked to the home for a sanctuary of "disinterested" love; because women at home presumably escaped exposure to competitive economic practices, they became representatives of "disinterestedness." (In fact, women at home who engaged in "given-out" industry, as increasing numbers did, brought the economic world into the home.) More profoundly and authentically, married women represented "disinterestedness" because they were economically dependent. Because their property and earnings by law belonged to their husbands, married women could not operate as economic individuals.[17] Wives lacked the means and motive for self-seeking. The laws of marriage made the social model of striving for wealth irrelevant to them. Beyond equating wives' economic dependence with disinterestedness, the canon of domesticity went a further step and prescribed women's appropriate attitude to be selflessness. The conventional cliché "that women were to live for others" was substantially correct, wrote the author of *Woman's Mission,* for only by giving up all self-interest did women achieve the purity of motive that enabled them to establish moral reference points in the home.[18] Thus women's self-renunciation was called upon to remedy men's self-alienation.

Furthermore, the canon of domesticity required women to sustain the milieu of task-oriented work that had characterized earlier family organization. This requirement made service to others and the diffusion of happiness in the family women's tasks. Women's household service alone remained from the tradition of reciprocal

17. Nor did wives, on the whole, fail to understand their dependence. "First when I received the $5. bill I kissed it," a Cambridge woman wrote to her absent husband in thanks, "because it seemed to me a proof that my dear Husband did not lose me from his mind as soon as from his sight; then, I thought I would use it very prudently." Elizabeth Gracter, Cambridge, Mass., to Francis Gracter, Aug. 14, 1836, Hooker Collection, SL.

18. *Woman's Mission,* pp. 48–52.

service by family members. Since it highlighted that aspect of women's role, the canon of domesticity in its early formulation directed them not to idleness or superficial gentility but to a special sort of usefulness. Sarah Hale maintained, for instance, that women's principles of unselfishness and magnanimity should be manifest in their acts of service. A female author of *Letters on Female Character* similarly preferred to view woman as "a rational being, whose intelligent and active exertions are to afford a perennial source of comfort to mankind," rather than as a romantic goddess to be worshipped.[19]

TILLIE OLSEN

I Stand Here Ironing

I stand here ironing, and what you asked me moves tormented back and forth with the iron.

"I wish you would manage the time to come in and talk with me about your daughter. I'm sure you can help me understand her. She's a youngster who needs help and whom I'm deeply interested in helping."

"Who needs help." Even if I came, what good would it do? You think because I am her mother I have a key, or that in some way you could use me as a key? She has lived for nineteen years. There is all that life that has happened outside of me, beyond me.

And when is there time to remember, to sift, to weigh, to estimate, to total? I will start and there will be an interruption and I will have to gather it all together again. Or I will become engulfed with all I did or did not do, with what should have been and what cannot be helped.

She was a beautiful baby. The first and only one of our five that was beautiful at birth. You do not guess how new and uneasy her

19. *Ladies' Magazine* 3 (Oct. 1830):p. 445; Cary, *Letters*, p. 174.

Tillie Olsen, excerpted from "I Stand Here Ironing," (1953–54) in *Tell Me a Riddle* (New York: Dell Publishing, 1976), pp. 1–12.

tenancy in her now-loveliness. You did not know her all those years she was thought homely, or see her poring over her baby pictures, making me tell her over and over how beautiful she had been—and would be, I would tell her—and was now, to the seeing eye. But the seeing eyes were few or nonexistent. Including mine.

I nursed her. They feel that's important nowadays. I nursed all the children, but with her, with all the fierce rigidity of first motherhood, I did like the books then said. Though her cries battered me to trembling and my breasts ached with swollenness, I waited till the clock decreed.

Why do I put that first? I do not even know if it matters, or if it explains anything.

She was a beautiful baby. She blew shining bubbles of sound. She loved motion, loved light, loved color and music and textures. She would lie on the floor in her blue overalls patting the surface so hard in ecstasy her hands and feet would blur. She was a miracle to me, but when she was eight months old I had to leave her daytimes with the woman downstairs to whom she was no miracle at all, for I worked or looked for work and for Emily's father, who "could no longer endure" (he wrote in his good-bye note) "sharing want with us."

I was nineteen. It was the pre-relief, pre-WPA world of the depression. I would start running as soon as I got off the streetcar, running up the stairs, the place smelling sour, and awake or asleep to startle awake, when she saw me she would break into a clogged weeping that could not be comforted, a weeping I can hear yet.

After a while I found a job hashing at night so I could be with her days, and it was better. But it came to where I had to bring her to his family and leave her.

It took a long time to raise the money for her fare back. Then she got chicken pox and I had to wait longer. When she finally came, I hardly knew her, walking quick and nervous like her father, looking like her father, thin, and dressed in a shoddy red that yellowed her skin and glared at the pockmarks. All the baby loveliness gone.

She was two. Old enough for nursery school they said, and I did not know then what I know now—the fatigue of the long day, and the lacerations of group life in nurseries that are only parking places for children.

Except that it would have made no difference if I had known.

It was the only place there was. It was the only way we could be together, the only way I could hold a job.

And even without knowing, I knew. I knew the teacher that was evil because all these years it has curdled into my memory, the little boy hunched in the corner, her rasp, "why aren't you outside, because Alvin hits you? that's no reason, go out, scaredy." I knew Emily hated it even if she did not clutch and implore "don't go Mommy" like the other children, mornings.

She always had a reason why we should stay home. Momma, you look sick, Momma. I feel sick. Momma, the teachers aren't there today, they're sick. Momma, we can't go, there was a fire there last night. Momma, it's a holiday today, no school, they told me.

But never a direct protest, never rebellion. I think of our others in their three-, four-year-oldness—the explosions, the tempers, the denunciations, the demands—and I feel suddenly ill. I put the iron down. What in me demanded that goodness in her? And what was the cost, the cost to her of such goodness?

The old man living in the back once said in his gentle way: "You should smile at Emily more when you look at her." What *was* in my face when I looked at her? I loved her. There were all the acts of love.

It was only with the others I remembered what he said, and it was the face of joy, and not of care or tightness or worry I turned to them—too late for Emily. She does not smile easily, let alone almost always as her brothers and sisters do. Her face is closed and sombre, but when she wants, how fluid. You must have seen it in her pantomimes, you spoke of her rare gift for comedy on the stage that rouses a laughter out of the audience so dear they applaud and applaud and do not want to let her go.

Where does it come from, that comedy? There was none of it in her when she came back to me that second time, after I had had to send her away again. She had a new daddy now to learn to love, and I think perhaps it was a better time.

Except when we left her alone nights, telling ourselves she was old enough.

"Can't you go some other time, Mommy, like tomorrow?" she would ask. "Will it be just a little while you'll be gone? Do you promise?"

The time we came back, the front door open, the clock on the floor in the hall. She rigid awake. "It wasn't just a little while. I didn't cry. Three times I called you, just three times, and then I ran downstairs to open the door so you could come faster. The clock talked loud. I threw it away, it scared me what it talked."

She said the clock talked loud again that night I went to the hospital to have Susan. She was delirious with the fever that comes before red measles, but she was fully conscious all the week I was gone and the week after we were home when she could not come near the new baby or me.

She did not get well. She stayed skeleton thin, not wanting to eat, and night after night she had nightmares. She would call for me, and I would rouse from exhaustion to sleepily call back: "You're all right, darling, go to sleep, it's just a dream," and if she still called, in a sterner voice, "now go to sleep, Emily, there's nothing to hurt you." Twice, only twice, when I had to get up for Susan anyhow, I went in to sit with her.

Now when it is too late (as if she would let me hold and comfort her like I do the others) I get up and go to her at once at her moan or restless stirring. "Are you awake, Emily? Can I get you something?" And the answer is always the same: "No, I'm all right, go back to sleep, Mother."

They persuaded me at the clinic to send her away to a convalescent home in the country where "she can have the kind of food and care you can't manage for her, and you'll be free to concentrate on the new baby." They still send children to that place. I see pictures on the society page of sleek young women planning affairs to raise money for it, or dancing at the affairs, or decorating Easter eggs or filling Christmas stockings for the children.

They never have a picture of the children so I do not know if the girls still wear those gigantic red bows and the ravaged looks on the every other Sunday when parents can come to visit "unless otherwise notified"—as we were notified the first six weeks.

Oh it is a handsome place, green lawns and tall trees and fluted flower beds. High up on the balconies of each cottage the children stand, the girls in their red bows and white dresses, the boys in white suits and giant red ties. The parents stand below shrieking up to be heard and the children shriek down to be heard, and between them the invisible wall "Not To Be Contaminated by Parental Germs or Physical Affection."

There was a tiny girl who always stood hand in hand with Emily. Her parents never came. One visit she was gone. "They moved her to Rose College," Emily shouted in explanation. "They don't like you to love anybody here."

She wrote once a week, the labored writing of a seven-year-old. "I am fine. How is the baby. If I write my letter nicely I will have a star. Love." There never was a star. We wrote every other day, letters she could never hold or keep but only hear read—once. "We simply do not have room for children to keep any personal possessions," they patiently explained when we pieced one Sunday's shrieking together to plead how much it would mean to Emily, who loved so to keep things, to be allowed to keep her letters and cards.

Each visit she looked frailer. "She isn't eating," they told us.

(They had runny eggs for breakfast or mush with lumps, Emily said later, I'd hold it in my mouth and not swallow. Nothing ever tasted good, just when they had chicken.)

It took us eight months to get her released home, and only the fact that she gained back so little of her seven lost pounds convinced the social worker.

I used to try to hold and love her after she came back, but her body would stay stiff, and after a while she'd push away. She ate little. Food sickened her, and I think much of life too. Oh she had physical lightness and brightness, twinkling by on skates, bouncing like a ball up and down up and down over the jump rope, skimming over the hill; but these were momentary.

She fretted about her appearance, thin and dark and foreign-looking at a time when every little girl was supposed to look or thought she should look a chubby blonde replica of Shirley Temple. The doorbell sometimes rang for her, but no one seemed to come and play in the house or be a best friend. Maybe because we moved so much.

There was a boy she loved painfully through two school semesters. Months later she told me how she had taken pennies from my purse to buy him candy. "Licorice was his favorite and I brought him some every day, but he still liked Jennifer better'n me. Why, Mommy?" The kind of question for which there is no answer.

School was a worry to her. She was not glib or quick in a world where glibness and quickness were easily confused with ability to learn. To her overworked and exasperated teachers she was an overconscientious "slow learner" who kept trying to catch up and was absent entirely too often.

I let her be absent, though sometimes the illness was imaginary. How different from my now-strictness about attendance with the others. I wasn't working. We had a new baby, I was home anyhow. Sometimes, after Susan grew old enough, I would keep her home from school, too, to have them all together.

Mostly Emily had asthma, and her breathing, harsh and labored, would fill the house with a curiously tranquil sound. I would bring the two old dresser mirrors and her boxes of collections to her bed. She would select beads and single earrings, bottle tops and shells, dried flowers and pebbles, old postcards and scraps, all sorts of oddments; then she and Susan would play Kingdom, setting up landscapes and furniture, peopling them with action.

Those were the only times of peaceful companionship between her and Susan. I have edged away from it, that poisonous feeling between them, that terrible balancing of hurts and needs I had to do between the two, and did so badly, those earlier years.

Oh there are conflicts between the others too, each one human, needing, demanding, hurting, taking—but only between Emily and Susan, no, Emily toward Susan that corroding resentment. It seems so obvious on the surface, yet it is not obvious. Susan, the second child, Susan, golden- and curly-haired and chubby, quick and articulate and assured, everything in appearance and manner Emily was not; Susan, not able to resist Emily's precious things, losing or sometimes clumsily breaking them; Susan telling jokes and riddles to company for applause while Emily sat silent (to say to me later: that was *my* riddle, Mother, I told it to Susan); Susan, who for all the five years' difference in age was just a year behind Emily in developing physically.

I am glad for that slow physical development that widened the difference between her and her contemporaries, though she suffered over it. She was too vulnerable for that terrible world of youthful competition, of preening and parading, of constant measuring of yourself against every other, of envy, "If I had that copper hair," "If I had that skin. . . ." She tormented herself enough about not looking like the others, there was enough of the unsureness, the having to be conscious of words before you speak, the constant caring—what are they thinking of me? without having it all magnified by the merciless physical drives.

Ronnie is calling. He is wet and I change him. It is rare there is such a cry now. That time of motherhood is almost behind me when the ear is not one's own but must always be racked and listening for the child cry, the child call. We sit for a while and I hold him, looking out over the city spread in charcoal with its soft aisles of light. *"Shoogily,"* he breathes and curls closer. I carry him back to bed, asleep. *Shoogily.* A funny word, a family word, inherited from Emily, invented by her to say: *comfort.*

In this and other ways she leaves her seal, I say aloud. And startled at my saying it. What do I mean? What did I start to gather together, to try and make coherent? I was at the terrible, growing years. War years. I do not remember them well. I was working, there were four smaller ones now, there was not time for her. She had to help be a mother, and housekeeper, and shopper. She had to set her seal. Mornings of crisis and near hysteria trying to get lunches packed, hair combed, coats and shoes found, everyone to school or Child Care on time, the baby ready for transportation. And always the paper scribbled on by a smaller one, the book looked at by Susan then mislaid, the homework not done. Running out to that huge school where she was one, she was lost, she was a drop; suffering over the unpreparedness, stammering and unsure in her classes.

There was so little time left at night after the kids were bedded down. She would struggle over books, always eating (it was in those years she developed her enormous appetite that is legendary in our family) and I would be ironing, or preparing food for the next day, or writing V-mail to Bill, or tending the baby. Sometimes, to make me laugh, or out of her despair, she would imitate happenings or types at school.

I think I said once: "Why don't you do something like this in the school amateur show?" One morning she phoned me at work, hardly understandable through the weeping: "Mother, I did it. I won, I won; they gave me first prize; they clapped and clapped and wouldn't let me go."

Now suddenly she was Somebody, and as imprisoned in her difference as she had been in anonymity.

She began to be asked to perform at other high schools, even in colleges, then at city and statewide affairs. The first one we went to, I only recognized her that first moment when thin, shy, she almost drowned herself into the curtains. Then: Was this Emily? The control, the command, the convulsing and deadly clowning, the spell, then the roaring, stamping audience, unwilling to let this rare and precious laughter out of their lives.

Afterwards: You ought to do something about her with a gift like that—but without money or knowing how, what does one do? We have left it all to her, and the gift has as often eddied inside, clogged and clotted, as been used and growing.

She is coming. She runs up the stairs two at a time with her light graceful step, and I know she is happy tonight. Whatever it was that occasioned your call did not happen today.

"Aren't you ever going to finish the ironing, Mother? Whistler painted his mother in a rocker. I'd have to paint mine standing over an ironing board." This is one of her communicative nights and she tells me everything and nothing as she fixes herself a plate of food out of the icebox.

She is so lovely. Why did you want me to come in at all? Why were you concerned? She will find her way.

She starts up the stairs to bed. "Don't get me up with the rest in the morning." "But I thought you were having midterms." "Oh, those," she comes back in, kisses me, and says quite lightly, "in a couple of years when we'll all be atom-dead they won't matter a bit."

She has said it before. She *believes* it. But because I have been dredging the past, and all that compounds a human being is so heavy and meaningful in me, I cannot endure it tonight.

I will never total it all. I will never come in to say: She was a child seldom smiled at. Her father left me before she was a year old. I had to work her first six years when there was work, or I sent her home and to his relatives. There were years she had care she hated. She was dark and thin and foreign-looking in a world where the prestige went to blondeness and curly hair and dimples, she was slow where glibness was prized. She was a child of anxious, not proud, love. We were poor and could not afford for her the soil of easy growth. I was a young mother, I was a distracted mother. There were the other children pushing up, demanding. Her younger sister seemed all that she was not. There were years she did not want me to touch her. She kept too much in herself, her life was such she had to keep too much in herself. My wisdom came too late. She has much to her and probably nothing will come of it. She is a child of her age, of depression, of war, of fear.

Let her be. So all that is in her will not bloom—but in how many does it? There is still enough left to live by. Only help her to know—help make it so there is cause for her to know—that she is more than this dress on the ironing board, helpless before the iron.

* * *

War years. I do not remember them well. I was working, there were four smaller ones now, there was not time for her. She had to help be a mother, and housekeeper, and shopper. She had to set her seal. Mornings of crisis and near hysteria trying to get lunches packed, hair combed, coats and shoes found, everyone to school or Child Care on time, the baby ready for transportation. And always the paper scribbled on by a smaller one, the book looked at by Susan then mislaid, the homework not done. Running out to that huge school where she was one, she was lost, she was a drop; suffering over the unpreparedness, stammering and unsure in her classes.

There was so little time left at night after the kids were bedded down. She would struggle over books, always eating (it was in those years she developed her enormous appetite that is legendary in our family) and I would be ironing, or preparing food for the next day, or writing V-mail to Bill, or tending the baby.

* * *

I will never total it all. I will never come in to say: She was a child seldom smiled at. Her father left me before she was a year old. I had to work her first six years when there was work, or I sent her home and to his relatives. There were years she had care she hated. She was dark and thin and foreign-looking in a world where the prestige went to blondeness and curly hair and dimples, she was slow where glibness was prized. She was a child of anxious, not proud, love. We were poor and could not afford for her the soil of easy growth. I was a young mother, I was a distracted mother. There were the other children pushing up, demanding. Her younger sister seemed all that she was not. There were years she did not want me to touch her. She kept too much in herself, her life was such she had to keep too much in herself. My wisdom came too late. She has much to her and probably nothing will come of it. She is a child of her age, of depression, of war, of fear.

Let her be. So all that is in her will not bloom—but in how many does it? There is still enough left to live by. Only help her to know—help make it so there is cause for her to know—that she is more than this dress on the ironing board, helpless before the iron.

PART FIVE

THERAPEUTIC THINKING AND SOCIAL RELATIONS

Self-realization and personal growth, empathic communication and supportive relationships: such therapeutic ideas have come to signify life's meaning and guide its conduct for rising numbers of Americans. Grown from psychological theories through affinity with our everyday experience into a popular morality, these ideas transmit a picture of selfhood and society that carries with it distinctive values, norms, and ideals of character. Therapeutic thinking has emerged as a powerful ethic of middle-class life in America today. Evidence of its importance can be found in surveys of mental-health trends, outcries over "the new narcissism," and serious cultural criticism of psychotherapeutic theory.

Among the latter is social critic Philip Rieff's sweeping typology of political, religious, economic, and psychological forms of selfhood. It has strong affinities with the four "languages" of *Habits of the Heart.* Rieff links alternative ideals of character to the social predominance of alternative institutions in the history of Western civilization. The ideal political self is the citizen whose virtue lies in reasoned and responsible participation in public affairs. A just and virtuous public order depends on the proper subordination of passion to intellect in the moral hierarchy of personal character, and a classical republic fosters such character in educating public-spirited citizens. Modern democracy broadens the base of citizenship, says Rieff, but it also saps the virtue of public life by breeding economic individuals who enjoy the privileges of citizenship while avoiding its responsibilities. These "defaulted citizens" place the pursuit of private interests over public virtues and duties with assurances that the market's invisible hand will providentially arrange the general satisfaction of public needs.

Religious ideals of character first challenge and then adapt to these political and economic selves. The faithful salvation of Christianity takes the classical vision of reasoned citizenship and turns it inward in ways that will later aid the pious "economic man" in justifying his self-interested privatism. In the twentieth century, a psychological ideal of selfhood democratizes morality by leveling earlier hierarchies of "higher" and "lower" impulses. Civilization becomes suburbia, a sea of small islands of intimate communities of two. Normality becomes a new norm, detached from natural law, divine authority, and love of neighbor. The "analytic attitude" arises to soften guilt and relativize the moral demands of love, work, and citizenship upon the private self. Therapeutic ascetics are quintessential individualists. They seek "better living" instead of a good way of life, by learning "not to attach oneself exclusively or too passionately to any one particular meaning or object," not even family or friends. In Rieff's view, the psychological individual lives alone because she or he likes it, and he has learned to like it because he believes there exists no alternative to using other persons and social institutions to serve the self.

Against the ironic generalizations of Rieff's essay, social scientists Joseph Veroff, Elizabeth Douvan, and Richard Kulka set the comparative results of two national surveys in which Americans reported their sense of themselves and their "mental health" in 1957 and 1976. They describe a "psychological revolution" in child-rearing, family relations, work, and politics. Over these two decades the meaning of life has grown more psychological and interpersonal, and less "moral or material," for the broad middle class as well as the highly educated. Social rules, norms, and organizations appear less relevant to a person's core identity, paradoxically making self-definition even more a matter of individual achievement than social consensus. As a consequence, Americans today experience less guilt at falling short of the moral mark, but more anxiety about finding themselves and reaching out to others.

A quickened search for warm, intimate relationships reflects this loss of meaning in role performance and social status, especially for men at work. More working women and more egalitarian gender-ideals, meanwhile, have made for more interactive, shared authority within the family, based on more forceful negotiation and more empathic communication. By contrast, the search for warmly expressive and "meaningful" relationships has gone largely unfulfilled in the workplace, particularly for men. This has spurred recognition of a turnabout in marital relations. Where once women were seen finding in their husbands and children vicarious experience of successful achievement, now men, who are typically less close to friends and kin, have grown increasingly dependent on marriage for emotional "support" and vicarious self-expression.

Work has lost its savor for many less repressed and task-oriented men, Veroff, Douvan, and Kulka report, even as dissatisfaction has grown over relationships at work. But it is also true that the increase of face-to-face work in the growing white-collar and personal-services sectors of the economy has placed a greater premium on the management of interpersonal relationships and feelings in bureaucratic settings, and it has encouraged the therapeutic skills and sensitivity this requires. Managers of the "new" middle class must sell their smiles and their personalities, not only their time and energy, C. Wright Mills observed a generation ago in *White Collar*. In *The Managed Heart*, sociologist Arlie Hochschild dramatizes the demands and discontents of such instrumentally "emotional labor" among airline flight attendants. In processing people, the product is a state of mind, and achieving it takes not only a professional smile but the therapeutic "engineering of a managed heart" to make that smile feel genuine. As a culture we have begun to place such unprecedented value on spontaneous, "natural" feeling because as a society faced with occupational demands for emotional self-management we are finding such a scarcity of feeling expressed for its own sake. Instead, it is being packaged as a commodity for the sake of commercial exchange.

In the minimalist celebration of therapeutic thinking psychotherapist Fritz Perls offers in "The Gestalt Prayer," the world consists fundamentally of unique individuals. Each is possessed of her own identity. Each does his "own thing" and pursues his own destiny. What holds this world together? It is not the "expectations" individuals project and seek to impose on each other, whether moral or conventional. Indeed, tolerance and communication are the only norms that transcend convention. All that links individuals is the sort of spontaneous fellow-feeling through which "we find each other." Like romantic love, it occurs by chance, and cannot be counted on or obliged. Like good fortune in a laissez-faire market, its absence cannot be helped.

By contrast, psychiatrist and storyteller Robert Coles argues that the most fearful human prospect is to live unprotected from our own drives and unreleased from our own individual feelings, wishes, and worries by transcendent communal commitments. Coles finds popularized psychology carrying just such a solipsistic concentration on the self as the axis of reality throughout America, among Indians and Eskimos as well as educated urbanites. For Coles, "civility" as a counterbalance to collective egoism begins with membership in a society seen as a moral community, and it makes possible such membership. It holds up to us the need to "live honorable lives in a big and complicated country which has so many problems that have little to do with psychology." Civility means subordinating personal feelings to shared moral imperatives and giving up emotional impulses for the order of civilization, discontents and all: "In losing we gain, in giving up we receive; the old Biblical paradoxes are built into what is called a republic, a civilization."

The problem posed by therapeutic thinking is not that personal intimacy is tyrannically taking over too much of public life, though Rieff and others have suggested as much. It is instead that too much of the purely contractual and procedural structures of today's economic and bureaucratic world—not the competitive "jungle" of the early modern market—have become an ideological model for personal life and thence public life. Therapeutic thinking etches the social contract into our intimacy. It echoes in our hearts the "go along to get along" idea of regulated cooperation with others for the sake of utilities with which to purchase our own private satisfactions. This model of life's meaning rings true to the experience of much of the urban middle class as interpersonal feelings do more and more of the face-to-face work in a mangerial and personal-services economy. The ideological overgrowth of contractual intimacy and procedural cooperation, carried over from boardroom to bedroom and back again, is what threatens to blur the ideals of compassion, civic duty, and reasoned discourse which distinguish public life as moral community from a marketplace or an administrative center.

Therapeutic thinking meshes smoothly with the administrative state and its group-interest politics. But in assuming extensive obligations for its citizens' welfare and enabling their self-support within a highly interdependent economy, the modern state tends to release them from a sense of duty to one another and service to the commonweal. If such a moral paradox is embedded in our central institutions, how can therapeutic aspirations to grow and get better strengthen our commitment to a just and humane society, instead of eroding it? The answers lie not only in changing our popular cultural conceptions of psychology and civility, but in changing our institutions to make them more able to merit our commitment to accept responsibility for the world we actually share.

JOSEPH VEROFF, ELIZABETH DOUVAN, RICHARD KULKA

The Inner American

Between 1957 and 1976, our culture underwent what can reasonably be described as a psychological revolution. We can contrast themes which dominated social criticism in the periods of our two surveys. David Riesman et al.'s *The Lonely Crowd*[1] struck the keynote of the fifties—that Americans had become slavish conformers who guided their behavior by the expectations of others, hoping thereby to win approval, to "fit in." By 1976, on the other hand, we had become, in Christopher Lasch's view a "culture of narcissism".[2] While both of these theses contrasted contemporary society with the golden age of the Victorian era when men were men and behavior was dictated by strong moral principles internalized during childhood and operating autonomously through individual conscience and standards of taste, the pass we had come to, according to the two visions, differ dramatically. According to Riesman, in the 1950s we had become too social, guided by the compass of social norms; in Lasch's view, by the 1970s we didn't care at all about social norms and were entirely preoccupied with looking out for "Number 1." While American social criticism tends to the hyperbolic, these assertions undoubtedly picked up and reflected themes that had some base in reality. Though they may have relied too heavily on and generalized too widely from observations of special

1. David Riesman, with Nathan Glazer and Reuel Denney, *The Lonely Crowd: A Study of the Changing American Character* (New Haven: Yale University Press, 1950).
2. Christopher Lasch, *The Culture of Narcissism* (New York: Norton, 1978).

Joseph Veroff, Elizabeth Douvan, and Richard Kulka, excerpted and abrideged from *The Inner AmericanL A Self-Portrait from 1957 to 1976* (New York: Basic Books, 1981) pp.14–25.

groups in the population (particularly intellectuals and the media elites), both Riesman and Lasch were probably on the trail of something real.

At least some thoughtful critics would see the two themes as stages of a single process: secularization. When religious authority waned, the autonomous, well-internalized moral code no longer served to guide behavior. The individual, then, looked to others for direction, and finally, recognizing the relativity of all judgment, came to measure all things by their ability to provide individual gratification, narcissistic pleasure. Family historians described a parallel process in the relation between family and the larger society; whereas in Colonial America family and state were integrated closely, the public and private aspects of life deeply interpenetrating and family life accessible to public scrutiny, by the nineteenth century, an adversarial, compensatory relation between the two spheres had become dominant. The world was now cast as a dangerous, competitive jungle, and the private family world a protective haven that held all that was warm, supportive, moral, and sustaining.

The problem with much of this social criticism and prediction is that it is based on limited information; it is a problem of generalization. Facts are observed correctly: the divorce rate has increased; women have left families in order to realize their individual talents or needs; the best-seller lists are dominated by books on self-improvement, personal growth, narcissistic preoccupation. But the facts are then interpreted too broadly, accorded a centrality and power in the broad population which they may in fact hold only for a part, for a highly articulate, "leading," powerful subgroup—but a subgroup all the same.

Our analyses of two national studies permit us to depict broad changes in American society with considerable confidence; they also permit us to isolate phenomena occurring only in certain social groups. As we approach these analyses, we can preview some of the general themes about social-psychological changes in the American population that occurred between 1957 and 1976. We will also describe changes that are especially characteristic of one group or another.

REDUCED SOCIAL INTEGRATION

A central theme . . . concerns what we judge to be a *reduced integration of American adults into the social structure.* Social organization, social norms, the adaptation to and successful performance of social roles all seem to have lost some of their power to provide people with meaning, identity elements, satisfaction. In fact, role and status designations have become objects of suspicion. The feminist movement objects to the use of "Miss" and "Mrs." as titles, pointing to the fact that marital status is used in a nonsymmetrical way to define women but not men. The use of status titles like Doctor or Professor, and inquiry about the vocation/profession of an individual on first encounter are considered bad form, somehow contravening genuine response to and interest in the core of the person so designated or questioned. Any allusion to status is taken as a preoccupation with status and a disregard for personal, egalitarian, human values. Reflecting an interest in what a person does (in the vocational realm) is taken as preoccupation with status and a disinterest in the authentic, the essential, the personal qualities and style of that person.

This reduced tie to the structural givens of the social order represents a potential psychological loss. Knowing what a person does can reveal a good deal of information about the personal organization, the essential and authentic aspects of a person. Knowing that a man works in a factory will not tell you whether he is gathering material for a book on automation or earning money to support a passion for painting, or never thought about work except as a means of earning a living. But it will tell something about his organization of life and experience and will open the door to further questions which may reveal more telling aspects of himself. Knowing that a woman is a physician, an inventor, or a professor of French literature will reveal more and more detailed information about her, and not only about prestige and wealth. Since Veblen's time, the connection between what people do for forty or more hours a week in work and the ways in which they will structure perception, knowledge, meaning, and relationships has been noted and studied by social scientists of various disciplines and persuasions. If a man spends most of his waking, attending hours thinking of human beings as resources to be deployed in the winning of wars, or as objects to be manipulated in the service of business profit, this activity will in all likelihood influence the way in which he relates to his children, his wife, his friends. What a person does is related to what he is—in his core.

The paradoxical truth is that disregard for status, which is urged as a counterthrust to formalism and status consciousness out of desire to reduce obstacles to close interaction between people, actually *increases* distance between people by insisting that they turn inward for the derivation of meaning and self-definition, by placing the burden of self-definition entirely on the individual—and making it a matter of individual achievement rather than a consensual and shared reality. No longer do we allow the individual to derive some of his sense of self and legitimacy from a position in a social structure. Rather, he must rediscover meaning in the spring of his individual detached self each day. Individual achievement becomes the whole story, and it urges distance from rather than connections to structure or to others.

None of this is to deny that preoccupation with status can be dehumanizing. The person who can see others only as representatives of status categories, who cannot see or relate to the personhood, the reality of a secretary or plumber or grocery clerk, or refers to "my little seamstress" or "little butcher," surely dehumanizes those others with whom s/he interacts. If *all* we ask is what people do in the occupational world, we fail to know them. If we *judge* people by the criterion of status, we lose the color and richness of human personality.

But the misuse of knowledge does not contradict its validity. Status, position in a social structure, connections to groups and to other people are all valid and informing and have traditionally signified meaning to the individual and to others about the individual's self. People do not play roles in quite the way that the implied analogy to theater conveys. We play roles, but our roles also enter—and alter—our selves. In a real sense, we *become* our roles, not just to an audience but also to ourselves. Aspects of the self which are role-derived (an American, a painter, a husband and father) are no less authentic and are usually more central to self-definition than those aspects based on extra-role dimensions (tall, nearsighted, melancholy, cheerful). They are aspects of the self, and they are facts of interest to anyone who would know the self.

When status and roles are discredited as legitimate information about people, as we believe they increasingly are in our society, they lose their meaning and their capacity to lend meaning to people's own lives and self-definitions.

* * *

What about other work roles and roles outside of the occupational sphere entirely? Have they also suffered an attrition in meaning? As we shall see in our analyses, we have to conclude that they have, although perhaps not as profoundly as the popular press would lead us to believe. They are no longer adult roles which are acquired and settled and then automatically give one meaning and stability. They depend on performance and achievement, and they have lost their implication of permanence, their unidirectional conferring of adult status and identity elements.

There are paradoxical consequences for the subjective experiences of people in a social system in which the binding power of roles has been diluted. On the one hand, there is a larger freedom to work out a legitimate life without conforming to rigid prescription or without comparing one's efforts to overidealized standards that so often demoralize. On many counts, Americans now feel better about themselves because they are more self-reliant and less dependent on social rules. On the other hand, the comforts of the social system are also given up when social roles lose their moral force. Although we obviously have not given up all role demands—or else we could no longer exist in a cooperative society—we have given up some easy rules that would guarantee legitimacy among those we know and among those we do not know. Without these easy guarantees, we have become a somewhat more anxious people. We see more problems in many parts of our lives. As many people have learned, it is often difficult to discover the authentic self. Freedom from a constraining authority often becomes a burden; the freedom to choose often a haunting personal problem.

AN INCREASED SEARCH FOR INTIMACY

Related to this thinning of the social commitment and social investment, we note an increased sensitivity to interpersonal relations—a desire for friendship, warm relationships at work and in the family, a desire for personal impact in everyday encounters. In all of the major life roles we looked at—work, marriage, and parenthood—respondents in 1976 stress interpersonal aspects in their definitions and in describing their satisfactions, problems, and inadequacies. The search for satisfying warm relationships which was primarily a feature of middle-class, educated life in 1957 has spread more broadly in 1976.

Men, in particular, seem to have suffered a loss of meaning from this shift in cultural emphasis from social integration and role performance to interpersonal and individual sources of meaning. The traditional male role depended critically on status differentiation, role performance, legitimate authority—more so than the traditional female role. Head of household, ultimate authority, breadwinner, and worker all took their meaning and criteria for performance from their integration into a structured set of reciprocal roles. They carried status, power, and the implication of uniqueness. As authority has come more and more to be questioned and challenged, it no longer comes automatically with a particular position, but must be achieved and legitimized on the basis of performance. As a result, people—and men in particular—began to emphasize more personal needs in their relationships with others. A search for intimacy was launched by a people who had traditionally depended on interaction rituals to guide their behavior and feelings. This happened both in the workplace and in the family.

At work, many forces coalesce to reduce the automatic meaning for men in attaining a secure job. Women and minorities have entered the boardroom as well as the factory. While occupational segregation is still a dominant pattern, these previously marginal groups assert their right to an equal share of any work. Given recent history and their successes, however restricted, even the highest levels of managerial and professional jobs are less immune to the possibility of democratization. Dominant majority males must lose some measure of their assured uniqueness at work. For women and minorities, on the other hand, the yielding of traditional discriminatory barriers has opened up new fields and contributed new stimulus for work aspirations which up to now would have been impossible fantasies. The promise of meaningful work, opportunities for advancement, and material rewards commensurate with talent and effort leaven the work motivation and achievement strivings of the disadvantaged. Our data yield evidence of the meaningfulness of work to women that is not so clearly shared by men. For many women, even those who start working to meet the needs of a family, merely assuming the role of worker contributes to a sense of resourcefulness that compensates for problems experienced on the job.

Other forces have contributed to the questioning of uniqueness in work for majority males. The counterculture movement of the sixties mounted a frontal assault on the work ethic. The term "workaholic" entered our vocabulary. Sons of workaholics rejected the "rat race" and confronted their parents with the irony that they had won the world but lost their own children. These young men swore that they would not trade life for financial success.

The development of social-welfare policy slipped one more support from under the work ethic. If welfare legislation, insurance programs, and workmen's compensation provide for minimal subsistence without work, then clearly work is not necessary for survival

If work has lost savor for many men, some of its automatic payoff in the sense of a unique contribution and significant impact, what then? Within the workplace itself, an emphasis on relationships developed. No small factor in this focus was the intensification of the bureaucratic organization of most people's work. More jobs required that people negotiate a web of hierarchical distinctions that were very unreal. The popularity of the T-group and sensitivity training in the 1960s originated in the resocialization of managers often embedded in a tangle of overbureaucratized organizations. Neophytes in focusing their attention on the interpersonal life, men approached their search for meaning in relationships as they did everything else. They objectified it as a commodity, a skill that could be packaged and taught to consumers hungry for interpersonal meaning. This approach only made matters worse for many people. We will find in our data that there is a growing dissatisfaction with the nature of interpersonal relationships at work.

If the workplace itself is inadequate for most people's search for intimacy, interpersonal exchange in family life may offer an alternative in which people can find meaning and validate their sense of significance. The family arena had gone through its own disruptions, as we noted earlier, and these disruptions often accentuated the search for intimacy. In addition, the nature of family life made it a far easier arena for people's search for closeness and impact than the workplace.

The shift in the meaning of family roles occurred over a fairly brief period of our recent social history. Returning from World War II, chastened about the possibilities of personal influence in the larger world of affairs, American men—and the women they married—launched an era of familism and family building in reaction to their loss of hope for significant influence on the world. If they lacked the hope to affect congressional decisions, they could still hope to influence their children and the local school board. Men and women at the end of the 1940s and 1950s launched the baby boom and reinforced traditional concepts of sex roles. Both were severely questioned in the late 1960s and 1970s.

Gratifications automatically generated from being the authoritative breadwinner/husband/father fell apart during the period between our two studies. The feminine mystique as a guide for mothers and wives was clearly demystified. The role of breadwinner was soon shared, and the husband/father could not assume a *unique* contribution in this role. As wives assumed a greater economic role in family support, they acquired more equal power in family decision making as well. Decisions became subject to more negotiation and debate, and the traditional pattern of unquestioned authority associated with both the father's and the husband's role yielded to a more interactive, shared authority. Wives who may once have wielded subtle feminine power on significant family choices came to expect direct participation.

Power and authority no longer automatically redound to those who parent—the positions of father or mother, the head-of-household, the final authority—all have lost the element of power ascription. Children have come to expect rationalized authority and the possibility of participating in decisions. Evaluation of performance and satisfaction in parenting have increasingly come to depend on the development of warm interpersonal relationships with one's children. It is not enough for a man to support his children and see that they obey him and learn to live by society's rules. It is not enough for women to say to their children, "Be nice." They have to justify their demands. Mothers have learned to listen harder for their child's idiosyncratic feelings and goals in their desire to raise ideal children. Both fathers and mothers have come to want and need warm relationships with their children and to feel inadequate without them. Love and warmth form the new basis for socializing children—the basis to substitute for the unquestioned authority which previously came with the role of parent. Men and women now feel guilty if they get angry with their children.

As family roles have undergone this transformation they have become fertile arenas for people's search for intimacy, particularly for men who have found their newly generated interpersonal goals largely unfulfilled at the workplace. The emphasis on relationship issues in fathers' and mothers' discussions of parenting and in husbands' and wives' discussions of marriages is one of the clearest trends we see in our study.

Experts perceptive of the changes we have been discussing tell men—and men feel on their own—that they will succeed as fathers to the extent that they develop warm, close, "meaningful" relationships with their children. But who is resocializing them with the skills they need to realize such relationships—skills in openness to feelings and fantasy, skills in self-disclosure and emotional sharing, the capacity to play, ease and expressiveness? Most of today's adult males were not taught such skills as they were growing up. They interacted within traditional authority-based families with fathers who were themselves models of task orientation and emotional repression. The only experience of fathering they know from their own lives is one specifically designed to make them emotionally retentive and interpersonally cool, inept in all the behaviors now asked of them in the contemporary ideal of the warm, sharing, expressive father. In school and the peer group rewards attached to "manliness," toughness, and competitive achievement.

So we find that men are sensitive to the interpersonal criteria of parenthood, they want warm relationships with their children, but they feel that such relationships elude them. The lack of warmth and closeness with their children is what men think of most often when asked what kinds of problems they have had with their children and what inadequacies they have experienced in the parent role. They don't refer to warm, loving relationships as often as mothers do when they are asked in the surveys to think of the "nicest things about having children" or the ways in which "having children change(s) a person's life."

THE INCREASING DEPENDENCE OF MEN ON
THE INSTITUTION OF MARRIAGE

What do men do with all of their unmet needs for interpersonal warmth? With both work and parenthood somehow falling short of providing these needs, where do they turn? Predictably, and entirely in keeping with traditional expectations of "masculine" behavior, they look to marriage for the warmth and expressiveness they fail to find (or develop) in the rest of their lives. Men look to their wives for warmth, nurturance, emotional sharing, expressiveness. Many adult men in our society experience emotional expressiveness only vicariously through the expressiveness of the women in their lives. When asked in the surveys how they handle problems, worries, or periods of unhappiness, married men often talk about the support they experience *only* from their wives. The wife represents the only resource short of formal help. Women—whether married or unmarried—have more informal resources to use in troubled times. When asked whether they are close enough to friends or relatives to talk over problems and troubles with them, men—more than women—say that they are not so close.

This series of themes reflecting men's needs for warm interpersonal relationships, their inability to satisfy such needs at work or in their parenting functions, and their exclusive reliance on marriage as an arena for emotional sharing and satisfaction of needs for interpersonal warmth and expressiveness—casts light on statistical data about marriage and divorce. It clarifies findings that seem to indicate that marriage is more crucial to the health and well-being of men than women and that men almost always remarry after divorce or widowhood. If marriage provides the only access to warmth and emotional statisfaction, it is both highly desirable and salutary to people's experience of life.

But this emphasis may also place an impossible burden on a

single relationship, and in this sense it may contribute heavily to increased divorce rates. If men need so much and are so undeveloped in the skills of interpersonal sharing and emotional expressiveness, they may ask too much and give too little to support marriage. It is not surprising that in the 1976 survey more wives than husbands say that they wish their spouse understood them better and shared more thoughts and feelings.

During the early days of the recent women's movement, a good deal was said about women's vicarious living. Women were seen as depending on their husbands and children for vicarious realization of achievement needs and success experience. Our data reveal that men also use marriage vicariously to experience warmth and expressiveness. As women have moved into the occupational world and experienced achievement directly, they may have less need to use marriage for vicarious achievement. And they may be less available and willing to supply their husbands' needs for vicarious experience of emotionality. The symbiosis which had served mutual expression has been unhinged and dislocated.

A GENERAL INCREASE IN TAKING A PSYCHOLOGICAL ORIENTATION TO EXPERIENCE

The increased orientation toward interpersonalism in work and family roles, the diminution of the importance of roles, can be seen as part of a broader cultural change, the introduction of the "era of psychology." The 1957 report spoke of a psychological orientation, as distinguished from material or moral orientations, and suggested that this way of looking at life experiences and life problems might increase significantly in the future.

By 1976 we have evidence that this shift had indeed occurred. In all areas covered by the studies, psychological orientation is palpably greater in 1976 than it was in 1957. American people are more likely to frame their satisfactions, problems, and inadequacies in psychological and relational terms—whether they speak of work or marriage or parenthood. In 1976 they less often attribute inadequacies or satisfactions to external and material conditions. They less often externalize problems and less often attribute blame.

The psychological and interpersonal orientation, which was almost exclusively a characteristic of the highly educated in 1957, had become common coin by 1976.

PHILIP RIEFF

Therapy and Technique

Four character ideals have competed for dominance over the conduct of life in Western civilization. First, the ideal of *political* man, formed and handed down to us from classical antiquity. Plato was the greatest student of political man, and his most persuasive teacher. From Plato we first learned systematically to divide human nature into higher and lower energies, each level of energy having its appropriate function and assigned a relative value in the proper conduct of life. As it turns out, in Plato, the health and stability of a person is analogous to—and, moreover, dependent upon—the health and stability of the political order; that is, a proper subordination of passions to intellect will follow from the subordination of the uneducated classes to the educated. An ordered inner life depends upon the constituting of the right public order, a correct hierarchy of classes makes for the good private life.

Every society has its own version of a good man. From Plato to the present, the ideal political man has been considered to be the one who participates rationally and responsibly in the processes of public decision. Political man is, in effect, the citizen.

Rooted in the ideals of classical antiquity, the entire political effort of democracy has been to broaden the base of citizenship. But democracy, as it became more popular, developed a powerful alternative to the classical ideal, one in which the citizen could enjoy the privileges of citizenship while avoiding responsibilities. Tocqueville rightly called this type, which he saw flourishing in both the America

Philip Rieff, excerpted from the introduction to *Therapy and Technique* (New York: Collier, 1963) pp. 8–24.

and France of his time, the "individual." There is a great chapter in the finest and still most informative book on America, and on democracy, ever written: *Democracy in America.* That chapter is called "Of Individualism in Democratic Countries." Tocqueville defines individualism in a psychological rather than a political or economic way; it is a "mature and calm feeling, which disposes each member of the community to sever himself from the mass of his fellows and to draw apart with his family and his friends, so that after he has thus formed a little circle of his own, he willingly leaves society at large to itself." Thus Tocqueville saw individualism sapping the "virtues of public life," until that life is "at length absorbed in downright selfishness." Tocqueville's analysis amounts to a heavy indictment of democratic culture. For he concludes by saying: "Thus not only does democracy make every man forget his ancestors, but it hides his descendants and separates his contemporaries from him; it throws him back forever upon himself alone and threatens in the end to confine him entirely within the solitude of his own heart." In short, himself trained to belief in the classical ideal of political man, Tocqueville saw the highly individualistic American as a defaulted citizen.

Tocqueville was measuring the American character entirely from the character ideal of political man. But in the century before Tocqueville wrote, another character ideal had fully matured: *economic* man, exactly the type Tocqueville called the "individual." Economic man feared and suspected the public life, aiming to stay out of it and cultivate rationally his very own garden, proud in his sense of isolation. In his ideological prime the "individual" met all criticisms that he was a defaulted citizen with the reply that by attending primarily to his own private needs a general satisfaction of the public needs would automatically occur. A moral revolution was the result: what had been lower in the established rank order of responsibilities, the private, was now asserted to be higher.

In the slow accretion of self-images that is the mortar between periods in the history of our civilization, yet a third character ideal persisted, challenging and then adapting first the political ideal and then the economic, but with gradually weakening effect, until, in our own time, it is being replaced by a fourth. That fourth character ideal is the main subject of this essay. The third borrowed the Platonic dichotomy between higher and lower energies, using it for different cultural purposes. Although originally a naïve and straightforward, even ecstatic, faith, Christianity could not resist going to the Greek philosophical schools, as later it could not resist accommodating itself to the desires of economic individualism. As a result of its historic compromise with classical antiquity, Christianity shaped and handed down to us a *religious* man who continues to show certain recognizably Greek traits. The Christian doctrine of human nature grafted faith onto the place once occupied by the idea of life as a continuing intellectual and moral reeducation for better public service. Both therapeutic functions merged, and the church became at once a saving and a pedagogic institution. Certainly, "The Republic," in the Greek conception, is one vast school, complete with intellectual and vocational programs, for the better training of more or less capable citizens. In the Gospels, the Church is set up as a teaching institution superior to the Republic; instead of a universal state, one universal church is to exist for the better training of the human capacity for faith. Thus, adapting Greek intellectualism to its own purposes, the main Christian institution developed a personality type that organized itself around the expectation of achieving faith, asserting it as superior to reason, which could, at best, merely support and confirm the religious gift of saving grace. Christianity represented a turning inward of the Greek criterion of well-being which would, later, prove useful to the nominally Christian economic man, in rationalizing the privacy and self-centeredness of his way of life.

The religious man, idealized during the long Christian period, carried with him two alternative strategies for the saving expression of his character. He could achieve his ideal self in two opposing ways: either mystic or ascetic. Of these two alternative procedures, what I have here called the mystic was first considered the better for achieving perfection in the religious sense, not involving, as did the ascetic way, the exercise of Reason.

These two character ideals persist competitively in our contemporary culture, yet in different degrees of attractiveness. For example, President Kennedy's Inaugural Address aimed at the American "individual" in the Tocquevillean sense of the word, in order to bring him back to an essentially classical ideal of public service. Yet it is possible that economic man, comfortably confined in the solitude of his own heart, will turn out to be a transitional type, with the shortest life-expectancy of all. When, by the turn of the twentieth century, this typical character of the Enlightenment and the great democratic revolutions, American and French, showed a faltering belief in his own superiority to his political and religious predecessors, a successor began to emerge—the *psychological* man of the twentieth century. In what follows, I shall try to present this new motivating idea that Western men, and Americans in particular, have of themselves.

It was at the frayed end of the period at which economic man grew nervous about himself, alone, that Freud first began to see his patients. Because they were unprepared for an ideal of ever-shifting insight as a way of accommodating their lives to a rapidly changing moral environment, Freud's patients of the turn of the century were incredulous and naïve. They demanded some doctrine of right, or a substitute faith. All Freud could give them, in the unyielding honesty of his own insight, was what he himself called the "analytic attitude." Such an attitude, if strictly held, allows for no return to religion, nor to any special doctrine of justice. Freud's concern is entirely with the emotions of the private man, and never with his aims or beliefs except so far as these prove to be mistaken therapies of action, appearing as symptoms rather than cures. Indeed, as I have implied, the earlier therapies of action had failed; Freud offered, instead, the action of therapy. Although it was not always the case, the classical ways of making life worth living, whether religious or political or economic, no longer were adequate to preserve the health of man and give him some measure of self-control and satisfaction. All the received therapies of action were efforts to find an ultimate cure for the difficulties of living where, as experience demonstrated time and again, no cure could possibly exist. All those cures had merely created the conditions for fresh outbursts of the nervous condition from which man suffers when he develops too high a set of aims for himself, and beyond himself.

Thus Freud led an increasingly successful attack on the ancient dichotomizing of human nature into categories of higher and lower, with respect to both ends and means. What is new—indeed revolutionary—about this latest image that Western men have of themselves is that it repudiates the hierarchical master assumption of "higher" and "lower" to which all the predecessors of psychological man have been addicted. Yet, perhaps in part because of this repudiation of both the classical and religious therapies of action, the new character ideal generates its own peculiar nervous tensions. After all, the aims of the individual have not changed. Freud took those aims for granted, as essentially the correct ones. He had the difficult problem of treating a character no longer content to live within the isolation of his own heart but unwilling to give his heart to anything other than himself. Freud could seek only to reconcile Tocqueville's "individual" to his present discontent, and somehow help him continue to live privately within the now rather constricting circle of his family and friends. It is the "individual" that Freud was seeking to defend as best he could, for he saw no alternative way of life.

The anxieties of this isolated individual and defaulting citizen (who, at best, sees the public life as yet another way of helping himself get through his own life) reflect not merely the pressures mounting inside his closed little circles of love and friendship; those anxieties also reflect the lines of personal competition that surround his new-found freedom from public responsibility and theological sovereignty. To meet these double anxieties, Freud taught the analytic attitude; his only alternative would have been to reassert some doctrine curtailing the very individuality that he sought to protect.

Developed for the private needs of private men, shifting with each individual case, the analytic attitude is not easily generalized. Indeed, this doctrinal aspect of psychological manhood is best described, I think, as an anti-doctrine, one that opposes the therapeutic compulsions of all doctrine as finally ineffective. Psychological man takes on the attitude of a scientist, with himself alone as the ultimate object of his science. If the action of the analytic therapy has been effective, he has learned not to prejudge the options around which the conduct of his own life might be organized, considering all options live, and, theoretically, equally legitimate. What matters is not so much the action as the determinants that have led up to the action. According to the analytic attitude, what counts is not what we do but why we do it. Thus there may be a kindness that is neurotic, if it develops out of unconscious compulsions, and a cruelty that is perfectly normal, if it is consciously determined upon in a controlled way. Sainthood, when determined by unconscious and uncontrolled motives, is neurotic; sinning, when determined by conscious and examined motives, is normal. Of course, the saint may be socially more valuable than the sinner; he may also be more neurotic. Freud was honest enough to discover that there was no inherent relation between normality and the norm, such as had been established in the ages of political and religious man through the mediating myth that there were natural laws. Freud could discover no natural harmony of goals worth striving for in life, no value built into conduct and inscribed upon the universe. With the destruction of natural law, only the analytic attitude could protect the individual from the folly of being drawn too far outside the protective isolation of his own self-interest.

To reserve the capacity for neutrality between choices even while making them, as required by this new science of moral management, creates a great strain, both intellectually and emotionally. It demands the capacity to entertain multiple perspectives upon oneself and even upon beloved others, and the finesse to shift from one perspective to another, in order to soften the demands upon oneself in all the major situations of life—love, parenthood, friendship, work, citizenship. Such flexibility is not easily acquired. In fact, the attainment of psychological manhood is more difficult than any of the older versions of maturity precisely because that manhood is no longer protected by any childish fantasy of having arrived at some saving place where meanings reside, like gods in their heavens. The best there is to say for oneself in life is that one has lived—"*really* lived," as the American saying goes.

Freud understood the dangers inherent in a situation in which the precious individual was vulnerable to the charge that his life had become meaningless. In answer, he asserted that no fresh access of doctrine could for long decrease that vulnerability. In such cases, the individual merely built his neurosis the more deeply into his character, combining it with some system of belief and action. All such systems of belief and action, with the neurotic factor as the mediating agent, brought more grief than relief to an individual now trying to complete not his task but himself. When the contemplation of self became a vocation, then the old therapies of action based on a saving belief in something other than oneself no longer relieved the individual of the most oppressive of his tensions—those developing in his own private circles of love and friendship. For these therapies were based on now irrelevant attempts to bring the individual too far out of himself, into some relation with a public end that no longer made private sense. What was needed was a therapy the action of which would take place entirely within the circle of the private life; the public life could, perhaps, in time be altered too by the success of the therapeutic effort in the private sphere. Thus, against the clear implication of his analysis of life as devoid of anything more than an endless network of essentially private and individually relevant meanings, Freud offered no large new cosset of a public philosophy—such as those offered by the philosophers, theologians and economists who had preceded him. His is a severe and chill anti-doctrine; for private consumption only, in which the final dichotomy to which Western man is prey—that between an ultimately meaningful and meaningless life—must also be abandoned. Such dichotomies belong to periods of public philosophies and communal theologies. In the era of the individual, each man belongs to an intimate society of his own devising. Civilization has become one vast suburbia, something like Tocqueville's nightmare of the United States and of France, populated by divided communities of two, with perhaps two junior members caught in the middle of a private and not always civil war: in relation to these intimate, though divided, communities of two, the public world is constituted as one vast stranger, who appears at inconvenient times and makes impossible demands, because he still proclaims one of the old ethics, whether political or religious.

In the time of public philosophies and social religions, all communities were positive. A positive community is characterized by the fact that it guarantees some kind of salvation to the private person by virtue of his membership and participation in that community. That sort of community seemed corrupt to the economic man, with his particular version of the ascetic ideal as tested mainly by self-reliance and personal achievement. It appears not so much corrupt as impossible to the psychological man, with his awareness of both ideology and rationalization as neurotic factors in social life. As an individualist, psychological man can only choose to live in negative communities, barren little islands surrounded by therapeutic activities; but he must live there without any pretense at a doctrine of salvation. Positive communities were, according to Freud, held together by guilt. They may be attractive now, in distant retrospect, but the modern individual, faced with merging his own into the communal effort, would have found them suffocating. Instead, the individual can use the community only as the necessary basis for a life-long effort to complete himself—if not always, or necessarily, to enrich himself. In this way, the therapeutically inclined individual apparently resembles his predecessor, the ascetic.

Therapeutic reeducation is at once a very difficult and yet very modest procedure. It teaches the patient-student how to live with the contradictions that constrict him into a unique personality; this in contrast to the older moral pedagogies, which tried to reorder the contradictions into a hierarchy of superior and inferior, good and evil, capabilities. To become a psychological man is thus to become kinder to the whole self, the private parts as well as the public, the formerly inferior as well as the formerly superior. While older character types were concentrated on the full-time job of trying to order the warring parts of personality into a hierarchy, the Freudian pedagogy, reflecting the changing self-conception of the times, is far more egalitarian: it is the task of psychological man to develop an informed (i.e., healthy) respect for the sovereign and unresolvable basic contradictions that galvanize him into the singularly complicated human being that he is. Not the good life but better living is the Freudian standard. It is a popular standard, not difficult to follow, as Americans, despite Freud's wish to make it difficult, were the first to recognize in any significant numbers.

Americans no longer model themselves after the Christian or the Greek. Nor are they such economic men as Europeans believe. The political man of the Greeks, the religious man of the Hebrews and Christians, the enlightened economic man of the eighteenth-century European (the original of that mythical present-day character, the "good European"), has been superseded by a new model for the conduct of life: the psychological man native to the American. This uniquely American type has outgrown his immediate ancestor in one clear sense, for both Socrates and Christ taught economic man to be at least slightly ashamed of himself when he failed to sacrifice lower to higher capacity. Freud is America's great teacher, despite his ardent wish to avoid that fate. For it was precisely the official and parental shams of high ideals that Freud questioned. In their stead, Freud taught lessons which Americans, prepared by their own national experience, learn easily: survive, resign yourself to living within your moral means, suffer no gratuitous failures in a futile search for ethical heights that no longer exist—if ever they did. Freud proclaims the superior wisdom of choosing the second best. He is our Crito, become intellectually more supple than a sick and old Socrates, who might still be foolish enough to justify his own death sentence rather than escape from the prison of his own crippling inhibitions about the sanctity of the State, which he mistakes for his father. Freud appeals so because his wisdom is so tired. Surely he is not to be blamed for living in a time when the inherited aspirations of the Greek, Christian and Humanist past had gone stale, when both Athens and Jerusalem, not to mention Paris, Oxford or the Italian Renaissance cities, have become tourist spots rather than the aim of pilgrims in search of spiritual knowledge. With no place to go for lessons on the conduct of contemporary life, every man must learn, as Freud teaches, to make himself at home in his own grim and gay little Vienna.

The alternatives with which Freud leaves us are grim only if we view them from the perspective of some possibility passed, either as political or religious men. Assuming that these character types are, in his terms, regressive, the grimness is relieved by the gaiety of being free from the historic Western compulsion of seeking large and general meanings for small and highly particular lives. Indeed, the therapy of all therapies, the secret of all secrets, the interpretation of all interpretations, in Freud, is not to attach oneself exclusively or too passionately to any one particular meaning or object. There is discernible in those who practice professionally the analytic attitude, the psychoanalysts themselves, a certain cultivated detachment and calm that is perhaps the finest expression of that individualism to which Tocqueville first referred. In the relation between analyst and patient, one member of that unique community of two must remain an almost total stranger to the other; only if the analyst draws a veil across his own life does he maintain his therapeutic effectiveness. The patient must, in turn, learn how to draw the veil properly around himself. To accomplish this much he needs to develop the full power and liberty of his emotions without paying the price of fixing them too firmly on any object or idea. This he is taught by the experience of ending his relation of intimacy to the analyst himself. Here, again, is the ascetic ideal, shorn of any informing goal or principle; thus divested of the need for compulsive attachments, the ascetic becomes the therapeutic. With Freud, individualism took a great and perhaps final step: the mature and calm feeling that must keep the individual a safe distance from the mass of his fellows can now, in therapy, be so trained that the individual can withdraw an even safer distance from his family and friends. With Freud, Western man has learned truly the technical possibility of living his inward life alone, at last rid of that crowd of shadows eternally pressing him to pay the price for a past, in his childhood, when he could not have been for himself. This isolation, however, is no longer confining, as Tocqueville, with his classical prejudices favoring political man, thought it must be; rather, in Freud's opinion, it is liberating. At last, in the assurance and control of his consciousness, the Western individual can live alone because he likes it. Left to ourselves, we will use each other; that is, in Freud's mind, the best that can be said about the value of love. All other relations, except those of use, are pretenses with which psychological man, in the sophisticated calm of his detachment, can do without—as he should, for relations that are too close and fixed lead to symptoms that destroy the capacity of an individual to meet the unexpected (e.g., the death of love, or the beloved) in ways of his own choosing.

This does not mean that psychological man is a loner. To live inwardly alone does not imply an absence of company, or even an absence of company manners. On the contrary, psychological man is more circumspect and better behaved than his ascetic forbears: he even has a measured, calculated sense of the therapeutic value of spontaneity. He is no less able to work successfully in organizations than the ascetic. The first organization men of our culture were members of the clergy, dedicated body and soul to their divine institution. Freed from all suspicions of divinity, psychological man can continue to work efficiently in all kinds of institutions, but without permitting his feelings to be dedicated to the service of those institutions. Indeed, this is precisely what Whyte, the author of the famous book *Organization Man,* asks of him: not that he quit work but that he work without such a naïve and corrupting sense of dedication; that the man use the organization rather than that the organization use the man. David Riesman, too, in his equally famous book, *The Lonely Crowd,* calls for an "autonomous" personality type to succeed the "other-directed" type of the late ascetic period in our business civilization. What both Riesman and Whyte desire, however much they derive in their analysis from Tocqueville, is not a revival of the classical ideal of political man, but far more subtly the creation of a new ideal, the individual free in the sobriety and modesty of his egoism. For this ideal, America already has its theoretician in Sigmund Freud.

Within the elaborate framework of a highly organized society, the ideal of psychological man, filtered through the popularizers of Freud, is gaining in popularity. In a society with so many rules, it is useful to realize, as the psychological man does, that all rules, even therapeutic ones, are made to be broken. The one standard of breakage is that the exception be "self-realizing" and not self-defeating. Freud could not conceive of an action that was not, however disguised and transformed, self-serving; neither could the best minds of the ascetic tradition. It was considered that in serving God one was, properly, serving oneself. Psychological man would phrase the matter somewhat differently: in serving the self one is serving "God." The notion of serving the self through some superior service to another has been in jeopardy throughout the era of economic man. Now that jeopardy has been resolved, the notion destroyed. For, in the era of psychological man, the self is the only reputable and effective god-term.

Perhaps the image of psychological man presented here is the one most appropriate and safe for use in this age. It is the self-image of a traveling man rather than a missionary. Unfortunately for culture and good taste, the salesman always cruelly parodies the preacher—without being able to help doing so, for his cultural history has dictated to the salesman the rhetorical style of the missionary. Freud distrusted that style, even for medical missionaries— or, more precisely, for missionaries of a saving medicine; he never "sold" his doctrine, as now some of his successors have done, to their real profit, with the patient elixir of "self-realization." Freud's own personal style is more suited to the American temper, with its characteristic lack of piety toward "higher" things, a respectful interest in the "lower," and a detachment from both. Like Freud, the American feels most comfortable when he is the man in the middle, neither on one side nor the other. How the American will preserve his sense of individuality finally, I do not know. Perhaps he will give up the struggle and return to some more profoundly social doctrine. It is certain, I think, that Freud has supplied the most subtly powerful technique of self-defense in the history of individualism. There is a guiding genius in Freud that Americans have been quick to recognize, for they, most of all, want to achieve that mature and calm feeling of detachment which prevents religious outburst or political experiment.

ARLIE HOCHSCHILD

The Managed Heart

> *The one area of her occupational life in which she might be "free to act," the area of her own personality, must now also be managed, must become the alert yet obsequious instrument by which goods are distributed.* *
>
> —*C. Wright Mills*

In a section in *Das Kapital* entitled "The Working Day," Karl Marx examines depositions submitted in 1863 to the Children's Employment Commission in England. One deposition was given by the mother of a child laborer in a wallpaper factory: "When he was seven years old I used to carry him [to work] on my back to and fro through the snow, and he used to work 16 hours a day. . . . I have often knelt down to feed him, as he stood by the machine, for he could not leave it or stop." Fed meals as he worked, as a steam engine is fed coal and water, this child was "an instrument of labor."[1] Marx questioned how many hours a day it was fair to use a human being as an instrument, and how much pay for being an instrument was fair, considering the profits that factory owners made. But he was also concerned with something he thought more

---

*C. Wright Mills, *White Collar* (New York: Oxford University Press, 1956
1. Marx, *Capital* (New York: Vintage, 1977), pp. 356–357, 358.

Arlie Hochschild, excerpted from *The Managed Heart: Commercialization of Human Feeling* (Berkeley and Los Angeles: University of California Press, 1983).

fundamental: the human cost of becoming an "instrument of labor" at all.

On another continent 117 years later, a twenty-year-old flight attendant trainee sat with 122 others listening to a pilot speak in the auditorium of the Delta Airlines Stewardess Training Center. Even by modern American standards, and certainly by standards for women's work, she had landed an excellent job. The 1980 pay scale began at $850 a month for the first six months and would increase within seven years to about $20,000 a year. Health and accident insurance is provided, and the hours are good.

The young trainee sitting next to me wrote on her notepad, "Important to smile. Don't forget smile." The admonition came from the speaker in the front of the room, a crew-cut pilot in his early fifties, speaking in a Southern drawl: "Now girls, I want you to go out there and really *smile*. Your smile is your biggest *asset*. I want you to go out there and use it. Smile. *Really* smile. Really *lay it on*."

The pilot spoke of the smile as the *flight attendant's* asset. But as novices like the one next to me move through training, the value of a personal smile is groomed to reflect the company's disposition— its confidence that its planes will not crash, its reassurance that departures and arrivals will be on time, its welcome and its invitation to return. Trainers take it as their job to attach to the trainee's smile an attitude, a viewpoint, a rhythm of feeling that is, as they often say, "professional." This deeper extension of the professional smile is not always easy to retract at the end of the workday, as one worker in her first year at World Airways noted: "Sometimes I come off a long trip in a state of utter exhaustion, but I find I can't relax. I giggle a lot, I chatter, I call friends. It's as if I can't release myself from an artificially created elation that kept me 'up' on the trip. I hope to be able to come down from it better as I get better at the job." At first glance, it might seem that the circumstances of the nineteenth-century factory child and the twentieth-century flight attendant could not be more different. To the boy's mother, to Marx, to the members of the Children's Employment Commission, perhaps to the manager of the wallpaper factory, and almost certainly to the contemporary reader, the boy was a victim, even a symbol, of the brutalizing conditions of his time. We might imagine that he had an emotional half-life, conscious of little more than fatigue, hunger, and boredom. On the other hand, the flight attendant enjoys the upper-class freedom to travel, and she participates in the glamour she creates for others. She is the envy of clerks in duller, less well-paid jobs.

But a close examination of the differences between the two can lead us to some unexpected common ground. On the surface there is a difference in how we know what labor actually produces. How could the worker in the wallpaper factory tell when his job was done? Count the rolls of wallpaper; a good has been produced. How can the flight attendant tell when her job is done? A service has been produced; the customer seems content. In the case of the flight attendant, the *emotional style of offering the service is part of the service itself,* in a way that loving or hating wallpaper is not a part of producing wallpaper. Seeming to "love the job" becomes part of the job; and actually trying to love it, and to enjoy the customers, helps the worker in this effort.

In processing people, the product is a state of mind. Like firms in other industries, airline companies are ranked according to the quality of service their personnel offer. Egon Ronay's yearly *Lucas Guide* offers such a ranking; besides being sold in airports and drugstores and reported in newspapers, it is cited in management memoranda and passed down to those who train and supervise flight attendants. Because it influences consumers, airline companies use it in setting their criteria for successful job performance by a flight attendant. In 1980 the *Lucas Guide* ranked Delta Airlines first in service out of fourteen airlines that fly regularly between the United States and both Canada and the British Isles. Its report on Delta included passages like this:

> [Drinks were served] not only with a smile but with concerned enquiry such as, "Anything else I can get you, madam?" The atmosphere was that of a civilized party—with the passengers, in response, behaving like civilized guests. . . . Once or twice our inspectors tested stewardesses by being deliberately exacting, but they were never roused, and at the end of the flight they lined up to say farewell with undiminished brightness. . . .
>
> [Passengers are] quick to detect strained or forced smiles, and

they come aboard wanting to *enjoy* the flight. One of us looked forward to his next trip on Delta "because it's fun." Surely that is how passengers ought to feel."[2]

The work done by the boy in the wallpaper factory called for a coordination of mind and arm, mind and finger, and mind and shoulder. We refer to it simply as physical labor. The flight attendant does physical labor when she pushes heavy meal carts through the aisles, and she does mental work when she prepares for and actually organizes emergency landings and evacuations. But in the course of doing this physical and mental labor, she is also doing something more, something I define as *emotional labor*.[3] This labor requires one to induce or suppress feeling in order to sustain the outward countenance that produces the proper state of mind in others—in this case, the sense of being cared for in a convivial and safe place. This kind of labor calls for a coordination of mind and feeling, and it sometimes draws on a source of self that we honor as deep and integral to our individuality.

Beneath the difference between physical and emotional labor there lies a similarity in the possible cost of doing the work: the worker can become estranged or alienated from an aspect of self— either the body or the margins of the soul—that is *used* to do the work. The factory boy's arm functioned like a piece of machinery used to produce wallpaper. His employer, regarding that arm as an instrument, claimed control over its speed and motions. In this situation, what was the relation between the boy's arm and his mind? Was his arm in any meaningful sense his *own?*[4]

This is an old issue, but as the comparison with airline attendants suggests, it is still very much alive. If we can become alienated from goods in a goods-producing society, we can become alienated

2. Egon Ronay, *Lucas Guide 1980* (New York: Penguin, 1979) pp. 66, 76.

3. I use the term *emotional labor* to mean the management of feeling to create a publicly observable facial and bodily display; emotional labor is sold for a wage and therefore has *exchange value*. I use the synonymous terms *emotion work* or *emotion management* to refer to these same acts done in a private context where they have *use value*.

4. Marx, in his *Economic and Philosophic Manuscripts*, may have provided the last really basic idea on alienation. See Robert Tucker, ed., *The Marx-Engels Reader* (New York: Norton, 1972).

from service in a service-producing society. This is what C. Wright Mills, one of our keenest social observers, meant when he wrote in 1956, "We need to characterize American society of the mid-twentieth century in more psychological terms, for now the problems that concern us most border on the psychiatric."[5]

When she came off the job, what relation had the flight attendant to the "artificial elation" she had induced on the job? In what sense was it her *own* elation on the job? The company lays claim not simply to her physical motions—how she handles food trays—but to her emotional actions and the way they show in the ease of a smile. The workers I talked to often spoke of their smiles as being *on* them but not *of* them. They were seen as an extension of the make-up, the uniform, the recorded music, the soothing pastel colors of the airplane decor, and the daytime drinks, which taken together orchestrate the mood of the passengers. The final commodity is not a certain number of smiles to be counted like rolls of wallpaper. For the flight attendant, the smiles are a *part of her work*, a part that requires her to coordinate self and feeling so that the work seems to be effortless. To show that the enjoyment takes effort is to do the job poorly. Similarly, part of the job is to disguise fatigue and irritation, for otherwise the labor would show in an unseemly way, and the product—passenger contentment—would be damaged. Because it is easier to disguise fatigue and irritation if they can be banished altogether, at least for brief periods, this feat calls for emotional labor.

The reason for comparing these dissimilar jobs is that the modern assembly-line worker has for some time been an outmoded symbol of modern industrial labor; fewer than 6 percent of workers now work on assembly lines. Another kind of labor has now come into symbolic prominence—the voice-to-voice or face-to-face delivery of service—and the flight attendant is an appropriate model for it. There have always been public-service jobs, of course; what is new is that they are now socially engineered and thoroughly organized from the top. Though the flight attendant's job is no worse and in many ways better than other service jobs, it makes the worker

5. C. Wright Mills, *The Power Elite* (New York: Oxford University Press, 1956), p. xx.

more vulnerable to the social engineering of her emotional labor and reduces her control over that labor. Her problems, therefore, may be a sign of what is to come in other such jobs.

Emotional labor is potentially good. No customer wants to deal with a surly waitress, a crabby bank clerk, or a flight attendant who avoids eye contact in order to avoid getting a request. Lapses in courtesy by those paid to be courteous are very real and fairly common. What they show us is how fragile public civility really is. We are brought back to the question of what the social carpet actually consists of and what it requires of those who are supposed to keep it beautiful. The laggards and sluff-offs of emotional labor return us to the basic questions. What is emotional labor? What do we do when we manage emotion? What, in fact, is emotion? What are the costs and benefits of managing emotion, in private life and at work?

* * *

Emotional labor does not observe conventional distinctions between types of jobs. By my estimate, roughly one-third of American workers today have jobs that subject them to substantial demands for emotional labor. Moreover, of all *women* working, roughly one-half have jobs that call for emotional labor. Thus this inquiry has special relevance for women, and it probably also describes more of their experience. As traditionally more accomplished managers of feeling in private life, women more than men have put emotional labor on the market, and they know more about its personal costs.

This inquiry might at first seem relevant only to workers living under capitalism, but the engineering of a managed heart is not unknown to socialism; the enthusiastic "hero of labor" bears the emotional standard for the socialist state as much as the Flight Attendant of the Year does for the capitalist airline industry. Any functioning society makes effective use of its members' emotional labor. We do not think twice about the use of feeling in the theater, or in psychotherapy, or in forms of group life that we admire. It is when we come to speak of the *exploitation* of the bottom by the top in any society that we become morally concerned. In any system, exploitation depends on the actual distribution of many kinds of profits—money, authority, status, honor, well-being. It is not emotional labor itself, therefore, but the underlying system of recompense that raises the question of what the cost of it is.

THE SEARCH FOR AUTHENTICITY

In a social system animated by competition for property, the human personality was metamorphosed into a form of capital. Here it was rational to invest oneself only in properties that would produce the highest return. Personal feeling was a handicap since it distracted the individual from calculating his best interest and might pull him along economically counterproductive paths. *

— *Rousseau (Berman's paraphrase)*

When Jean-Jacques Rousseau observed that personality was becoming a form of capital he was writing about eighteenth-century Paris, long before there were stewardess training schools. If Rousseau could sign on as a flight attendant for Delta Airlines in the second half of the twentieth century, he would doubtless be interested in learning just *whose* capital a worker's feelings are and just *who* is putting this capital to work. He would certainly see that although the individual personality remains a "medium of competition," the competition is no longer confined to individuals. Institutional purposes are now tied to the workers' psychological arts. It is not simply individuals who manage their feelings in order to do a job; whole organizations have entered the game. The emotion management that sustains the smile on Delta Airlines competes with the emotion management that upholds the smile on United and TWA.

What was once a private act of emotion management is sold now as labor in public-contact jobs. What was once a privately negotiated rule of feeling or display is now set by the company's Standard Practices Division. Emotional exchanges that were once idiosyncratic and escapable are now standardized and unavoidable. Exchanges that were rare in private life become common in commercial life. Thus a customer assumes a right to vent unmanaged hostility against a flight attendant who has no corresponding right— because she is paid, in part, to relinquish it. All in all, a private emotional system has been subordinated to commercial logic, and it has been changed by it.

---

*This, in Marshall Berman's words, is what Rousseau concluded about the impersonality of personal relations in the eighteenth century. See Berman, *The Politics of Authenticity* (New York: Atheneum, 1970), p. 140.

Estrangement from display, from feeling, and from what feelings can tell us is not simply the occupational hazard of a few. It has firmly established itself in the culture as permanently imaginable. All of us who know the commercialization of human feeling at one remove—as witness, consumer, or critic—have become adept at recognizing and discounting commercialized feeling: "Oh, they have to be friendly, that's their job." This enables us to ferret out the remaining gestures of a private gift exchange: "Now *that* smile she really meant just for me." We subtract the commercial motive and collect the personal remainders matter-of-factly, almost automatically, so ordinary has the commercialization of human feeling become.

But we have responded in another way, which is perhaps more significant: as a culture, we have begun to place an unprecedented value on spontaneous, "natural" feeling. We are intrigued by the unmanaged heart and what it can tell us. The more our activities as individual emotion managers are managed by organizations, the more we tend to celebrate the life of unmanaged feeling. This cultural response found its prophets in late eighteenth-century philosophers like Rousseau and its disciples in the Romantic movement of the nineteenth-century; but widespread acceptance of the view that spontaneous feeling is both precious and endangered has occurred only recently, in the mid-twentieth century.

According to Lionel Trilling, in his classic work *Sincerity and Authenticity,* there have been two major turning points in the public evaluation of expressed feeling. The first was the rise (and subsequent fall) of the value that people put on sincerity. The second was a rise in the value placed on authenticity. In the first case, the value attached to sincerity rose as its corresponding flaw, insincerity or guile, became more common. In the second case, I think the same principle has been at work: the value placed on authentic or "natural" feeling has increased dramatically with the full emergence of its opposite—the managed heart.

Before the sixteenth century, Trilling says, insincerity was neither a fault nor a virtue. "The sincerity of Achilles or Beowulf cannot be discussed; they neither have nor lack sincerity."[6] It simply

6. Lionel Trilling, *Sincerity and Authenticity* (Cambridge, Mass.: Harvard University Press, 1972), p. 9.

had no relevance. Yet during the sixteenth century, sincerity came to be admired. Why? The answer is socioeconomic. At this period in history, there was an increasing rate of social mobility in England and France; more and more people found it possible, or conceivable, to leave the class into which they had been born. Guile became an important tool for class advancement. The art of acting, of making avowals not in accord with feeling, became a useful tool for taking advantage of new opportunities. As mobility became a fact of urban life, so did guile and people's understanding that guile was a tool.

Sincerity for its part came to be seen as an inhibition of the capacity to act before a multiplicity of audiences or as an absence of the psychic detachment necessary to acting. The sincere, "honest soul" came to denote a "simple person, unsophisticated, a bit on the dumb side."[7] It was considered "dumb" because the art of surface acting was increasingly understood as a useful tool. When mobility became a fact of urban life, so did the art of guile, and the very interest in sincerity as a virtue declined.[8] Modern audiences, in contrast to nineteenth-century ones, became bored with duplicity as a literary theme. It had become too ordinary, too unsurprising: "The hypocrite-villain, the conscious dissembler, has become marginal, even alien, to the modern imagination of the moral life. The situation in which a person systematically misrepresents himself in order to practice upon the good faith of another does not readily command our interest, scarcely our credence. The deception we best understand and most willingly give our attention to is that which a person works upon himself.[9] The point of interest has moved inward. What fascinates us now is how we fool ourselves.

What seems to have replaced our interest in sincerity is an interest in authenticity. In both the rise and the fall of sincerity as a virtue, the feeling of sincerity "underneath" was assumed to be something solid and permanent, whether one was true to it or betrayed it. Placing a value on guile amounted to placing a value on

7. Trilling 1972, p. 9.
8. "If sincerity has lost its former status, if the word itself has for us a hollow sound and seems almost to negate its meaning, that is because it does not propose being true to one's self as an end but only as a means" (Trilling 1972, p. 9).
9. Trilling 1972, p. 16.

detachment *from* that solid something underneath. The present-day value on "authentic" or "natural" feeling may also be a cultural response to a social occurrence, but the occurrence is different. It is not the rise of individual mobility and the *individual* use of guile in pleasing a greater variety of people. It is the rise of the *corporate* use of guile and the organized training of feeling to sustain it. The more the heart is managed, the more we value the unmanaged heart.

Rousseau's Noble Savage was not guided by any feeling rules. He simply felt what he felt, spontaneously. One clue to the modern-day celebration of spontaneous feeling is the growing popularization of psychological therapies, especially those that stress "getting in touch with" spontaneous feeling.[10] Consider them: Gestalt, bio-energetics, biofeedback, encounter, assertiveness training, transactional analysis, transcendental meditation, rational-emotive therapy, LSD therapy, feeling therapy, implosive therapy, EST, primal therapy, conventional psychotherapy, and psychoanalysis. Therapy books, as the linguist Robin Lakoff has said, are to the twentieth century what etiquette books were to the nineteenth. This is because etiquette has itself gone deeper into emotional life.

The introduction of new therapies and the extension of older ones have given a new introspective twist to the self-help movement that began in the last century.[11] To that twist is now added the value on unmanaged feelings. As practitioners of Gestalt therapy put it:

10. For an excellent essay on this subject, see Ralph Turner, "The Real Self: From Institution to Impulse," *American Journal of Sociology* 81(1976):989–1016.

11. The significance of the growth of new therapies cannot be dismissed by the argument that they are simply a way of extending jobs in the service sector by creating new needs. The question remains, why *these* needs? Why the new need to *do* something about how you feel? The new therapies have also been criticized, as the old self-help movement was, for focusing on individual solutions to the exclusion of social ones and for legitimating the message "Look out for Number One." [See Christopher Lasch, "The Narcissist Society." *New York Review of Books* 23 (September 30, 1976):5–13.] This critique is not wrong in itself, but it is partial and misleading. It is my own view that the capacity to feel is fully analogous to the capacity to see or hear; and if that capacity is lost or injured, it is wise to restore it in whatever way one can. But to attach the cure to a solipsistic or individualistic philosophy of life or to assume that one's injury can only be self-imposed is to contribute to what I have called (with optimism) a "prepolitical" stance.

"The childish feelings are important not as a past that must be undone but as some of the most beautiful powers of adult life that must be recovered: spontaneity, imagination."[12] Again, in *Born to Win*, two popularizers of transactional analysis collapse a more general viewpoint into a simple homily: "Winners are not stopped by their contradictions and ambivalences. Being authentic, they know when they are angry and can listen when others are angry with them."[13] Winners, the suggestion is, do not *try to know* what they feel or *try to let themselves* feel. They just know and they just feel, in a natural, unprocessed way.

Ironically, people read a book like *Born to Win* in order to *learn* how to *try* to be a natural, authentic winner. Spontaneity is now cast as something to be *recovered;* the individual learns how to treat feeling as a recoverable object, with ego as the instrument of recovery. In the course of "getting in touch with our feelings," we make feelings more subject to command and manipulation, more amenable to various forms of management.[14]

While the qualities of Rousseau's Noble Savage are celebrated in modern pop therapy, he did not act in the way his modern admirers do. The Noble Savage did not "let" himself feel good about his garden. He did not "get in touch with" or "into" his resentment. He had no therapist working on his throat to open up a "voice block." He did not go back and forth between hot and cold tubs while hyperventilating to get in touch with his feelings. No therapist said to him, "Okay, Noble Savage, let's try to really get into your sadness." He did not imagine that he owed others any feeling or that they owed him any. In fact, the utter absence of calculation and will as they have become associated with feeling is what nowadays makes the Noble Savage seem so savage. But it is also—and this is my point—what makes him seem so noble.

Why do we place more value now on artless, unmanaged feel-

12. Perls et al. (1951), p. 297.
13. Muriel James and Dorothy Jongeward, *Born to Win* (Center City, Minn.: Hazelden, 1971).
14. The ego detachment necessary to do emotion work is fostered by many modern therapies that aim, in part, to increase control over feelings. The individual is inducted into the belief that he or she *already has control over feeling*, a control that simply has to be brought to awareness.

ing? Why, hopelessly and romantically, do we imagine a natural preserve of feeling, a place to be kept "forever wild"? The answer must be that it is becoming scarce. In everyday life, we are all to some degree students of Stanislavski; we are only poorer or better at deep acting, closer or more remote from incentives to do it well. We have carried our ancient capacity for gift exchange over a great commercial divide where the gifts are becoming commodities and the exchange rates are set by corporations. Jean-Jacques Rousseau as a flight attendant for Delta Airlines might add to his eighteenth-century concern for the faceless soul beneath the mask a new concern for the market intrusion into the ways we define ourselves and for how, since his day, that intrusion has expanded and organized itself.

FRITZ PERLS

The Gestalt Prayer

I do my thing, and you do your thing.
I am not in this world to live up to your expectations
And you are not in this world to live up to mine.
You are you, and I am I,
And if by chance, we find each other, it's beautiful.
If not, it can't be helped.

Fritz Perls, "The Gestalt Prayer," from *Gestalt Therapy Verbatim* (Moab, Utah: Real People Press, 1972).

Civility and Psychology

There was a time when the major discordance in American political and cultural life was regional; specifically, a matter of North and South—terms that represented not only two regions, but two ways of thinking about life and living it. The question of slavery dominated the argumentative discourse, needless to say, but even before our Constitution was ratified by the states of Colonial America, the great Virginia eccentric (and statesman and singularly shrewd social observer) John Randolph had prophesied the increasing polarization of a future nation: the pull of a strong central government, so convenient to urban manufacturing centers intent on getting resources and doing business, no matter the cost to this person or that community; as against the tug of a rural aristocracy, heavily slave-connected as well as dependent on a white yeomanry, but also devoted to ways of leisure and aspects of a cultural tradition (that of ancient Greece and Rome) at variance with the habits and interests of, say, the burghers of New England, New York, and Pennsylvania. William Taylor's felicitously stated polarity in *Cavalier and Yankee*[1]—the South as a repository of one set of apprehensions and aspirations, the North as a place where a rather different social and economic agenda predominated—was deeply embedded in our national life well into this century. Even now, as the "New South" becomes, in fact, a *déjà vu* North ("commerce, everywhere commerce" we heard a member of Alabama's gentry say, with respect to Birmingham and Atlanta, in 1965), some of the distinctions Mr. Taylor emphasized haven't quite disappeared.

* * *

If, as some would insist, there are still two principal opposites in American life, yet again they are grounded in geography; but

1. William Taylor, *Cavalier and Yankee* (New York: George Braziller, 1961).

Robert Coles, excerpted and abridged from "Civility and Psychology," in *Dædalus* 109 (Summer 1980), pp. 133–41.

today they are the East as against the West. There is, without question, a cultural tradition specifically and intimately Western. . . . And without question, the West's political life these days lends itself to the speculation that there most certainly are a number of felt assumptions that set apart, at least to a degree, many of the people who live west of the Mississippi River: a preoccupation with land and, more subjectively, with a sense of space; a continuing apprehension about the availability of water; a feeling of distance from the federal city of Washington, and a desire to extend rather than shorten that distance. "Space is everything here—and movement, the right to pick up and go and be yourself and no one hassling you"—these are the words of a New Mexico cowboy we knew when living in the state. In contrast, we heard this from a Mississippi lawyer in the early spring of 1963: "Kin is what matters in the South—your people, in your town. If we lose that, we'll become just another bunch of American gypsies, going here and there and anywhere, because someone is singing the tune of cash."

* * *

Even the farthest West is a place to which something was brought—culture as baggage of sorts, unselfconsciously worked into the lives of both those who stay put and those who travel a good distance in a strenuous search for a supposedly new or different life. Put differently, if the texture of our national life is changing, the supposedly more remote parts of the geographic entity will most decidedly feel the effect, especially in this age of the airplane, the television set, the telephone—as anyone knows who has landed in an Eskimo village way up the Arctic coast, or along the Kobuk River, and found pizzas, Coca-Cola, hi-fi sets, snowmobiles, pictures everywhere of the Grateful Dead.

But technology is not the only ingredient of our contemporary life that penetrates even our apparently inaccessible and forbidding territorial extremities. In the middle 1970s as my wife and sons and I visited one Indian reservation after another, one Eskimo community after another, we came upon (inevitably, we now realize) a number of what, I assume, some future archaeologist will call a species of North American artifacts, circa the twentieth century, late (?1970–1990). On a Hopi reservation (yes, *Hopi,* arguably the most persistent cultural critics this country has harbored within its midst) we found the following message, printed on a mimeographed handout: "Something on your mind? Don't be silent. We will meet to discuss a new Hopi life. Come, and feel a lot better afterwards!" In Alaska's Kotzebue, and in Noorvik, not far away, we saw several copies of a book titled *Child and Baby Care,* by one Benjamin Spock. On the wall of a school in Kotzebue, this meeting was announced: "Weekly group to discuss teacher-student attitudes, Wednesday at 3." On a bulletin board in a town named Corrales, close by the Rio Grande River, north and west of Albuquerque, a pamphlet presented questions, and also some advice: "Unable to sleep? Overweight? Having Marriage Problems? Come talk about it! You'll feel better!" Then came the details (the place, the time) of a phenomenon surely not regional in nature: life's personal troubles as a subject for strangers (of course!) to mull over long and hard. One of my sons. He was even allowed, indeed encouraged, to take pictures of a meeting in a small Utah town, where teachers were insisting to each other that they were "interacting" and "letting out" what they kept calling their "hostilities." The result would be "a more honest approach in the classroom." Such phrases belong, alas, to all of us in every region of America; they are not merely handed down, out of memory, as part of one roaming family's "oral literature."

What about another kind of "literature," our national best-sellers; what is their cumulative, transparent message? An endless story, it seems, of self-cultivation—what we can do for ourselves, say for ourselves, eat for ourselves. If we are "O.K.," everyone else is. If we consume X or Y or Z, we have our "health," and that is "everything." But, of course, it isn't; one must keep in mind other parts of the self—the sexual organs, say, or the appearance we give, or the "relationships" we have. And those relationships, Lord spare us—they determine whether we'll really get where we ought naturally want to be: "number one" in our minds, "best friends" to ourselves, knowing "where we're coming from," hence possessed of "mental health." I don't think there is a great need for an extended analysis of, or argument about, the collective impact of such a line of thinking. All the books on psychology, food, exercise, sex; all the sermons on how to win friends, on the importance of releasing tensions, on how to "cope," on how to "rear" children so they won't have "conflicts" or "problems," as if that were either possible or desirable—there is a high mound of evidence, in print, of what we are like culturally. The heart of the matter, I fear, is psychology, though not the kind fairly often taught in college and university courses (a scholarly discipline conveyed as such), and not the kind taught under the name of this kind of psychoanalysis:

> . . . at the time when psychoanalysis laid great emphasis on the seductive influence of sharing the parents' bed and the traumatic consequences of witnessing parental intercourse, parents were warned against bodily intimacy with their children and against performing the sexual act in the presence of even their youngest infants. When it was proved in the analyses of adults that the withholding of sexual knowledge was responsible for many intellectual inhibitions, full sexual enlightenment at an early age was advocated. When hysterical symptoms, frigidity, impotence, etc., were traced back to prohibitions and the subsequent repressions of sex in childhood, psychoanalytic upbringing put on its program a lenient and permissive attitude toward the manifestations of infantile, pregenital sexuality. When the new instinct theory gave aggression the status of a basic drive, tolerance was extended also to the child's early and violent hostilities, his death wishes against parents and siblings, etc. When anxiety was recognized as playing a central part in symptom formation, every effort was made to lessen the children's fear of parental authority. When guilt was shown to correspond to the tension between the inner agencies, this was followed by the ban on all educational measures likely to produce a severe super-ego. When the new structural view of the personality placed the onus for maintaining an inner equilibrium on the ego, this was translated into the need to foster in the child the development of ego forces strong enough to hold their own against the pressure of the drives. Finally, in our time, when analytic investigations have turned to earliest events in the first year of life and highlighted their importance, these specific insights are being translated into new and in some respects revolutionary techniques of infant care.[2]

The author of those words, Anna Freud, takes note, a bit further on, of the intense hope and great (messianic) faith, if not sadly instructive and desperate gullibility, involved in all this: "In the unceasing search for pathogenic agents and preventive measures, it

2. Anna Freud, *Normality and Pathology in Childhood* (New York: International Universities Press, 1965).

seemed always the latest analytic discovery which promised a better and more final solution of the problem." But then, the disappointment: "Above all, to rid the child of anxiety proved an impossible task. Parents did their best to reduce the children's fear of them, merely to find that they were increasing guilt feelings, i.e., fears of the child's own conscience. Where in its turn, the severity of the super-ego was reduced, children produced the deepest of all anxieties, i.e., the fear of human beings who feel unprotected against the pressure of their drives." And too, the discovery that yet another fantasied perfectionism had been tried, been found wanting: "It is true that the children who grew up under its influence were in some respects different from earlier generations; but they were not freer from anxiety or from conflicts, and therefore not less exposed to neurotic and other mental illnesses."

But Anna Freud was not only addressing her psychoanalytic colleagues with such penetrating and ironic remarks. She wrote as a social historian; and the tale she was telling has by no means come to an end. It is a story that has to do with widespread notions—in sum, psychology as a dominant theme, if not an obsession, in our national life: among those belonging to the higher realms, whom Miss Freud is gently educating, if not, ever so tactfully, reprimanding for a certain self-important and self-centered variety of fatuity; among those so-called ordinary people who see the best sellers on the counters of stores located in each of our fifty states—including, I've noticed, the markets of obscure villages of the West or the South, where few know of or pay heed to the "important" (national) newspapers or magazines. Psychology, in this instance, means a concentration, persistent, if not feverish, upon one's thoughts, feelings, wishes, worries—bordering on, if not embracing, solipsism: the self as the only or main form of (existential) reality. Our two regional informants above, poor backward souls from New Mexico and Mississippi, talked about "kin" or "land" as of transcendent importance (even as God and later the nation-state once were held in such commanding esteem). Today it is "groups" that matter, people who know how to talk and talk and talk.

The hallmark of our time[3] seems to be lots of psychological

3. There are several theoretical ways to approach this question of twentieth century "psychological man" Philip Rieff has done so through a critique of psychoa-

chatter, lots of self-consciousness, lots of "interpretations." As the saying goes, "Let it all hang out," and then we'll "talk about it." Asks Soren Kierkegaard in *The Present Age*, written in 1846: "What is *talkativeness?* It is the result of doing away with the vital distinction between talking and keeping silent." Imagine that, a notion that it is important, often enough, to keep one's mouth shut—rather than, for instance, to say something about someone's "behavior" or "motives" or "problems." At one point Kierkegaard even insisted that "silence is the essence of inwardness, of the inner life." Such an observation tells us today exactly what Kierkegaard meant it to tell his Copenhagen neighbors almost a century and a half ago—how far we've gone in a given direction.

Here is Kierkegaard again, also in *The Present Age*, letting us know that at least one nineteenth century observer was able to prophesy our time of "cool"—a time in which a crude kind of popularized psychology has become the moral standard many, many people rely upon: "A father no longer curses his son in anger, using all his parental authority, nor does a son defy his father, a conflict which might end in the inwardness of forgiveness; on the contrary, their relationship is irreproachable, for it is really in process of ceasing to exist, since they are no longer related to one another within the relationship; in fact it has become a problem in which the two partners observe each other as in a game, instead of having any relation to each other, and they note down each other's remarks instead of showing a firm devotion." And he could take the next step, to see the self becoming our moral *ne plus ultra*. No longer are we as persons subordinate to Yaweh or Christ, to a particular flag and all it stands for, to explicitly avowed and handed-down ethical principles which one tries desperately to live by, if necessary to die for. The self is our guide, our standard—those psychological "needs" we experience, those psychological "passages" through

---

nalysis as a social phenomenon in *Freud: The Mind of the Moralist* (Chicago: University of Chicago Press, 1979). Richard Sennett has done so historically in *The Fall of Public Man* (New York: Alfred A. Knopf, 1977.) Christopher Lasch has done so, brilliantly, by using narcissism as an angle of approach to the contemporary American social scene in *The Culture of Narcissism* (New York: W. W. Norton, 1978). In my work with children of well-to-do families I have had to comment repeatedly on the self-centeredness one finds, the "narcissistic entitlement"—see, Robert Coles, *Privileged Ones*, vol. 5 of *Children of Crisis* (Boston: Atlantic-Little, Brown, 1978).

which we journey, those "emotions" we boastfully proclaim to each other. "Now everyone can have an opinion," Kierkegaard observed, and then added, "but they have to band together numerically in order to have one. Twenty-five signatures make the most frightful stupidity into an opinion, and the considered opinion of a first-class mind is only a paradox." If the self must at all costs put its banal cards on the table, then subjective universals (exactly who is without "hostility," "anxiety," and all the rest?) become a public phenomenon (Kierkegaard's "opinion"), and "group psychology" becomes a major aspect of social reality (as in so-called encounter groups, T-groups, Esalen groups, EST groups—the lot of them).

Even a modest consideration of civility brings us into territory smack in between psychology and politics. When John Milton reminded his fellow citizens of seventeenth century England how important it is "to inbreed and cherish in a great people the seeds of virtue, and public civility," he was making an important connection between educational principles and a nation's political life. Civility for him had to do with citizenship, membership in a particular national community—not a T-group or a single "cause" or a neighborhood or even a collection of them, called a region. He understood that a given social order was only as strong as the commitment to it of the men and women who, in their sum, make up that order. For him, politeness was no superficial attribute of human behavior, something to be stripped away in the interest of a supposed verbal bluntness that turns out to be, so often, an exercise in truculence, rudeness, self-display, if not a mix of self-promotion and self-indulgence. Civility has to do with allegiance—a sense that one's behavior ought to be, under a range of circumstances, responsive to, and respectful of, certain standards: historically, they have been state-connected; more recently, they have tended increasingly to be social or conventional (in the nonpejorative sense of that last word). Now we have moved to the standard of the intensely private—ironically, a public phenomenon. Citizens show earnest, even exclusive respect for the autobiographical disclosures of other citizens, no matter that they might be pronouncements of an agitated or even ailing mind. The entire point is to "communicate."

When a culture begins to turn its back on civility, ought it be called "civilized"? One is not just playing with cognate words here,

Latin roots. "Without politeness, without a tight lid on our big mouths at certain critical moments, it's a quick plunge into the old swamp we once called home"—the words of William Carlos Williams, as he contemplated the ornery, sticky, frustrating, galling side of the urban life he knew so well and worked so hard to improve as a doctor who climbed tenement house stairs every day. Maybe he needed a little of that "help" we're all told to go get. Or is it we who need "help"—because we've got so much of it, we've forgotten what else we have to do in this world besides keep getting more of it: live honorable lives in a big and complicated country which has so many problems that have little to do with psychology.

Is it making too brash a leap to say that there is a connection between, on the one hand, the insistent emphasis on self, buttressed by reductionist psychology as a secular, philosophical *raison d'être*, along with a consumerism fueled significantly by an "applied psychology" that tells us what's "in it" for ourselves; and on the other hand, the proliferation of single-issue political activity, whereby one gives one's all to what one feels most strongly about, and the devil with any notion of a larger personal, never mind social, responsibility? A long question, but I've heard it reduced all too readily to a terse statement, indeed: "I'm in this struggle because it means a lot to me; it's where I'm at." I'm afraid I can't describe the person as a poorly educated fool, so for that reason full of the usual encounter-group gibberish one learns to wince at or, if one can, ignore. A graduate of an Ivy League college and law school, a dedicated, hardworking environmentalist, he had the above justification for what amounted to a political yardstick. "They're with me or they're against me," he kept saying. All right, he lived in New Mexico, and had good reason to worry about the land, so stunning in its beauty, yet so vulnerable; the water, so necessary, yet so precarious in supply; the air, so clear and bracing, yet so thin and fragile, and already violated cruelly in parts of the Southwest. Still, here was an American citizen, talking about a vote for an occupant of a seat in the U.S. Senate, and nothing else mattered—*to him,* he frankly admitted. And if he and all the rest of us are told all the time that what matters is what matters to us personally, and that what happens to matter to us must at all costs be spoken, then why not grab on for dear life and with all one's passion to one or another cause, movement, issue? The point is to fulfill *your* potential, do *your* thing, live and act in a way *you* wish and find comfortable—sexually, with friends, with respect to a career. Why not politically, too? True, millions can't find the kind of leeway ("liberation") a collection of newspaper columnists, book writers, and psychological experts, if not hustlers, tell them they require. But the cultural standards are there, the courts of last appeal: advice handed down in response to letters addressed to newspaper columnists; articles on what to do in just about every "psychologically significant" situation; and always that inquiry as to how one *feels* about something, anything.

Civility means all of us subordinating our feelings to certain shared imperatives; and in politics it means choosing candidates on the basis of not only one's personal tastes and inclinations but the entire country's requirements. If the country itself, however, has been very much taken by the notion that the overriding requirement is that each person follow his or her emotional dictates, respond to initiatives that he or she has found *within* (an examination not of political and economic and social reality, but of the mind's and/or the body's rhythms), then we surely are at a decisive point in Ameri can history. When the self becomes our transcendence, politics becomes, along with everything else, a matter of impulse, whim, fancy, exuberant indulgence, bored indifference, outright angry rejection. A political analogue to "doing one's own thing" is a one-issue politics. Civility is meant to guard diversity—because the unifying object of transcendence is something, by definition, above and beyond personal taste or inclination: a loyalty to constitutional principles and obligations, to a process meant to mediate, arbitrate, adjudicate, and yes, promulgate (laws, administrative decisions, acts of policy carried out). It is true that our Constitution explicitly refers to an "inalienable right" we have for "the pursuit of happiness"; but that is connected, immediately, to other issues (life itself, and liberty) and it is part of a long statement, with all sorts of provisions, cautions, reminders, denials, and prohibitions. Moreover, it is a *pursuit* that is mentioned—the task of sifting and sorting, saying yes, but also saying no. And if one person's "happiness" becomes another's pain and sorrow—by God, the Constitution and its Bill of Rights (a clear bill of responsibilities) makes quite clear a particular "civilized" bias, an inclination toward, an insistence upon, actually, civility: the checks and balances, the elaborate political courtesies, hesitations, curbs, second guesses, nay-saying prerogatives of a government, a national authority set up, finally, to make decisions, to govern. At some point, such an activity demands more than the responsive listening of duly elected authorities. It demands a commitment from us—not us as persons, "whole" or otherwise, but as citizens. A surrender has to be made—not of values and principles, and not of the right to fight for one's (chief) cause or collection of ideas and ideals (ideology, or general political convictions), but of one's right to hoard allegiances—give them only as the property of a particular mind, a certain emotional life.

In losing we gain, in giving up we receive; the old Biblical paradoxes are built into what is called a republic, a civilization. Civility means losing a chance to have one's emotional, wordy say, giving up impulse. For what? For the sake of procedure, order, restraint; for the sake of a thankful absence of the other person's torrent of emotional impulses, visited on oneself and those near at hand. As Anna Freud has pointed out in a quotation above, nothing can be more fearful and disintegrating than being "unprotected against the pressure of [our] drives." The gift for the act of renunciation (civility) is, of course, civilization. Yes, with Freud's "discontents," but that is a small price to pay for sparing ourselves thousands, indeed millions, of breast-beating, fist-clenching, constantly jabbering and self-scrutinizing I's, with their haunting, unsettling refrain of recent years; *I* am all right; *I* have figured myself out; *I* know what *I* want—and that's all that counts. The sad paradox of a collective egoism.

PART SIX

THE CULTURAL FORMS AND LIMITS OF INDIVIDUALISM

The individualism that constitutes the core of our American culture is a very complex system of ideas about the nature of social life and the foundations of morality. The readings in this chapter illustrate some of the moral ambiguities that this complex of ideas gives rise to; they show how modern developments in American forms of individualism can lead to unresolvable moral dilemmas; and they point toward ways out of these dilemmas.

John G. Cawelti, a professor of American literature, explores the mythic individualism that finds expression in popular literature. In the selection reprinted here he focuses on the hard-boiled detective story. Like the hero of the classic cowboy story, the hero of the detective story achieves his (the hero is usually a man) moral stature only by standing alone against a corrupt society. But if this vision is pushed to its extreme, if society is so rotten that all its leading citizens are secretly criminals, its legal institutions unable to establish justice, its canons of success and respectability completely destructive of moral initiative, and if the hero for all his effort has no hope of contributing to a better legal system or a more decent social order, then what is the point of continuing in a lonely struggle for what is good?

That our most popular myths of individualism lead to such troubling questions is a sign of fundamental ambiguities in middle-class American culture. As the anthropologists David M. Schneider and Raymond T. Smith portray it, the "middle class" is as much a state of mind as a matter of wealth. Most Americans—the relatively affluent as well as the relatively poor—like to think of themselves as middle-class. To be middle-class is to have "certain attitudes, aspirations, and expectations towards status mobility." It is to have some reason to hope that by disciplined, calculating effort one can move beyond the station into which one was born—or some reason to fear that by failure to exercise such effort one can sink below it. It is to expect that one's status in life will be the result of one's own individual achievement in a competition for success with similar strivers rather than the result of qualities ascribed to one by the accidents of birth, class, or race.

Practically all Americans except those who are so very poor that they have no realistic hope of "getting ahead" and those who are so very rich that they have no realistic fear of losing their wealth share these middle-class aspirations—and even the very poor tend to wish they could be middle-class, while the very rich at least pay lip service to middle-class values. To the extent that to be middle-class is to be preoccupied with "making something of oneself," members of the middle class tend to ignore the ways in which their identities are constituted by their ties to society. Ignoring this reality won't make it go away. It will, however, make it difficult to attach any positive moral value to the institutions that connect us with one another—thus the detective hero can only prove his worth by working outside of social institutions, not by patiently constructing the foundations for a better society.

"Reflections in a Glass Eye," a commentary by the novelist David Black, on a week's Top 10 videocassettes, indicates how pervasive is the theme that moral worth is only to be achieved by standing outside of and over against institutions. Not only hard-boiled detectives but heroes as diverse as Rambo, Luke Skywalker, Jane Fonda, and Pinocchio find salvation by standing outside of mainstream society, by resisting the corrupting pull of established institutions, and, in the act of resistance, engaging in moral choices that will liberate them. But these heroes of a typical week's best-selling videocassettes each make very different kinds of moral choice. Is there any way to say that the path to moral salvation chosen by Jane Fonda is any better than that of, say, Rambo? As long as these different kinds of choices are each made with lonely authenticity, as long as they each genuinely feel right to the moral hero and his or her supporters, it is difficult for people immersed in American culture to say that one choice is better than another. The moral philosophy that predominates not only among academic philosophers but in the common sense of ordinary Americans is what Alasdair MacIntyre calls "emotivism."

As the moral philosopher MacIntyre describes it in his *After Virtue*, emotivism is a theory based on the idea that all moral judgments are nothing but expressions of individuals' subjective preferences, that there are ultimately no objective criteria that can be used to determine whether one judgment is better than another. How can a society composed of individuals who think this way keep from degenerating into anarchy? In the selections from *After Virtue* reprinted here, Alasdair MacIntyre argues that it is only the overwhelming dominance of bureaucratic institutions that can hold us together. Modern individualism is what he calls "bureaucratic individualism," and emotivism is its moral creed.

The great irony of modern individualism is that the belief that individuals should define themselves independently of social institutions flourishes against a backdrop of ever expanding systems of social control. To "make something of themselves" in modern society, the vast majority of middle-class Americans have to work within bureaucratic institutions (like the mass communications organizations that publish and market stories about lonely American heroes) devoted to ensuring that other people—employees, customers, clients, and so forth—will act in predictable ways. This dominance of bureaucratic institutions renders the emotivist celebration of individual autonomy ultimately illusory.

MacIntyre contrasts the way of life embodied in modern bureaucratic individualism with a way of life centered around the performance of what he calls "practices," shared activities that are good in themselves, not simply means to some other end like wealth, status, or power. To see an activity—like playing chess, or creating a work of art, or raising a family, or governing a nation—as a practice is to acknowledge that there is an objectively good way to carry it out, defined by the historical tradition through which the practice has been transmitted to the present and by the community of persons committed to maintaining that tradition and creatively extending it into the future. The performance of a practice requires those human qualities that the Aristotelian philosophical tradition calls virtues. The conception of the virtues requires an overriding conception of the *telos*— the goal—of a whole human life. A coherent morality and a coherent social life can only be achieved through commitment to intrinsically good practices, and practices can be sustained only through cultivation of the virtues.

Modern culture renders such moral and social coherence problematic. Modern emotivism is based on a denial that there is any objective way to conceive of the goal of a whole human life, and modern society tends to transform all activities into means for the achievement of extrinsic goals like wealth and power. The traditional notions of virtue and of intrinsically good practices are thus alien to modern society.

Habits of the Heart suggests, however, that Americans have not totally lost a sense of the importance of practices and of virtues. Americans still retain "second languages" that can give substance to these ideas, and *Habits* emphasizes the importance of preserving, revitalizing, and restoring these second languages to cultural centrality.

John G. Cawelti

Adventure, Mystery, and Romance

PATTERNS OF THE FORMULA

The hard-boiled formula resembles the main outlines of the classical detective story's pattern of action. It, too, moves from the introduction of the detective and the presentation of the crime, through the investigation, to a solution and apprehension of the criminal. Significant differences appear in the way this pattern is worked out in the hard-boiled story. Two are particularly important: the subordination of the drama of solution to the detective's quest for the discovery and accomplishment of justice; and the substitution of a pattern of intimidation and temptation of the hero for the elaborate development in the classical story of what Northrop Frye calls "the wavering finger of suspicion" passing across a series of potential suspects.

The hard-boiled detective sets out to investigate a crime but invariably finds that he must go beyond the solution to some kind of personal choice or action. While the classical writer typically treats the actual apprehension of the criminal as a less significant matter than the explanation of the crime, the hard-boiled story usually ends with a confrontation between detective and criminal. Sometimes this is a violent encounter similar to the climactic shootdown of many westerns. This difference in endings results from a greater personal involvement on the part of the hard-boiled detective. Since he becomes emotionally and morally committed to some of the persons involved, or because the crime poses some basic crisis in his image of himself, the hard-boiled detective remains unfulfilled until he has taken a personal moral stance toward the

John G. Cawelti, excerpted from *Adventure, Mystery, and Romance: Formula Stories as Art and Popular Culture* (Chicago: University of Chicago Press, 1976), pp. 142–54.

criminal. In simpler hard-boiled stories like those of Spillane, the detective, having solved the crime, acts out the role of judge and executioner. In the more complex stories of Raymond Chandler and Dashiell Hammett, the confrontation between detective and criminal is less violent and more psychological. In both cases we find the detective forced to define his own concept of morality and justice, frequently in conflict with the social authority of the police. Where the classical detective's role was to use his superior intellect and psychological insight to reveal the hidden guilt that the police seemed unable to discover, the hard-boiled detective metes out the just punishment that the law is too mechanical, unwieldy, or corrupt to achieve. As [Spillane's] Mike Hammer puts it in his forthright way:

> By Christ, I'm not letting the killer go through the tedious process of the law. You know what happens, damn it. They get the best lawyer there is and screw up the whole thing and wind up a hero! . . . No, damn it. A jury is cold and impartial like they're supposed to be, while some snotty lawyer makes them pour tears as he tells how his client was insane at the moment or had to shoot in self-defense. Swell. The law is fine. But this time I'm the law and I'm not going to be cold and impartial.

Chandler's Philip Marlowe, a bit more subtly, also views the law as an impediment to the accomplishment of true justice:

> Let the law enforcement people do their own dirty work. Let the lawyers work it out. They write the laws for other lawyers to dissect in front of other lawyers called judges so that other judges can say the first judges were wrong and the Supreme Court can say the second lot were wrong. Sure there's such a thing as law. We're up to our necks in it. About all it does is make business for lawyers.

Because the hard-boiled detective embodies the threat of judgment and execution as well as exposure, the pressure against his investigation is invariably more violent than in the classical story. Philip Marlowe, Sam Spade, Mike Hammer, and the rest are threatened by physical violence to a degree unknown to the classical detective whose activities are largely confined to the examination of clues, the taking of testimony, and the reconstruction of the crime. The hard-boiled detective faces assault, capture, drugging, blackjacking, and attempted assassination as a regular feature of his investigations. Moreover, he is frequently threatened with loss of his license or tempted with bribes of various kinds to halt his investigations, for the criminal is commonly a person of considerable political and social influence. Inevitably there comes a point in the hard-boiled detective's investigation when he can lament with Philip Marlowe: "I get it from the law, I get it from the hoodlum element, I get it from the carriage trade. The words change, but the meaning is the same. Lay off."

These two differences of emphasis—the detective becoming judge as well as investigator, and the intimidation and temptation of the detective—shape the pattern of action in the hard-boiled story into a formula different in many respects from its classical counterpart. Like the classical story, we usually begin with the introduction of the detective, but instead of the charming bachelor apartment of Holmes and Watson, or the elegant establishment of Lord Peter Wimsey, the hard-boiled detective belongs to the dusty and sordid atmosphere of an office located in a broken-down building on the margin of the city's business district. Sometimes the story begins in this office but, more often, the detective is already in motion to the scene of the crime, on his way to visit a client, or, like Philip Marlowe in the opening to *Farewell, My Lovely*, simply sucked violently in:

> The doors swung back outwards and almost settled to a stop. Before they had entirely stopped moving they opened again, violently, outwards. Something sailed across the sidewalk and landed in the gutter between two parked cars. . . . A hand I could have sat in came out of the dimness and took hold of my shoulder and squashed it to a pulp. Then the hand moved me through the doors and casually lifted me up a step. . . . The big man stared at me solemnly and went on wrecking my shoulder with his hand.

Sometimes instead of plunging the hero immediately into violence, the story opens in a context of decadent wealth. *The Big Sleep* begins with Marlowe visiting rich old General Sternwood in a hothouse atmosphere redolent of corruption and death:

> The air was thick, wet, steamy and larded with the cloying smell of tropical orchids in bloom. The glass walls and roof were heavily

misted and big drops of moisture splashed down on the plants. The light had an unreal greenish color, like light filtered through an aquarium tank. The plants filled the place, a forest of them, with nasty meaty leaves and stalks like the newly washed fingers of dead men.

These opening scenes immediately establish a number of the central motifs of the hard-boiled story. We see the detective as a marginal professional carrying on his business from the kind of office associated with unsuccessful dentists, small mail-order businesses, and shyster lawyers. However, we soon realize that he has chosen this milieu. His way of life may look like failure, but actually it is a form of rebellion, a rejection of the ordinary concepts of success and respectability. As Raymond Chandler puts it:

> The other part of me wanted to get out and stay out, but this was the part I never listened to. Because if I ever had I would have stayed in the town where I was born and worked in the hardware store and married the boss's daughter and had five kids and read them the funny paper on Sunday morning and smacked their heads when they got out of line and squabbled with the wife about how much spending money they were to get and what programs they could have on the radio and TV set. I might even have got rich— small town rich, an eight-room house, two cars in the garage, chicken every Sunday and the Reader's Digest on the living room table, the wife with a cast-iron permanent and me with a brain like a sack of Portland cement. You take it, friend.

Or as Shell Scott puts it:

> I suppose I should be—oh, more orthodox. Nose to the old grind-stone, up at the crack of dawn, charge around with an expression of severe pain on my face. Like right now, for example. But that wouldn't be *me,* and if I lost me, where would I be.

The beginning of the hard-boiled story usually represents both this marginal, rebellious aspect of the hero and his capacity to function effectively in a world of wealth, corruption, and violence. Since his office is scruffy and his salary and mode of life that of the lower middle class we see the detective not as a brilliant eccentric with transcendent powers of ratiocination but as an ordinary man. At the same time the opening incidents reveal that his commonness is a mask for uncommon qualities. For this antihero, this seemingly frustrated and cynical failure knows how to handle himself in the midst of violence. The rich, the powerful, and the beautiful desperately need his help with their problems.

As the pattern of action develops, the rich, the powerful, and the beautiful attempt to draw the detective into their world and to use him for their own corrupt purposes. He in turn finds that the process of solving the crime involves him in the violence, deceit, and corruption that lies beneath the surface of the respectable world. [Ross Macdonald's] Lew Archer enters on his investigation in *The Doomsters* with a typical hard-boiled reflection on what he knows will come of his quest:

> We passed a small-boat harbor, gleaming white on blue, and a long pier draped with fishermen. Everything was as pretty as a postcard. The trouble with you, I said to myself: you're always turning over the postcards and reading the message on the underside. Written in invisible ink, in blood, in tears with a black border around them, with postage due, unsigned, or signed with a thumbprint.

As in the classical story, the introduction of the hard-boiled detective leads immediately to the presentation of the crime, but substantial differences in the treatment of the crime give it rather different implications. The classical detective generally faces a *fait accompli*. The crime has left behind its mysterious clues. The detective is called to the quarantine site and challenged to expose the hidden guilt. This proceeding emphasizes the abnormality and isolation of the crime, its detachment from the detective and the reader. The hard-boiled story, on the other hand, typically implicates the detective in the crime from the very beginning. In many hard-boiled stories, the detective is given a mission—usually a deceptive one—which seemingly has little to do with murder and violence. Pursuing this mission, the detective happens upon the first of a series of murders that gradually reveal to him the true nature of his quest. In this way, the hard-boiled detective's investigation becomes not simply a matter of determining who the guilty person is but of defining his own moral position. For example, Sam Spade in *The Maltese Falcon* is asked by a beautiful young lady to investigate the disappearance of her sister. While pursuing this investigation, Spade's partner is mysteriously murdered. Then Sam himself is confronted by a mysterious Levantine who first asks him puzzling questions about a bird and then attempts to hold him up and search his office. Gradually events accumulate, more murders take place, and additional mysterious characters are introduced. The shape of Sam's mission keeps changing from the search for the client's sister, to the investigation of his partner's death, to the hunt for the falcon until finally it turns out that his real problem is not to find the killer but what to do about a woman he has fallen in love with and who has turned out to be a murderess. A similarly shifting definition of the detective's mission occurs in many Mike Hammer stories. In *The Body Lovers,* Mike undertakes to locate the sister of a convict. His investigations lead to a ring of rich and powerful sadists who get their kicks from torture-murders. But with this discovery the problem changes, for the sadist group is largely made up of UN diplomats from the Middle East who have "diplomatic immunity" and therefore cannot be punished by the police. Finally, Mike must take up his usually climactic role of personal judge and executioner and work out some way of blowing up the dirty foreigners. It only remains to be added that in a fashion almost invariable to Spillane but common to the hard-boiled story, Mike discovers that the beautiful and fashionable woman who has thrown herself at his feet is actually the procuress for the sadist ring. In the end, like Sam Spade, Mike faces a personal moral and emotional decision: must he destroy the woman he loves but who has turned out to be a vicious killer? That Mike has so little trouble with such decisions suggests some of the more disturbing psychological undercurrents of the hard-boiled story.

Thus, while the classical detective's investigation typically passes over a variety of possible suspects until it lights at last on the least-likely person, his hard-boiled counterpart becomes emotionally involved in a complex process of changing implications. Everything changes its meaning: the initial mission turns out to be a smoke screen for another, more devious plot; the supposed victim turns out to be a villain; the lover ends up as the murderess and the faithful friend as a rotten betrayer; the police and the district attorney and often even the client keeps trying to halt the investigation; and all the seemingly respectable and successful people turn out to be members of the gang. While all these discoveries of the villainy of the seemingly innocent, the duplicity of the seemingly faithful, and the corruption of the seemingly respectable do not occur in every hard-boiled story, what can be called the rhythm of exposure is almost invariable in one form or another. In many ways this rhythm is the antithesis of the classical story where the detective always shows that the corruption is isolated and specific rather than general and endemic to the social world of the story.

Like the classical story, the hard-boiled formula develops four main character roles: *(a)* the victim or victims; *(b)* the criminal; *(c)* the detective; and *(d)* those involved in the crime but incapable of resolving the problems it poses, a group involving police, suspects, and so on—in effect, the set of characters who represent society in the story. To this set of relationships, the hard-boiled formula very often adds one central role, that of the female betrayer.

I have already noted the characteristic multiplicity of victims in the hard-boiled story. While the classical story typically maintains an emotional detachment from the victim by making him relatively obscure and by stressing the complicated and exotic circumstances surrounding his death instead of its brutality and violence, the hard-boiled story more often encourages readers to feel strongly about the crimes by eliminating most of the complex machinery of clues. Often, the initial victim is a friend of the detective or some other person whose death seems not simply mysterious but regrettable. For example, in *The Maltese Falcon* the first victim is the detective's partner; in *The Big Sleep* he is a noble and handsome son-in-law much loved by the detective's client; in *I, the Jury* he is the detective's best friend. In many stories, the emotion roused by the sympathetic victim is intensified by a threat to the detective or one of his friends. Mike Hammer's beautiful secretary Velda commonly faces a horrible fate at the hands of the criminal before she is rescued by the opportune appearance of her boss. (The criminal here nearly succeeds in carrying out what the detective can never quite steel himself to perform: violation of the ideal and chaste sweetheart and companion.)

The sympathetic victim and the threat to the detective stimulate the reader's feelings of hostility toward the criminal and his wish for the detective to pass beyond solutions and attributions of guilt to the judgment and execution of the criminal. In contrast to the classical pattern of making the criminal a relatively obscure, marginal figure, a "least-likely" person, the hard-boiled criminal usually plays a central role, sometimes *the* central role after the detective. Since Dashiell Hammett first created the pattern in *The Maltese Falcon*, one hard-boiled detective after another has found himself romantically or sexually involved with the murderess. In other hard-boiled stories, the criminal turns out to be a close friend of the detective, as in *The Dain Curse*, where the criminal has been in a Watson-like association with the detective throughout the story. In this respect the pattern of the hard-boiled story is almost antithetical to the classical formula. In Agatha Christie, Dorothy Sayers, and their fellow writers, sympathetically interesting or romantic characters frequently appear to be guilty in the middle of the story but are invariably shown to be innocent when the detective finally unveils the solution. (The great prototype of all such stories is Wilkie Collins's *The Moonstone* where the two lovers are successively suspected and exonerated of the crime.) In Dorothy Sayers's *Strong Poison*, for example, Harriet Vane, with whom Lord Peter Wimsey falls in love (a gesture rather uncharacteristic of the classical detective), is thought to be guilty of a murder. The action of the story focuses on Lord Peter's successful demonstration of her innocence. The exact opposite is the case in *I, the Jury*, where the detective's romantic object is the one character who appears to be innocent throughout most of the story but who is finally revealed as the killer.

Thus the hard-boiled criminal plays a complex and ambiguous role while the classical villain remains an object of pursuit hiding behind a screen of mysterious clues until the detective finally reveals his identity. The hard-boiled villain is frequently disguised as a friend or lover, adding to the crimes an attempted betrayal of the detective's loyalty and love; when revealed, this treachery becomes the climax of that pattern of threat and temptation noted earlier. To support this pattern of threatened betrayal, the hard-boiled criminal is often characterized as particularly vicious, perverse, or depraved, and, in a striking number of instances as a woman of unusual sexual attractiveness. Facing such a criminal, the detective's role changes from classical ratiocination to self-protection against the various threats, temptations, and betrayals posed by the criminal.

A second important characteristic of the hard-boiled culprit is his involvement with the criminal underworld. Rarely is the classical criminal more than a single individual with a rational and specific motive to commit a particular crime. The hard-boiled criminal, on the other hand, usually has some connection with a larger criminal organization. Sometimes, as in Dashiell Hammett's *Red Harvest,* the detective's mission is to battle a criminal syndicate that has taken over a town. More characteristically, the criminal is a highly respectable member of society whose perverse acts have involved him with the underworld. In *The Big Sleep,* Carmen, the daughter of the wealthy General Sternwood, has killed Rusty Regan in a pathological sexual rage. Her sister has called on a local racketeer to help dispose of the body and to cover up the crime. By the time Marlowe enters the story, the racketeer has moved in to blackmail the Sternwood family. Marlowe finds that he must cope not only with Carmen's perversities but with the threats and attacks of a gang of racketeers somehow connected with the wealthy and respectable Sternwoods. This, as we have seen, is the typical hard-boiled pattern of action: the detective is called in to investigate a seemingly simple thing, like a disappearance; his investigation comes up against a web of conspiracy that reflects the presence of a hidden criminal organization; finally, the track leads back to the rich and respectable levels of society and exposes the corrupt relationship between the pillars of the community and the criminal underground.

What sort of a hero confronts, exposes, and destroys this web of conspiracy and perversion? Like many formula heroes, the hard-boiled detective is a synthesis of antithetical traits. Where the classical detective combined scientific ratiocination with poetic intuition, the hard-boiled detective's character paradoxically mixes cynicism and honor, brutality and sentimentality, failure and success. The hard-boiled detective is first and foremost a tough guy. He can dish it out and he can take it. Accustomed to a world of physical violence, corruption, and treachery, the detective's hard and bitter experience shows in his face:

> Samuel Spade's jaw was long and bony, his chin a jutting v under the more flexible v of his mouth. His nostrils curved back to make another, smaller, v. His yellow-grey eyes were horizontal. The v *motif* was picked up again by thickish brows rising outward from twin creases above a hooked nose, and his pale brown hair grew down—from high flat temples—in a point on his forehead. He looked rather pleasantly like a blond satan.

Even an exotic costume cannot hide the rugged and battered look of a later avatar of Sam Spade like Shell Scott:

> The effect of sheer beauty was perhaps marred only by the bent-down-at-the-ends inverted-V eyebrows over my gray eyes, since those brows were also obtrusively white. . . . And naturally, nothing could be done about my twice-broken and still bent nose, the bullet-clipped ear top, the fine scar over my right eye, and the general impression of recent catastrophe I've been told I sometimes present.

Behind this face, the detective's mind has become knowing about the persuasive corruption of society. Unlike the classical detective, for whom evil is an abnormal disruption of an essentially benevolent social order caused by a specific set of criminal motives, the hard-boiled detective has learned through long experience that evil is endemic to the social order:

> "When I went into police work in 1935, I believed that evil was a quality some people were born with, like a harelip. A cop's job was to find those people and put them away. But evil isn't so simple. Everybody has it in him, and whether it comes out in his actions depends on a number of things. . . ."
> "Do you judge people?"
> "Everybody I meet. The graduates of the police schools make a big thing of scientific detection, and that has its place. But most of my work is watching people, and judging them."
> "And you find evil in everybody?"
> "Just about. Either I'm getting sharper or people are getting worse. And that could be. War and inflation always raise a crop of stinkers, and a lot of them have settled in California."

Philip Marlowe explains the inescapable relation between crime and society:

> "Crime isn't a disease. It's a symptom. We're a big rough rich wild people and crime is the price we pay for it, and organized crime is the price we pay for organization. We'll have it with us a long time. Organized crime is just the dirty side of the sharp dollar."
> "What's the clean side?"
> "I never saw it."

John G. Cawelti / 209

In this respect, Mike Hammer's world is much the same. As one of his newspaperman friends puts it, "in every man's past there's some dirt."

Though his sense of an all-pervasive evil and violence is similar, a writer with right-wing political leanings like Mickey Spillane dramatizes the cause of the corruption as the worldwide Communist conspiracy, with its American dupes. More recently, with the improvement of Soviet-American relationships, Spillane seems to have shifted his animus to other foreign sources. His 1967 *The Body Lovers* projected corruption onto a group of middle eastern sadist-diplomats centered at the UN. But whatever the specific foreign source, the evil encountered by Mike Hammer most frequently manifests itself in that same group of internationalist-minded, upper-class, intellectual easterners that Senator Joseph McCarthy and his disciples used to attack. A more liberal writer like Raymond Chandler ascribes the evil to American materialism and greed, rather than to some foreign source of corruption. Dashiell Hammett, despite his radical political leanings, implies a more philosophical basis for the detective's sense of a world full of evil in a pessimistic vision of the universe that goes beyond the parochial political animosities and frustrations of Spillane. But whether his vision of evil is political or metaphysical, the hard-boiled detective has rejected the ordinary social and ethical pieties and faces a world that he has learned to understand as fundamentally corrupt, violent, and hostile. To put it more abstractly, he is a man who has accepted up to a point the naturalistic view of society and the universe and whose general attitude toward society and God resembles that alienation so often and fashionably described as the predicament of "modern man."

As R. V. Cassil suggests, modern democratic man "uses the fiction of violence for its purgative effect [but] what needs to be noted is that whatever his brow level, he doesn't really want to be purged very hard. Not really scoured . . ." So, the hard-boiled detective, below his surface of alienated skepticism and toughness, tends to be as soft as they come. No one has asserted the essential sentimentality as well as the power of the conception of the hard-boiled detective more eloquently than Raymond Chandler, one of his major creators:

Down these mean streets a man must go who is not himself mean, who is neither tarnished nor afraid. The detective in this kind of story must be such a man. He is the hero, he is everything. He must be a complete man and a common man and yet an unusual man. He must be, to use a rather weathered phrase, a man of honor, . . ."

Chandler's characterization suggests that though the hard-boiled detective's world bears some resemblance to the bitter, godless universe of writers like Crane, Dreiser, and Hemingway, his personal qualities also bear more than a little resemblance to the chivalrous knights of Sir Walter Scott. Not above seducing, beating, and even, on occasion, shooting members of the opposite sex, he saves this treatment for those who have gone bad. Toward good girls his attitude is as chaste as a Victorian father. The very thought of anyone touching his virginal secretary Velda reduces Mike Hammer to a gibbering homicidal maniac. Such knightly attitudes determine much of the hard-boiled detective's behavior: he is an instinctive protector of the weak, a defender of the innocent, an avenger of the wronged, the one loyal, honest, truly moral man in a corrupt and ambiguous world.

DAVID M. SCHNEIDER AND RAYMOND T. SMITH

Class Differences and Sex Roles in American Kinship and Family Structure

Itis sometimes said that the United States is a classless society, but this is always a statement of intent, designed to separate American society as a type from the class-ridden Old World societies from

David M. Schneider and Raymond T. Smith, excerpted from *Class Differences and Sex Roles in American Kinship and Family Structure* (Englewood Cliffs, N.J.: Prentice-Hall, 1973), pp. 19–29, 42–44.

which most Americans are descended. Some antipathy to class consciousness remains, but few Americans deny the existence of social classes in their society; most like to think of themselves as being "middle class," which is perhaps indicative of the wish to escape into classlessness by a peculiarly neutral route.[1] In this monograph we do not profess to explore the complexities of the American class system, either at the cultural or social system levels. We beg many difficult questions by simply regarding the middle class as a broad but not undifferentiated category which includes those who have certain attitudes, aspirations, and expectations toward status mobility, and who shape their actions accordingly. The lower and the upper classes are at rest, relatively speaking. They do not act as though they seriously believe that they are headed "up" or "down," although certain individuals may harbor fantasies of sudden wealth or poverty, and even act in terms of those fantasies. It is true that all lower-class people in this society, as in most others, yearn for an improvement in their physical condition. This is very different from the calculating attempts of the middle class to move up the ladder of success by the solid virtues of thrift, hard work, and calculated self-interest. As one of our informants said, "To be a square dude is hard work, man."

CLASS AS A CULTURAL CONSTRUCT

The tendency to think of society as divided into three classes is at least as old as Aristotle, but the modern urban and suburban middle class is a relatively new phenomenon. Karl Marx and Max Weber laid the groundwork for the analysis of the emergence and historical role of the modern middle class, and although it might be difficult to recognize the hero-villains of the rise of the bourgeoisie, the growth of capitalism, and the emergence of the Protestant Ethic in

1. R. W. Hodge and D. J. Treiman, "Class Identification in the United States," *American Journal of Sociology*, 73, No. 5 (1968). This national sample survey shows that, in unstructured questioning, fully three-quarters of the sample identified with some variety of "middle class." In a precoded question 2.2 percent identified with the upper class, 2.3 percent with the lower class, 16.6 percent with upper middle, 44.0 percent with middle, and 34.3 percent with the "working class." The last was rarely resorted to when respondents were asked to provide their own categories for self-identification.

the average suburban commuter, he is nonetheless the embodiment of a particular cultural tradition, developed in particular historical circumstances.

That cultural tradition can be brought into sharp focus by considering the question of individualism, which is often thought of as a particularly American characteristic. A gross comparison between the ideology of Indian caste society and that of the Euro-American Judeo-Christian tradition points up the emphasis upon the individual (or the "person") as the unit of action in the latter, as opposed to the corporate status group in traditional India. This contrast has been drawn sharply by Dumont,[2] but the main argument is not new. The transformation of European societies from collections of closed estates to relatively open class societies was accompanied by the growth of complex ideologies which ranged from religious doctrines, such as Calvinism, to classical economic theory and modern political nationalism, all of which emphasize the rational individual as the fundamental moral entity out of which society is composed through individual acts of association. Dumont argues brilliantly that even doctrines of the corporate state, such as those of German National Socialism, are ultimately predicated upon a view of society as a collection of individuals, rather than as a true organic entity.

American culture is not merely heir to this tradition, but is perhaps its most extreme expression. A constant stream of European writers, of whom de Tocqueville is merely the best known, have looked to the United States for an image of Europe's future—if not the future of the world—and all have been impressed by the sentiments of egalitarianism and individualism, and their expression in forms of social life apparently so different from those of Europe.

What is variously termed "the American Creed," the "dominant value system," or the "ideal system" clearly embodies this ideological stress upon the contradictory values of equality and individual status achievement or mobility. Lloyd Warner, for example, says:

2. See L. Dumont, *Homo Hierarchicus* (Chicago: The University of Chicago Press, 1970); "Caste, Racism and 'Stratification,' " in *Contributions to Indian Sociology,* No. V (October 1961), pp. 20–43.

In the bright glow and warm presence of the American Dream all men are born free and equal. Everyone in the American Dream has the right, and often the duty, to try to succeed and to do his best to reach the top. Its two fundamental themes and propositions, that all of us are equal and that each of us has the right to the chance of reaching the top, are mutually contradictory, for if all men are equal there can be no top level to aim for, no bottom one to get away from. . . .[3]

Seymour Martin Lipset has documented at length the proposition that the United States is dominated by the values of egalitarianism and achievement, and that these values have, through the interplay of their contradictions, been instrumental in shaping American institutions. He says:

The value we have attributed to achievement is a corollary to our belief in equality. For people to be equal they need a chance to become equal. Success, therefore, should be attainable by all, no matter what the accidents of birth, class, or race. Achievement is a function of equality of opportunity. That this emphasis on achievement must lead to new inequalities of status and to the use of corrupt means to secure and maintain high position is the ever recreated and renewed American dilemma.[4]

The most extreme conclusion which has been drawn from these observations is that America is essentially a classless society characterized by a continuous rank-order scale upon which individuals are ranged according to objective criteria stressing individual performance. Individuals may then be grouped into a number of categories, sometimes called "classes." This is a use of the term very different from that which stresses the group nature of social class, whereby classes are, or may become, self-conscious, acting units.

The most difficult problem encountered in this view of American society as essentially classless, open, mobile, and achievement-oriented is the position of the so-called "nonwhite" population of

3. W. Lloyd Warner, Marcia Meeker, and Kenneth Eells, *Social Class in America* (New York: Harper Torchbooks, 1960), p. 3.
4. Seymour Martin Lipset, *First New Nation* (New York: Anchor Books, Doubleday & Co., Inc., 1967), p. 2.

Blacks, American Indians, Mexican-Americans, Puerto Ricans, and Asiatics. Lipset asserts that "American egalitarianism is, of course, for white men only. The treatment of the Negro makes a mockery of this value now as it has in the past."[5] Dumont manages to make the best of the difficulty by arguing that racism is a disease of democracy; it is *only* where individualism is the encompassing value that individuals are systematically discriminated against on the basis of physical characteristics.[6] Such simple ignoring of the socioeconomic context in which racial discrimination has developed in the United States is only possible when one is exclusively concerned with the logical structure of values and ideologies, but it is precisely those politicoeconomic contexts which we must examine if we are to understand the way in which class and ethnicity affect the construction of kinship roles.

To see Blacks, or other ethnic groups, as being outside the "mainstream" is another, and related, way of resolving the problem. The poor can also be placed in this marginal, residual, or peripheral position in which they become a social aberration, marked by a "culture of poverty," "disorganization," "a tangle of pathology," or some other negative, abnormal bundle of characteristics. Such a view depends upon the analyst's taking his position in the mainstream, or at the center, and by-passes any objective analysis of the content of the cultural system of the supposedly peripheral groups. In fact, it is not an exaggeration to say that these theories are really an integral part of middle-class ideology.

Not all analysts view the United States as a classless society. Lloyd Warner's well-known study of Newburyport, Massachusetts, took quite the opposite view, and argued that it is not only possible to sort the population of American towns and cities into classes, but that these are recognized to exist by the inhabitants themselves, so that class is rooted in the consciousness of Americans as well as in the objective facts of their existence.[7] Richard Centers' study was one of the best-known attempts to demonstrate the reality of class consciousness in American society,[8] and Kornhauser's follow-up

5. Lipset, *First New Nation,* pp. 379–80.
6. Dumont, "Caste, Racism and Stratification," pp. 38–43.
7. W. Lloyd Warner and Paul Lunt, *The Social Life of a Modern Community* (New Haven: Yale University Press, 1945).

survey, while it did not entirely confirm Centers' assertions, certainly demonstrated the existence of significant variations in attitude and belief among income and occupational groups.[9]

The issues at stake here are considerable, for they involve the basic questions of the nature of the society, internal variations in American culture, and the manner in which cultural symbols are articulated with action in the most strategic areas of the social system.

It could be argued that the American class system is precisely that system of continuous rank gradation which is seen by the broad middle as the normal outcome of the operation of individual achievement. The system would thus be an expression of the logical principles which inhere in the cultural definition of equality and achievement. The significant unit in the system is the individual, unfettered by family or other group affiliation, afforded equality of opportunity to make himself into the "best" expression he can of the most valued characteristics of the society. What are those most valued characteristics? Here we come face-to-face with a most interesting fact. Just as an individual's position on the scale of rank is not determined by ascribed characteristics, that is, by his intrinsic qualities, so there are no fixed standards of behavior which serve to mark status. The only clearly defined cultural standards against which status can be measured are the gross standards of income, consumption, and conformity to rational procedures for attaining ends. There is a constant search for new ends which are defined as desirable because they are in conformity with a rationally elaborated image of the meaning of the world, which image is constantly liable to change because of the discovery of new "facts."

The cultural values of equality and achievement, important though they are as components of the American status system, are derived from the more general cultural stress upon individualism. In American culture, the person is defined as the basic unit of

8. Richard Centers, *The Psychology of Social Classes* (Princeton: Princeton University Press, 1949).

9. Arthur Kornhauser, "Public Opinion and Social Class," *American Journal of Sociology,* 55 (1950), pp. 333–345. See also John C. Leggett, *Class, Race and Labor* (New York: Oxford University Press, 1968).

action, rather than the group, the aggregate, or the collectivity. When some larger assemblage is involved, it is *personified,* and thus redefined as a person capable of acting or doing things. In law a corporation can be treated as a person and held responsible for its acts quite apart from the acts of any of its officers. But even when corporate groups or collectivities are personified in this way, the relationship between the unit and any member is such that the member's whole social identity is never defined by his membership in that unit alone. The emphasis in American culture is upon dealing with the person on his own merits as a unique individual, despite whatever associations he may have. The ideal is that each person's identity, his position, should derive from his own actions and not from the actions of any group with which he may be associated.

American society, like any other, is faced with organizational problems which require a subjugation of individual desire to collective ends. Although the cultural stress is upon the person as the significant unit of action, this does not mean that social structure is merely the outcome of a series of individual acts unconstrained by normative factors and situational exigencies. It is precisely the tension between cultural stress upon the individual as the unit of action, and the necessity for a very complex organizational structure which makes class such a difficult concept to deal with in this case.

"Social class" in American culture is not conceived as a closed corporate entity whose members have a special rank within the society by virtue of their membership in that group, a rank which can change only when the formal rank of the whole group changes within the system. Such a closed entity is represented by a caste in Hindu culture. In America, a person's membership in a particular class is thought to depend upon his actions and their conformity to class standards.

We said earlier that the standards of class are difficult to describe because they are not fixed. Apart from size of income and scale of consumption, there are no clear markers of class, a fact which is closely related to the absence of fixed groups.

However, there is a differential cultural stress upon the selection of ends and the mode of evaluating means for attainment of ends. The culturally middle-class value for judging both ends and the relationship between means and ends is the value of *rationality.*

In this context, application of the value of rationality involves the use of universalistic standards in making choices.[10] The culturally lower-class value lays stress upon *security*, a procedure which involves the use of particularistic standards and traditional criteria. Upper-class values do not stress security, but they do emphasize particularistic standards, stability, and continuity or "tradition" in a way that has more in common with lower- than with middle-class culture.

Culturally, then, "class" takes its structure from the primacy of evaluation placed upon different modes of relating ends to means.

These cultural characteristics do not exist apart from their bearers, no matter how analytically expedient it may be to represent them in this way, and the bearers of cultural values are concrete individuals involved in a multiplicity of social relationships. As such, they activate different, and perhaps contradictory, values at different times. For all Americans rationality is an active element in the norms of action, but we recognize a lower-class cultural complex by the fact that rationality is subordinated to the dominant value of security, and its traditionalistic, particularistic concomitants. We thus expect to find, in the lower class as in the upper class, rationality harnessed to the service of traditionalistic, particularistic ends and means. In the middle class the opposite obtains, with traditionalistic, particularistic elements being harnessed in the service of rationality, permitting its free application to limited areas while other areas are maintained in a given position. But in each case one set of values is held primary, with the other in a secondary position; the one encompasses the other, and it is this relationship that yields the striking differences in cultural orientation among classes.

The cultural system of class thus depends upon the secular nature of the social order, on the predominance of the person rather than the group as the unit which is conceptualized and evaluated in the system, on the value of equality predominating over (though not eliminating) the value of hierarchy, and upon the premise that the person is, or should be, autonomous. That is, he should be free to

10. Needless to say, this view of "class" derives from the dominating ideology of American society, that of bourgeois individualism. It does not speak to the historically important issue of class conflict, which requires a different mode of analysis.

pursue his ends in a rational manner, unencumbered by family, fate or station in life.

It is worth repeating that classes, even at the cultural level, are not isolates. They constitute part of a wider order or system of classes which are always thought of in relation to each other. In this wider context class values are ranked, or, more properly, are accorded significance in proportion to their appropriateness for the continuation of the society as a whole in its present form. From this perspective middle-class values can be said to encompass both lower- and upper-class values. This is particularly clear as regards the lower class, where considerable deference is paid to middle-class values, and where people often explain their inferior position in terms of circumstances which have prevented them from behaving in a middle-class fashion. That is, in contrast to middle-class norms of rationality, lower-class norms of security and tradition are judged inferior even by members of the lower class. Upper-class values of tradition and particularism are also considered to be "wrong," or at least an indulgence, when contrasted with middle-class values of rationality. The upper class sees itself as a privileged stratum which really ought to pay deference to middle-class values because they are the driving force of the whole social system. While the upper class may take advantage of particularistic ties in order to achieve individual ends, its members do not attempt to alter institutions to accord with upper-class values; on the contrary, they are the staunchest upholders of the norms of rationality and achievement—for others.

CLASS AS A DIMENSION OF THE SOCIAL SYSTEM

Shifting from the cultural to the social structural level, one can see that American society is made up of a series of interrelated organizational structures, highly differentiated and specialized. Virtually all studies of status ranking in the United States emphasize occupation as the primary determinant of social position. Since there is no single univalent rank order, we would not expect to find a perfect scale of occupational prestige. But we do discover that, in this highly urbanized, industrialized society, the occupational milieu is the important formative influence so far as class culture is concerned.

As we pointed out, concern with the structure of American values, "national identity," or "American character" leads many writers to view the United States as an essentially classless society. The fact that most Americans will choose, under certain circumstances, to identify with the middle class is taken as evidence of the fact that recognition of rank or gradation of status does not lead to the formation of disjunctive classes. There is acknowledgment of a lower class, but, as Gunnar Myrdal observed, this could more properly be designated an "under-class that is not really an integrated part of the nation but a useless and miserable substratum."[11] Theories of the "culture of poverty" take a similar view of this "external" and self-perpetuating group which has a particular culture shaped by the degeneration of its social condition.

Rather than class consciousness in contemporary American society, one finds a multiplicity of overlapping status groups based upon occupation, income, style of life, ethnicity, and race. Still, we have been able to distinguish markedly different clusters of attitudes which find expression in kinship and family behavior, and the contrasts in these attitudes are most sharp between well-off professional, managerial, and white-collar workers and poor, unemployed, partially-employed, or unskilled workers. We have thus far referred to the lower, middle, and upper classes, but this is a preliminary orienting use of these terms which merely points the way toward a more detailed examination of the empirical variations in status and in associated cultural patterns.

At the very center of our assumptions is a recognition of differences between social classes which are more than differences of position upon some objective scale of ranking. There are differences of life-style and of culture, though we do not share the common anthropological tendency to confuse "subculture" with the existence of differentiated groups. On the contrary, it seems to us that it is possible neither to construct univalent scales of rank or prestige which serve to divide American society into disjunctive

11. Gunnar Myrdal, *Challenge to Affluence* (New York: Pantheon Books, 1963).

strata,[12] nor to divide American society into a series of clearly bounded and relatively self-contained groups which are the bearers of distinctive subcultures. The cultural differences to which we refer are parts of a single system which varies according to internally consistent logical principles, and are, at the same time, an expression of the different and varying life experiences of individuals, particularly in relation to the occupational milieu. These cultural differences are not isolated from each other; they are available to all individuals. In general they are present in all individuals as potential means of constructing social reality, though the emphasis and mode of patterning varies in a systematic way between classes.

One must avoid the error of assuming that the cultural system is unchanging. It is precisely the varying experiences of social groups which lead to the institutionalization of new symbolic orientations. In order to anchor our discussion at a more concrete level, we now turn to a brief examination of the social background of the families we studied.

* * *

Whereas the middle class lays strong emphasis upon the self-sufficiency and solidarity of the nuclear family against all other kinship ties and groupings, the lower class (whatever its household group structure may be) does not emphasize nuclear family self-sufficiency. On the contrary, the emphasis is on help, cooperation, and solidarity with a wide range of kin. This is not to say that there is a stress on "the extended family," or that there are clearly structured kinship groups of wide span; the emphasis is upon keeping open the options—upon maximizing the number of relationships which involve diffuse solidarity. It is for this reason that one finds a tendency to *create* kinship ties out of relationships which are originally ties of friendship. For example, we found the category "play-kin" to be important for many of our lower-class Black informants. These are individuals who are "just like" a mother, sister, brother,

12. Edward A. Shils, "Deference," in John A. Jackson, ed., *Social Stratification* (Cambridge: Cambridge University Press, 1968), pp. 104–132. An excellent discussion of the multiple and overlapping bases of prestige evaluations and the impossibility of constructing simple univalent rankings.

aunt, uncle, or, less frequently, some other category of kinsman. Liebow has described the phenomenon of "going for brothers" among lower-class Black men in Washington.[13] Apart from this kind of semiformalized relationship, lower-class persons develop close and intimate bonds of friendship, particularly with persons of the same sex who are frequently described as being very close, "like a member of my family."

There is a sense in which the middle-class pattern of nuclear family solidarity is undifferentiated: everyone must work together for the good and betterment of all.[14] But the family has a life span. It starts with the marriage of a man and woman, proceeds through procreation and the raising of children who grow up and leave home to found their own families, leaving the parents together until one or both die. Of necessity the top priority concerning solidarity must be that of husband and wife, who become mother and father, but must also continue to be husband and wife "until death do them part." They are the solid core around which the whole system revolves; they are the beginning and the end. If one of them long survives the other, he or she becomes a problem, as myriad nursing homes and retirement colonies testify. Although mother and children constitute a most important focus of solidary relations, it is felt to be wrong to sacrifice the relationship of husband and wife to the demands of children. Husband, wife, son, and daughter all pull together, go out together, take vacations together, do things together at home—but it is known that the children will grow up and leave home, while husband and wife have a permanent life together.

The lower-class pattern places the primary stress elsewhere—upon the solidarity of mother and children—while it stresses the separateness of men and women.

Although our primary concern here is with the shape and internal ordering of the immediate family, these differences affect the patterning of wider kinship ties. Briefly, the outcome of the middle-class pattern is what might be called a "chain kindred"; that is, a structure something like a charm bracelet, in that a series of families

13. Elliot Liebow, *Tally's Corner* (Boston: Little, Brown & Co., 1967).
14. Of course the cultural value stress upon individualism is a constant factor at all class levels and penetrates to the very core of kinship units, so that the emphasis upon family solidarity is also seen as serving the end of facilitating individuality.

are linked together through the sibling bond or the parent-child bond, but with the nuclear family as the fundamental unit. The outcome of the lower-class pattern of solidary emphasis is a reticulated pattern of person-to-person ties. It may not be a perfectly uniform network, for there will be both bunching and unevenness of mesh, but there is an openness of pattern which contrasts with the middle-class emphasis on closed nuclear family units. One also sees a tendency for a collection of kin often referred to as "close family" to be important in both solidary and interactive terms, and to be different from the household group.

ALASDAIR MACINTYRE

After Virtue

The self, as distinct from its roles, has a history and a social history and that of the contemporary emotivist self is only intelligible as the end product of a long and complex set of developments.

Of the self as presented by emotivism we must immediately note: that it cannot be simply or unconditionally identified with *any* particular moral attitude or point of view (including that of those *characters* which socially embody emotivism) just because of the fact that its judgments are in the end criterionless. The specifically modern self, the self that I have called emotivist, finds no limits set to that on which it may pass judgment, for such limits could only derive from rational criteria for evaluation and, as we have seen, the emotivist self lacks any such criteria. Everything may be criticised from whatever standpoint the self has adopted, including the self's choice of standpoint to adopt. It is in this capacity of the self to evade any necessary identification with any particular contingent state of affairs that some modern philosophers, both analytical and existentialist, have seen the essence of moral agency. To be a moral agent

Alasdair MacIntyre, excerpted from *After Virtue: An Essay in Moral Theory* (South Bend, Ind.: University of Notre Dame Press, 1981), pp. 30–33, 175–182, 188–89.

is, on this view, precisely to be able to stand back from any and every situation in which one is involved, from any and every characteristic that one may possess, and to pass judgment on it from a purely universal and abstract point of view that is totally detached from all social particularity. Anyone and everyone can thus be a moral agent, since it is in the self and not in social roles or practices that moral agency has to be located. The contrast between this democratization of moral agency and the elitist monopolies of managerial and therapeutic expertise could not be sharper. Any minimally rational agent is to be accounted a moral agent; but managers and therapists enjoy their status in virtue of their membership within hierarchies of imputed skill and knowledge. In the domain of fact there are procedures for eliminating disagreement; in that of morals the ultimacy of disagreement is dignified by the title 'pluralism.'

This democratized self which has no necessary social content and no necessary social identity can then be anything, can assume any role or take any point of view, because it *is* in and for itself nothing. This relationship of the modern self to its acts and its roles has been conceptualized by its acutest and most perceptive theorists in what at first sight appear to be two quite different and incompatible ways. Sartre—I speak now only of the Sartre of the thirties and forties—has depicted the self as entirely distinct from any particular social role which it may happen to assume; Erving Goffman by contrast has liquidated the self into its role-playing, arguing that the self is no more than 'a peg' on which the clothes of the role are hung. For Sartre the central error is to identify the self with its roles, a mistake which carries the burden of moral bad faith as well as of intellectual confusion; for Goffman the central error is to suppose that there *is* a substantial self over and beyond the complex presentations of role-playing, a mistake committed by those who wish to keep part of the human world 'safe from sociology.' Yet the two apparently contrasting views have much more in common than a first statement would lead one to suspect. In Goffman's anecdotal descriptions of the social world there is still discernible that ghostly 'I,' the psychological peg to whom Goffman denies substantial selfhood, flitting evanescently from one solidly role-structured situation to another; and for Sartre the self's self-discovery is characterized as the discovery that the self is 'nothing,' is not a substance but a set of perpetually open possibilities. Thus at a deep level a certain agreement underlies Sartre's and Goffman's surface disagreements; and they agree in nothing more than in this, that both see the self as entirely set over against the social world. For Goffman, for whom the social world is everything, the self is therefore nothing at all, it occupies no social space. For Sartre, whatever social space it occupies it does so only accidentally, and therefore he too sees the self as in no way an actuality.

What moral modes are open to the self thus conceived? To answer this question, we must first recall the second key characteristic of the emotivist self, its lack of any ultimate criteria. When I characterize it thus I am referring back to what we have already noticed, that whatever criteria or principles or evaluative allegiances the emotivist self may profess, they are to be construed as expressions of attitudes, preferences and choices which are themselves not governed by criterion, principle or value, since they underlie and are prior to all allegiance to criterion, principle or value. But from this it follows that the emotivist self can have no rational history in its transitions from one state of moral commitment to another. Inner conflicts are for it necessarily *au fond* the confrontation of one contingent arbitrariness by another. It is a self with no given continuities, save those of the body which is its bearer and of the memory which to the best of its ability gathers in its past. And we know from the outcome of the discussions of personal identity by Locke, Berkeley, Butler and Hume that neither of these separately or together are adequate to specify that identity and continuity of which actual selves are so certain.

The self thus conceived, utterly distinct on the one hand from its social embodiments and lacking on the other any rational history of its own, may seem to have a certain abstract and ghostly character. It is therefore worth remarking that a behaviorist account is as much or as little plausible of the self conceived in this manner as of the self conceived in any other. The appearance of an abstract and ghostly quality arises not from any lingering Cartesian dualism, but from the degree of contrast, indeed the degree of loss, that comes into view if we compare the emotivist self with its historical predecessors. For one way of re-envisaging the emotivist self is as having suffered a deprivation, a stripping away of qualities that were once believed to belong to the self. The self is now thought of as lacking any necessary social identity, because the kind of social identity that it once enjoyed is no longer available; the self is now thought of as criterionless, because the kind of *telos* in terms of which it once judged and acted is no longer thought to be credible. What kind of identity and what kind of *telos* were they?

In many pre-modern, traditional societies it is through his or her membership of a variety of social groups that the individual identifies himself or herself and is identified by others. I am brother, cousin and grandson, member of this household, that village, this tribe. These are not characteristics that belong to human beings accidentally, to be stripped away in order to discover 'the real me.' They are part of my substance, defining partially at least and sometimes wholly my obligations and my duties. Individuals inherit a particular space within an interlocking set of social relationships; lacking that space, they are nobody, or at best a stranger or an outcast. To know oneself as such a social person is however not to occupy a static and fixed position. It is to find oneself placed at a certain point on a journey with set goals; to move through life is to make progress—or to fail to make progress—toward a given end. Thus a completed and fulfilled life is an achievement and death is the point at which someone can be judged happy or unhappy. Hence the ancient Greek proverb: "Call no man happy until he is dead."

This conception of a whole human life as the primary subject of objective and impersonal evaluation, of a type of evaluation which provides the content for judgment upon the particular actions or projects of a given individual, is something that ceases to be generally available at some point in the progress—if we can call it such—towards and into modernity. It passes to some degree unnoticed, for it is celebrated historically for the most part not as loss, but as self-congratulatory gain, as the emergence of the individual freed on the one hand from the social bonds of those constraining hierarchies which the modern world rejected at its birth and on the other hand from what modernity has taken to be the superstitions of teleology. To say this is of course to move a little too quickly beyond my present argument; but it is to note that the peculiarly modern self, the emotivist self, in acquiring sovereignty in its own realm lost its traditional boundaries provided by a social identity and a view of human life as ordered to a given end. Nonetheless, as I have already suggested, the emotivist self has its own kind of social definition. It is at home in—it is an integral part of—one distinctive type of social order, that which we in the so-called advanced countries presently inhabit. Its definition is the counterpart to the definition of those *characters* which inhabit and present the dominant social roles. The bifurcation of the contemporary social world into a realm of the organizational in which ends are taken to be given and are not available for rational scrutiny and a realm of the personal in which judgment and debate about values are central factors, but in which no rational social resolution of issues is available, finds its internalization, its inner representation, in the relation of the individual self to the roles and *characters* of social life.

This bifurcation is itself an important clue to the central characteristics of modern societies and one which may enable us to avoid being deceived by their own internal political debates. Those debates are often staged in terms of a supposed opposition between individualism and collectivism, each appearing in a variety of doctrinal forms. On the one side there appear the self-defined protagonists of individual liberty, on the other the self-defined protagonists of planning and regulation, of the goods which are available through bureaucratic organization. But in fact what is crucial is that on which the contending parties agree, namely that there are only two alternative modes of social life open to us, one in which the free and arbitrary choices of individuals are sovereign and one in which the bureaucracy is sovereign, precisely so that it may limit the free and arbitrary choices of individuals. Given this deep cultural agreement, it is unsurprising that the politics of modern societies oscillate between a freedom which is nothing but a lack of regulation of individual behavior and forms of collectivist control designed only to limit the anarchy of self-interest. The consequences of a victory by one side or the other are often of the highest immediate importance; but, as Solzhenitzyn has understood so well, both ways of life are in the long run intolerable. Thus the society in which we live is one in which bureaucracy and individualism are partners as well as antagonists. And it is in the cultural climate of this bureaucratic individualism that the emotivist self is naturally at home.

* * *

By a "practice" I am going to mean any coherent and complex form of socially established cooperative human activity through which goods internal to that form of activity are realized in the course of trying to achieve those standards of excellence which are appropriate to, and partially definitive of, that form of activity, with the result that human powers to achieve excellence, and human conceptions of the ends and goods involved, are systematically extended. Tic-tac-toe is not an example of a practice in this sense, nor is throwing a football with skill; but the game of football is, and so is chess. Bricklaying is not a practice; architecture is. Planting turnips is not a practice; farming is. So are the enquiries of physics, chemistry and biology, and so is the work of the historian, and so are painting and music. In the ancient and medieval worlds the creation and sustaining of human communities—of households, cities, nations—is generally taken to be a practice in the sense in which I have defined it. Thus the range of practices is wide: arts, sciences, games, politics in the Aristotelian sense, the making and sustaining of family life, all fall under the concept. But the question of the precise range of practices is not at this stage of the first importance. Instead let me explain some of the key terms involved in my definition, beginning with the notion of goods internal to a practice.

Consider the example of a highly intelligent seven-year-old child whom I wish to teach to play chess, although the child has no particular desire to learn the game. The child does however have a very strong desire for candy and little chance of obtaining it. I therefore tell the child that if the child will play chess with me once a week I will give the child 50¢ worth of candy; moreover, I tell the child that I will always play in such a way that it will be difficult, but not impossible, for the child to win and that, if the child wins, the child will receive an extra 50¢ worth of candy. Thus motivated the child plays and plays to win. Notice however that, so long as it is the candy alone which provides the child with a good reason for playing chess, the child has no reason not to cheat and every reason to cheat, provided he or she can do so successfully. But, so we may hope, there will come a time when the child will find in those goods specific to chess, in the achievement of a certain highly particular kind of analytical skill, strategic imagination and competitive intensity, a new set of reasons, reasons now not just for winning on a particular occasion, but for trying to excel in whatever way the game of chess demands. Now if the child cheats, he or she will be defeating not me, but himself or herself.

There are thus two kinds of good possibly to be gained by playing chess. On the one hand there are those goods externally and contingently attached to chess-playing and to other practices by the accidents of social circumstance—in the case of the imaginary child, candy, in the case of real adults such goods as prestige, status and money. There are always alternative ways for achieving such goods, and their achievement is never to be had *only* by engaging in some particular kind of practice. On the other hand there are the goods internal to the practice of chess which cannot be had in any way but by playing chess or some other game of that specific kind. We call them internal for two reasons: first, as I have already suggested, because we can only specify them in terms of chess or some other game of that specific kind and by means of examples from such games (otherwise the meagerness of our vocabulary for speaking of such goods forces us into such devices as my own resort to writing of "a certain highly particular kind of"); and secondly because they can only be identified and recognized by the experience of participating in the practice in question. Those who lack the relevant experience are incompetent thereby as judges of internal goods.

This is clearly the case with all the major examples of practices: consider for example—even if briefly and inadequately—the practice of portrait painting as it developed in Western Europe from the late middle ages to the eighteenth century. The successful portrait painter is able to achieve many goods which are, in the sense just defined, external to the practice of portrait painting—fame, wealth, social status, even a measure of power and influence at courts upon occasion. But those external goods are not to be confused with the goods which are internal to the practice. The internal goods are those which result from an extended attempt to show how Wittgenstein's dictum "The human body is the best picture of the human soul" might be made to become true by teaching us "to regard . . . the picture on our wall as the object itself (the men, landscape and so on) depicted there" in a quite new way. What is misleading about Wittgenstein's dictum as it stands is its neglect of the truth in George Orwell's thesis "At 50 everyone has the face he deserves". What painters from Giotto to Rembrandt learned to show was how the face at any age may be revealed as the face that the subject of a portrait deserves.

Originally in medieval paintings of the saints the face was an icon; the question of a resemblance between the depicted face of Christ or St. Peter and the face that Jesus or Peter actually possessed at some particular age did not even arise. The antithesis to this iconography was the relative naturalism of certain fifteenth-century Flemish and German painting. The heavy eyelids, the coifed hair, the lines around the mouth undeniably represent some particular woman, either actual or envisaged. Resemblance has usurped the iconic relationship. But with Rembrandt there is, so to speak, synthesis: the naturalistic portrait is now rendered as an icon, but an icon of a new and hitherto inconceivable kind. Similarly in a very different kind of sequence mythological faces in a certain kind of seventeenth-century French painting become aristocratic faces in the eighteenth century. Within each of these sequences at least two different kinds of good internal to the painting of human faces and bodies are achieved.

There is first of all the excellence of the products, both the excellence in performance by the painters and that of each portrait itself. This excellence—the very verb "excel" suggests it—has to be understood historically. The sequences of development find their point and purpose in a progress towards and beyond a variety of types and modes of excellence. There are of course sequences of decline as well as of progress, and progress is rarely to be understood as straightforwardly linear. But it is in participation in the attempts to sustain progress and to respond creatively to moments that the second kind of good internal to the practices of portrait painting is to be found. For what the artist discovers within the pursuit of excellence in portrait painting—and what is true of portrait painting is true of the practice of the fine arts in general—is the good of a certain kind of life. That life may not constitute the whole of life for someone who is a painter by a very long way or it may at least for a period, Gauguin-like, absorb him or her at the expense of almost everything else. But it is the painter's living out of a greater or lesser part of his or her life *as a painter* that is the second kind of good internal to painting. And judgment upon these goods requires at the very least the kind of competence that is only to be acquired either as a painter or as someone willing to learn systematically what the portrait painter has to teach.

A practice involves standards of excellence and obedience to rules as well as the achievement of goods. To enter into a practice is to accept the authority of those standards and the inadequacy of my own performance as judged by them. It is to subject my own attitudes, choices, preferences and tastes to the standards which currently and partially define the practice. Practices of course, as I have just noticed, have a history: games, sciences and arts all have histories. Thus the standards are not themselves immune from criticism, but none the less we cannot be initiated into a practice without accepting the authority of the best standards realised so far. If, on starting to listen to music, I do not accept my own incapacity to judge correctly, I will never learn to hear, let alone to appreciate, Bartok's last quartets. If, on starting to play baseball, I do not accept that others know better than I when to throw a fast ball and when not, I will never learn to appreciate good pitching let alone to pitch. In the realm of practices the authority of both goods and standards operates in such a way as to rule out all subjectivist and emotivist analyses of judgment. *De gustibus* est *disputandum*.

We are now in a position to notice an important difference between what I have called internal and what I have called external goods. It is characteristic of what I have called external goods that when achieved they are always some individual's property and possession. Moreover, characteristically they are such that the more someone has of them, the less there is for other people. This is sometimes necessarily the case, as with power and fame, and sometimes the case by reason of contingent circumstance as with money. External goods are therefore characteristically objects of competition in which there must be losers as well as winners. Internal goods are indeed the outcome of competition to excel, but it is characteristic of them that their achievement is a good for the whole community who participate in the practice. So when Turner transformed the seascape in painting or W. G. Grace advanced the art of batting in cricket in a quite new way, their achievement enriched the whole relevant community.

But what does all or any of this have to do with the concept of the virtues? It turns out that we are now in a position to formulate a first, even if partial and tentative definition of a virtue: *A virtue is an acquired human quality the possession and exercise of which tends to enable us to achieve those goods which are internal to practices and the lack of which effectively prevents us from achieving any such goods.* Later this definition will need amplification and amendment. But as a first approximation to an adequate definition it already illuminates the place of the virtues in human life. For it is not difficult to show for a whole range of key virtues that without them the goods internal to practices are barred to us, but not just barred to us generally, barred in a very particular way.

It belongs to the concept of a practice as I have outlined it—and as we are all familiar with it already in our actual lives, whether we are painters or physicists or quarterbacks or indeed just lovers of good painting or first-rate experiments or a well-thrown pass—that its goods can only be achieved by subordinating ourselves to the best standard so far achieved, and that entails subordinating ourselves within the practice in our relationship to other practitioners. We have to learn to recognize what is due to whom; we have to be prepared to take whatever self-endangering risks are demanded along the way; and we have to listen carefully to what we are told about our own inadequacies and to reply with the same carefulness for the facts. In other words we have to accept as necessary components of any practice with internal goods and standards of excellence the virtues of justice, courage and honesty. For not to accept these, to be willing to cheat as our imagined child was willing to cheat in his or her early days at chess, so far bars us from achieving the standards of excellence or the goods internal to the practice that it renders the practice pointless except as a device for achieving external goods.

We can put the same point in another way. Every practice requires a certain kind of relationship between those who participate in it. Now the virtues are those goods by reference to which, whether we like it or not, we define our relationships to those other people with whom we share the kind of purposes and standards which inform practices. Consider an example of how reference to the virtues has to be made in certain kinds of human relationship.

A, B, C, and D are friends in that sense of friendship which Aristotle takes to be primary: they share in the pursuit of certain goods. In my terms they share in a practice. D dies in obscure circumstances, A discovers how D died and tells the truth about it to B while lying to C. C discovers the lie. What A cannot then intelligibly claim is that he stands in the same relationship of friendship to both B and C. By telling the truth to one and lying to the other he has partially defined a difference in the relationship. Of course it is open to A to explain this difference in a number of ways; perhaps he was trying to spare C pain or perhaps he is simply cheating C. But some difference in the relationship now exists as a result of the lie. For their allegiance to each other in the pursuit of common goods has been put in question.

Just as, so long as we share the standards and purposes characteristic of practices, we define our relationships to each other, whether we acknowledge it or not, by reference to standards of truthfulness and trust, so we define them too by reference to standards of justice and of courage. If A, a professor, gives B and C the grades that their papers deserve, but grades D because he is attracted by D's blue eyes or is repelled by D's dandruff, he has defined his relationship to D differently from his relationship to the other members of the class, whether he wishes it or not. Justice requires that we treat others in respect of merit or desert according to uniform and impersonal standards; to depart from the standards of justice in some particular instance defines our relationship with the relevant person as in some way special or distinctive.

The case with courage is a little different. We hold courage to be a virtue because the care and concern for individuals, communities and causes which is so crucial to so much in practices requires the existence of such a virtue. If someone says that he cares for some individual, community or cause, but is unwilling to risk harm or danger on his, her or its own behalf, he puts in question the genuineness of his care and concern. Courage, the capacity to risk harm or danger to oneself, has its role in human life because of this connection with care and concern. This is not to say that a man cannot genuinely care and also be a coward. It is in part to say that a man who genuinely cares and has not the capacity for risking harm or danger has to define himself, both to himself and to others, as a coward.

I take it then that from the standpoint of those types of relationship without which practices cannot be sustained truthfulness, justice and courage—and perhaps some others—are genuine excellences, are virtues in the light of which we have to characterise ourselves and others, whatever our private moral standpoint or our society's particular codes may be. For this recognition that we cannot escape the definition of our relationships in terms of such goods is perfectly compatible with the acknowledgment that different societies have and have had different codes of truthfulness, justice and courage. Lutheran pietists brought up their children to believe that one ought to tell the truth to everybody at all times, whatever the circumstances or consequences, and Kant was one of their children. Traditional Bantu parents brought up their children not to tell the truth to strangers, since they believed that this could render the family vulnerable to witchcraft. In our culture many of us have been brought up not to tell the truth to elderly great-aunts who invite us to admire their new hats. But each of these codes embodies an acknowledgment of the virtue of truthfulness. So it is also with varying codes of justice and of courage.

Practices then might flourish in societies with very different codes; what they could not do is flourish in societies in which the virtues were not valued, although institutions and technical skills serving unified purposes might well continue to flourish. (I shall have more to say about the contrast between institutions and technical skills mobilized for a unified end, on the one hand, and practices on the other, in a moment.) For the kind of cooperation, the kind of recognition of authority and of achievement, the kind of respect for standards and the kind of risk-taking which are characteristically involved in practices demand, for example, fairness in judging oneself and others—the kind of fairness absent in my example of the professor, a ruthless truthfulness without which fairness cannot find application—the kind of truthfulness absent in my example of A, B, C and D—and willingness to trust the judgments of those whose achievement in the practice give them an authority to judge, which presupposes fairness and truthfulness in those judgments, and from time to time the taking of self-endangering, reputation-endangering and even achievement-endangering risks. It is no part of my thesis that great violinists cannot be vicious or great chess players mean-spirited. Where the virtues are required, the vices also may flourish. It is just that the vicious and mean-spirited necessarily rely on the virtues of others for the practices in which they engage to flourish and also deny themselves the experience of achieving those internal goods which may reward even not very good chess players and violinists.

To situate the virtues any further within practices it is necessary now to clarify a little further the nature of a practice by drawing two important contrasts. The discussion so far I hope makes it clear that a practice, in the sense intended, is never just a set of technical skills, even when directed towards some unified purpose and even if the exercise of those skills can on occasion be valued or enjoyed for its own sake. What is distinctive of a practice is in part the way in which conceptions of the relevant goods and ends which the technical skills serve—and every practice does require the exercise of technical skills—are transformed and enriched by these extensions of human powers and by that regard for its own internal goods which are partially definitive of each particular practice or type of practice. Practices never have a goal or goals fixed for all time—painting has no such goal nor has physics—but the goals themselves are transmuted by the history of the activity. It therefore turns out not to be accidental that every practice has its own history and a history which is more and other than that of the improvement of the relevant technical skills. This historical dimension is crucial in relation to the virtues.

To enter into a practice is to enter into a relationship not only with its contemporary practitioners, but also with those who have preceded us in the practice, particularly those whose achievements extended the reach of the practice to its present point. It is thus the achievement, and a fortiori the authority, of a tradition which I then confront and from which I have to learn. And for this learning and the relationship to the past which it embodies the virtues of justice, courage and truthfulness are prerequisite in precisely the same way and for precisely the same reasons as they are in sustaining present relationships within practices.

It is not only of course with sets of technical skills that practices ought to be contrasted. Practices must not be confused with institutions. Chess, physics and medicine are practices; chess clubs, laboratories, universities and hospitals are institutions. Institutions are characteristically and necessarily concerned with what I have called external goods. They are involved in acquiring money and other material goods; they are structured in terms of power and status, and they distribute money, power and status as rewards. Nor could they do otherwise if they are to sustain not only themselves, but also the practices of which they are the bearers. For no practices can survive for any length of time unsustained by institutions. Indeed so intimate is the relationship of practices to institutions—and consequently of the goods external to the goods internal to the practices in question—that institutions and practices characteristically form a single causal order in which the ideals and the creativity of the practice are always vulnerable to the acquisitiveness of the institution, in which the cooperative care for common goods of the practice is always vulnerable to the competitiveness of the institution. In this context the essential function of the virtues is clear. Without them, without justice, courage and truthfulness, practices could not resist the corrupting power of institutions.

Yet if institutions do have corrupting power, the making and sustaining of forms of human community—and therefore of institutions—itself has all the characteristics of a practice, and moreover of a practice which stands in a peculiarly close relationship to the exercise of the virtues in two important ways. The exercise of the virtues is itself apt to require a highly determinate attitude to social and political issues; and it is always within some particular community with its own specific institutional forms that we learn or fail to learn to exercise the virtues. There is of course a crucial difference between the way in which the relationship between moral character and political community is envisaged from the standpoint of liberal individualist modernity and the way in which that relationship was envisaged from the standpoint of the type of ancient and medieval tradition of the virtues which I have sketched. For liberal individualism a community is simply an arena in which individuals each pursue their own self-chosen conception of the good life, and political institutions exist to provide that degree of order which makes such self-determined activity possible. Government and law are, or ought to be, neutral between rival conceptions of the good life for man, and hence, although it is the task of government to promote law-abidingness, it is on the liberal view no part of the legitimate function of government to inculcate any one moral outlook.

By contrast, on the particular ancient and medieval view which I have sketched, political community not only requires the exercise of the virtues for its own sustenance, but it is one of the tasks of government to make its citizens virtuous, just as it is one of the tasks of parental authority to make children grow up so as to be virtuous adults. The classical statement of this analogy is by Socrates in the *Crito*. It does not of course follow from an acceptance of the Socratic view of political community and political authority that we ought to assign to the modern state the moral function which Socrates assigned to the city and its laws. Indeed, the power of the liberal individualist standpoint partly derives from the evident fact that the modern state is indeed totally unfitted to act as moral educator of any community. But the history of how the modern state emerged is of course itself a moral history. If my account of the complex relationship of virtues to practices and to institutions is correct, it follows that we shall be unable to write a true history of practices and institutions unless that history is also one of the virtues and vices. For the ability of a practice to retain its integrity will depend on the way in which the virtues can be and are exercised in sustaining the institutional forms which are the social bearers of the practice. The integrity of a practice causally requires the exercise of the virtues by at least some of the individuals who embody it in their activities; and conversely the corruption of institutions is always in part at least an effect of the vices.

* * *

Without an overriding conception of the *telos* of a whole human life, conceived as a unity, our conception of certain individual virtues has to remain partial and incomplete. Consider two examples. Justice, from an Aristotelian view, is defined in terms of giving each person his or her due or desert. To deserve well is to have contributed in some substantial way to the achievement of those goods, the sharing of which and the common pursuit of which provide foundations for human community. But the goods internal to practices, including the goods internal to the practice of making and sustaining forms of community, need to be ordered and evaluated in some way if we are to assess relative desert. Thus only substantive application of an Aristotelian concept of justice requires an understanding of goods and of the good that goes beyond the multiplicity of goods which inform practices. As with justice, so also with patience. Patience is the virtue of waiting attentively without complaint, but not of waiting thus for anything at all. To treat patience as a virtue presupposes some adequate answer to the question: waiting for what? Within the context of practices a partial, although for many purposes adequate, answer can be given: the patience of a craftsman with refractory material, of a teacher with a slow pupil, of a politician in negotiations, are all species of patience. But what if the material is just too refractory, the pupil too slow, the negotiations too frustrating? Ought we always at a certain point just to give up in the interests of the practice itself? The medieval exponents of the virtue of patience claimed that there are certain types of situation in which the virtue of patience requires that I do not ever give up on some person or task, situations in which, as they would have put it, I am required to embody in my attitude to that person or task something of the patient attitude of God towards his creation. But this could only be so if patience served some overriding good, some *telos* which warranted putting other goods in a subordinate place. Thus it turns out that the content of the virtue of patience depends upon how we order various goods in a hierarchy and *a fortiori* on whether we are able rationally so to order these particular goods.

DAVID BLACK

Reflections in a Glass Eye

While it is reckless to abstract a moral about the American mind—or heart—from a single week's Top 10 videocassette list, it may at least be fair to take the list as a hint of what concerns us. By the middle of May, *Jane Fonda's Workout* had been on *Billboard*'s Top 10 videocassette sales list for 209 weeks. *Jane Fonda's New Workout,* which was number 1 that week, had been on *Billboard*'s list for twenty-eight weeks. If the videotapes Americans buy give a glimpse of what Americans care about and who they are, exercises—or, at least, women in leotards—loom large on the national agenda.

Ever since Adah Isaacs Menken shocked society by wearing a flesh-colored bodysuit in a production of *Mazeppa* during the Flash Age of post–Civil War New York, women in leotards—or the equivalent (step-ins for flappers, no bras for 1960s hippies)—have typified freedom from convention.

David Black, "Reflections in a Glass Eye," from *Harper's,* August 1986, pp. 73–75.

And freedom from convention has frequently been justified as hygienic. Early in the nineteenth century, shortly after women started wearing underpants, Catherine Beecher advocated flannel undergarments for hygiene—a fad revived a generation later by Dr. Gustav Jaeger.

Health and rebellion against convention frequently have been linked to reform movements—like temperance. William Lloyd Garrison, Sylvester Graham (the inventor of the the graham cracker and one of America's first promoters of health food), Theodore Weld, and William Alcott and his cousin Bronson Alcott were among the nineteenth-century advocates of social change who supported women's rights, abolitionism, calisthenics, and diet reform—and saw them all as parts of a unified movement.

Jane Fonda's tapes fall into this long tradition. Her workouts are political—small revolutions in perception. Her tapes—not just the two on the Top 10 list—and her books, the products of the whole Fonda workout industry, are less about aerobics than about a redefinition of beauty. By presenting models of various shapes and conditions, young and old, lithe and pregnant, they undercut the myth of the ideal female body—an ideal that changes with every generation, from the thin, small-busted women popular in Elizabethan England and the 1920s to the voluptuousness of the late nineteenth century and the 1950s *Playboy* centerfold. The participants may all be attractive, but they are not all attractive in the same way: they are the workout tape equivalent of the platoon in a war movie, with one WASP, one black, one Jew, one Italian, one Indian . . .

This democratization of the body makes Fonda's workout tapes so popular. Women are led through the routines not by goddesses—beauties like Victoria Principal or body-builders like Rachel McLish—but by mortals, who are, at least by Hollywood standards, ordinary. Not Titian's reclining Venuses but Degas's nudes contorting as they bathe.

Divorcing health from a single ideal of beauty is an attractive idea for normally shaped women who have been raised to believe that a particular type of good looks means health, that to be different is to be infirm. *Jane Fonda's Workout* and *Jane Fonda's New Workout* are not at all silly; they are subversive in the best sense. Although, with their emphasis on being fit, they seem to reflect the new American Puritanism, they actually undermine it. Anyone—everyone, they affirm—is beautiful.

If the appeal of this notion is obvious, the dangers are hidden. Fonda is offering a generation of American women a model comparable to the one Teddy Roosevelt gave American males nearly a century ago—what used to be called "muscular Christianity," a linking of the healthy body with the healthy soul. According to the myth, Roosevelt transformed himself from a sickly kid to a vigorous adult through acts of will; he conquered his body the way he would break a wild horse.

His influence—through Hemingway, who did his best to look like T.R.—has conned four generations of Americans into believing that control of the body somehow translates into control of the spirit, a myth that would damn roly-poly G. K. Chesterton and hypochondriacal Marcel Proust.

Two tapes on *Billboard*'s Top 10 list feed this myth: *Commando* and *Rambo: First Blood Part II*, a title that (I assume) is supposed to be epic but that, with its three parts, seems pompous—the movie equivalent of an office belonging to an insecure professional who has covered his walls with diplomas. In *Rambo* (number 10 on *Billboard*'s list), Sylvester Stallone plays a half-Indian/half-German warrior who, true to Hollywood racial stereotypes (the closest America has to Jonsonian humors), is half noble savage/half *Übermensch.*

Early in the movie, Rambo, who is being parachuted into enemy territory, gets caught under the wing of the airplane. To free himself, he must cut away all the high-tech gear he has been given by the United States government; and he lands, equipped with only a bow and quiver of arrows. He survives not so much by his wits as by his instincts. In physical violence, Rambo finds transcendence, a romance of the gut.

Unlike Fonda, Stallone is manufacturing an ideal: Rambo is what a *real* (that is, an *unreal*) man looks and acts like. But, like Fonda, he has plugged into an American tradition—in his case, the tall-tale hero. Rambo is larger than life, America's Golem, out to right the wrongs done to GIs in the Vietnam War. He is to the servicemen of the late 1960s what Paul Bunyan was to loggers and Joe Magarac was to steelworkers, what Pecos Bill was to cowboys and Stormalong Jones was to sailors. Although liberals feel uncomfortable with what they believe to be the reactionary political message of *Rambo,* the movie is not really about politics. Rambo is an American archetype: Natty Bumppo in Southeast Asia.

In *Commando* (number 8 on *Billboard*'s list), Arnold Schwarzenegger does an intelligent variation on the American tall-tale hero. The character he plays with self-deprecating humor and considerable wit is not a fantasy like Paul Bunyan; he is closer to heroes of American history who actually existed, men like Daniel Boone, Kit Carson, and Davy Crockett. And the movie has all the verve of one of Crockett's "brags," a popular art that today is rare in literature (recently, only Thomas Pynchon and T. Coraghessan Boyle have carried it off successfully) but is flourishing on the streets in the form of "rankouts," the poetry of invective.

Rambo is a killing machine: his previous incarnation in the nineteenth century decimated Indian tribes. He is the forerunner of civilization, the human ax used to clear the land. Schwarzenegger's Commando is a homesteader who—like every homesteader in American movie history—wants to be left alone; he is self-sufficient and ready to create his private utopia. He begins the movie—after a brief show of strength—with ice cream on his nose, something inconceivable for Rambo (whose closest approach to losing his dignity is to be buried and then emerge, like Lazarus, from mud). Schwarzenegger, human and humorous, goes berserk only when his family (in this case, his daughter) is threatened. In the mythology of film, Schwarzenegger is Jimmy Stewart in *Destry Rides Again,* forced into action against his will, and Stallone is Jack Palance in *Shane,* the killer who enjoys murder as an art.

What Fonda in her workout tapes, Stallone in *Rambo: First Blood Part II,* and Schwarzenegger in *Commando* share is the role of the reformer, someone outside mainstream society who offers a corrective—a corrective that, while different in each case, varying from jumping jacks to revenge, involves spiritual growth through physical activity.

Luke Skywalker in *Return of the Jedi* (number 4 on *Billboard*'s list) is also an outsider—a rebel against the Empire that controls the galaxy. Like Schwarzenegger's Commando, he begins his saga on a homestead, the cosmic equivalent of the Oklahoma Territory at the turn of the century; and, against his will, he is drawn into his adventure—which is no less than saving the galaxy.

As the unacknowledged heir to greatness (he is the son of the most powerful man in this particular creation, Darth Vader, who is the fist behind the emperor, a kind of sidereal Bismarck), Luke seems at first not so much an American as a classical archetype: Theseus, brought up in the boondocks and fated to rule Athens, or Jason, raised in the country by centaurs for his destiny as captain of the Argonauts—one of the company of legendary and fairy tale heroes who discover in puberty that they are not simple peasants but leaders of men. In the end, it is a myth that is not so different from the American belief that any boy can grow up to be president.

Luke, like Fonda, Stallone, and Schwarzenegger, finds virtue in the natural, which in the *Star Wars* epic is called The Force. The Force is an Emersonian oversoul, a vital current into which one can plug—energy that can be turned to good or evil use. Luke masters The Force by going through a series of exercises, which are not that different from those on the Fonda tapes—with a fillip of Zen as interpreted by Saint Paul. Or, rather, as interpreted by Friedrich Ludwig Jahn, the early-nineteenth-century German prophet of the folk-soul.

Darth Vader and his storm troopers may look like Nazis, but it is Luke who abandons his own will, surrenders to the folk-soul of The Force, and through The Force gains superpowers. He is Siegfried, Parsifal, the galactic Redeemer, dancing through battles as if they were ballets.

Just as Luke seeks to graduate from human to superhuman, Pinocchio (in the Walt Disney film of the same name, which was number 7 on *Billboard*'s list) seeks to graduate from puppet to human. Both want to be more physically perfect. Both achieve their apotheosis through right choice. And both have personified consciences that are cute creatures: Yoda for Luke and Jiminy Cricket for Pinocchio.

Stallone's Rambo and Schwarzenegger's Commando also have consciences, both represented by nonwhite women. Stallone's is Oriental, Schwarzenegger's is black. (And for the folks at home, trying to decide whether to join in the exercises demonstrated on the workout tapes, Jane Fonda is the conscience.) These consciences perform the function that women did in popular fiction in the nineteenth century. Their role is to civilize brute men—which is what Julie Andrews does in *The Sound of Music* (number 2 on *Billboard*'s list), Deborah Kerr does in *The King and I* (number 9 on the list), Ingrid Bergman does in *Casablanca* (number 6), and Kelly McGillis does in *Witness* (number 3). They spur men not to action but to feeling. In *The Sound of Music,* the baron is taught to express his love for his children. The king learns the same lesson in *The King and I.* The urban cop, John Book, is initiated into nonviolence in *Witness.* And love redeems Rick in *Casablanca.*

The baron, the king, the cop, the expatriate—all, like Pinocchio, are faced with moral choices that will humanize them. And all, like Luke, rebel against a threatening power: the baron and the expatriate defy the Nazis, the king struggles against colonialism, the cop fights a corrupt police force. They are political outsiders who through moral choice become ethical insiders.

All the tapes on *Billboard*'s Top 10 videocassette list present a world divided between the strong and the weak. In half—the two Jane Fonda workout tapes, *Rambo: First Blood Part II, Commando,* and *Return of the Jedi*—strength is seen as virtue. In half—*Pinocchio, The Sound of Music, The King and I, Casablanca,* and *Witness*—strength is seen as criminal. From the evidence, Americans seem to be grappling with the obvious: How does a nation with monstrous power reconcile this with an equally monstrous belief in its own virtue? We are torn between flexing our muscles and flexing our morals.

If these tapes are popular, it may be because they give us a simple vision, and whether that vision plumps for violence or nonviolence doesn't matter. All suggest that the world is a dangerous place, that the strong dominate the weak, and that living may be a second-by-second choice between good and evil.

A vision that, in fact, is true.

PART SEVEN

COMMUNITY

To say that Americans are individualistic is not to imply that they prefer being alone to belonging to groups. By the logic of individualism, though, the only kind of belonging that is meaningful is that which is freely chosen by individuals. Americans emphasize "getting involved" over "being involved." This characteristic emphasis on voluntary association tends to lead Americans to live in what *Habits of the Heart* calls "lifestyle enclaves" rather than communities "in the strong sense." A community in the strong sense is a group of people who are different yet interdependent, who are bound together by mutual responsibilities arising out of a common history, a history which they have not simply chosen to be a part of but which they are nonetheless responsible for carrying on. A lifestyle enclave is a group of people who choose to be together because they are similar in some dimension of life that is important to them—for example, the amount of money that they have or the kind of professional status they have achieved or the kind of leisure activities that they enjoy.

As used here, "lifestyle enclave" and "community" are ideal types, abstract definitions of the limits toward which certain social tendencies are headed. In real life, most American associations retain at least some of the elements of real community. But the tendencies that predominate are those that lead them toward becoming lifestyle enclaves. To the extent that our society is composed mainly of lifestyle enclaves rather than communities, it will be difficult for us to understand how and why we should act justly and decently toward those who are so different from ourselves that we would not voluntarily choose to be associated with them—and difficult therefore to give any substantive content to the idea of the "public good." The short readings that begin this section illustrate some of these difficulties.

In his study of Canarsie, a neighborhood in Brooklyn composed mostly of lower-middle-class Jews and Italians, sociologist Jonathan Rieder describes the bitter hostilities that can be engendered when one lifestyle enclave finds itself threatened by another. Canarsie is composed of hardworking, family-oriented people who have invested most of their economic resources in purchasing small single-family homes in what they had hoped would be a secure, safe neighborhood, inhabited by families who shared similar ways of life. Canarsie, however, is surrounded by neighborhoods of largely unemployed blacks who live in housing projects and many of whom have had children out of wedlock. Canarsians deeply fear that their enclave will be engulfed by this underclass. Many of them feel betrayed by upper-middle-class "liberal" politicians who advocate racial integration while living in secure enclaves far away from the underclass. Canarsians' fears and resentments often take the form of bitter, racist hatred and sometimes vigilante violence. One relatively poor enclave desperately battles another while members of more affluent enclaves insulate themselves from the problems of the lower strata of their society.

Too often, then, Americans have sought to solve the problems of poverty simply by segregating the poor into ghettos. The worst victims of this have been impoverished blacks. Until a generation ago, as the journalist Nicholas Lemann reminds us in his recent article on "The Origins of the Underclass," urban whites in the northern metropolises blatantly used the power of restrictive housing laws to confine black migrants from the rural south into ghettos. Thanks to the civil rights movement, most such laws have now been abolished. The ghettos have lost much of their population. Yet the ugly realitites of segregation persist, imposed now by subtle economic and social pressures. Many individuals with the economic, educational, and cultural resources to compete successfully for rungs on the middle class ladder of success have taken advantage of the legal reforms and have left the ghetto. Many others, though, suffering from a heritage of extreme poverty and powerless, are unable to compete for middle class occupations, especially in a tight job market and in a society still permeated with subtle forms of racial discrimination. They remain trapped in ghettos, which, though shrunken in size, still breed the self-defeating social pathologies that come from alienation and despair. In this context, the opportunities that have opened up for the middle class to escape the ghetto have made life even worse for those forced to remain.

"Rich Friends," a short essay by the documentary filmmaker, Howard Husock, invokes a much more tolerant, cosmopolitan social world than that of the previous two readings. And yet, for all its openness to a wide range of experiences and for all its diversity, Husock's neighborhood is also a kind of enclave. All the people who live there are professionals. Some make much more money than others, but nobody is poor. And all have jobs that give them great personal satisfaction. Disparities of wealth nonetheless give rise to the feelings of insecurity and guilty envy reported by less affluent neighbors like Husock.

The socially destructive potential of this envy is held in check by a sense that those who have less money voluntarily chose careers that did not pay well. "If we feel the rules are fair, that fair warning is provided, that opportunity is relatively equivalent, then we can proceed without upheaval and ennui. But jealousy is a partner of competition. If those in the middle doubt the propriety of wealth, and if those below the middle feel altogether excluded, then our house of plastic cards can collapse." Husock, a person in the middle, does not feel excluded and for this reason is not goaded into doubting the propriety of wealth. But what about those in Canarsie, and those in the ghettos surrounding it? And what responsibilities do those securely in the middle classes have toward those who are excluded from the opportunity to live a life of security and dignity in our society?

The tendency of modern Americans to retreat into lifestyle enclaves is the outcome of a long process of historical development. America, the distinguished historian Robert H. Wiebe argues in his book *The Segmented Society,* has always been fragmented into segments of similar people who try to keep themselves separate from those who are different. Throughout our history, he says, "what held Americans together was their ability to live apart." However, the principal bases upon which Americans have built their separate segments have changed over time, and the problems of building a national community out of a segmented society have gotten more serious.

In the eighteenth century, the main elements of life that held Americans together in segments of similar people while separating them from the rest of their fellow citizens were common religious and moral beliefs and common family ties. The emphasis on rigid orthodoxies entailed by this pattern of associations made large-scale social change difficult. The development of an industrial economy in the nineteenth century demanded a society geared to rapid change, and as this happened, the basis for the formation of America's most important segments changed accordingly. Instead of common beliefs or common familial origins, the things that now bound people together were common economic opportunities, usually associated with common residence in a particular geographical locality. Across the nation, social order could be (precariously) maintained in spite of this segmentation because the country was big enough with enough material resources for all that each segment could usually pursue its interests without clashing with those of other segments. Nineteenth-century American society was divided into "countless, isolated lanes where Americans, singly and in groups, dashed like rows of racers toward their goals."

By the end of the nineteenth century, industrialization had finally led to a highly interdependent national and international economy that made it impossible for Americans to seek their goals in isolation from a wide array of diverse fellow citizens. Nevertheless, America carried on its tradition of segmentation. Now, however, the most important thing binding people together into their primary units of life was not where one lived or what one believed, but what kind of job one performed within the interlocking system of occupations that constituted the national economy. At least that is what constituted the most meaningful units of life for relatively successful Americans, those who acquired secure jobs with at least moderate amounts of income within the new occupational system. Large numbers of less successful Americans retained attachments to particular places or cultural values that were irrelevant to an occupational system, causing the "national collection of segments" to display "an intricate pattern of gaps and tiers."

Today, the most important units of association for successful professionals like Howard Husock are indeed occupational. The main factor that determines whom they will associate with and whom they will feel sympathy toward is not where they live or how much money they have but how much status they have gained in the occupational hierarchy. Typically, a professional will find his or her most important friends and associates among fellow professionals scattered throughout the country; and in pursuit of professional success he or she must be ready to travel to wherever the most important available opportunities for practicing his or her profession happen to be.

But for people like those in Canarsie who have no opportunity to climb (at least, not very high) on national ladders of occupational success, and who realistically have no way to seek a better life by moving out of their neighborhoods, the most important units of life are defined, somewhat as they were in the nineteenth century, by where exactly one lives and, somewhat as they were in the eighteenth century, by what beliefs and values constitute the way of life of one's neighbors. Not surprisingly, people like those in Canarsie often feel threatened by people too poor to adopt their standards of respectability and feel looked down upon by those professionals who are able to identify their self-worth with the attainment of a high degree of occupational success.

To confront the moral and political issues raised for all of us by our complexly interdependent society, we cannot any longer afford to remain isolated in our homogeneous enclaves. We have to find ways to see ourselves as part of a political whole, part of a commonwealth. In this section's descriptions of Canarsie, of the professional neighborhood in "Rich Friends," and even of the urban ghettos of the underclass, there are echoes of moral traditions that could be used by a committed leadership to anchor those enclaves in the life of a national community. In subsequent sections of this book, we will further explore how this can be done.

JONATHAN RIEDER

Canarsie

NEIGHBORHOOD INTEGRATION

*"Maybe they used to be liberals, but not after they
were scared out of East Flatbush."*

Real and imaginary threats to property values and racial balance
quickened the struggle over territory. Resistance to integration
went beyond cupidity, but the economics of land, housing capital,
and debt payments best explain the residents' fear of racial change.
A school official, who once had cheered George Wallace at a Madison Square Garden rally, described to me one source of Canarsians'
demonic perceptions in the mid-1970s. "With the economy so bad,
people are getting crazy. If busing goes in, they figure, 'Hey, I can't
make a living, I'm falling behind and now they're going to ram this
busing down my throat and take my house away.'"

The apparent racial stability of Canarsie did not console its
nervous residents. For two decades they had been watching white
Brooklyn shrink down to a thin sliver along its south shore, extending from Bay Ridge in the west to Bensonhurst, Sheepshead Bay,
and lower Flatbush in the center, to Canarsie in the east. "We're
finished here in Brooklyn, I tell you," one man avowed. "It's like
we're the Israelis. They are surrounded by fifty million Arabs, they
have to fight, but there's no place to retreat. Their back is against
the water. Well, the white middle class in Canarsie is up against the
same wall."

Signs of incipient change in the late 1970s lent some credence
to the fear of engulfment. The central core of Canarsie remained lily
white. In all but seven of its thirty-three census tracts between 1970

Jonathan Rieder, excerpted from *Canarsie* (Cambridge, Mass.: Harvard University
Press, 1985), pp. 79–83.

and 1980, the number of blacks remained constant at zero or increased from two or three to less than a dozen. Yet change was coming to the peripheral tracts that abutted adjacent neighborhoods and to anomalous zones like the two projects.

Bayview Homes, a middle-income high-rise public project, went from 15 to 22 percent black in the 1970s, and the increase in Puerto Rican tenants brought the minority population to one-third. At the northwestern threshold of Canarsie, in a tract that looked across Ralph Avenue toward East Flatbush, the black population of 47 quadrupled, rising by 1980 to 161 blacks, or 4 percent of the total. In Canarsie's northeastern quadrant north of Flatlands Avenue, a striking exodus of whites left the low-income Breukelen Houses a minority enclave of youth gangs, female-headed households, and welfare recipients. The halo effect of the project touched the surrounding blocks. Directly to the west was a buffer zone between the project and all-white Italian Old Canarsie across Rockaway Parkway; that tract jumped from a dozen to four hundred blacks in a decade. Most ominously to Canarsians, the commercial strip along the south side of Flatlands Avenue across from the project had an increasingly seedy and abandoned appearance. And dozens of middle-income black and Hispanic families were moving into the eleven front-line blocks south of Flatlands Avenue opposite the project. They had penetrated only one block deep into the heartland of eastern Canarsie, but the direction of movement, south toward Seaview Village and Jamaica Bay, was obvious.

People's forebodings varied with the steepness of their investment, their reserves, and their options for disengagement. One Jewish woman had lived most of her life in walkup apartments and middle-income projects in Brownsville before buying a home in Canarsie in the early 1960s. "Canarsie people don't have a lot of money. We got a little house and it's a big achievement. We don't want to lose what it took our entire life to build."

Caution underwrote stiff resistance to integration. In 1976, at the first meeting of a block association in the central section of New Canarsie, a speaker told the audience, "Jimmy Carter used the phrase 'ethnic purity' and had to apologize for it. But I use the term and I won't apologize for it. I am not a racist. I just want to keep my community pure. I sunk every dime I have into my house and I don't want to be chased. I won't be chased."

Canarsians had an earthy, materialistic view of the link between attitudes and property. A carpenter dismissed his sister's self-righteousness as the luxury of transience. "She don't even care who lives next door to her. She wouldn't care if an Eskimo moved into the neighborhood. But what do you expect? She lives in an apartment in Manhattan." To some extent, attitudes toward laws against discrimination in selling homes reflect property interests. The motives that created an informal version of apartheid in Canarsie, however, cannot be reduced to the racist greed of a privileged segment of the housing market trying to hang onto its advantages. White views of blacks moving in resulted from forces of ideology and environment as well as of investment, and all three forces influenced the others.

Nationally, urban Catholics score respectably high on measures of integrationist sympathy when compared to nonsouthern Protestants. They come close to the stereotype of know-nothing ethnics only when compared to Jews, whose support for civil rights laws is striking. A Jewish teacher insisted that race was an invidious, even un-American, criterion for selecting a home buyer—adding the proviso that the buyer should have attained the same level of social rank and respectability as she had. "It's the American way. Minorities should live where they want. It's part of our philosophy: life, liberty, and freedom for all." In contrast to this universalist statement is the virtually phobic fear expressed by an Italian machinest. "I bag all the niggers together. They do nothing for themselves. They are a useless people. They have different traits from us. I don't want to mingle with them."

Comparing a Jewish teacher with a master's degree, whose father was a Socialist tailor, to an Italian machinist with eight years of education, whose father liked Joseph McCarthy, hardly offers a fair test of ethnicity, a tag that partially hides influences of education, class, and occupation. Surveys permit the analyst to weigh factors that may remain hidden from the ethnographer; their drawback, however, is that the respondents are treated as lonely atoms with no ties to local communities that impart to their members distinct moral learning.

The commandments and taboos that pervaded the speech of Jewish political and school leaders signaled the vibrancy of a public culture of democracy. A PTA leader stated, "Of course it's the blacks' right to move in. Everybody has the right to civil rights." Her tolerance was not a mysterious gift, something she had merely by virtue of being Jewish. Cultural teachers, by harping on a set of precious "shoulds," had imbued her with a self-conscious striving toward universalism. "I try not to see color. I wouldn't care if a black bought a house next to me. You should take each person on their own merits."

Italian leaders in the Republican party, the North Canarsie Civic Association, and the Conservative party had different notions of "should." Unabashedly defending the exclusion of blacks from Canarsie, they affirmed the personal wishes of kith and kin rather than the canons of formal law. The acceptance of prejudice as inevitable upheld a strict division between the rights of citizenship, which prevailed in the larger society, and the rights of settlement, which applied to the smaller world of community. "Some prejudice is legal," insisted one Italian man who was active in Old Canarsie civic affairs. "You have to do it to keep out undesirables. It's a cooperative effort of neighbors. They have the right to pick their neighbors. The social and the business world are two entirely different things." Citing human nature rather than human rights, a Republican leader rejected the perfectionist ideal of law as an instrument of social change or guarantor of liberty. "The government is trying to equalize the races by moving people around, but law can't accomplish this sort of thing. Brothers like to be close to brothers. People moved into communities because they wanted to be close to people who are like them. It's not up to the government to throw things over."

His claim evokes the naturalistic sensibility that weakens the persuasiveness of law in provincial neighborhoods, as well as the realistic ethos that lies at the core of white ethnic culture. A far cry from individualism, ethnic provincialism views life as a field of social entanglements. Its conservatism rests on deference to communal prejudices, on the belief in the natural quality of personal ties, and on its suspicion of the formal remedies of strangers, including those of the state.

Provincial people tend to shy away from airy generalities in favor of judgments conditioned by local context and immediate experience. "That's completely different out there on [Long] Island with those blacks," exclaimed an Italian blue-collar worker, who moments before had insisted, "We don't want them blacks in Canarsie, I tell you, I wouldn't want to live next door to them." The material differences between the worlds of here and there made the comparison academic. "The [black] ones who live out on the Island, you never hear of an incident out there. Not really." Incidents, his euphemism for crime, was the relevant issue, not race. "The only incidents you ever hear of is right here—in Bedford Stuyvesant, the ghetto, East New York, and Brownsville. All the incidents are mostly out this way."

A policeman's mistrust of abstract moralism made him angry over sanctimonious condemnations of white racism:

> We aren't racist pigs. We are only people looking out for the survival of our community and children. Did you ever notice anyone who talks of an area being prejudiced? I love this, I look at this: We had a Nyquist on the Board of Regents. Where does he live? Where does his kid go to school? They ain't never lived in Brooklyn, they ain't never lived in East New York. A Kennedy who says this, "Oh, we got to live together, we'll have busing," or a Nyquist, why do you live out in Long Island, why is there an eight-foot fence around your property with armed guards, how come your kids don't go to public schools?

NICHOLAS LEMANN

The Origins of the Underclass

In Chicago and other northern cities there was a direct link between the magnitude of the black migration from the South and the degree of residential segregation imposed by whites. In 1898 only 11 percent of black Chicagoans lived in neighborhoods more than 75 percent black. In 1900 thirty-three of Chicago's thirty-five wards were at least 0.5 percent black. As soon as the flow of migrants became significant, though, white hostility toward blacks surged, growing partly from pure prejudice, partly from fear of the importa-

Nicholas Lemann, "The Origins of the Underclass," *Atlantic Monthly,* June 1986, pp. 51–53.

tion of the social ills created by Jim Crow, partly from intense competition in the labor market. It is a pattern of long standing, a primal white antipathy toward the black masses, which always leads to the creation of iron restrictions on where blacks can live and work. In the summer of 1919, just as Chicago was absorbing the first big concentrated wave of southern migrants, white gangs started a riot at a Lake Michigan beach when a black swimmer ventured into a de facto white stretch of water. Violence, by both blacks and whites, spread through much of the South Side, lasted a week, and left thirty-eight people dead and 537 injured.

In the late forties, with southern blacks again pouring into the city and racial tensions rising (there were riots when black veterans tried to move into temporary housing in white neighborhoods), Chicago, like many cities, began building many public-housing projects. At the time, integrated public housing was one of the great liberal causes, and it was also a constant, long-standing political demand of blacks. In the liberal dream, housing projects would be filled by a racially integrated, clean-living, well-educated working class. Ward politicians with white constituents to keep happy were adamantly opposed to integration, though, and in 1949 the state legislature passed a law that boxed out the liberals by requiring that the Chicago City Council approve all public-housing sites. This virtually ensured that projects would be segregated. In 1950 Robert Taylor, the black chairman of the Chicago Housing Authority, resigned in frustration at his inability to get the sites he wanted past the council. In 1953 there were protracted riots when one black family moved into a white housing project. In 1954 Elizabeth Wood, a Jane Addams–style reformer who was the CHA's director and longtime guiding spirit, and a great believer in integration, was forced out. From 1957 to 1968 the CHA built 15,591 housing units—almost all in high-rise buildings, almost all with black tenants, almost all in existing black ghettos. The private housing market was, by unwritten law, strictly segregated in most places. By 1970 Chicago was the most residentially segregated city in America.

But because the segregation was by race, the ghetto was fairly well integrated by class. It was a community, with leaders and institutions—poor, with unusual difficulties, but a community nonetheless. From the First World War through the mid-sixties the black leadership regarded the high crime and low marriage rates of the black lower class as problems it had to solve, sometimes with a sigh (the white folks on the Gold Coast weren't held responsible for the rough-and-tumble of poor-white Chicago). It would, in sociologists' language, help the lower class to acculturate. For years the Chicago *Defender* published what a city commission called "instructions on dress and conduct [that] had great influence in smoothing down improprieties of manner which were likely to provoke criticism and intolerance in the city." The big South Side churches all had memberships across the black economic spectrum, in contrast to the segregation by class that prevailed in white Protestant churches. The Urban League was founded with the purpose of teaching lower-class southern migrants the ways of city life. Drake and Cayton, commenting on a slogan made popular by the *Defender*, wrote, "When upper-class and middle-class [black] people speak of 'advancing The Race,' what they really mean is creating conditions under which lower-class traits will eventually disappear and something approaching the middle-class way of life will prevail in Bronzeville." The black middle class knew that the black lower class would constantly be held up as the reason that all blacks had to be kept in certain neighborhoods and certain jobs; this was a grievous wrong, which had the side effect of giving the black middle class a strong vested interest in the uplift of the black middle class. Then the grievous wrong was righted.

In January of 1966 Martin Luther King, Jr., moved into an apartment in North Lawndale and announced that he and the Southern Christian Leadership Conference would be focusing their energies on Chicago for a while. He called his Chicago project the "End Slums Campaign" and said it would be aimed at improving the conditions in overcrowded, poorly maintained inner-city black neighborhoods. During his time in Chicago his campaign underwent a crucial shift, though it may not have seemed that way then. John A. McDermott, at the time a young Catholic activist working in the civil-rights movement and later the publisher of a distinguished Chicago newsletter on race relations, says, "King would try one issue after another to see what would get a response. 'End Slums' did not generate a tremendous amount of popular support. It was not a simple good-versus-evil issue. This was not Montgomery, Alabama. There were no overt racist laws or institutions. The problem of racism was more subtle. It was not clear it was a conspiracy. Some of the slumlords were black.

"Then a group tried the issue of open housing. We held demonstrations in white neighborhoods that wouldn't let blacks in. The white reaction was one of panic and outrage. It was on the nightly news, and suddenly people saw that a) the laws were not being enforced, and b) white people were full of hate and anger. People suddenly woke up and literally *poured* into the movement."

With the last great wave of southern migrants just arrived, North Lawndale was frustrated, tense, and swollen—in 1960 its population was 25 percent higher than it had been ten years earlier, when North Lawndale was a white neighborhood, and nearly half the population was under twenty years old, compared with less than 30 percent in 1950. Gangs were starting to become a severe problem. In July of 1966 there was rioting on the West Side that required 1,500 National Guardsmen to restore order. The working, married, better-established part of the population desperately wanted to get out of the neighborhood. On August 5 King led an open-housing demonstration in Marquette Park, then an all-white neighborhood, on the Southwest Side. The protection of more than 1,200 policemen did not stop his being hit in the head by a rock thrown by whites from the neighborhood. A knife thrown at him hit someone else. The demonstrators had to be evacuated in buses. On August 26 Mayor Richard Daley, under intense pressure from his white precinct captains to stop the demonstrations, finally sat down with King at the negotiating table. The result was a "summit agreement" devoted almost exclusively to the fair-housing issue rather than to ending slums.

What happened in Chicago is an especially dramatic version of what happened all over the country: just as the number of new, poor, migrant blacks in the cities reached its all-time peak, the country decided to mount a real attack on segregation in housing and employment, and otherwise to help those blacks capable of moving closer to the mainstream of American society to do so. The result is evident in the census data, as we have already seen: there has been another major migration of blacks over the past twenty years, out of the ghettos. Even more pronounced than the social and economic deterioration of the ghettos between 1970 and 1980 is their depopulation. North Lawndale was already losing population in the late sixties, and in the seventies more than half its black population moved away. The tenement house where King lived is a vacant lot now. In the same decade the area around Forty-seventh and South Parkway, the old vibrant heart of the South Side ghetto, lost 38 percent of its black population. The Robert Taylor Homes, whose extremely low rents and solid construction for years attracted long waiting lists, are now 20 percent vacant. All the ghetto schools, the overcrowding of which in the sixties was supposed to be a major cause of low achievement levels, have lost enrollment. This isn't happening just in Chicago. The South Bronx lost 37 percent of its population between 1970 and 1980. More than 100,000 black Chicagoans moved to the suburbs in the seventies; 224,000 blacks moved from Washington, D.C., to its suburbs, 124,000 from Atlanta to its suburbs. These are unusually high numbers for neighborhood population loss, and the comparable numbers today would be even higher.

There's no mystery to why so many people left the ghettos. They wanted to feel safe on the streets, to send their children to better schools, and to live in more pleasant surroundings; in particular, riots drove many people away. Probably everyone who could leave did. Many businesses and churches (except for tiny "storefront" churches, which often are unaffiliated with any organized religion) left with them. What was unusual about the migration of the black working population out of the ghettos, compared with that of other immigrant groups, is that it was for many years delayed and then suddenly made possible by race-specific government policies. That's why it happened so fast. One reason that the numbers for unemployment and poverty and female-headed families in the ghettos have gone up so much is that nearly everyone who was employed and married moved away (also, the fertility rate of black married women has dropped substantially, which is a sign of assimilation into the middle class). Very quickly, around 1970, the ghettos went from being exclusively black to being exclusively black lower-class, and there was no countervailing force to the venerable, but always carefully contained, disorganized side of the ghetto culture. No wonder it flourished in the seventies. The "losing ground" phenomenon, in which black ghettos paradoxically became worse during the time of the War on Poverty, can be explained partly by the abrupt disappearance of all traces of bourgeois life in the ghettos and the complete social breakdown that resulted.

Howard Husock

Rich Friends

We all moved to the neighborhood about the same time—time of year and time of life. Young couples with first houses, planning families to fill them. But first, there were rotten porches and downspouts to fix, careers to establish. That sense of common purpose and situation drew us all to the local civic association, where we got to know one another better. We won the fight for new playground equipment in the park and began having the children who would play together on the Timberforms.

A decade later, much of that sense of shared experience persists, but there has been an important change. Two of my neighbors have become rich. They started as struggling architects with offices in an old building that badly needed repairs. As high-tech industry surged into the Boston area, they went on to renovate much more than that old house. They found big money in the real estate boom, designing and undertaking those tasteful renovations that you see in the backdrops of "Cheers" and "Spencer: For Hire." (One of their penthouse condos was even featured in the latter. They got bit parts as compensation.)

The results were predictable but still striking: the Mercedes, the BMW, the second home. Their once-empty rooms are filled with furniture now. While most of us in the neighborhood still cast worried glances at the outstanding balance column on our Master-

Howard Husock, "Rich Friends," *The New York Times Magazine,* September 7, 1986, p. 98.

Card statements, the partners are off to the Caribbean and on to even bigger projects.

Inevitably, such success changes the relationships among young husbands, in whom a competitive ethic is so deeply ingrained. In the career competition in which we all engage, but which we seldom acknowledge, the two have, on one universally recognized score card, taken a commanding lead. Of course, we all know that a competitive system will reward us all in different ways and at different financial levels, but one is still unprepared for such differences as they actually develop. Hesitancy creeps into conversations. Are they looking askance at my old parka from their vantage point in topcoats and pin stripes? Am I saying something foolish? Conversely, their comments seem more important. They must be pretty smart, after all.

In conversations with oneself, there is nagging self-doubt. Am I lagging? Compared to whom? Come on, think of the poor. Look at all you have. Yes, but the poor don't live just across the street or around the corner. Talking on the car phone, waving to me on my bicycle, the partners are there to see every day. Does having only one car mean I'm a failure?

More is involved here than the practical results of uneven distribution of wealth. There is a realization of fate, of having made choices. Not that I'd wanted to be rich. Just the opposite, I'd said any number of times. But subconsciously, deep in the masculine psyche, something has never wanted to rule wealth out, either. To see some—neighbors in fact—find the pot of gold, is to know that time's a-wasting, if it hasn't already slipped away. It is not unlike the adolescent realization that you will not pitch a no-hitter nor hit that last-second jumper, except in your bedroom, posting up five feet from the wastebasket.

The funny thing, though, is that as I've gotten used to the situation, I've found our ability to live as neighbors—notwithstanding radically different income levels—to be oddly reassuring, a kind of personal proof of the flexibility of the social compact. After all, I still go to work every day. I'm still capable of work and love. And down deep, I really don't think our situations are unfair. I had my eyes open when I chose public television. They saw the market and took risks. We all knew the rules. Beyond that, there are a variety of potent rationalizations: if they can buy anything, nothing means much to them; the discipline of choices is actually good for our children. There is an intrinsic value to work that rivals money as reward.

And so it is, I think, that, armed with such constructs, most of us are able to face the day, knowing that not everyone will share equally in the rewards spread out before us. But still, there are moments, instants in which envy simply can't be suppressed. When my wife and I priced the preschool overlooking the apple orchard and had to settle for sending our son to the school in the church basement, there was envy and worry. What if, when our children are older, private school really would be better? Why should my kids be denied?

Then there are what I call the babysitter wars. Ten years ago was the time of the baby bust. Now the neighborhood is thick with Aprica strollers and Transformers T-shirts. Demand for babysitters simply exceeds supply. Those who can pay more for help go out on Saturday nights. The rest of us rent video cassettes—and recall, with some longing, dinners out and first-run films. The sense of resentment that can, involuntarily, well up on such occasions, serves as a reminder of how fragile our system is. If we feel the rules are fair, that fair warning is provided, that opportunity is relatively equivalent, then we can proceed without upheaval and ennui. But jealousy is a partner of competition. If those in the middle doubt the propriety of wealth, and if those below the middle feel altogether excluded, then our house of plastic cards can collapse. We simply can't allow envy—the unavoidable emotion—to be coupled with a sense of injustice. This must be what we are really discussing when we plot tax reform and welfare revision: how to allow some to succeed without demoralizing others, how to protect the needy without negating the value of ambition.

So far, I can happily report, the real estate partners and I remain friends.

ROBERT H. WIEBE

The Segmented Society

A sense of historical continuity depends upon an appreciation of change. The meaning of a common American experience, therefore, must begin with the distinct societies of the eighteenth, the nineteenth, and the twentieth centuries, for each enduring quality has had to fit their very different requirements.

American society in the eighteenth century operated according to the logic of a closed system. Whatever the scope of concern—a family, a community, a new nation, an empire—the guiding assumptions in each case established a framework of rules or principles, a container of truth that defined relationships and consequences inside its bounds. Sometimes the source of these principles lay in heavenly writ, sometimes in natural law, more often in some blend of the sacred and the secular. Always, however, they existed above and prior to human actions, and therefore they always stood ready as a measure of virtue in the present and a basis for prescriptions about the future. Rarely were these truths considered incomprehensible. Although ordinary citizens might require a learned elite to explain them, their meaning nevertheless fell within the ken of human reason. Hence everyone was obligated to adapt their ways to these overarching rules, as they were commonly understood, and anyone could reasonably judge others, wherever they lived, by their degree of conformity to the same immutable principles.

Applying these principles was a delicate art that demanded quite different skills in a familiar, local setting than in a broad, impersonal one. The center of eighteenth-century society was the family in a community. Across an impressive American diversity, family and community interconnected in a great many forms, ranging from Mennonite settlements where the community almost swallowed its families to kinship systems in South Carolina and Virginia

Robert H. Wiebe, excerpted from *The Segmented Society: An Historical Preface to the Meaning of America* (New York: Oxford University Press, 1975), pp. 14–27, 42–46.

with a very loose attachment to a county seat or a region. Every variation, however, set family units to manage the particulars of everyday life in a manner that constrained each unit by the values all of them held in common. These controls, in turn, were reinforced by an assumption of the community's permanence. People expected to spend a lifetime with the same faces, the same family names, the same pattern of institutions, the same routines of work and pleasure, and as they judged these intimate relations by their superstructure of truths, they drew upon an accretion of knowledge about individuals and families and customary ways to estimate, day by day, the state of their immediate society.

The farther their vision extended beyond the community, however, the more people relied upon an explicit demonstration that the affairs concerning them in a wider environment were actually abiding by the correct principles. An obsession with the exact privileges of a colonial legislature and the precise extent of Britain's imperial power, the specifics of a state constitution and the absolute necessity of a federal one, all expressed this urge for a careful articulation as proof that the right relationship with external powers did indeed prevail. Unlike the calculations of a community's health, which gave significance to everybody's accumulated knowledge about their neighbors and their traditions, these broad applications of principle belonged almost exclusively to an elite. The more a wider world affected the life of a community, the more its members looked to an elite for mediation—to explain distant events, to negotiate with distant authorities. During times of crisis relationships inside a community that might otherwise have been quite fluid tended to solidify behind a very few leaders in order to meet an external danger. Late in the eighteenth century when Americans showed less and less willingness to deal with the outside world exclusively through elite channels, they signaled trouble at a central point in their society's operation.

Eighteenth-century America could absorb no more than gradual changes. When measured against immutable principles, the slightest shift in an important area automatically sounded the alarm, not only because it threatened greater changes to come but because it was crucial in its own right as a disruption to an extremely sensitive network of relationships. Whether the test was a religious orthodoxy or a harmony of political powers, any deviation meant a critical impurity or a crippling imbalance. What appeared in retrospect as minor differences between Old Light and New Light during the Great Awakening, as nuances in the procedure of government following the Revolution, aroused the kind of emotions that split communities and shattered friendships. Would the lower and upper houses of a legislature meet in the same building or in separate ones? Was the new chief executive His Excellency or the President? The future of republicanism might hinge on the answer.

In part, Americans could enter these debates with such passion because they understood their own character as the same careful adjustment of components, the same minute approximations of purity, that governed their society, and character, the most precious commodity of the eighteenth century, always deserved a fiery defense. No one thought it extraordinary that James Monroe would invest about as much energy in justifying his public career as in the career itself. Microcosm or macrocosm, the imperative was stability, the security of a perfect fit between principles and practice. Consequently, when the Revolution did bring important changes to a society with no natural means of assimilating them, most of its leaders devoted themselves to resisting its radical implications, explaining its consonance with eternal truths and American traditions, then embodying that conservative judgment in the laws of the land; and voters responded by returning these same men to office. The bitter exchanges that did occur, rather than pitting demands for a grand departure against cries for reaction, almost always matched competing claims to a purer application of principles.

Abstractions that made eighteenth-century society so brittle and unyielding in some areas kept it very elastic in others. Neither time nor space shaped the minds of eighteenth-century Americans as both would for later generations. Although people obviously recognized differences between age and youth, they found little that was inevitable in the flow of life except its culmination in death. A change for the better or the worse might occur to any individual at any time; the old as well as the young studied their souls and their books in the expectation that one age was as eligible as the other to receive new insights, to improve character. Wisdom might appear in a youthful Hamilton or Madison, or in an elderly Franklin or Washington. Family, breeding, and station revealed a great deal, but the cumulative effect of the passing years told scarcely more than the moment could verify.

Eighteenth-century Americans roamed through history with a similar freedom. If civilizations, like individuals, completed a cycle of life, they also, like individuals, left a record that made sense only as immutable principles explained it. Hence Americans could cull the past for the good and the bad, the apt illustration of rules honored or violated, with a sole concern for their deductive logic from eternal truths. The Roman Republic, the Hanseatic League, the Swiss Confederation, each contained an assortment of lessons to extract and set against the verities. As late as the War of 1812, those founding fathers who still held federal office exhibited no particular embarrassment when America's declaration of war crossed in mid-Atlantic with the announcement of a major change in British policy. To Madison and Monroe it had not been a sequence of events but a violation of principles that justified the war, and any new information belonged on the scales of justice, not along a line of time.

Geography, in its usual concrete meaning, was a dependent variable in eighteenth-century America. Ties of family and belief held a prior sovereignty, and loyalties ran to the people and the ideas, wherever they were located, who served these needs. Seceding members of a church congregation either moved, carrying their community with them, or turned their backs to their neighbors, creating a community by the paths they walked. Letters united parents and children, even friends, with an immediacy that obliterated physical distance, and the deep, personal excitement that was generated by events in Europe during the French Revolution effortlessly transcended an ocean. When Americans cheered Citizen Genêt in 1793, they were greeting a brother in the cause of liberty, not a visitor from France. Place names conveyed the same orientation—the endless echoes of English towns, or the string of Republican settlements in southern Ohio that one after another memorialized Napoleon's great victories. Operating from this outlook, the founding fathers experienced no pangs of contradiction as they expanded and contracted the geographical range of their ambitions. The Federalist, who had dreamed of empire in 1799, stood behind his New England fortress in 1803 as naturally as Jefferson, who had speculated grimly on a separate nation of Virginia and North Carolina in 1799, envisaged a continental republic in 1803. Each was using geography to fulfill a purpose, not to define it.

The new society of the nineteenth century was geared to rapid change, and in order to accommodate it, Americans radically redesigned these concepts of space and time. Their world became a series of simple lines or channels along which change irrevocably flowed, and their lives a series of tests that pitted inherent worth against the hazards of change. One set of channels represented economic opportunities, and in almost all instances these followed specific, geographic lines, often related to the multiplying shoots of transportation—roads, canals, railways. Because each unit—individual or family, company or community, region or nation—perceived economic challenge as a measure of its intrinsic merit, it presumed the right to choose its own route and seek its own objectives without interference from any other unit. A properly ordered society, therefore, would comprise countless, isolated lanes where Americans, singly and in groups, dashed like rows of racers toward their goals. What happened along other tracks might be a matter of intense interest, for competitors, after all, were sprinting there, but it was seldom a matter for emulation. Each lane, testing a unique virtue, would trace a unique experience. Hundreds of communities had to learn all over again that silkworms died in America, that plank roads rotted, that imported laborers rarely revived a flagging agriculture or industry. Nineteenth-century America, as Frederick Jackson Turner observed in another context, recorded an endless recapitulation of the same experiences—a continuous demonstration of myopic pragmatism.

In a scheme of parallel endeavors, competition and monopoly were not only compatible but actually normal companions. Whatever the scope of enterprise, from a local store to a transcontinental railroad, Americans expected an exclusive realm appropriate to their ambitions where they, like their competitors in other realms, would prosper to the limits of their merit. Even when cities vied for the commerce of a common territory—Philadelphia against New York or Chicago against St. Louis—it was assumed that after no more than an interlude of uncertainty, the superior of the two would then absorb the contested area into its domain: a prolonged period of indeterminate, interlocking competition was always unnatural. Hence the primary tasks of public policy were twofold. First, it should provide sufficient space for the parallel enterprises of all its citizens, a requirement of such vast proportions that it made nineteenth-century America a study in insatiable land hunger. Second, public policy should guarantee freedom within each lane. A legal system to delineate the boundaries between parallel enterprises, and the passionate differences this system generated, defined the most critical public issues of the century. During these angry debates, charges of "monopoly" were directed not at exclusive privilege itself but at the intrusion of someone else's privilege into a sphere that the accusers considered their own.

A second set of lines marked the life span of individuals. As a corollary to their economic ambition, Americans assumed that they would normally move in search of better opportunities and that their initial departure would probably occur as soon as they became adults. Lives were now charted in sequences of time, with childhood as the crucial period of preparation, young adulthood as the most severe period of testing, and the later years as the increasingly predictable consequence of what had accumulated over a previous lifetime. To ready them for the unknown, children were taught a few, simple truths as their inviolable guides in life, and young adults were then scrutinized to see how thoroughly they had internalized these absolutes and how effectively they could operate from them. The models of success were invariably people of full maturity who could display a long record of strength against temptations and vacillations; the youthful patrician had disappeared from the gallery of American leaders. Although middle age brought a degree of security, nothing fully released individuals from the imperative to prove themselves, to verify that their lines were indeed ascending ones. Life's path was determined by a ceaseless flow of cause and effect, and at any time the force of a bad decision might wreck the work of many decades. Who knew the flaws hiding in even the finest careers? For individuals as for all units of enterprise in the nineteenth century, the commandment was grow or die. Any pause risked decline in a world of sudden challenges and shifting opportunities, and males in particular were driven on a lifelong quest for improvement that would repeatedly validate their personal worth.

What might have seemed the atomization of American society was in fact an age of unusual community strength. It was an internalized community that individuals carried with them, and it was a replica of this community which they sought as a place to settle. Rootlessness, as distinct from mobility, implied the absence of both a moral base and an adequate setting for economic enterprise. The community, like so much else in nineteenth-century America, acquired a new geographical exactness to meet the responsibilities it was now expected to manage. Inside its boundaries lay a preserve where members prepared themselves to meet the challenges of a wider world. There they amassed their moral and economic resources for a successful outward thrust, and they guarded their community against any influence that might damage their peculiar values and rights, their special moral stamina and special cluster of ambitions. Because strange people constituted an omnipresent threat to the community in an era of mobility, members devoted particular attention to the sifting of newcomers. In this task, as well as in interpreting the good and the bad tendencies of a broader society, they came to rely upon shorthand devices that sorted people by their surface characteristics: their skin color, their demeanor, their public habits. These very surface qualities, in fact, were the ones they emphasized in the rearing of their children. In a society of small, absolutistic domains and compelling material ambitions, it was perfectly consistent to resist cultural novelty with the same sort of intensity that they invested in economic or technological innovations.

Institutions extending beyond the community operated by the same formula of a few absolutes thoroughly internalized, infinitely applicable. Political parties and religious denominations, the public school movement and civil service reform, a legal profession and a fraternal organization, all relied upon a small set of principles and procedures—a kernel of truths—that could enable people widely dispersed and scarcely in communication to pursue their activities with a firm sense of common purpose. A carefully marked Bible or Blackstone, Theodore Weld on slavery or Horace Mann on education held the essentials, and an unwavering dedication to the simple truth completed the links of an effective, if almost invisible institution. In its broadest application, this logic explained the course of the entire society. The nation, like any other unit, was following its own irresistible sequence of cause and effect, and it also was bound by the truths at its core. Because anything that violated its absolutes—the wrong tariff law, one slave, an evil President, or whatever seemed critical from the perspective of a particular community—threatened to bring disastrous results, Americans remained constantly alert for that first, perhaps half-hidden sign of a momentous turn. A change at the core of society would affect the whole pattern of tracks inside it, ultimately altering the destinies of individual, community, and nation together.

The Civil War demonstrated the operations of this social system without significantly damaging it. The Missouri Compromise, banning slavery above 36'30° and allowing it below, had established channels of parallel growth for the North and the South that eventually merged in the trans-Mississippi territories. By the 1850s the natural urge to comprehend a complex course of events by a crucial absolute—a central cause—had elevated slavery and free soil to the level of explanatory truths about the South and the North, and the imperative to grow or die now applied to the triumph of a section's truth in the territories. Either one or the other would have to prevail; the issue could not linger. In a world of inevitable expansion or contraction, people in both the North and the South increasingly interpreted the pieces of evidence about them as a sequence of cause and effect that would extend either slavery or free soil throughout the nation. To more and more southern leaders, the evidence told them that their grand vistas of space and opportunity were rapidly closing, a prospect that Daniel Webster among others had already pictured for them, and they made a dramatic shift at the core—secession—in order to break the deadly flow of events, preserve their special sources of moral and economic strength, and demarcate their own safe paths for development. In the North, secession violated fundamental law and conjured visions of an expansive evil permanently at hand. By a comparable logic from central absolutes to inevitable consequences, the decision for war followed.

The mark of war branded millions of lives. Slavery was abolished. With major changes in the southern economy came a new centrality for its towns and small cities. A general process of industrialization was greatly facilitated. Yet contemporaries overwhelmingly interpreted the war as abnormal, and the lessons they drew from it were largely negative and heavily conservative. The willingness of so many southerners to read the war as a judgment of failure and seek new leaders for a new departure, the willingness of so many northerners to accept adjustments in the law as proof of a redeemed society, and the eagerness of people everywhere to return to their economic channels indicated how well the fundamentals of nineteenth-century society had survived the war. It would require several decades more to undermine the economics of parallel development and force Americans to reconsider this open, expansive system of geographical lines.

In the twentieth century these parallel tracks were redesigned to form the interlocking pieces of a puzzle. According to a pattern that was organized around productive and distributive business, the units of the new society acquired their definition from the functions that they performed in a single, national system. A logic of relationships within this system replaced a nineteenth-century logic of countless scattered enterprises, each of which American society had been expected to honor and accommodate. Just as citizens had once contested boundaries across space, they now competed along the borders of occupational privilege, and the antagonists were determined by business specialties, agricultural products, professions, and labor skills rather than by communities, states, regions, and the economic ambitions that these units of nineteenth-century society had supported. In the twentieth century, what one did superseded where one did it as the initial, controlling question.

A system based on social functions splintered the elements of wholeness that had characterized nineteenth-century America. Instead of assuming an essential sameness at every level of society— individual, family, community, nation—each functional unit accentuated its own particular qualities that related to its role in the system, and the system itself was then presumed to operate by still another set of rules. Rather than acknowledging the presence of general absolutes, each subdivision claimed a separate truth, one accessible only to insiders with a unique training and experience. A multitude of functions, a multitude of specializations, yet each person could master very few, probably only one. In order to succeed, individuals had to concentrate on a single specialty; in order to survive, they had to rely upon an array of specialists in those many critical areas beyond their knowledge. What originated as a way of organizing work and responsibilities in an urban-industrial world thus spread into a pattern of life. Without expert guidance, who could prepare a balanced meal, evaluate candidates for the local judiciary, understand one's children, relieve headaches, enjoy sex? An endless parceling of expertise transformed individuals themselves into an agglomeration of functions—wife or husband, mother or father, consumer or citizen, hostess or handyman—each offered as a solemn, sovereign obligation and none necessarily integrated with the others outside the individual's schedule of daily activities.

New national elites inspired and dominated this society. It was the requirements of their work, the pursuit of their objectives, that created a system of functions transcending the older geographical attachments, and it was they who monopolized its primary benefits. Although Americans could never agree on one scale of importance to rate the members of the modern system, the usual measures—significance in economic production and distribution, degree of specialization, amount of wealth—promised little recompense for the majority with routine or menial jobs. In the nineteenth century a society of innumerable little communities had multiplied local winners, held the distance between the top and the bottom of a community to manageably human proportions, and protected the self-respect of many citizens with small incomes but good reputations. A single national standard, on the other hand, funnelled a few winners to the top, dramatically extended the distance from there to the bottom, and stripped an anonymous poor of their residual sources for respect. Millions of Americans resisted these consequences. As supplements or replacements for this encompassing national scale, a wide variety of people—local elites, ordinary citizens in the countryside and the cities, and the impoverished everywhere—turned instead to some version of the old-fashioned cultural norms, personal networks, and attachments to place as their defense against the national system's demeaning evaluation of their lives. Although no one could ignore the omnipresent values of the new elites, the casualties of the modern system could modify or even defy its judgments, and as a result they developed subtle shadings of qualitative difference throughout a society that was now divided not by many applications of a single social formula, as in the nineteenth century, but by many social formulas with contradictory elements: education versus ethnicity, impersonal skills versus personal connections, economic function versus place of residence, in complex variations and combinations.

What mitigated the effect of these new social divisions was a common commitment among almost all Americans to the rewards that the national system generated. Whether their source was a corporation or a distributor of credit, a law or an administrative agency, a direct government payment or an indirect government subsidy, an overwhelming majority depended upon the modern scheme of economic functions for their well-being. Even those who rejected its values fought grimly for their place in a structure that determined their livelihood, and such an intense involvement gave a deep, national toughness to the system. A common commitment to the goods and services that this system so grandly displayed served as an equally powerful source of social cohesion. Indeed, less successful participants in the system, as compensation for their meager satisfactions from work, proved to be especially ardent consumers. The cardinal test of the system, therefore, became its capacity to guarantee each constituent group a regular flow of rewards, a predictable payoff, and weak and strong alike combined to defend it against any radicals who might jeopardize these crucial procedures of distribution.

A society of interrelated parts required leaders with a refined talent for management. To motivate those who endlessly repeated a single routine and to regulate a multitude of groups in the service of economic productivity and social peace would have taxed any leadership. Yet this system was also dedicated to change. Because it was predicated on a continual economic growth, it welcomed new products, services, and technologies, and it accepted the arrival of new functional groups whenever these seemed necessary either to increasing productivity or to maintaining peace. Imaginative responses to flux placed the highest valuation on leaders who could maneuver with the forces around them—adapting here, pressuring there, always remaining alert to the use of one group's ambitions for another group's goals. Premier leadership was sensitive manipulation, the deft guidance of diverse people by means and toward ends that they would never recognize. As these skills came also to cover a complex pattern of international involvements, the touch of the invisible hand required even more delicacy. Like all members of the system, its leaders received their rewards for results, not for the procedures producing them. Their particular specialty was the technique of management, and their public policies were judged by the only standards inherent in the system: the social functions they performed.

* * *

These conditions created a society of segments, each presuming autonomy in its domain, each requiring homogeneity of its membership, and each demanding the right to fulfill its destiny without interference. They wrought this pattern of compartments through a complex process of interaction and reinforcement. Cultural diversity separated the units of society so effectively because military security and a thin institutional overlay invited its influence, open land provided it with an appropriate setting, and abundance underwrote its indulgence; an institutional framework gave these units so much latitude because space stretched its span, security justified its looseness, cultural particularism softened its discipline, and abundance promised it a steady flow of returns; and thus from any vantage point they joined. This interweaving was neither simple nor self-evident. Institutional diffusion, for example, did not lessen fears of a centralizing power any more than military security removed those of an enemy looming outside. What these strands did produce was a broad foundation delimiting the kind of system that Americans could construct.

In its everyday operations perhaps no Western society more closely approximated the sum of its parts. Yet Americans still managed to survive massive changes without breaking the critical threads of continuity or destroying their basic institutional channels—their constitutions and courts, churches and schools, political parties and economic enterprises. They built remarkably tough societies. What held Americans together was their ability to live apart. Society depended upon segmentation. From this elementary principle emerged a pattern of beliefs and behavior that was recognizably American.

PART EIGHT

CALLINGS:
WORK AND CITIZENSHIP

Work has long had for Americans something of the quality of a calling, a dedication that goes beyond what is merely necessary and touches what is intrinsically worthwhile, even sacred. Work has also had a quality of romance. Tocqueville found that Americans of his day seemed always busy. *Habits of the Heart* found that work continues to be central to identity, even the primary way in which an individual establishes a sense of self-worth. Work simultaneously provides Americans with their primary experience of interconnection with others outside family and the immediate local community. Work is thus typically the most significant link between private and public life.

Americans seek in their work many of the qualities of an activity good in itself, or a practice as described in part VI. Yet, as the earlier selections from Alasdair MacIntyre (part VI) and Robert Wiebe (part VII) have shown, modern work does not necessarily integrate individuals into the public sphere in a morally coherent way. Often, the opposite is true. The causes for this situation lie, as we have seen, in the structure and workings of economic relationships in our society. But the persistent cultural tendency to conceive all social relationships in the languages of utilitarian or expressive individualism also inhibits our capacity to make moral sense of our complex interdependencies. Without a morally meaningful comprehension of the relations that bind us to other individuals, groups and institutions, the ideals of citizenship that animated the nation's founding have little chance of realization.

For the founding tradition of the nation, work and citizenship were thought to complement one another, so that economic efforts for the well-being of the individual, family, and group should support rather than undermine concern for the common good. Work as a practice and a calling, with the public and even religious connotations of those words, was integral to that vision, and it remains a widely shared aspiration among Americans. However, realizing this purpose has always been difficult and often elusive. It continues to define the continuing task of citizenship.

The selections in this section explore some of the dimensions of this complex task. They begin with two contrasting depictions of what it can mean to live one's work as a practice, while illustrating the complex social, moral, and political ramifications an organized livelihood gives rise to. In the first selection, from *Moby Dick,* Herman Melville, one of the great writers of nineteenth-century America, portrays the intensely physical, challenging character of nineteenth-century work. The second selection, from the well-known scientist Lewis Thomas's *Lives of a Cell,* provides a colorful insider's view of the excitement of one quintessential twentieth-century work-as-practice, that of the research scientist.

Melville pictures the demanding labor of the whaling ship as in many ways a practice—it is disciplined labor that fully engages the worker's energies and even enthusiasms in a nearly ecstatic pitch of cooperative effort. Yet, it is also described as "man-killing," and indeed destructive of the great sea creatures as well as of the bodies of their pursuers. The whaling ship, like the mine or factory, is an extractive enterprise, exploiting natural and human resources alike for economic gain. Does such work, even if it is considered a practice, ultimately promote or harm the greater good? So does a consideration of work lead to the concerns of the public realm and citizenship.

By contrast, Lewis Thomas leaves the reader in no doubt as to the constructive social consequences of the practice he describes in the reading from *Lives of a Cell.* Unlike the modern factory or bureaucratic organization, scientific research is best treated as "more a kind of game than a systematic business." And here, in the serene and antiseptic environment of the twentieth-century laboratory, we encounter the same driven, ecstatic quality Melville saw in the practice of whaling: "the people engaged in it are so caught up, so totally preoccupied, so driven beyond their strength and resources." The researchers so driven undoubtedly make contributions to the public welfare through their work. And yet, one senses, despite Thomas's talk of play, excitement, and disinterested striving, that considerations of the social or moral aspects of their work are not an integral part of the way the work of these researchers is conceived or organized. The scientists may be judged perfectly competent professionals without raising such questions.

In *The Culture of Professionalism,* contemporary historian Burton Bledstein pursues the question of how it is that the notion of a professional career has developed in such a way that professional practice can be conceived without reference to its public and moral dimensions. Bledstein finds the answer in the shift from the earlier American conception of work as a calling pronounced by God, to the notion that the best work is one which allows an individual to advance in wealth and station for personal benefit. This shift from calling to career Bledstein dates to the latter half of the nineteenth century, and presents as a twofold process. On the one hand, the shift signaled the loosening of older social bonds and controls over individuals, while, on the other, it marked the emergence of a new ethic.

For Bledstein, the United States in the nineteenth century more and more defined its promise with reference to expanding economic opportunity, alledgedly for all, though this opportunity was meant in practice for native-born, white male Protestants. In this period, the new ideal of "economic man," prefigured by Benjamin Franklin (part II) and described by Philip Rieff (part V) came to shape the aspirations of the middle class. (See also the selection from David Schneider and Raymond Smith in part VI). The notion of a "career"—and the social organization of the expanding commercial-industrial economy—provided for the middle class, in Bledstein's words, "a great opportunity to identify themselves without the support of a community and in the absence of the kind of rigid barriers found in Europe." The cultural form of the career fit well into the social context of private goal-seeking, laying a basis for the "bureaucratic individualism" that Alasdair MacIntyre identified in part VI as widespread in modern work-life.

In counterpoint to the privatizing tendencies of much modern work, historian Sara M. Evans and Harry C. Boyte, activist scholar, explore the possibilities for reconnecting private and public aspirations in a reanimation of citizenship. In a selection from *Free Spaces: The Sources of Democratic Change in America,* Evans and Boyte argue for a tradition of American citizenship based upon "free spaces . . .

settings between private lives and large-scale institutions where ordinary citizens can act with dignity, independence and vision." Evans and Boyte conceive a kind of political practice adapted to modern conditions, yet based upon biblical and republican moral and civic ideals. The citizenship they describe must be local enough to engage people in the concerns of their everyday lives, and yet sufficiently universal in claim and vision to effectively mediate local with wider, cosmopolitan concerns. Evans and Boyte take up again the problems of local versus national politics which were raised in the selections of part VII, tracing the historical links between the development of an industrial economy and the eclipse of "free spaces."

Martin Luther King, Jr., is one of the figures Evans and Boyte point to as an example of leadership that is rooted in the life of a particular community and yet reaches beyond the local enclave to reanimate and restructure the national life. King's "Letter from Birmingham Jail," written during the height of the intensely fought struggle King led against racial segregation in the South, shows a politics of reforming citizenship in action. In the "Letter," Martin Luther King speaks as a Baptist pastor and political activist. He speaks for his community of black Americans with their painful memories of slavery and continuing oppression at the hands of the white majority. King gives voice to other disturbing parts of that memory—of justice affirmed in the ideal but betrayed in practice, and of fellowship, both civic and religious, celebrated and yet denied. The "Letter" sets out King's explanation for his campaign of militant nonviolence, but it also extends that struggle into a direct challenge to the conscience of his fellow citizens, both white and black.

In his "Letter" King continually alludes to memories and traditions in the idiom of the black church of the South, but he does this in a way that resonates with the biblical and republican heritage of Americans more generally. He continually describes his actions and those of his movement by analogies drawn from the Bible, while stressing that he writes not from the position of an outsider but as a fellow citizen. His stance is contentious; he has outraged the leaders of the "white power structure," and King challenges that structure, not by merely mobilizing resentment, but by calling it into judgment in terms of the values of justice and peace that both he and his opponents profess. No American institution, least of all the church, escapes King's moral censure; he brings discretion and discord, just as his movement must break unjust laws to reveal the need for justice. Yet, in the end the goal is peace, and a wider solidarity: "[T]he present tension in the South is merely a necessary phase of the transition from an obnoxious negative peace, where the Negro passively accepted his unjust plight, to a substance-filled positive peace, where all men will respect the dignity and worth of human personality."

HERMAN MELVILLE

Moby Dick

STOWING DOWN AND CLEARING UP

Already has it been related how the great leviathan is afar off de-
scried from the mast-head; how he is chased over the watery moors,
and slaughtered in the valleys of the deep; how he is then towed
alongside and beheaded; and how (on the principle which entitled
the headsman of old to the garments in which the beheaded was
killed) his great padded surtout becomes the property of his execu
tioner; how, in due time, he is condemned to the pots, and, like
Shadrach, Meshach, and Abednego, his spermaceti, oil, and bone
pass unscathed through the fire;—but now it remains to conclude
the last chapter of this part of the description by rehearsing—singing, if I may—the romantic proceeding of decanting off his oil into
the casks and striking them down into the hold, where once again
leviathan returns to his native profundities, sliding along beneath
the surface as before; but, alas! never more to rise and blow.

While still warm, the oil, like hot punch, is received into the
six-barrel casks; and while, perhaps, the ship is pitching and rolling
this way and that in the midnight sea, the enormous casks are slewed
round and headed over, end for end, and sometimes perilously
scoot across the slippery deck, like so many land slides, till at last
man-handled and stayed in their course; and all round the hoops,
rap, rap, go as many hammers as can play upon them, for now, *ex
officio,* every sailor is a cooper.

At length, when the last pint is casked, and all is cool, then the
great hatchways are unsealed, the bowels of the ship are thrown

---

Herman Melville, "Stowing Down and Clearing Up," chap. 98 of *Moby Dick* (New
York: Albert Boni, 1933), pp. 380–82.

open, and down go the casks to their final rest in the sea. This done, the hatches are replaced, and hermetically closed, like a closet walled up.

In the sperm fishery, this is perhaps one of the most remarkable incidents in all the business of whaling. One day the planks stream with freshets of blood and oil; on the sacred quarter-deck enormous masses of the whale's head are profanely piled; great rusty casks lie about, as in a brewery yard; the smoke from the try-works has besooted all the bulwarks; the mariners go about suffused with unctuousness; the entire ship seems great leviathan himself; while on all hands the din is deafening.

But a day or two after, you look about you, and prick your ears in this self-same ship; and were it not for the tell-tale boats and try-works, you would all but swear you trod some silent merchant vessel, with a most scrupulously neat commander. The unmanufactured sperm oil possesses a singularly cleansing virtue. This is the reason why the decks never look so white as just after what they call an affair of oil. Besides, from the ashes of the burned scraps of the whale, a potent ley is readily made; and whenever any adhesiveness from the back of the whale remains clinging to the side, that ley quickly exterminates it. Hands go diligently along the bulwarks, and with buckets of water and rags restore them to their full tidiness. The soot is brushed from the lower rigging. All the numerous implements which have been in use are likewise faithfully cleansed and put away. The great hatch is scrubbed and placed upon the try-works, completely hiding the pots; every cask is out of sight; all tackles are coiled in unseen nooks; and when by the combined and simultaneous industry of almost the entire ship's company, the whole of this conscientious duty is at last concluded, then the crew themselves proceed to their own ablutions; shift themselves from top to toe; and finally issue to the immaculate deck, fresh and all aglow, as bridegrooms new-leaped from out the daintiest Holland.

Now, with elated step, they pace the planks in twos and threes, and humorously discourse of parlors, sofas, carpets, and fine cambrics; propose to mat the deck; think of having hangings to the top; object not to taking tea by moonlight on the piazza of the forecastle. To hint to such masked mariners of oil, and bone, and blubber, were little short of audacity. They know not the thing you distantly allude to. Away, and bring us napkins!

But mark: aloft there, at the three mast heads, stand three men intent on spying out more whales, which, if caught, infallibly will again soil the old oaken furniture, and drop at least one small grease-spot somewhere. Yes; and many is the time, when, after the severest uninterrupted labors, which know no night; continuing straight through for ninety-six hours; when from the boat, where they have swelled their wrists with all day rowing on the Line,—they only step to the deck to carry vast chains, and heave the heavy windlass, and cut and slash, yea, and in their very sweatings to be smoked and burned anew by the combined fires of the equatorial sun and the equatorial try-works; when, on the heel of all this, they have finally bestirred themselves to cleanse the ship, and make a spotless dairy room of it; many is the time the poor fellows, just buttoning the necks of their clean frocks, are startled by the cry of "There she blows!" and away they fly to fight another whale, and go through the whole weary thing again. Oh! my friends, but this is man-killing! Yet this is life. For hardly have we mortals by long toilings extracted from this world's vast bulk its small but valuable sperm; and then, with weary patience, cleansed ourselves from its defilements, and learned to live here in clean tabernacles of the soul; hardly is this done, when—*There she blows!*—the ghost is spouted up, and away we sail to fight some other world, and go through young life's old routine again.

Oh! the metempsychosis! Oh! Pythagoras, that in bright Greece, two thousand years ago, did die, so good, so wise, so mild; I sailed with thee along the Peruvian coast last voyage—and, foolish as I am, taught thee, a green simple boy, how to splice a rope!

Lewis Thomas

Lives of a Cell

The essential wildness of science as a manifestation of human behavior is not generally perceived. As we extract new things of value from it, we also keep discovering parts of the activity that seem in need of better control, more efficiency, less unpredictability. We'd like to pay less for it and get our money's worth on some more orderly, businesslike schedule. The Washington planners are trying to be helpful in this, and there are new programs for the centralized organization of science all over the place, especially in the biomedical field.

It needs thinking about. There is an almost ungovernable, biologic mechanism at work in scientific behavior at its best, and this should not be overlooked.

The difficulties are more conspicuous when the problems are very hard and complicated and the facts not yet in. Solutions cannot be arrived at for problems of this sort until the science has been lifted through a preliminary, turbulent zone of outright astonishment. Therefore, what must be planned for, in the laboratories engaged in the work, is the totally unforeseeable. If it is centrally organized, the system must be designed primarily for the elicitation of disbelief and the celebration of surprise.

Moreover, the whole scientific enterprise must be arranged so that the separate imaginations in different human minds can be pooled, and this is more a kind of game than a systematic business. It is in the abrupt, unaccountable aggregation of random notions, intuitions, known in science as good ideas, that the high points are made.

The most mysterious aspect of difficult science is the way it is done. Not the routine, not just the fitting together of things that no one had guessed at fitting, not the making of connections; these are

Lewis Thomas, excerpted from *Lives of a Cell: Notes of a Biology Watcher* (New York: Viking, 1974), pp. 117–20.

merely the workaday details, the methods of operating. They are interesting, but not as fascinating as the central mystery, which is that we do it at all, and that we do it under such compulsion.

I don't know of any other human occupation, even including what I have seen of art, in which the people engaged in it are so caught up, so totally preoccupied, so driven beyond their strength and resources.

Scientists at work have the look of creatures following genetic instructions; they seem to be under the influence of a deeply placed human instinct. They are, despite their efforts at dignity, rather like young animals engaged in savage play. When they are near to an answer their hair stands on end, they sweat, they are awash in their own adrenalin. To grab the answer, and grab it first, is for them a more powerful drive than feeding or breeding or protecting themselves against the elements.

It sometimes looks like a lonely activity, but it is as much the opposite of lonely as human behavior can be. There is nothing so social, so communal, so interdependent. An active field of science is like an immense intellectual anthill; the individual almost vanishes into the mass of minds tumbling over each other, carrying information from place to place, passing it around at the speed of light.

There are special kinds of information that seem to be chemotactic. As soon as a trace is released, receptors at the back of the neck are caused to tremble, there is a massive convergence of motile minds flying upwind on a gradient of surprise, crowding around the source. It is an infiltration of intellects, an inflammation.

There is nothing to touch the spectacle. In the midst of what seems a collective derangement of minds in total disorder, with bits of information being scattered about, torn to shreds, disintegrated, deconstituted, engulfed, in a kind of activity that seems as random and agitated as that of bees in a disturbed part of the hive, there suddenly emerges, with the purity of a slow phrase of music, a single new piece of truth about nature.

In short, it works. It is the most powerful and productive of the things human beings have learned to do together in many centuries, more effective than farming, or hunting and fishing, or building cathedrals, or making money.

It is instinctive behavior, in my view, and I do not understand how it works. It cannot be prearranged in any precise way; the minds cannot be lined up in tidy rows and given directions from printed sheets. You cannot get it done by instructing each mind to make this or that piece, for central committees to fit with the pieces made by the other instructed minds. It does not work this way.

What it needs is for the air to be made right. If you want a bee to make honey, you do not issue protocols on solar navigation or carbohydrate chemistry, you put him together with other bees (and you'd better do this quickly, for solitary bees do not stay alive) and you do what you can to arrange the general environment around the hive. If the air is right, the science will come in its own season, like pure honey.

There is something like aggression in the activity, but it differs from other forms of aggressive behavior in having no sort of destruction as the objective. While it is going on, it looks and feels like aggression: get at it, uncover it, bring it out, grab it, it's mine! It is like a primitive running hunt, but there is nothing at the end of it to be injured. More probably, the end is a sigh. But then, if the air is right and the science is going well, the sigh is immediately interrupted, there is a yawping new question, and the wild, tumbling activity begins once more, out of control all over again.

BURTON BLEDSTEIN

The Culture of Professionalism

The culture of professionalism is the neglected theme in American history. Frederick Jackson Turner explored the significance of the frontier in American history, Charles A. Beard described industrial capitalism as a social force, and Perry Miller analyzed the impact of Puritanism. But the significance of the culture of professionalism, its total influence upon American lives, including those of Turner, Beard, and Miller, remains undefined. Indeed, the culture of profes-

Burton Bledstein, excerpted from *The Culture of Professionalism: The Middle Class and the Development of Higher Education in America* (New York: W. W. Norton, 1976), pp. ix–xi, 4–8, 171–77.

sionalism has been so basic to middle-class habits of thought and action that a majority of twentieth-century Americans has taken for granted that all intelligent modern persons organize their behavior, both public and private, according to it. This book describes a cultural process by which the middle class in America matured and defined itself.

By the middle of the nineteenth century, social perceptions about the uses of space, time, and words had begun to change dramatically. These perceptions were not wholly mental or imaginary, but corresponded to the reality of how people saw themselves—a reality that affected human lives. The middle class in America appeared as a new class with an unprecedented enthusiasm for its own forms of self-expression, peculiar ideas, and devices for self-discipline. Here was a great opportunity for people to identify themselves without the support of a community and in the absence of the kind of rigid barriers found in Europe.

Ambitious individuals in America were instrumental in structuring society according to a distinct vision —the vertical one of career. The most emphatically middle-class man was the professional, improving his worldly lot as he offered his services to society, expressing his expanding expectations at ascending stages of an occupation. Professionalism emerged as more than an institutional event in American life, more than an outward process by which Americans made life more rational. It was a culture—a set of learned values and habitual responses—by which middle-class individuals shaped their emotional needs and measured their powers of intelligence. When men had to make crucial decisions about the directions of their lives, the culture of professionalism was usually decisive in influencing their future. Though this culture was not totally homogeneous, not the single influence that ordered the events of an age, it did present Americans with a pattern of acceptable options.

The middle-class person in America owns an acquired skill or cultivated talent by means of which to provide a service. And he does not view his "ability" as a commodity, an external resource, like the means of production or manual labor. His "ability" is a human capacity—an internal resource—as unlimited in its potential expansion and its powers to enrich him financially and spiritually as the enlarging volume of his own intelligence, imagination, aspirations, and acquisitiveness. "A salesman is got to dream, boy. It comes with the territory": the requiem for Willy Loman caught the spirit of men desperate to establish their own importance and respectability.[1]

And middle-class Americans have dreamed about upgrading their occupations: from distributing a commodity to offering a service based on an acquired skill. Only in America, for example, did undertakers in the nineteenth century sever their historical ties with cabinet-makers, manufacturers of funeral furniture, and liverymen. They enhanced their prestige by calling themselves "funeral directors," proposing to provide a full personal service for the bereaved from the moment of a cherished one's death to the maintenance of a grave site. The professional importance of an occupation was exaggerated when the ordinary coffin became a "casket," the sealed repository of a precious object; when a decaying corpse became a "patient" prepared in an "operating room" by an "embalming surgeon" and visited in a "funeral home" before being laid to rest in a "memorial park." In the 1890s, the title *mortician* appeared, suggested by the word *physician*, and the subject "mortuary science" soon entered the curriculum of accredited colleges. After all, as one embalming school advertised in the 1880s, "When your fluid fails, who pays the damage?"[2] The American public demanded service and at least the appearance of an acquired skill; middle-class Americans quickly cashed in on this demand, appropriating and inventing the titles that glorified their status. A mortician was a "Doctor of Grief."[3]

1. Arthur Miller, *Death of a Salesman: Certain Private Conversations in Two Acts and a Requiem* (New York: The Viking Press, 1969), p. 138.

2. Robert W. Habenstein and William M. Lamers, *The History of American Funeral Directing* (Milwaukee: Bulfin Printers, Inc., 1955), p. 316; H. L. Mencken, *The American Language: An Inquiry into the Development of English in the United States,* 4th ed. rev. (New York: Alfred A. Knopf, 1916), pp. 287–88; Philippe Aries, *Western Attitudes toward Death from the Middle Ages to the Present* (Baltimore and London: The Johns Hopkins University Press, 1974), pp. 97–103; Stanley French, "The Cemetery as Cultural Institution: the Establishment of Mount Auburn and the 'Rural Cemetery' Movement," *American Quarterly* 26 (March 1971), pp. 37–59; Adolphus Strauch, *Spring Grove Cemetery* (Cincinnati: Robert Clarke & Co., 1869); Jessica Mitford, *The American Way of Death* (New York: Simon & Schuster, 1963); Geoffrey Goner, "The Pornography of Death," in *Death, Grief, and Mourning* (Garden City, N.Y.: Anchor Books, 1967), pp. 192–99.

3. Mencken, "Honorifics," *American Language*, pp. 271–84.

Historically, the middle class in America has defined itself in terms of three characteristics: acquired ability, social prestige, and a lifestyle approaching an individual's aspirations. Neither restrictions of income nor even differences between occupations have delimited the scope of the middle class in America. And it has been the breadth of that class which has struck observers who have compared it with middle classes elsewhere.

Being middle class in America has referred to a state of mind any person can adopt and make his own. It has not referred to a person's confined position in the social structure, a position delimited by common chances in the market and by preferred occupations. The popular imagination has so closely identified being middle class with pursuing the so-called American dream that "middle class" has come to be equated with a good chance for advancement, an expanding income, education, good citizenship—indeed, with democracy. Most middle-class Americans have convinced themselves that neither communism nor any other social system would, in current slang, give the "average working stiff" as great a "piece of the action" as does American society. No other social system, especially one in which the government makes a habit of distributing free goods, would give the individual the opportunity to "get ahead" on the basis of his personal capacity for enterprise, ambition, and the ability to serve others by winning their trust.

The middle-class American has traditionally rejected the idea that any classes and any permanent forms of privilege divide American society. On the one hand, he has believed that those ambitious individuals who take full advantage of their opportunities will be rewarded by society with a rising material standard of consumption. Stories of success, self-help, and self-confidence have pervaded the popular media; and many accounts have appeared to document the claim that the future holds for the middle-class American with positive attitudes both more fortunate circumstances and a higher standard of living. His opportunities for advancement are better than his parents', and his children's opportunities—especially with higher levels of education—will surpass his own. On the other hand, the middle-class American has believed that society must preserve obedience to the law, order, and conventions necessary for stable civilization. The ambitious individual must present himself as a good citizen, one who defends images of moral probity and ethical integrity, whose character and clean-cut appearance could be held up to youth, who respects religious values and affiliation, who condemns license and intolerance, and who bequeaths democratic freedoms to posterity.

The majority of Americans have aspired to belong to the "fortunate middle class" as the best of all possible alternatives in an imperfect world. Moreover, it has been significant that admission to this group has cut across all lines of social division: black and white, female and male, poor and rich, uneducated and educated, young and old, non-Protestant and Protestant. The enduring capacity of Americans with middle-class biases to ward off threatening values has been more than historical accident and luck. Yet, why middle-class attitudes have persisted in satisfying a basic need in American lives, and what that need is, remain unclear. In order to explain this phenomenon, the American historian must reach into the past and recover the original source of interest.

* * *

The word *career* derives from forms meaning "carry." The original definitions of *career* all referred to rapid and continuous action, movement, and procedure. For instance, an 1819 American edition of Samuel Johnson's eighteenth-century *Dictionary of the English Language* listed the following items: "1. The ground on which a race is run; the length of a course. 2. A course, a race. 3. Height of speed; swift motion. 4. Course of action; uninterrupted procedure." The most common usage of the word related to horse racing and falconry. As the nineteenth century progressed, however, the meaning of *career* took on a new dimension, cultural rather than physical, abstract rather than visual. The *Oxford English Dictionary* dated as 1803 the first example of the following usage: "A person's course or progress through life (or a distinct portion of life) so of a nation, party, etc. A profession affording opportunities of advancement." But it was not until midcentury that *Oxford* found an example of a person actively being told to "go and make a career for himself." The usage of the word was maturing. In American English by the late nineteenth century, to make the career meant to make a success, to become famous. The 1893 edition of the *Funk and Wagnalls* dictionary in America added the following definitions of *career* to the familiar ones: "1. A complete course or progress extending through the life or a portion of it, especially when abounding in remarkable actions or incidents, or when publicly conspicuous: said of persons, political parties, nations, etc. 2. A course of business activity, or enterprise: especially, a course of professional life or employment, that offers advancement or honor."

When speaking of occupational activities in the new usage of *career*, an individual no longer confined himself to the description of a random series of jobs, projects, or businesses which provided a livelihood. The individual could now speak of a larger and more absorbing experience—a career: a pre-established total pattern of organized professional activity, with upward movement through recognized preparatory stages, and advancement based on merit and bearing honor. By the late nineteenth century, *The Century Dictionary* and *Funk and Wagnalls* were acknowledging a new social concept, and they were citing examples of the new use of the word by such contemporary writers as Herbert Spencer and James Bryce.[4]

The new notion of career was striking for its totality and self-sufficiency. The new individual professional life had gained both an inward coherence and self-regulating standards that separated and defined it independently of the general community. The inner intensity of the new life oriented toward a career stood in contrast to that of the older learned professional life of the eighteenth and early nineteenth centuries. In the earlier period such external attributes of gentlemanly behavior as benevolence, duty, virtue, and manners circumscribed the professional experience. Competence, knowledge, and preparation were less important in evaluating the skills of the professional than were dedication to the community, sincerity, trust, permanence, honorable reputation, and righteous behavior. The qualifying credentials of the learned professional were honesty, decency, and civility. Hence, he did not think of a professional life in terms of ascending stages, each preparatory in training for the next, but as a series of good works or public projects, performed within a familiar and deferential society which heaped respectability on its first citizens.

4. The 1893 edition of *Funk and Wagnalls*, for instance, cited the following example from Bryce: " 'It is easier for women to find a *career* [in America], to obtain remunerative work of an intellectual as of a commercial or mechanical kind, than in any part of Europe,' *American Commonwealth* vol. II, Ch. 105, p. 585 [MACM, '88]".

In order to witness how the idea of community held the more specialized idea of career at bay, one need only turn to a well-known example of mobility in the eighteenth century, Ben Franklin. Despite his many occupations—printer, publicist, postmaster, scientist, diplomat, statesman—Franklin thought of his professional activities as a linear series of projects and good works. The end was the welfare of the public, which included Franklin's own "modest" return of Affluence, Reputation, and Felicity. In Franklin's mind, no structured or graduated career pattern, culminating in a senior professional stage associated with the height of accomplishment, knowledge, maturity, and recognition imposed itself on his life. Significantly, he began the *Autobiography* by writing his own epitaph, which revealed the man's self-identity. Who was Ben Franklin? For posterity he wished to project the image of his original vocation—printer. Here had lived the dutiful and common servant of the local community. Moreover, Franklin did not conclude the *Autobiography* by describing his acclaimed successes as a cosmopolitan scientist, diplomat, and statesman. He recounted the many and random community improvement projects in which he participated and took pride. The *Autobiography* was intended to advise youth, and Franklin's improvement projects testified to both a successful public life and a good character.[5]

A review of the ministry, the most admired and sought after of the learned professions, documents the changes that became noticeable within the first generation of the nineteenth century. By the 1820s, the previous century's notion of "permanency" in the ministry had been seriously eroded in the expanding national society. The Lord's "calling" had committed His servant to perform his duties in a single congregation and community for a lifetime. But the meaning of an organic ministry, slowly maturing in intimate and familiar surroundings in which social order was paramount, was disappearing.[6] The profession of the ministry had entered a com-

5. See John William Ward, " 'Who was Benjamin Franklin?'," *The American Scholar* 32 (Autumn 1963): pp. 541–53. On Franklin as autobiographer see Robert F. Sayre, *The Examined Self: Benjamin Franklin, Henry Adams, Henry James* (Princeton, N.J.: Princeton University Press, 1964), pp. 3–43; Daniel B. Shea, Jr., *Spiritual Autobiography in Early America* (Princeton, N.J.: Princeton University Press, 1968), pp. 234–48.

6. See Daniel H. Calhoun, *Professional Lives in America: Structure and Aspiration, 1750–1850* (Cambridge, Mass.: Harvard University Press, 1965), pp. 88–177.

petitive society in which unrestrained individual self-determination undermined traditional lifestyles. No longer did Americans feel the restrictions imposed by a "calling" in which dependent man subordinated himself to the summons of an autonomous God who had determined the station in which every man could work most diligently for the public good and avoid idleness.[7]

Individual choice in a "calling" had never really been a choice at all. Few vocational alternatives presented themselves in a colonial society in which most people farmed. The professional class committed its children at a young age to early apprenticeships or college education, which most people, including the youth concerned, presumed would make entrance into the occupation selected by the parent practically irreversible. However, the fluid environment of the nineteenth century made it possible for an ambitious young man with a will of his own to decline God's invitation in a calling, put his own feelings before social duty, and find easier access than ever before to a growing array of professions, including a number of new semi-public professions. A former minister himself, Emerson illustrated the case. With considerable wit and personal dismay, he described "[The New Professions:] The phrenologist; the railroad man; the landscape gardener; the lecturer; the sorcerer, rapper, mesmeriser, medium; the daguerreotypist. [Proposed:] The Naturalist, and the Social Undertaker."[8]

7. The classic source for the definition of "calling" was William Perkins, "A treatise of the Vocations or Callings of Men with the Sorts and Kinds of Them and the Right Use Thereof," The Works of . . . Mr. William Perkins, 3 vols. (London: John Legatt, 1626), 1:pp. 747–79. On the importance of the concept in America, see J. E. Crowley, This Sheba, Self: The Conceptualization of Economic Life in Eighteenth-Century America (Baltimore and London: The Johns Hopkins University Press), pp. 50–75; Stephen Foster, Their Solitary Way: The Puritan Social Ethic in the First Century of Settlement in New England (New Haven, Conn., and London: Yale University Press, 1971), pp. 99–103; Edmund S. Morgan, The Puritan Family: Religion and Domestic Relations in Seventeenth-Century New England, rev. (New York: Harper & Row, Publishers, 1966), pp. 66–79; James Axtell, The School Upon a Hill: Education and Society in Colonial New England (New Haven, Conn., and London: Yale University Press, 1971), pp. 100–101; T. H. Breen, The Character of the Good Ruler: A Study of Puritan Political Ideas in New England, 1630–1730 (New York: W. W. Norton & Company, 1974), pp. 6–7. See also Michael Walzer, The Revolution of the Saints: A Study in the Origins of Radical Politics (New York: Atheneum, 1969), pp. 210–19.

8. Ralph Waldo Emerson Journals, 8: p. 574.

Confronted by both irreverence and competition, a traditional profession like the ministry came under intense pressures to approve of some internal changes. In part, the sociology of the profession played a role. Supported by scholarships and professional charity, a first generation of poor boys from the New England hills, displaced from family farms, began entering the ministry in the first quarter of the nineteenth century.[9] And these men began rejecting the social intimacy and family dominance of the older guild. There was an unprecedented element of individual effort and even drudgery in the new vision, which the older generation tended to deplore as corrupt, degenerate, and materialistic. New expectations displayed themselves in a new style. In a social environment now offering vocational alternatives, young men could criticize, calculate, envision a ladder of advancement, and act with some measure of impunity toward their less flexible elders. Above all, young men could begin thinking in vertical rather than horizontal imagery. They meant, very literally, to move *up* and away.

The new minister thought more in terms of a career which he actively made than a "calling" into which he had been summoned. Lacking either a sense of permanency or commitment to a single congregation, the ambitious young minister now could express his concern with a rising salary. He could attend to the outward trappings of growing success, and the need to please laymen who were as ambitious, irritable, and status-conscious as himself. In the nineteenth-century world of movement, the social motives of the minister did not always differ greatly from the social motives of his congregation. Far from setting an elevated moral example of clerical detachment, the minister often appeared to be an entrepreneur, privately negotiating the contractual terms of a successful career as he moved upward from congregation to congregation. In the course of an individual's career, every congregation now became a conquest, a stepping-stone to the next challenge.

9. See David F. Allmendinger, Jr., *Paupers and Scholars: The Transformation of Student Life in Nineteenth-Century New England* (New York: St. Martin's Press, 1975), pp. 64–78; Lois Kimball Mathews, *The Expansion of New England: The Spread of New England Settlement and Institutions to the Mississippi River, 1620–1865* (Boston and New York: Houghton Mifflin Company, 1909), pp. 139ff. Refer to the implications for crowding in New England in Kenneth Lockridge, "Land Population and the Evolution of New England Society," Chapter 1, 11, 12.

The new professional man often had nowhere to return, nothing to fall back upon except his own self-reliance and his own will. He balked at "inability," he deplored enervation and drift, he expected "commitment," and he accentuated "decision." He respected the trained capacity of his own mind to organize and control his surroundings. He believed in mental concentration and the spontaneous release of emotional energy.[10] He no longer heard William Perkins's classic definition of a calling, "a certain kind of life, ordained and imposed on man by God for the common good."[11] Describing the events of the twenty years following 1820, Emerson recalled that,

> there was a new consciousness. . . . The young men were born with knives in their brain, a tendency to introversion, self-dissection, anatomizing of motives. . . . The key to the period appeared to be that the mind had become aware of itself. . . . It is the age of severance, of dissociation, of freedom, of analysis, of detachment. Every man for himself. . . . People grow philosophical about native land and parents and relations. There is an universal resistance to ties and ligaments once supposed essential to civil society.[12]

Perhaps close to thirty years old when he entered a profession, after having tasted life and rejected a series of pursuits; mature, competitive, and calculating about his prospects, believing in his expectations—the new type of professional man personally struggled to create his career, he did not inherit it. He rejected the social forms and the public conviviality associated with the shallow intellect of the older learned professions.

A profession no longer circumscribed a man, confining him to a preestablished station in life, including a calling toward which sympathetic parents guided him. A man now actively chose his profession, perhaps in defiance of parents and friends. The world of movement and expectation focused on the spirited individual, his specialized nature, his self-discipline, and the continuity of his rise

10. See Perry Miller, *The Life of the Mind in America: From the Revolution to the Civil War* (New York: Harcourt Brace & World, 1965), pp. 3–95.

11. Perkins, *Works*, 1: p. 750.

12. "Life and Letters in New England," in *The Complete Works of Ralph Waldo Emerson*, 12 vols. (Boston: Houghton Mifflin Company, 1903–4), 10, *Lectures and Biographical Sketches*, 326–27, 329.

rather than his humility, his self-subordination to the social order, and his dependence upon God's will. In the steps of a career, an individual progressively discovered his potential, and his sense of worldly power rose accordingly.

SARA M. EVANS AND HARRY C. BOYTE

Free Spaces

DEMOCRATIC HERITAGE OF THE AMERICAN REVOLUTION

America's founders were divided. For most, drawing on biblical and republican traditions, the concepts of participation and civic virtue were central—though very few indeed imagined "citizens" as including women, slaves, or the very poor. Private property, for instance, was rarely seen as an end in itself. Even our archetypical entrepreneur, Benjamin Franklin, held that "property" is simply "the creature of Society . . . subject to the calls of that Society." The independence which small amounts of property—small farms, for example, or small stores or artisanal skills—allowed was important in this view, in fact, because it thereby freed citizens to participate in the public life of the self-governing community, or commonwealth.

Such participation was seen as the foundation of a free society— indeed, the only way in which skills of active public life, values of communal responsibility, and consciousness of the broader common good or commonwealth could be renewed and sustained. Thus, Thomas Jefferson contrasted the Europeans, who he claimed "have divided their nations into two classes, wolves and sheep," with the Indians. Groups like the Iroquois, he believed, furnished a model for self-government because of their reliance on the moral force of community opinion instead of government action to control

Sara M. Evans and Harry C. Boyte, excerpted from *Free Spaces: The Sources of Democratic Change in America* (New York: Harper & Row, 1986), pp. 6, 7, 11–13, 15–20.

crime and other social problems: "Controls are their manners and the moral sense of right and wrong." From such perspectives, great extremes of wealth or speculative sale of property, like the squandering of the means of one's independence, were seen in the most unfavorable light because of the clear danger that the community might be eroded or disrupted. The values prized included service to the community, frugality, hard work, independence, and self-restraint. Their opposites—extravagance, self-indulgence, idleness, and so forth—had no place in a virtuous and just republic.

Tied to the principles of this republican political tradition, which can be traced back to classic Greek and Roman thought, Americans repeatedly turned to apocalyptic themes, largely inherited from the Bible, to describe their mission in a "new world" and to reinforce their sense of communal obligation. For settlers naming communities Salem or Shiloh, Canaan, Jerusalem, Nazareth, Bethlehem, Eden, and Paradise, the new continent represented the "promised land," a chance to create a Kingdom of God on earth. Immigrants readily identified themselves as being like the Hebrew children, fleeing corrupt and unjust societies in the Old World, beginning again as "chosen people" in the new. "The Lord will be our God and delight to dwell among us, as His own people, and . . . command a blessing upon us in all our ways," said John Winthrop aboard the *Arbella* in 1630. Biblically oriented interweaving of religious and political themes has, especially, been characteristic of populist and democratic endeavors. The preachers and pamphleteers of the 1740s and 1750s decried "selfishness and avarice" and called for a "vital communion of kindred spirits" against the new "Lords of Mammon." And their populist sentiments laid powerful groundwork for the democratic spirit of the Revolutionary period.

For all the potency of American democratic traditions, certain flaws are unmistakable and they weakened the very movements those traditions nourished. At times, such flaws also furnished material for subsequent democratic protest, as groups excluded or marginalized by the original terms of citizenship and democracy came to point out the chasm between myth and reality.

* * *

"Democracy" suggested New England town meetings, or more informally, decision-making in religious congregations or the discussion of local affairs in voluntary groups. Government was seen, in these terms, not as the primary arena of democracy but, more authentically, as the instrument of citizens joined together. Even for popular protest movements, political engagement was seen as an expression of the values and activities of community life, not as an end in itself. Thus, for instance, the nineteenth-century Knights of Labor, a movement of laboring men and women protesting the rise of giant trusts and cartels and their threat to artisan traditions, "looked to self-organized society—not to the individual and not to the state—as the redeemer of their American dream," as labor historian Leon Fink put it. "Neither ultimate antagonist nor source of salvation, the state represented a mediator in the conflict between the civil forces of democracy and its enemies."

But the developments of the late nineteenth and early twentieth centuries—technological change, urbanization, industrialization, waves of immigration, the growth of new professions and scientific knowledge applied to social life—radically changed the very texture of life in America. In enormous cities, one could scarcely know one's neighbors, much less those down the street or on the other side of the tracks. Waves of immigrants brought new customs, traditions, and languages. Communications technologies like the railroad, telegraph, and mass newspaper began to shatter the boundaries of the local community; technologies at work and in professions sharply eroded older patterns of craft and community tradition. Civic involvement in town meetings and voluntary groups became less and less the model of "democracy." In its place emerged corrupt big-city political machines and the manipulation of a mass electorate by techniques of public relations and sloganeering. Modernity, as Lippmann observed, "had upset the old life on the prairies, made new demands upon democracy, introduced specialization and science, had destroyed village loyalties . . . and created the impersonal relationships of the modern world."

Middle-class reformers, meanwhile, adapted to the changes with alacrity—but in ways that further eclipsed any notion of small-scale, participatory, and community-based democracy. According to the Progressive thinkers like Lippmann, *New Republic* editor Herbert Croly, Theodore Roosevelt, and others in the early twentieth century, the erosion of local community ties and a sense of civic responsibility was more than compensated for by possibilities for broader involvement. Local community life had had positive features, sustaining values like participation, egalitarianism, and a sense of civic involvement. But the new changes had great potential, in the view of such observers, to bring in the place of small communities a far better great community that would dissolve all differences of nationality, ethnicity, religion, and region into a "melting pot." Thus, Herbert Croly argued that "the responsibility and loyalty which the citizens of a democratic nation must feel one towards another is comprehensive and unmitigable." The communal feeling of small-town life would be re-created by the "loyal realization of a comprehensive democratic social ideal." And the new techniques of science and the professions could be applied to solve age-old problems and social ills. As Frederick Taylor, pioneer in scientific management techniques in the world of business, put it: "The same principles can be applied with equal force to all social activities."

Progressives—and those who followed in their tradition, like many liberal reformers of the New Deal—continued to advocate direct involvement of citizens in decision-making processes. But the locus of civic involvement shifted from voluntary association and community activity to government itself. Through various public agencies and electoral reforms—regulatory commissions, civil service reform, nonpartisan local elections, direct election of senators, referenda and initiative, and the like—citizens would shape the "great community" of the country. Women's suffrage, in this understanding, would be democracy's greatest realization. And democracy itself, in Croly's words, no longer meant that citizens "assemble after the manner of a New England town-meeting" since there existed "abundant opportunities of communications and consultation without any meeting. . . . The active citizenship of the country meets every morning and evening and discusses the affairs of the nation with the newspaper as an impersonal interlocutor."

But the reality proved to be radically different. Aside from the new, rising middle class of professionals and white-collar workers in large private and public bureaucracies, most Americans continued to identify with their locales, their traditions, their heritages and cultures. But their worlds seemed increasingly shaped by distant forces over which they had no control whatsoever. Corner grocers gave way to chain stores; local decisions over education were removed to state or national bureaucracies; ways of doing things—from child-rearing to family home remedies—that had been passed down for generations were replaced by "expert advice" from professionals who claimed specialized knowledge.

* * *

Thus, on the face of it, the emergence of democratic movements is a puzzle—and, undoubtedly, the exception. Popular movements, it has now been widely enough documented, normally arise in defense of rights or ways of life that a changing world threatens to destroy. Examples of defensive and limited protests abound, from the nativist movements of the nineteenth century to the Ku Klux Klan and the White Citizens Council of the 1960s, from the National Union for Social Justice of the 1930s to fights against "dangerous books" in the present. Backward-looking in their central construction, such protests are in a basic sense survival efforts, aimed at returning things to "the way they were" at best, and at the least retaining whatever elements of identity, culture, and place that can be salvaged.

Whatever the diminished sense of possibility afflicting modern thought, however, ordinary men and women have also found the courage and spirit again and again to imagine the possibility of an active, participatory democracy—to seek something radically *different*, rather than simply a "bigger piece of the pie" or a return to the way things were. From nineteenth-century farmers' populist struggles and women's fight for citizenship and suffrage to modern movements like the rise of the CIO in the 1930s, the southern civil rights struggle and the youth movement in the 1960s, and the neighborhood and citizen movements in the 1970s and 1980s, Americans have again and again articulated a broad and inclusive vision of direct participation and civic virtue that renews and enriches earlier conceptions of democracy. With varying degrees of success they have fashioned the practical skills and organizational means to seek to realize their aspirations.

The most radical challenges to conventional American politics have drawn their vocabulary and power from core issues remembered from the past. Thus, Sarah Grimké replied to a group of ministers who questioned her right as a woman to speak publicly against slavery in the 1830s, "How monstrous, how anti-Christian is the doctrine that woman is to be dependent on man! Where in all the sacred Scriptures is this taught? This doctrine of dependence upon man is utterly at variance with the doctrine of the Bible." Black Americans, for whom the notion of America as the promised land contained no small irony, inverted the imagery: in black song and religion, America was like Egypt, the land of bondage, if also like Canaan-in-potential—someday to be the land of milk and honey. Similarly, Eugene Debs, visionary spokesman for the American Socialist Party in its halcyon days of the early twentieth century, built his denunciations of corporate greed and business concentration on "the eighteenth century Revolutionary heritage," according to his biographer, Nicholas Salvatore, "the concept that the government will rest upon the intelligence and virtue of the people." Martin Luther King, Jr., described the civil rights movement as "bringing the entire nation back to the great wells of democracy that were dug deep by the founding fathers."

To understand the inner life of democratic movements, one must rethink such traditional categories as "politics," "private life," "public activity," "reaction," and "progress." Only then can we hope to fathom how people draw upon their past for strength, create out of traditions—which may seem on their face simply to reinforce the status quo—new visions of the future, gain out of the experiences of their daily lives new public skills and a broader sense of hope and possibility.

The central argument of this book is that particular sorts of public places in the community, what we call free spaces, are the environments in which people are able to learn a new self-respect, a deeper and more assertive group identity, public skills, and values of cooperation and civic virtue. Put simply, free spaces are settings between private lives and large-scale institutions where ordinary citizens can act with dignity, independence, and vision. These are, in the main, voluntary forms of association with a relatively open and participatory character—many religious organizations, clubs, self-help and mutual aid societies, reform groups, neighborhood, civic, and ethnic groups, and a host of other associations grounded in the fabric of community life. The sustained public vitality and egalitarianism of free spaces are strikingly unlike the "public" face of reactionary or backward-looking protests. Democratic action depends upon these free spaces, where people experience a schooling in citizenship and learn a vision of the common good in the course of struggling for change.[1]

Free spaces are never a pure phenomenon. In the real world, they are always complex, shifting, and dynamic—partial in their freedom and democratic participation, marked by parochialism of class, gender, race, and other biases of the groups which maintain them. There are no easy or simple ways to sustain experiences of democratic participation and values of civic virtue in the heart of broader environments that undermine them and demand, at least on the face of it, very different sorts of values. Democratic movements have had varying degrees of success in sustaining themselves, in spreading their values, symbols, and ideas to larger audiences, in changing the world. They have in different ways and with different outcomes addressed issues such as the bureaucratic state, the problem of size in organization, the role of experts, the power of conventional media. They have sought to hold leaders accountable through a variety of measures—from direct election and recall to

1. In more theoretical terms, a focus on the free spaces at the heart of democratic movements aids in the resolution of polarities that have long and bitterly divided modern observers and critics—expressive individualism versus ties of community; modernity versus tradition; public and private values, and so forth—by highlighting the living environments where people draw upon both "oppositions" to create new experiments. For earlier discussions of the concept of free space, see Harry C. Boyte, "The Textile Industry: Keel of Southern Industrialization," *Radical America* (March–April 1972); Sara M. Evans, *Personal Politics: The Roots of Women's Liberation in the Civil Rights Movement and the New Left* (New York: Knopf, 1979); Harry C. Boyte, "Populism and the Left," *Democracy* 1 (April 1981):pp. 53–66, and Sara M. Evans and Harry C. Boyte, "Schools for Action: Radical Uses of Social Space," *Democracy* 2 (Fall 1982):pp. 55–65. Though we have developed the concept in our explorations of American social movements, it clearly has application to other cultural and social settings. For interesting applications of the idea to other societies, see, for instance, Craig Calhoun, "Class, Place and Industrial Revolution," in N. Thrift and P. Williams, eds., *The Making of Urban Society: Historical Essays on Class Formation and Place* (London: Routledge & Kegan Paul, 1985); Allen Isaacman et al., " 'Cotton Is the Mother of Poverty': Peasant Resistance to Forced Cotton Production in Mozambique, 1938–1961," *The International Journal of African Historical Studies* 13 (1980); Allen Isaacman and Barbara Isaacman, *Mozambique: From Colonialism to Revolution, 1900–1982* (Hampshire, England: Gower, 1983); Ronald Aminzade, *Class, Politics and Early Industrial Capitalism: A Study of Mid-Nineteenth-Century Toulouse, France* (Albany: State University of New York Press, 1981).

frequent turnover in top leadership, and widespread dissemination of information—or they have failed to develop such measures. And they have drawn upon and transformed threads in peoples' cultures and traditions, weaving ideas into new sets of values, beliefs and interpretations of the world, codes of behavior, and visions of the future. Together, these new elements make up, in democratic movements, basic alternatives to the conventional ways of the world, what might be called "movement cultures," that suggest a different way of living.

Free spaces are the foundations for such movement countercultures. And for all their variations, free spaces have certain common features, observable in movements varying widely in time, aims, composition, and social environment. They are defined by their roots in community, the dense, rich networks of daily life; by their autonomy; and by their public or quasi-public character as participatory environments which nurture values associated with citizenship and a vision of the common good. In a full way, the spirit, dynamics, and character of free spaces can only be understood in the concrete-

---

We have used the terms "space" and "social space" to suggest the lived, daily character of those networks and relationships that form the primary base of social movements. The concept of social space grows from traditions of social geography, ethnology, and phenomenology. It suggests strongly an "objective," physical dimension—the ways in which places are organized and connected, fragmented, and so forth; and a subjective dimension, space as understood, perceived, and lived—what seems customary, familiar, part of daily experience. For discussions of the "socially constructed" nature of physical reality, see for instance Edward Hall, *The Hidden Dimension* (New York: Doubleday, 1966), and Anne Buttimer, "Social Space in Interdisciplinary Perspective," in John Gabree, ed., *Surviving the City* (New York: Ballantine Books, 1973). We stress, in addition to the communal nature of free space, the importance of voluntary organizational forms through which people can learn public skills and values and take sustained action over time. But it should be noted that informal, local relations themselves normally have an important element of independence from centers of power that can sustain brief forms of resistance. As Anthony Leeds put it, "The amorphousness, multiplicity and kaleidoscopic quality of the organization of localities . . . are virtually impossible to legislate for (or against) or to control by uniform sets of sanctions. . . . In this independence and its social and ecological bases is found a locus of power for cooperation with—but especially for resistance against the encroachments of—the supralocal institutions." "Locality Power in Relation to Supralocal Institutions," in Aidan Southall, ed., *Urban Anthropology: Crosscultural Studies of Urbanization* (New York: Oxford University Press, 1973), pp. 15–42.

ness of particular stories, where people gain new skills, a new sense of possibility, and a broadened understanding of whom "the people" include.

MARTIN LUTHER KING, JR.

Letter from Birmingham Jail

My dear fellow clergymen:

While confined here in the Birmingham city jail, I came across your recent statement calling my present activities "unwise and untimely." Seldom do I pause to answer criticism of my work and ideas. If I sought to answer all the criticisms that cross my desk, my secretaries would have little time for anything other than such correspondence in the course of the day, and I would have no time for constructive work. But since I feel that you are men of genuine good will and that your criticisms are sincerely set forth, I want to try to answer your statement in what I hope will be patient and reasonable terms.

I think I should indicate why I am here in Birmingham, since you have been influenced by the view which argues against "outsiders coming in." I have the honor of serving as president of the Southern Christian Leadership Conference, an organization operating in every southern state, with headquarters in Atlanta, Georgia. We have some eighty-five affiliated organizations across the South, and one of them is the Alabama Christian Movement for Human Rights. Frequently we share staff, educational and financial resources with our affiliates. Several months ago the affiliate here in Birmingham asked us to be on call to engage in a nonviolent direct-action program if such were deemed necessary. We readily consented, and when the hour came we lived up to our promise. So I,

Martin Luther King, Jr., excerpted from "Letter from Birmingham Jail," in *Why We Can't Wait* (New York: Harper & Row, 1963), pp. 77–100. Copyright © 1963 by Martin Luther King, Jr. Reprinted by permission of Harper & Row, Publishers.

along with several members of my staff, am here because I was invited here. I am here because I have organizational ties here.

But more basically, I am in Birmingham because injustice is here. Just as the prophets of the eighth century B.C. left their villages and carried their "thus saith the Lord" far beyond the boundaries of their home towns, and just as the Apostle Paul left his village of Tarsus and carried the gospel of Jesus Christ to the far corners of the Greco-Roman world, so am I compelled to carry the gospel of freedom beyond my own home town. Like Paul, I must constantly respond to the Macedonian call for aid.

Moreover, I am cognizant of the interrelatedness of all communities and states. I cannot sit idly by in Atlanta and not be concerned about what happens in Birmingham. Injustice anywhere is a threat to justice everywhere. We are caught in an inescapable network of mutuality, tied in a single garment of destiny. Whatever affects one directly, affects all indirectly. Never again can we afford to live with the narrow, provincial "outside agitator" idea. Anyone who lives inside the United States can never be considered an outsider anywhere within its bounds.

You deplore the demonstrations taking place in Birmingham. But your statement, I am sorry to say, fails to express a similar concern for the conditions that brought about the demonstrations. I am sure that none of you would want to rest content with the superficial kind of social analysis that deals merely with effects and does not grapple with underlying causes. It is unfortunate that demonstrations are taking place in Birmingham, but it is even more unfortunate that the city's white power structure left the Negro community with no alternative.

In any nonviolent campaign there are four basic steps: collection of the facts to determine whether injustices exist; negotiation; self-purification; and direct action. We have gone through all these steps in Birmingham. There can be no gainsaying the fact that racial injustice engulfs this community. Birmingham is probably the most thoroughly segregated city in the United States. Its ugly record of brutality is widely known. Negroes have experienced grossly unjust treatment in the courts. There have been more unsolved bombings of Negro homes and churches in Birmingham than in any other city in the nation. These are the hard, brutal facts of the case. On the basis of these conditions, Negro leaders sought to negotiate with the city fathers. But the latter consistently refused to engage in good-faith negotiation.

* * *

You may well ask: "Why direct action? Why sit-ins, marches and so forth? Isn't negotiation a better path?" You are quite right in calling for negotiation. Indeed, this is the very purpose of direct action. Nonviolent direct action seeks to create such a crisis and foster such a tension that a community which has constantly refused to negotiate is forced to confront the issue. It seeks so to dramatize the issue that it can no longer be ignored. My citing the creation of tension as part of the work of the nonviolent-resister may sound rather shocking. But, I must confess that I am not afraid of the word "tension." I have earnestly opposed violent tension, but there is a type of constructive, nonviolent tension which is necessary for growth. Just as Socrates felt that it was necessary to create a tension in the mind so that individuals could rise from the bondage of myths and half-truths to the unfettered realm of creative analysis and objective appraisal, so must we see the need for nonviolent gadflies to create the kind of tension in society that will help men rise from the dark depths of prejudice and racism to the majestic heights of understanding and brotherhood.

The purpose of our direct-action program is to create a situation so crisis-packed that it will inevitably open the door to negotiation. I therefore concur with you in your call for negotiation. Too long has our beloved Southland been bogged down in a tragic effort to live in monologue rather than dialogue.

One of the basic points in your statement is that the action that I and my associates have taken in Birmingham is untimely. Some have asked: "Why didn't you give the new city administration time to act?" The only answer that I can give to this query is that the new Birmingham administration must be prodded about as much as the outgoing one, before it will act. We are sadly mistaken if we feel that the election of Albert Boutwell as mayor will bring the millennium to Birmingham. While Mr. Boutwell is a much more gentle person than Mr. Connor, they are both segregationists, dedicated to maintenance of the status quo. I have hope that Mr. Boutwell will be reasonable enough to see the futility of massive resistance to desegregation. But he will not see this without pressure from devotees of civil rights. My friends, I must say to you that we have not made a single gain in civil rights without determined legal and nonviolent pressure. Lamentably, it is an historical fact that privileged groups seldom give up their privileges voluntarily. Individuals may see the moral light and voluntarily give up their unjust posture; but, as Reinhold Niebuhr has reminded us, groups tend to be more immoral than individuals.

We know through painful experience that freedom is never voluntarily given by the oppressor; it must be demanded by the oppressed. Frankly, I have yet to engage in a direct-action campaign that was "well timed" in the view of those who have not suffered unduly from the disease of segregation. For years now I have heard the word "Wait!" It rings in the ear of every Negro with piercing familiarity. This "Wait" has almost always meant "Never." We must come to see, with one of our distinguished jurists, that "justice too long delayed is justice denied."

We have waited for more than 340 years for our constitutional and God-given rights. The nations of Asia and Africa are moving with jetlike speed toward gaining political independence, but we still creep at horse-and-buggy pace toward gaining a cup of coffee at a lunch counter. Perhaps it is easy for those who have never felt the stinging darts of segregation to say, "Wait." But when you have seen vicious mobs lynch your mothers and fathers at will and drown your sisters and brothers at whim; when you have seen hate-filled policemen curse, kick and even kill your black brothers and sisters; when you see the vast majority of your twenty million Negro brothers smothering in an airtight cage of poverty in the midst of an affluent society; when you suddenly find your tongue twisted and your speech stammering as you seek to explain to your six-year-old daughter why she can't go to the public amusement park that has just been advertised on television, and see tears welling up in her eyes when she is told that Funtown is closed to colored children, and see ominous clouds of inferiority beginning to form in her little mental sky, and see her beginning to distort her personality by developing an unconscious bitterness toward white people; when you have to concoct an answer for a five-year-old son who is asking: "Daddy, why do white people treat colored people so mean?"; when you take a cross-country drive and find it necessary to sleep night after night in the uncomfortable corners of your automobile because no motel will accept you; when you are humiliated day in and day out by nagging signs reading "white" and "colored"; when your first name becomes "nigger," and your middle name becomes "boy" (however old you are) and your last name becomes "John," and your wife and mother are never given the respected title "Mrs."; when you are harried by day and haunted by night by the fact that you are a Negro, living constantly at tiptoe stance, never quite knowing what to expect next, and are plagued with inner fears and outer resentments; when you are forever fighting a degenerating sense of "nobodiness"—then you will understand why we find it difficult to wait. There comes a time when the cup of endurance runs over, and men are no longer willing to be plunged into the abyss of despair. I hope, sirs, you can understand our legitimate and unavoidable impatience.

You express a great deal of anxiety over our willingness to break laws. This is certainly a legitimate concern. Since we so diligently urge people to obey the Supreme Court's decision of 1954 outlawing segregation in the public schools, at first glance it may seem rather paradoxical for us consciously to break laws. One may well ask: "How can you advocate breaking some laws and obeying others?" The answer lies in the fact that there are two types of laws: just and unjust. I would be the first to advocate obeying just laws. One has not only a legal but a moral responsibility to disobey unjust laws. I would agree with St. Augustine that "an unjust law is no law at all."

Now, what is the difference between the two? How does one determine whether a law is just or unjust? A just law is a man-made code that squares with the moral law or the law of God. An unjust law is a code that is out of harmony with the moral law. To put it in the terms of St. Thomas Aquinas: An unjust law is a human law that is not rooted in eternal law and natural law. Any law that uplifts human personality is just. Any law that degrades human personality is unjust. All segregation statutes are unjust because segregation distorts the soul and damages the personality. It gives the segregator a false sense of superiority and the segregated a false sense of inferiority. Segregation, to use the terminology of the Jewish philosopher Martin Buber, substitutes an "I-it" relationship for an "I-thou" relationship and ends up relegating persons to the status of things. Hence segregation is not only politically, economically and sociologically unsound, it is morally wrong and sinful. Paul Tillich has said that sin is separation. Is not segregation an existential expression of man's tragic separation, his awful estrangement, his terrible sinfulness? Thus it is that I can urge men to obey the 1954 decision of the Supreme Court, for it is morally right; and I can urge them to disobey segregation ordinances, for they are morally wrong.

Let us consider a more concrete example of just and unjust laws. An unjust law is a code that a numerical or power majority group compels a minority group to obey but does not make binding on itself. This is *difference* made legal. By the same token, a just law is a code that a majority compels a minority to follow and that it is willing to follow itself. This is *sameness* made legal.

Let me give another explanation. A law is unjust if it is inflicted on a minority, that, as a result of being denied the right to vote, had no part in enacting or devising the law. Who can say that the legislature of Alabama which set up the state's segregation laws was democratically elected? Throughout Alabama all sorts of devious methods are used to prevent Negroes from becoming registered voters, and there are some counties in which, even though Negroes constitute a majority of the population, not a single Negro is registered. Can any law enacted under such circumstances be considered democratically structured?

Sometimes a law is just on its face and unjust in its application. For instance, I have been arrested on a charge of parading without a permit. Now, there is nothing wrong in having an ordinance which requires a permit for a parade. But such an ordinance becomes unjust when it is used to maintain segregation and to deny citizens the First-Amendment privilege of peaceful assembly and protest.

I hope you are able to see the distinction I am trying to point out. In no sense do I advocate evading or defying the law, as would the rabid segregationist. That would lead to anarchy. One who breaks an unjust law that conscience tells him is unjust, and who willingly accepts the penalty of imprisonment in order to arouse the conscience of the community over its injustice, is in reality expressing the highest respect for law.

Of course, there is nothing new about this kind of civil disobedience. It was evidenced sublimely in the refusal of Nebuchadnezzar, on the ground that a higher moral law was at stake. It was practiced superbly by the early Christians, who were willing to face hungry lions and the excruciating pain of chopping blocks rather than submit to certain unjust laws of the Roman Empire. To a degree, academic freedom is a reality today because Socrates practiced civil disobedience. In our own nation, the Boston Tea Party represented a massive act of civil disobedience.

We should never forget that everything Adolf Hitler did in Germany was "legal" and everything the Hungarian freedom fighters did in Hungary was "illegal." It was "illegal" to aid and comfort a Jew in Hitler's Germany. Even so, I am sure that, had I lived in Germany at the time, I would have aided and comforted my Jewish brothers. If today I lived in a Communist country where certain principles dear to the Christian faith are suppressed, I would openly advocate disobeying that country's antireligious laws.

I must make two honest confessions to you, my Christian and Jewish brothers. First, I must confess that over the past few years I have been gravely disappointed with the white moderate. I have almost reached the regrettable conclusion that the Negro's great stumbling block in his stride toward freedom is not the White Citizen's Councilor or the Ku Klux Klanner, but the white moderate, who is more devoted to "order" than to justice; who prefers a negative peace which is the absence of tension to a positive peace which is the presence of justice; who constantly says: "I agree with you in the goal you seek, but I cannot agree with your methods of direct action"; who paternalistically believes he can set the timetable for another man's freedom; who lives by a mythical concept of time and who constantly advises the Negro to wait for a "more convenient season." Shallow understanding from people of good will is more frustrating than absolute misunderstanding from people of ill will. Lukewarm acceptance is much more bewildering than outright rejection.

I had hoped that the white moderate would understand that law and order exist for the purpose of establishing justice and that when they fail in this purpose they become the dangerously structured dams that block the flow of social progress. I had hoped that the white moderate would understand that the present tension in the South is a necessary phase of the transition from an obnoxious negative peace, in which the Negro passively accepted his unjust plight, to a substantive and positive peace, in which all men will respect the dignity and worth of human personality. Actually, we who engage in nonviolent direct action are not the creators of tension. We merely bring to the surface the hidden tension that is already alive. We bring it out in the open, where it can be seen and dealt with. Like a boil that can never be cured so long as it is covered up but must be opened with all its ugliness to the natural medicines of air and light, injustice must be exposed, with all the tension its exposure creates, to the light of human conscience and the air of national opinion before it can be cured.

In your statement you assert that our actions, even though peaceful, must be condemned because they precipitate violence. But is this a logical assertion? Isn't this like condemning a robbed man because his possession of money precipitated the evil act of robbery? Isn't this like condemning Socrates because his unswerving commitment to truth and his philosophical inquiries precipitated the act by the misguided populace in which they made him drink hemlock? Isn't this like condemning Jesus because his unique God-consciousness and never-ceasing devotion to God's will precipitated the evil act of crucifixion? We must come to see that, as the federal courts have consistently affirmed, it is wrong to urge an individual to cease his efforts to gain his basic constitutional rights because the quest may precipitate violence. Society must protect the robbed and punish the robber.

* * *

You speak of our activity in Birmingham as extreme. At first I was rather disappointed that fellow clergymen would see my nonviolent efforts as those of an extremist. I began thinking about the fact that I stand in the middle of two opposing forces in the Negro community. One is a force of complacency, made up in part of Negroes who, as a result of long years of oppression, are so drained of self-respect and a sense of "somebodiness" that they have adjusted to segregation; and in part of a few middle-class Negroes who, because of a degree of academic and economic security and because in some ways they profit by segregation, have become insensitive to the problems of the masses. The other force is one of bitterness and hatred, and it comes perilously close to advocating violence. It is expressed in the various black nationalist groups that are springing up across the nation, the largest and best-known being Elijah Muhammad's Muslim movement. Nourished by the Negro's frustration over the continued existence of racial discrimination, this movement is made up of people who have lost faith in America, who have absolutely repudiated Christianity, and who have concluded that the white man is an incorrigible "devil."

I have tried to stand between these two forces, saying that we need emulate neither the "do-nothingism" of the complacent nor the hatred and despair of the black nationalist. For there is the more excellent way of love and nonviolent protest. I am grateful to God that, through the influence of the Negro church, the way of nonviolence became an integral part of our struggle.

If this philosophy had not emerged, by now many streets of the South would, I am convinced, be flowing with blood. And I am further convinced that if our white brothers dismiss as "rabble-rousers" and "outside agitators" those of us who employ nonviolent direct action, and if they refuse to support our nonviolent efforts, millions of Negroes will, out of frustration and despair, seek solace and security in black-nationalist ideologies—a development that would inevitably lead to a frightening racial nightmare.

Oppressed people cannot remain oppressed forever. The yearning for freedom eventually manifests itself, and that is what has happened to the American Negro. Something within has reminded him of his birthright of freedom, and something without has reminded him that it can be gained. Consciously or unconsciously, he has been caught up by the *Zeitgeist,* and with his black brothers of Africa and his brown and yellow brothers of Asia, South America and the Caribbean, the United States Negro is moving with a sense of great urgency toward the promised land of racial justice. If one recognizes this vital urge that has engulfed the Negro community, one should readily understand why public demonstrations are taking place. The Negro has many pent-up resentments and latent frustrations, and he must release them. So let him march; let him make prayer pilgrimages to the city hall; let him go on freedom rides—and try to understand why he must do so. If his repressed emotions are not released in nonviolent ways, they will seek expression through violence; this is not a threat but a fact of history. So I have not said to my people: "Get rid of your discontent." Rather, I have tried to say that this normal and healthy discontent can be channeled into the creative outlet of nonviolent direct action. And now this approach is being termed extremist.

But though I was initially disappointed at being categorized as an extremist, as I continued to think about the matter I gradually gained a measure of satisfaction from the label. Was not Jesus an extremist for love: "Love your enemies, bless them that curse you, do good to them that hate you, and pray for them which despitefully use you, and persecute you." Was not Amos an extremist for justice: "Let justice roll down like waters and righteousness like an ever-flowing stream." Was not Paul an extremist for the Christian gospel: "I bear in my body the marks of the Lord Jesus." Was not Martin Luther an extremist: "Here I stand; I cannot do otherwise, so help me God." And John Bunyan: "I will stay in jail to the end of my days before I make a butchery of my conscience." And Abraham Lincoln: "This nation cannot survive half slave and half free." And Thomas Jefferson: "We hold these truths to be self-evident, that all men are created equal . . ." So the question is not whether we will be extremists, but what kind of extremists we will be. Will we be extremists for hate or for love? Will we be extremists for the preservation of injustice or for the extension of justice? In that dramatic scene on Calvary's hill three men were crucified. We must never forget that all three were crucified for the same crime—the crime of extremism. Two were extremists for immorality, and thus fell below their environment. The other, Jesus Christ, was an extremist for love, truth and goodness, and thereby rose above his environment. Perhaps the South, the nation and the world are in dire need of creative extremists.

I had hoped that the white moderate would see this need. Perhaps I was too optimistic; perhaps I expected too much. I suppose I should have realized that few members of the oppressor race can understand the deep groans and passionate yearnings of the oppressed race, and still fewer have the vision to see that injustice must be rooted out by strong, persistent and determined action. I am thankful, however, that some of our white brothers in the South have grasped the meaning of this social revolution and committed themselves to it. They are still all too few in quantity, but they are big in quality. Some—such as Ralph McGill, Lillian Smith, Harry Golden, James McBride Dabbs, Ann Braden and Sarah Patton Boyle—have written about our struggle in eloquent and prophetic terms. Others have marched with us down nameless streets of the South. They have languished in filthy, roach-infested jails, suffering the abuse and brutality of policemen who view them as "dirty nigger lovers." Unlike so many of their moderate brothers and sisters, they have recognized the urgency of the moment and sensed the need for powerful "action" antidotes to combat the disease of segregation.

Let me take note of my other major disappointment. I have been so greatly disappointed with the white church and its leadership. Of course, there are some notable exceptions. I am not unmindful of the fact that each of you has taken some significant stands on this issue. I commend you, Reverend Stallings, for your Christian stand on this past Sunday, in welcoming Negroes to your worship service on a nonsegregated basis. I commend the Catholic leaders of this state for integrating Spring Hill College several years ago.

But despite these notable exceptions, I must honestly reiterate that I have been disappointed with the church. I do not say this as one of those negative critics who can always find something wrong with the church. I say this as a minister of the gospel, who loves the church; who was nurtured in its bosom; who has been sustained by its spiritual blessings and who will remain true to it as long as the cord of life shall lengthen.

When I was suddenly catapulted into the leadership of the bus protest in Montgomery, Alabama, a few years ago, I felt we would be supported by the white church. I felt that the white ministers, priests and rabbis of the South would be among our strongest allies. Instead, some have been outright opponents, refusing to understand the freedom movement and misrepresenting its leaders; all too many others have been more cautious than courageous and have remained silent behind the anesthetizing security of stained-glass windows.

In spite of my shattered dreams, I came to Birmingham with the hope that the white religious leadership of this community would see the justice of our cause and, with deep moral concern, would serve as the channel through which our just grievances could reach the power structure. I had hoped that each of you would understand. But again I have been disappointed.

I have heard numerous southern religious leaders admonish their worshipers to comply with a desegregation decision because it is the law, but I have longed to hear white ministers declare: "Follow this decree because integration is morally right and because the Negro is your brother." In the midst of blatant injustices inflicted upon the Negro, I have watched white churchmen stand on the sideline and mouth pious irrelevancies and sanctimonious trivialities. In the midst of a mighty struggle to rid our nation of racial and economic injustice, I have heard many ministers say: "Those are social issues, with which the gospel has no real concern." And I have watched many churches commit themselves to a completely otherworldly religion which makes a strange, un-Biblical distinction between body and soul, between the sacred and the secular.

I have traveled the length and breadth of Alabama, Mississippi and all the other southern states. On sweltering summer days and crisp autumn mornings I have looked at the South's beautiful churches with their lofty spires pointing heavenward. I have beheld the impressive outlines of her massive religious-education buildings. Over and over I have found myself asking: "What kind of people worship here? Who is their God? Where were their voices when the lips of Governor Barnett dripped with words of interposition and nullification? Where were they when Governor Wallace gave a clarion call for defiance and hatred? Where were their voices of support when bruised and weary Negro men and women decided to rise from the dark dungeons of complacency to the bright hills of creative protest?"

Yes, these questions are still in my mind. In deep disappointment I have wept over the laxity of the church. But be assured that my tears have been tears of love. There can be no deep disappointment where there is not deep love. Yes, I love the church. How could I do otherwise? I am in the rather unique position of being the son, the grandson and the great-grandson of preachers. Yes, I see the church as the body of Christ. But, oh! How we have blemished and scarred that body through social neglect and through fear of being nonconformists.

There was a time when the church was very powerful—in the time when the early Christians rejoiced at being deemed worthy to suffer for what they believed. In those days the church was not merely a thermometer that recorded the ideas and principles of popular opinion; it was a thermostat that transformed the mores of society. Whenever the early Christians entered a town, the people in power became disturbed and immediately sought to convict the Christians for being "disturbers of the peace" and "outside agitators." But the Christians pressed on, in the conviction that they were "a colony of heaven," called to obey God rather than man. Small in number, they were big in commitment. They were too God-intoxicated to be "astronomically intimidated." By their effort and example they brought an end to such ancient evils as infanticide and gladiatorial contests.

Things are different now. So often the contemporary church is a weak, ineffectual voice with an uncertain sound. So often it is an archdefender of the status quo. Far from being disturbed by the presence of the church, the power structure of the average community is consoled by the church's silent—and often even vocal—sanction of things as they are.

But the judgment of God is upon the church as never before. If today's church does not recapture the sacrificial spirit of the early church, it will lose its authenticity, forfeit the loyalty of millions, and be dismissed as an irrelevant social club with no meaning for the twentieth century. Every day I meet young people whose disappointment with the church has turned into outright disgust.

* * *

I hope the church as a whole will meet the challenge of this decisive hour. But even if the church does not come to the aid of justice, I have no despair about the future. I have no fear about the outcome of our struggle in Birmingham, even if our motives are at present misunderstood. We will reach the goal of freedom in Birmingham and all over the nation, because the goal of America is freedom. Abused and scorned though we may be, our destiny is tied up with America's destiny. Before the pilgrims landed at Plymouth, we were here. Before the pen of Jefferson etched the majestic words of the Declaration of Independence across the pages of history, we were here. For more than two centuries our forebears labored in this country without wages; they made cotton king; they built the homes of their masters while suffering gross injustice and shameful humiliation—and yet out of a bottomless vitality they continued to thrive and develop. If the inexpressible cruelties of slavery could not stop us, the opposition we now face will surely fail. We will win our freedom because the sacred heritage of our nation and the eternal will of God are embodied in our echoing demands.

Before closing I feel impelled to mention one other point in your statement that has troubled me profoundly. You warmly commended the Birmingham police force for keeping "order" and "preventing violence." I doubt that you would have so warmly commended the police force if you had seen its dogs sinking their teeth into unarmed, nonviolent Negroes. I doubt that you would so quickly commend the policemen if you were to observe their ugly and inhumane treatment of Negroes here in the city jail; if you were to watch them push and curse old Negro women and young Negro girls; if you were to see them slap and kick old Negro men and young boys; if you were to observe them, as they did on two occasions, refuse to give us food because we wanted to sing our grace together. I cannot join you in your praise of the Birmingham police department.

It is true that the police have exercised a degree of discipline in handling the demonstrators. In this sense they have conducted themselves rather "nonviolently" in public. But for what purpose? To preserve the evil system of segregation. Over the past few years I have consistently preached that nonviolence demands that the means we use must be as pure as the ends we seek. I have tried to make clear that it is wrong to use immoral means to attain moral ends. But now I must affirm that it is just as wrong, or perhaps even more so, to use moral means to preserve immoral ends. Perhaps Mr. Conner and his policemen have been rather nonviolent in public, as was Chief Pritchett in Albany, Georgia, but they have used the moral means of nonviolence to maintain the immoral end of racial injustice. As T. S. Eliot has said: "The last temptation is the greatest treason: To do the right deed for the wrong reason."

I wish you had commended the Negro sit-inners and demonstrators of Birmingham for their sublime courage, their willingness to suffer and their amazing discipline in the midst of great provocation. One day the South will recognize its real heroes. They will be the James Merediths, with the noble sense of purpose that enables them to face jeering and hostile mobs, and with the agonizing loneliness that characterizes the life of the pioneer. They will be old, oppressed, battered Negro women, symbolized in a seventy-two-year old woman in Montgomery, Alabama, who rose up with a sense of dignity and with her people decided not to ride segregated buses, and who responded with ungrammatical profundity to one who inquired about her weariness: "My feets is tired, but my soul is at rest." They will be the young high school and college students, the young ministers of the gospel and a host of their elders, courageously and nonviolently sitting in at lunch counters and willingly going to jail for conscience's sake. One day the South will know that when these disinherited children of God sat down at lunch counters, they were in reality standing up for what is best in the American dream and for the most sacred values in our Judaeo-Christian heritage, thereby bringing our nation back to those great wells of democracy which were dug deep by the founding fathers in their formulation of the Constitution and the Declaration of Independence.

Never before have I written so long a letter. I'm afraid it is much too long to take your precious time. I can assure you that it would have been much shorter if I had been writing from a comfortable desk, but what else can one do when he is alone in a narrow jail cell, other than write long letters, think long thoughts and pray long prayers?

If I have said anything in this letter that overstates the truth and indicates an unreasonable impatience, I beg you to forgive me. If I have said anything that understates the truth and indicates my having a patience that allows me to settle for anything less than brotherhood, I beg God to forgive me.

I hope this letter finds you strong in the faith. I also hope that circumstances will soon make it possible for me to meet each of you, not as an integrationist or a civil-rights leader but as a fellow clergyman and a Christian brother. Let us all hope that the dark clouds of racial prejudice will soon pass away and the deep fog of misunderstanding will be lifted from our fear-drenched communities, and in some not too distant tomorrow the radiant stars of love and brotherhood will shine over our great nation with all their scintillating beauty.

Yours for the cause of Peace and Brotherhood,

MARTIN LUTHER KING, JR.

PART NINE

RELIGION

By the usual numerical measures, the United States is the most religious society in the modern industrial world. Ninety-five percent of us say "yes" when asked if we believe in God. Nine of ten express a "religious preference." Two of three belong to a local church or synagogue, and four of ten participate in weekly services. At the same time, other numbers have recently grown all too familiar for many in the "mainline" Protestant churches, along with liberal Catholics and Jews. They have lost one tenth of their members and aged rapidly over the last two decades. Striking with generational abruptness, these losses were led by young, well-educated adults coming of age since the 1960s and becoming unchurched, while conservative Evangelical and Fundamentalist churches held onto their children and continued to grow.

Yet mainline Protestants, such as Methodists and Presbyterians, make up one-third of American church members, twice the 15 percent who are white conservative Protestants and triple the 9 percent who are unchurched. Moreover, as a result of upward social mobility and cultural assimilation in the last generation, growing numbers of Catholics, now one-quarter of the population, have come to resemble mainline Protestants in their social, political, and religious views. This suggests that the erosion of mainline religion's strength has been more a matter of ethos than numbers. It remains a strong majority but with a growing consciousness of itself as a beleaguered minority. The churches that have been most troubled since the mid-sixties are those that have upheld the synthesis of religious and political liberalism that has long defined the moral middle ground of American culture. These churches of the center now find themselves off-balance in a period of greater cultural conflict marked by resurgent Evangelicalism and spreading religious individualism.

To interpret this picture of increased religious pluralism and voluntarism, we must recognize that religion in America, historically and morally, is at once an intensely personal matter, centered around the family and the local church; *and* it lies at the core of our public life. In nineteenth-century American religion and society two characteristics come to the fore. The first is "institutional differentiation," the dividing up of institutions, so that public and private life grow more separated, with distinctive structures and ideals. As politics and the economy are freed of church authority, their moral ordering shifts further to a religious ethic of *personal* piety and discipline, and to overarching cultural ideals. This is what Tocqueville stresses when he says that religion is "the first of their political institutions," because it shapes our character in the form of moral sentiments, moods, and motives. Church and family are schools for character, teaching by practice and example, word and worship, believers who are also public-spirited citizens.

Religion also extends its sway over reason, says Tocqueville. Religious ideas anchor moral convictions and modes of discourse, affirming, for example, the ultimate worth of all persons as God's creatures and the universality of their duties and virtues as well as their rights. Such ideas underlie and order the moral argument of public life, and they justify political policy-making, as public statements by religious leaders such as Jerry Falwell and Jesse Jackson make resoundingly clear.

As the nineteenth-century church grows toward the denominational forms we recognize today, a personalizing and interiorizing of its ethics frame visions of the local church, in particular, as a community of pastoral care, warm intimacy, and loving harmony rather than moral casuistry. National denominational offices and voluntary societies meanwhile develop to address public issues and assume public responsibilities. This institutional division of moral labor goes hand in hand with a second characteristic social change, the "segmentation" or dividing up of communities into different social groups according to membership in different churches along with different occupations, political parties, and social classes.

French anthropologist Hervé Varenne brings such segmentation to life in his present-day portrait of "Appleton," a small Wisconsin town. There the intellectually "sophisticated" Presbyterian church appeals mainly to professionals and educated civil servants, the Methodists to established farmers and "up-and-coming" young businessmen, the Full Gospel church to poor white migrants, and so on. But despite their differences in doctrine, ritual, and social image, the actual social composition of many of the larger churches is similarly diverse. Why? Individuals choose one church or another chiefly for personal reasons, answers Varenne, but these intersect with the social attitudes and cultural conventions of a circle of members most actively involved in guiding the life of each congregation. At the same time, their members see through what are "just symbols" to the sacred truths that unite them in one essential humanity all "worshipping the same God."

The ambiguity of standing socially apart yet together, and theologically "in" yet not "of" the world, is nowhere more striking in American religion today than it is for Fundamentalism. This movement of Evangelicals in the revivalist tradition is socially diverse and culturally paradoxical, as American religious historian George Marsden describes it in "Preachers of Paradox." It is torn between controversial and uncivil rejection of unbelievers in a pluralistic society and their warm embrace to win souls for Christ. It actively engages larger public issues to help redeem the city of the world, and it forsakes a sinful world to seek the City of God. This ambiguity reflects Fundamentalists' sense of being outsiders in the twentieth century, a scorned minority in secular America, countered by their residually powerful heritage from Evangelicalism as the dominant religious establishment in nineteenth-century America.

Cultural outsiders who really represent America's "moral majority," Fundamentalists favor the individualism of laissez-faire economics and the church seen as a sect-like assembly of individual believers. But, in fact, their churches are some of the strongest nonethnic communities in America, with authoritative leaders and uniform beliefs and practices. Often labeled anti-intellectuals, they take ideas seriously and prize learning in God's service. Despite the subjectivism of Evangelical piety, Fundamentalists read Scripture with the unshaken faith in inductive rationalism of Enlightenment philosophers bent over a Baconian scientific treatise. This early modern faith in reason and biblical inerrancy justifies rejecting the historicist premises of late modern thinking which invites moral relativism and agnosticism among latter-day liberals. Masters of modern techniques of communication and organization, Fundamentalists preach a Christianity in step with the technological thought and circumstances of our age, yet one which offers solid answers to counter its uncertainties and tensions.

Tensions arising from conflicts of moral meaning since the 1960s set the backdrop for sociologist Steven Tipton's account of "Conversion and Cultural Change" among sixties youth joining new religious movements in the past two decades. Among these conservative Christian, neo-Oriental, and therapeutic groups is Erhard Seminars Training *(est)*, a human potential movement with particular appeal for unchurched young adults of the middle class. Its "rule-egoism" speaks to the moral predicament of those in a generation still seeking self-fulfillment and hoping for a better world, yet facing the need for emotional self-management in white-collar careers and "touch-and-go" relationships on the urban singles scene. As in *Habits of the Heart,* this "moral anthropology" uses philosophical categories to read "the living texts" of everyday moral discourse. Then it probes the social conditions that make moral ideas particularly plausible to those who hold them. Thus social and economic circumstances influence our thinking, but they do not do it for us.

The moral argument of public life includes struggling over how to construe traditions truly, not simply how to apply them to particular social issues. Such struggling is exemplified by the statements of Jerry Falwell and Jesse Jackson counterposed in this chapter. Both preach the Gospel and criticize the conduct of public life from the podium as well as the pulpit. Despite Evangelicalism's pietist zeal to separate church and state, as Marsden observes, Fundamentalism mixes a popularized Whig version of American history and folklore with Puritan social doctrines to envision a Christian America. Echoing Puritan jeremiads, Falwell charges that in the past "America has been great because her people have been good." Today, however, "our nation's problems," from poverty to energy, "are direct results of her spiritual condition," epitomized by the sins of abortion, homosexuality, pornography, fractured families, and secular humanism. Poised at the edge of eternity, America's only hope for survival lies in "a revival of righteous living based on a proper confession of sin and repentance of heart."

Jesse Jackson, by contrast, invokes "our faith in a mighty God" to charge the 1984 Democratic Convention with a moral calling "to feed the hungry, to clothe the naked, to house the homeless," teach the illiterate, employ the jobless, and choose "the human race over the nuclear race." Asking forgiveness for anti-Semitism stirred by his campaign, he describes America as a racial "rainbow" of peoples "all precious in God's sight." He recalls the shared pain and progress of the black and Jewish communities, "co-partners in a long and rich religious history—the Judeo-Christian traditions." Like Falwell, Jackson calls for "a revival of the spirit" in America today. But he stresses its passion for "social justice at home and peace abroad," and he takes to task laissez-faire social policies for violating Jesus' charge to care "for the least of these."

Writing sixty years ago, in the wake of World War I and in the midst of a newly prosperous middle class, theologian H. Richard Niebuhr recasts the themes of revival and repentance with a twentieth-century temper in exposing *The Social Sources of Denominationalism.* He criticizes denominationalism's moral compromise with the evils of caste, class, and nationalism for the sake of worldly power and organizational self-preservation. Compromise between worldly interests and the Gospel ethic of unselfish and freely forgiving love may be inevitable, Niebuhr recognizes. But denominationalism compromises too lightly and too pridefully with "the caste-system of human society." In so doing, it "draws the color line in the church of God," denies the equality of women and men, and "seats the rich and poor apart at the table of the Lord." Such moral failure within the churches undercuts their efforts to heal the world's divisions. Practicing the Gospel we preach, says Niebuhr, requires "the universal fellowship" of a church that gives "each their share in the common task and the common love." This is "the church which can save the churches from their secularism and consequent division," and light the world with the goodness of "a Kingdom of God that is among us."

In this light it appears that greater religious voluntarism and movement in American religious affiliation today does not signal the breakdown of institutional religious attachments. Instead it means that they are coming to depend less on established social sources of denominationalism and more on binding ties between the moral outlook and way of life to which persons actually hold, and the moral vision and community which their churches embody. It marks a need for the churches to renew the sacramental soul and fellowship they incarnate in worship, in critical social teaching, and in service to the larger human community. It invites them to rekindle our commitment to the common task and common love of a church unbound by caste, neither softened into mystical individualism nor hardened into self-righteous sectarianism.

HERVÉ VARENNE

Americans Together

At the most general level, the three main currents of American religious thought are represented in Appleton. There are the moderate Protestant churches, such as the Presbyterian and Methodist, characterized by a minimal insistence on any specific theological background. There are the fundamentalist Protestants, such as the Baptists or the Assembly of God, with a theoretical insistence on a literal interpretation of the Bible.

Finally, there is the Catholic Church, which includes, principally, recent immigrants from Catholic parts of Europe, their children, and a few converts interested in the more complex and systematic theological justification of the beliefs and liturgy of this church. The historical establishment of Catholicism in the United States is not really recent, but its ranks have constantly been renewed as immigrants came into the country, and its superficial organization is still more European than American. Yet the process of Americanizing the Catholic Church in Appleton is certainly well on its way, as the influx of new immigrants has almost stopped.

I will focus first and foremost on Protestant churches because they reveal organizational realities at the most visible levels.

The distinction between the two brands of Protestantism or between Protestantism and Catholicism can be made to seem much sharper at a theoretical level than it is in reality. It is well known that the Episcopal and Lutheran churches incorporate many traits typical of the Catholic Church, such as complex ritualism and a religious hierarchy that limits the autonomy of the local congregation. Similarly, the Church of Christ, with a theological orientation that

Hervé Varenne, excerpted from *Americans Together: Structured Diversity in a Midwestern Town* (New York: Teachers College Press, 1977), pp. 98–103, 107–110.

equates it with the moderate Protestants, incorporates the "coming-forward" ritual and baptism by immersion typical of fundamentalist churches. On the other hand, the Baptist church of Appleton held services whose structure was very close to that of the moderate Protestant churches. From that point of view, the Protestant churches are positioned along a continuum with "high ritualism" at one extreme and "high emotionalism" at the other, the order being: Episcopal, Lutheran, Methodist, Presbyterian, Church of Christ, Baptist, Seventh-day Adventist, Assembly of God, Jehovah's Witnesses, Church of God, Full Gospel Pentecostal. (The ranking could be different elsewhere.)

This order loosely conforms to a sociopolitical order insofar as members of moderate Protestant churches held all the direct political power and most of the wealth that Protestants possessed in Appleton. Fundamentalists rarely participated in any political or social activities with members of other churches, even though they were often invited and most of them would have been perfectly acceptable almost anywhere. The Catholic church was a special case, since it included many of the richest and most powerful people in town (those who were not Protestant) and also a wide selection of people from all social levels. Therefore, it would be meaningless to rank it with the Protestant churches. These churches were much more homogeneous in their membership and could easily be characterized socially if one accepts that the people who dominated each congregation in some way represented the sociological reality of these churches.

As perceived by many people in Appleton, the Presbyterian church, for example, was supposed to be "intellectual" and "sophisticated"; the Methodist was the church both of older, established small farmers and younger, "up-and-coming" businessmen in the town. Indeed, the Presbyterian church appealed mainly to professionals and high-level civil servants, the Methodist to merchants. The school board was dominated by Presbyterians, the town council by Methodists. There was clearly a feeling of competition between these two churches, the most important ones in Appleton. For the time being, the advantage appeared to lie with the Presbyterian church for the top spot in the ranking system.

The Episcopalian church, being very small, did not play a very noticeable role in the social and political life of the town. The income of some of its members was very high, but the most active members, a handful of them, congregated mostly with Presbyterians outside of church activities.

The Church of Christ was quite close to the Methodist in many ways, but its atmosphere was very quaint and its congregation did not try to compete socially with the others, although one could feel a certain desire among some members to do so. Its members were often close to people in the Baptist church, with whom they felt more at ease on religious matters than with the more liberal Methodists. They were generally not fundamentalists, but they preferred this position to the liberal Protestantism preached by other churches.

The Lutheran church was quite outside this ranking system, probably because a large number of its members came from areas outside the town and because of a strong plurality of German immigrants in its ranks. In outward appearance, its membership consisted of many people whose socioeconomic background was very similar to that of the Methodists, and they could have competed with them, but they did not, and remained withdrawn.

An absolute ranking for the fundamentalist churches would be even more difficult. The Full Gospel church appealed mainly to very poor white migrants from the South, many of them unemployed, and all with large families. They contrasted strikingly with the congregations of the moderate churches, in which people of this type were exceedingly rare. I could say that the Full Gospel church fell at the bottom of the social scale.

The status of the other fundamentalist churches, though certainly lower than that of any of the moderate churches, is much more difficult to determine. On the one hand, none of the people who held political power or offices, whether in the school system or the town or county government, belonged to any of these churches. On the other hand, most fundamentalist church members held jobs and, more importantly, followed a life-style totally acceptable to, and often encountered in, the moderate churches. As long as religious subjects were not approached, it was often hard to distinguish between a churchgoing Methodist and a Seventh-day Adventist or Baptist. They were, in fact, regularly invited to participate in the ecumenical activities planned by the moderate churches, and just as regularly refused.

It soon became evident to me that the absence of any Baptist or Seventh-day Adventist in most townwide activities was the result of an ideological choice: "worldly power" was evil and corrupting and should be avoided. This was not a rationalization in the face of segregation. Many individual Baptists would have been politically acceptable. But if they *had* joined the political cliques in town, they could not have remained Baptist. They would have been rejected and, conversely, accepted in, say, the Methodist church. Socioeconomic differences among the fundamentalist churches were minute. The only differences among most of these churches were religious and theological; they were essentially "equal" among themselves.

All fundamentalist churches were very small, each comprising only four dozen families. And the smaller they were, the tighter and more segregative they were. The Seventh-day Adventists were the best example of this process, with their insistence on keeping Saturday rather than Sunday as their holy day. Their reason for doing so was, of course, a typical fundamentalist statement: "This is what the Bible says." They believed themselves to be more fundamentalist than all other fundamentalist churches combined because *they* kept the Sabbath and the others did not. On the other hand, their interest in health, nonviolence, conscientious objection to military service, and social service did not derive from a wholly literal reading of the Bible. They seemed to insist relatively less on salvation than other churches.

All fundamentalist churches present such a mix of literalism and interpretation with regard to the Bible. They have to be literal to justify their existence, and they have to be interpretive not only because of the ambiguous character of many biblical passages but also to differentiate themselves from other fundamentalist churches. By keeping Saturday as their day of worship, the Seventh-day Adventists devised a particularly efficacious way of differentiating themselves from the rest of the population. It made communication with other churches a little more difficult, contributing thereby to the strength of the bond among church members.

The differences among churches were also expressed by the use of different prayers during Sunday services or by small shifts in the organization of the service: some churches would use both the Gloria Patri and the Doxology; others would use only one at a time; some would use neither. There were variations in the frequency of communion services or in the order of the different steps of a service; communion generally came after the sermon, but it might be placed before, and the consecrating prayers might be said by the pastor or by one or several elders. These variations were quite important symbolically because of the relatively large amount of communication that existed among the congregations of these churches. People frequently attended services at churches other than their own and thus found out how other churches went about doing things. Practical help was often exchanged, and friendship networks existed across churches. Here also segregation demands communication.

I characterized the Episcopalian congregation as rich and in the orbit of the Presbyterian church. It was rich because it was clear that it could count on more money per member than any other church in Appleton. In spite of the small size of the membership, it could afford a full-time minister and a church fellowship hall complex at least as large as the Presbyterians'. Proportionally, this made the Episcopalians richer than the Presbyterians. On the other hand, the Presbyterians were much more active in politics and other aspects of the life of the town, while the Episcopalians were underrepresented. What does all this mean?

There were 80 names on the mailing list of the Episcopal church and 200 baptized Episcopalians in Appleton. About 150 people practiced, and the average church attendance was around 80 (none of these subdivisions offered to me by the pastor cover exactly the same units; statistics cannot be very precise, just indicative). In general, people holding high-status jobs (professionals, managers, civil administrators, small businessmen) made up about 40 percent of the congregation. People with lower-status jobs (clerks, secretaries, blue-collar workers) comprised 35 percent. Retired persons (25 percent of the congregation) were, in general, not very well-to-do, except for the two widows of Chrysler and General Motors executives. Finally, no one in this church played the role of "old aristocrat." Even among the upper half of the congregation many were new, both to Appleton and to their social position. None of these people would have been unwelcome in the Presbyterian church. Nor were Episcopalians totally snobbish toward Presbyterians; there were many extra-church relationships between the two congregations.

The statistical composition of the Methodist congregation does not vary significantly from the Episcopalian: 35 percent of the people on the membership list (266 "units," 410 people) could be classified as "higher" (both in status and income), and 56 percent as "lower." There were also 9 percent who were retired and unaccounted for. (My criteria for determining higher or lower status are the same as those I used for the Episcopalians. My data are purely occupational; that was all I could get from my sources. Once again, these statistics are intended to be indicative of the type of people who were on the mailing lists of the respective churches.) The average and median incomes and jobs were thus most probably slightly lower for the Methodist than for the Episcopal church, a result well in keeping with the findings of sociological studies of American towns. The question is: To what extent is this difference in income averages relevant? To be more precise: Why is it that university professors, white-collar workers in a large chemical complex, and blue-collar workers in a Ford automobile factory could be found in all three churches—and, in fact, of course, in all the others? Why is it, furthermore, that the Episcopalian church gave an outward appearance of wealth and gentility, the Presbyterian one of intellectualism, the Methodist one of *nouveau riche* pride and self-consciousness, although the statistics reveal that the composition of the congregations did not vary significantly?

The answer to the first question is very simple: One belongs to one church or another primarily for *personal* reasons. A person does not join a group or a church *because* he is a university professor (or in spite of being one) but because he wants, for whatever reasons, to be a member of this or that church. A Methodist survey found that the three main answers given to this question were that one joins a church because it has a "good" minister, a "nice" church building, a "congenial" congregation.

*   *   *

There are also many examples, both in the sociological literature and in novels about American life, of people who would like to join a church, association, or clique they consider "higher" and are prevented from doing so by the resistance of the members of these groups to their application. Most of this literature (Dreiser, Lewis, Marquand, Warner) is critical of actual American life, and one can raise some doubts as to the validity of their analysis of motives, with their insistence on jealousy, envy, snobbery and other "evil" things as the primary motors of social stratification in America. But there is also little doubt that their descriptions correspond to a certain reality.

Most people in Appleton would insist on what they would consider to be the positive aspects of group formation; they would insist that anybody is welcome in their midst if he is an "interesting" or "good" or "respectable" person—which means, among established, successful, white middle-class persons, as well as among their young, "radical" children that the applicant for membership is willing to conform to the rules of the group as defined by its dominant clique at the time of the application.

If a blue-collar worker wanted to join the Episcopalian church or even simply to remain in it without feeling too uncomfortable, he certainly could do so in Appleton; there were several blue-collar workers in the church. His problem would be that he would not find many of his kind in the dominant clique, that he would have to play the game of sophistication in speech, dress, and outside interests, which he might be disinclined to do. On the other hand, the church might just happen to be dominated by blue-collar workers, and so he would not have to play a role too different from that of the majority of his fellow-workers. The Episcopalian minister had served in just such a parish before he came to Appleton. On the other hand, a blue-collar atmosphere might not appeal to the wife of a retired executive. But then again, it also might.

My argument here is that two things must be distinguished. First there is what might be called the sociological reality of the congregation, a reality dependent on the amount of money it controls and is willing to spend on church-related activities. Then there is the appearance it conveys by the use of certain symbols and by the activities of the group of people, always rather small even in the large churches, who hold most committee positions, meet informally regularly, and thus control the church. The interesting thing is that the two things are not necessarily related, something that has escaped many sociologists concerning American religion. There is a relationship between economic power and church membership only if one considers the churches in groups. But within each level there can be several competing churches, each a slight variation on the general theme. Thus the Presbyterian church in Appleton was not "intellectual" because there was a predominance of university professors and school teachers in it, but because several of the most active members of the congregation, those who planned and organized church activities, had enough influence on the minister to orient his sermons in a direction that they considered "intellectual," were interested in some sort of cultural life, and pushed the congregation to accept it.

* * *

What this choice of symbols to characterize a church reveals is that the true role of these symbols is not so much to express the inner reality of the particular group as to differentiate it from those groups closer to it and in interaction with it. Youth services and dancing, a new church, or a theatrical troupe play the same role in the social organization of moderate churches and belong to the same category of phenomena as the presence or absence of crosses in fundamentalist churches.

The manipulation of these symbols for purposes of differentiation and identification has a distinct totemic quality to it. Each group is differentiated from all others by the symbols it uses to express its existence. These symbols almost never spring from the infrastructural reality the groups may also possess. They are also very rarely invested with any emotional meaning for the members of the group: they are not sacred. They are essentially intellectual means by which the need for a multitude of groups and communities is solved.

The totems are not sacred, nor do they represent in any sense the "true" reality of the groups as seen by the members themselves. They are, as they would say, just "symbols" of the essential humanity of the members. I was told many a time: "What matters that we be Methodists, Baptists, Seventh-day Adventists (or even Jews)? We are all Christians (human beings) worshiping the same God." The totemic diversity of the social organization is a matter of surface appearance that hides an essential, and obviously very abstract and ideal, unity—the oneness that comes from the fact that all the members of these communities remain individuals whose attachment to their communities and its symbols is of the same nature.

George M. Marsden

Preachers of Paradox

IF HISTORY HAS LAWS, the first is that it is usually unpredictable. Who in the 1950s anticipated the upheavals of the 1960s? Or who in 1970 clearly projected the conservative religious resurgences of the next decade? So when we look at the religious New Right in America today we cannot say whether it marks the dawn of a new spiritual era, a phase in recurrent cycles of social and spiritual anxiety, or the last gasp of an old order. All we can agree on, perhaps, is that theories of secularization that predicted correlations of scientific-technological advance and spiritual decline are in deep trouble.

* * *

The purpose of this essay is to understand the religious New Right more clearly by looking at it from the perspective of the history of evangelicalism and fundamentalism in America. So considered, we find in current fundamentalism the amalgamation of a fascinating variety of traditions. Some are highly intellectualized and some highly emotional, some elitist-establishmentarian and some directed toward outsiders, some concerned with public policy and some privatistic, and all are mixed with various American assumptions and folklore. During the twentieth century these were fused together, transformed, and sometimes fragmented by intense efforts simultaneously to fight American secularists and to convert them. The result is a movement fraught with paradoxes that have made it sociologically mystifying. By employing a historical perspective we can perhaps sort out some of those paradoxes and show how the movement has the potential to point in more directions than is usually perceived.

* * *

George M. Marsden, excerpted from "Preachers of Paradox: The Religious New Right in Historical Perspective," in *Religion and American Life,* ed. Mary Douglas and Steven M. Tipton (Boston: Beacon Press, 1982), pp. 150–168. Copyright © American Academy of Arts and Sciences 1982, 1983.

THE PARADOXES OF THE FUNDAMENTALIST NEW RIGHT

The first thing to notice in considering the New Right in light of this fundamentalist and evangelical history is the diversity of the religious movement and hence its sometimes self-contradictory stances toward culture. Fundamentalism from the outset was both a distinct movement or impulse and a coalition of a number of movements. Nineteenth-century American evangelicalism, from which fundamentalism grew, was itself a coalition of several denominational traditions. Similarly, today we can identify at least fourteen varieties of evangelicalism.[1] While these evangelicals share many doctrines, their diversities in inherited stances toward culture and politics are especially pronounced. So on the issues of culture and politics generalizations about evangelicalism are particularly hazardous.

Central to the fundamentalist heritage is a basic tension between positive revivalism and polemics. Fundamentalism developed largely within the revivalist tradition, in which the highest goal was to win other souls to Christ. Controversy could aid revivalism for a time, but in the long run too much controversy and too much cantankerousness could hinder evangelistic efforts. This was one of the issues that divided neo-evangelicals from hard-line fundamentalists after 1940. Fundamentalist separatism, insistence on strict doctrinal purity, and incivility toward persons with other beliefs seemed to the new evangelicals to hinder the spread of the Gospel. The evangelism of Billy Graham well represented their impulse. Despite his traditionalist message and his efforts to change individuals, Graham was willing to live with American pluralism. Hard-line fundamentalists were unwilling to accept such compromise with pluralism and so continued the warfare on modern society from the position of strict separatists. The price of such polemics was that they remained on the fringe where fewer people would take their message seriously.

The tensions between positive revivalism and controversialism are complicated by a second tension that pulls evangelicalism simultaneously in two directions. Simply put, this is a tension between

1. Robert F. Webber, *Common Roots: A Call to Evangelical Maturity* (Grand Rapids: Zondervan, 1978), p. 32. Cullen Murphy, "Protestantism and the Evangelicals," *The Wilson Quarterly* (Autumn 1981), pp. 105–17, identifies twelve varieties.

being and not being politically and culturally oriented. This division cuts differently than does the positive revivalist versus polemicist division. Some evangelicals with political-cultural concerns are militant controversialists (fundamentalists) and others are not. Moreover, many evangelicals who stress positive revival also have political-cultural programs; but many others do not. So these two types of tensions produce four combinations of basic ideal types (positive-nonpolitical, positive-political, polemicist-nonpolitical, and polemicist-political).[2]

The tension between emphasizing political-cultural implications of the Gospel or eschewing them is also deeply rooted. It is inherent in Christianity itself, which always has wavered between Old Testament and New or between redeeming the city of the world and thinking of the City of God as wholly spiritual or otherworldly. Such ambivalence is particularly strong in American evangelicalism. This is so both because American evangelicalism and fundamentalism fuse so many traditions and because in America itself evangelicals have been cast in vastly different roles in different eras.

The most immediate heritage of fundamentalists comes from their twentieth-century experiences of being a beleaguered and ridiculed minority. Sin and secularism had run rampant over some key parts of American culture. Like twentieth-century sociologists, most fundamentalists believed in laws that declared that the process of secularization was irreversible. In the fundamentalists' case these laws were drawn from dispensational premillennialism, which posited the steady decline of the modern era in preparation for a final world calamity resolved only by the personal return of Christ with avenging armies. Fundamentalists in this world view were outsiders.[3] They were outsiders from the power centers of society, its politics, and its cultural life; they viewed themselves as separated from these worldly powers. This separation was indeed selective, not precluding full participation in the nation's economic life and

2. A more refined version of this sort of categorization is found in Richard J. Mouw, "The Bible in Twentieth-Century Protestantism: A Preliminary Taxonomy," in Nathan O. Hatch and Mark A. Noll, eds., *The Bible in America: Essays in Cultural History* (New York: Oxford University Press, 1982), pp. 139–62.

3. Laurence Moore, "Insiders and Outsiders in American Historical Narrative and American History," *American Historical Review*, 87, No. 2 (April 1982), pp. 390–412, provides a helpful account of this outsider theme and its inherent ambiguities.

usually not thwarting impulses to patriotism. Some fundamentalists stood as lonely prophets warning of the destruction that was to come and that could be seen in the growing strength of demonic world forces such as Catholicism or communism. More typically, however, fundamentalists and many other evangelicals, sensing themselves to be essentially outsiders, drew on those considerable strands in their revivalist and New Testament heritage that forsook political and cultural aspirations.

If one looks a little further back, however, one finds an almost opposite strand in the heritage. Throughout the nineteenth century, revivalist evangelicalism was the dominant religious force in America, strong enough to be a virtual establishment in this most religious of modern nations. Though often submerged, the images of this historical tradition retained a residual power through the hard days of the twentieth century. When in eras such as the early 1920s or 1980s, when the nation was in the midst of a conservative reaction and unfocused anxiety, this establishmentarian side of the tradition could be readily revived.

This political-cultural side of the heritage reflects not at all the premillennialism that was taught in twentieth-century fundamentalism but rather a residual postmillennialism that had dominated nineteenth-century evangelicalism. In this view America has a special place in God's plans and will be the center for a great spiritual and moral reform that will lead to a golden age or "millennium" of Christian civilization. Moral reform accordingly is crucial for hastening this spiritual millennium. Fundamentalists today reject postmillennialism as such, but genetically postmillennial ideals continue to be a formidable force in their thinking. Such ideals now appear not so much as Christian doctrine but as a mixture of piety and powerful American folklore. This folklore is a popularization of a version of the Whig view of history, in which true religion and liberty are always pitted against false religion and tyranny. America, in this view, was founded on Christian principles embodied in the Constitution and has been chosen by God to be a beacon of right religion and liberty for the whole world.[4]

4. Ronald A. Wells, "Francis Schaeffer's Jeremiad: A Review Article," *The Reformed Journal*, 32, No. 5 (May 1982), pp. 16–20, suggests the combination of Whig history and the jeremiad.

Puritanism is another powerful source of fundamentalist cultural views. Almost always, Puritan social doctrines are mixed with the Whig version of American history and folklore. One clue to the Puritan connection is the constant use of the jeremiad form. The light of true religion and liberty has dimmed, though only rather recently—sometime since the end of World War II.[5] Up to that time "America has been great because her people have been good," as Jerry Falwell puts it.[6] Her recent moral decline coincides with her recent international humiliations. These are, in fact, simply cause and effect. While the connections might not seem apparent to human wisdom, we can be sure that God is punishing America for her depravity, an idea inherited directly from the Puritan covenantal tradition. God's blessings and curses are, in Old Testament fashion, contingent on national righteousness or sinfulness. Falwell constantly repeats this theme, suggesting, for instance, that the spread of pornography is causally related, through God's providential control, to national distresses such as the oil crisis.[7] "Our nation's internal problems," he says, characteristically, "are direct results of her spiritual condition."[8]

The continuing strength of this combination of Whig and Puritan views in the religious outlook suggests that it is misleading to characterize the fundamentalist-evangelical heritage as generally "private."[9] One important strand of the revivalist heritage, drawn from pietism, Methodism, and Baptist zeal for separation of church and state, has tended to eschew identifications of the Kingdom of God with social-political programs. Evangelicalism has always been divided within itself on this point, however. During the nineteenth

5. For example, John R. Price, *America at the Crossroads: Repentence or Repression?* (Indianapolis: Christian House Publishing Co., 1976), pp. 3–7. Cf. Jerry Falwell, *Listen America!* (Garden City, New York: Doubleday, 1980).

6. Falwell, *Listen America!*, p. 243.

7. Jerry Falwell, interview, *Eternity* (July–August 1980), p. 19.

8. Falwell, *Listen America!*, p. 243.

9. Unfortunately, the identification of evangelicalism and revivalism as "private" in contrast to "public" Protestantism has been widely promoted by one of the most consistently astute interpreters of American religion, Martin Marty. See, for example, his *Righteous Empire: The Protestant Experience in America* (New York: Harper Torchbooks, 1970).

century the Puritan heritage was still a formidable force in shaping evangelicals' quasi-Calvinist visions of a Christian America. Such Puritan culture-dominating ideals persist in the Moral Majority today. Much of evangelicalism accordingly has been of two minds on the question of personal versus social applications of the Gospel. Fundamentalism has sometimes resolved its internal dilemma on this point by making distinctions between public "moral" questions that it supports as opposed to illicit mixing of "politics" with religion by liberal church leaders[10]

A related point is worth noting: Fundamentalists are reputedly highly individualistic. Indeed, fundamentalists are individualistic in the sense of advocating classical liberal economics and in emphasizing the necessity of an individual's personal relation to Jesus. Moreover, their view of the church is nominalistic: they see it essentially as a collection of individuals. Early in this century theological liberals who were building the Social Gospel movement were quick to point out such individualistic traits and to contrast them with their own more communal emphases. Ever since, this individualistic-privatistic image has dominated views of fundamentalism. Despite the substantial truth to this characterization, there is another side. In fact fundamental churches and national organizations are some of the most cohesive non-ethnic communities in America.[11] Certainly the fundamentalist churches offer far stronger community for their members than do their moderate-liberal Protestant counterparts. Moreover, despite the profession of individuality, fundamentalist churches and organizations tend to be highly authoritarian, typically under the control of one strong leader. Although fundamentalist preaching sometimes stresses making up one's own mind, in fact the movement displays some remarkable uniformities in details of doctrine and practice that suggest anything but real individualism in thought.

10. Carl McIntire, for instance, characteristically responded to accusations that he had made the Gospel too political with statements such as, "What men call politics, to me is standing up for righteousness."

11. Lowell D. Streiker and Gerald S. Strober, *Religion and the New Majority: Billy Graham, Middle America, and the Politics of the '70s* (New York: Association Press, 1972), pp. 139–40. Most fundamentalists are of northern European descent, but the unity of their communities is not usually based on more narrow ethnic ties.

Returning to the persistence of the quasi-Calvinist vision of cultural dominance, we can see yet another paradox within fundamentalism. Fundamentalism usually has been regarded as essentially anti-intellectual. Again, there is some truth to this accusation. A considerable tradition within American revivalism has always viewed higher education with suspicion. Early Methodists, many Baptists, and other American groups considered an educated clergy a stumbling block to true spirituality. Today some fundamentalist groups insist that education beyond high school be confined to their own Bible schools. Moreover, bitter opposition to the American intellectual establishment and accusations that too much learning has corrupted liberal and neo-evangelical Protestants are commonplace.

Nonetheless, as we have seen, fundamentalism also reflects the persistence of the Puritan heritage in the American Protestant psyche. This heritage includes a cultural vision of all things, including learning, brought into the service of the sovereign God. Fundamentalists accordingly retain vestiges of this ideal. Schools, including colleges and "universities," are central parts of their empires. Although they may only rarely attain excellence in learning, they seek it in principle and sometimes do attain it. No group is more eager to brandish honorary degrees. Perhaps more to the point, genuine degrees are more than welcome when in the service of the Lord. Nowhere is this clearer than in the creation-science movement, a predominantly fundamentalist effort. While decrying the scientific establishment and people who blindly follow the lead of "experts," the Creation Research Society emphasizes the hundreds of Ph.D.'s who make up its membership.

Even more centrally, fundamentalists are among those contemporary Americans who take ideas most seriously. In this respect they reflect, even if in a dim mirror, the Puritan heritage. For the fundamentalist, what one believes is of the utmost importance. They are, as Samuel S. Hill, Jr., observes, more "truth-oriented" than most evangelical groups.[12] The American intellectual establishment, in contrast, has a tendency to reduce beliefs to something else, hence

12. Samuel S. Hill, Jr., "Popular Southern Piety," in *Varieties of Southern Evangelicalism,* ed. David Edwin Harrell, Jr. (Macon, Ga.: Mercer University Press, 1981), p. 100.

devaluing the importance of ideas as such. So, for instance, fundamentalist ideas themselves have long been presented as though they were "really" expressions of some social or class interest. It seems fair to inquire in such cases as to who is really the anti-intellectual. To reduce beliefs to their social functions is to overemphasize a partial truth and so to underestimate the powers of the belief itself. Consider, for instance, the important fundamentalist belief that God relates to the nation convenantally, rewarding or punishing it proportionately to its moral record. This is a belief, deeply held on religious grounds, about some causal connections in the universe. Throughout the history of America this conception about causality has survived through a number of revolutionary changes in the class and status of its adherents. While, as suggested earlier, social and cultural circumstances strongly influence the expressions of this belief, there is no doubt that the belief itself is sometimes a powerful force in determining the way people behave.

Fundamentalist thought often appears anti-intellectual because of its proneness to oversimplification. The universe is divided in two—the moral and the immoral, the forces of light and darkness. This polarized thinking reflects a crass popularizing that indeed is subversive to serious intellectual inquiry and a world view that starts with a premise that the world is divided between the forces of God and of Satan and sorts out evidence to fit that paradigm. Another influence on this thinking reflects a modern intellectual tradition that dates largely from the Enlightenment. Fundamentalist thought has close links with the Baconian and Common Sense assumptions of the early modern era. Humans are capable of positive knowledge based on sure foundations. If rationally classified, such knowledge can yield a great deal of certainty. Combined with biblicism, such a view of knowledge leads to supreme confidence on religious questions. Despite the conspicuous subjectivism throughout evangelicalism[13] and within fundamentalism itself, one side of the fundamentalist mentality is committed to inductive rationalism.

This commonsense inductive aspect of fundamentalist thinking,

13. James Davidson Hunter, "Subjectivism and the New Evangelical Theodicy," *Journal for the Scientific Study of Religion*, 20, No. 1 (1982), pp. 39–45, documents the subjectivist side of evangelicalism.

rather than being anti-intellectual, reflects an intellectual tradition alien to most modern academics. What is most lacking is the contemporary sense of historical development, a Heraclitean sense that all is change. This contemporary conception of history invites relativism or at least the seeing of ambiguities. Fundamentalists have the confidence of Enlightenment philosophies that an objective look at "the facts" will lead to the truth.[14] Their attacks on evolutionism reflect their awareness that the developmentalist, historicist, and culturalist assumptions of modern thought undermine the certainties of knowledge. Correspondingly, persons attracted to authoritarian views of the Bible are often also attracted to the pre-Darwinian, ahistorical, philosophical assumptions that seem to provide high yields of certainty.

It is incorrect then to think of fundamentalist thought as essentially premodern. Its views of God's revelation, for example, although drawn from the Bible, are a long way from the modes of thought of the ancient Hebrews. For instance, fundamentalists' intense insistence on the "inerrancy" of the Bible in scientific and historical detail is related to this modern style of thinking. Although the idea that Scripture does not err is an old one, fundamentalists accentuate it partly because they often view the Bible virtually as though it were a scientific treatise. For example, southern Baptist fundamentalist Paige Patterson remarks: "Space scientists tell us that minute error in the mathematical calculations for a moon shot can result in a total failure of the rocket to hit the moon. A slightly altered doctrine of salvation can cause a person to miss Heaven also."[15] To the fundamentalist the Bible is essentially a collection of true and precise propositions. Such approaches may not be typical of most twentieth-century thought, but they are more nearly early modern than premodern.

Fundamentalist thought is in fact highly suited to one strand of contemporary culture—the technological strand. Unlike theoretical

14. For example, the apologetics of Josh McDowell, *Evidence that Demands a Verdict: Historical Evidences for the Christian Faith* (San Bernardino, Calif.: Campus Crusade, 1972). Such objectivist apologetics were dominant in nineteenth-century American evangelicalism.

15. Patterson, *Living in the Hope of Eternal Life* (Grand Rapids: Zondervan, 1968). p. 26.

science or social science, where questions of the supernatural raise basic issues about the presuppositions of the enterprise, technological thinking does not wrestle with such theoretical principles. Truth is a matter of true and precise propositions that classified and organized, will work. Fundamentalism fits this mentality because it is a form of Christianity with no loose ends, ambiguities, or historical developments. Everything fits neatly into a system. It is revealing, for instance, that many of the leaders of the creation-science movement are in applied sciences or engineering.[16] The principal theories of creation science were in fact designed by an engineer, Henry Morris. Morris, in typically fundamentalist Baconian terms, describes his quest for scientific confirmation of the Bible: "In trying to lead others to Christ, I needed answers and this led me to research. And being an engineer, I looked for solid evidence."[17]

Fundamentalists in more general ways have proved themselves masters of modern technique. The skillful use of organizational mass mailing and media techniques by the fundamentalist New Right during the 1980 election demonstrates this mastery of an aspect of modern culture. Such expertise in rationalized technique should hardly be surprising in a Protestant American tradition. Moreover, evangelicalism has long depended for support on effectively mobilizing masses of potential constituents. Evangelist Charles Finney in the early nineteenth century was in fact one of the pioneers in rationalized techniques of modern advertising and promotion.

The fundamentalist message is also peculiarly suited for large segments of society in the technological age. Fundamentalists have been particularly adept at handling mass communication.[18] If there

16. Dorothy Nelkin, *Science Textbook Controversies and the Politics of Equal Time* (Cambridge: MII Press, 1977), p. 72.
17. Quoted in Nelkin, *Science Textbook Controversies*, pp. 71–72.
18. This side of evangelicalism makes it unclear exactly how the movement fits the scheme suggested by Peter Berger, who argues that the real conflict within American Protestantism is a "class struggle" between two elites, the "new knowledge class" and "the old business class" (Berger, "The Class Struggle in American Religion," *The Christian Century*, February 25, 1981, p. 197). If the knowledge class is "a new elite composed of those whose livelihood derives from the manipulation of symbols—intellectuals, educators, media people, members of the 'helping professions,' and a miscellany of planners and bureaucrats," then many conservative evan-

is a rule of mass communications that the larger the audience the simpler the message must be, fundamentalists and similar evangelicals came to the technological age well prepared. Television ministries flourish best when they provide answers in simple polarities.[19] By contrast, one could hardly imagine a widely popular neo-Orthodox television ministry; subtleties and ambiguities would kill it immediately.[20] Such aptness of the message to the age is not confined to TV. Although not often acknowledged by the controllers of public opinion, evangelicals have also dominated the actual best-seller statistics during the past decade.[21] The key to such success is again a simple message. Such simplicity itself bears a paradoxical relationship to contemporary life. On the one hand, it is a reaction against the tensions, uncertainties, and ambiguities that surround modern life and always shape the human condition. At the same time, the ancient simplicities have been given a contemporary shape by the same forces that produce the efficient production and sales of, let's say, McDonald's hamburgers. As the Cathedral at Chartres symbolized the essence of the medieval era, so perhaps the McDonald's golden arches may symbolize ours. For better or worse, fundamentalism is a version of Christianity matched to its age.

Fundamentalism, then, is fraught with paradoxes. It is torn between uncivil controversialism and the accepting attitudes neces-

gelical media people, educators, evangelists, pop psychologists, and so forth would seem to qualify admirably ("Class Struggle," p. 197). Manipulation of symbols has long been an evangelical forte. A simpler explanation for the conflict is preferable. The conflict is at root ideological, a version of avowed secularism versus a version of Christianity. Some secularists have championed a "new class" and helped create it; but they approve only of secularist manifestations of it.

19. Many of these ministries were enhanced also by salting the Gospel with promises of personal success and healing, often by implication related to contributions to the ministry. Such themes have been relatively stronger among evangelists with pentecostal heritage or ties. Throughout much of evangelicalism, traditional themes of sin and judgment have been muted. This latter point is well documented in James D. Hunter, *American Evangelicalism* (New Brunswick, N.J.: Rutgers University Press, 1983).

20. This point is suggested in Jerry Falwell, *The Fundamentalist Phenomenon, The Resurgence of Conservative Christianity* (Garden City, N.Y.: Doubleday, 1981), p. 172, regarding the media advantage of fundamentalists versus "left-wing Evangelicalism."

21. Jeremy Rifkin and Ted Howard, *The Emerging Order: God in the Age of Scarcity* (New York: G.P. Putnam's Sons, 1979), p. 112.

sary for being influential and evangelizing effectively. Often it is otherworldly and privatistic; yet it retains intense patriotism and interest in the moral-political welfare of the nation. It is individualistic, yet produces strong communities. It is in some ways anti-intellectual, but stresses right thinking and true education. It accentuates the revivalists' appeal to the subjective, yet often it is rationalistic-inductivist in its epistemology. It is Christianity derived from an ancient book, yet shaped also by the technological age. It is antimodernist, but in some respects strikingly modern. Perhaps most ironically, it offers simple answers phrased as clear polarities; yet it is such a complex combination of traditions and beliefs that it is filled with more ambiguity and paradox than most of its proponents, or its opponents, realize.

STEVEN M. TIPTON

Conversion and Cultural Change

Widespread interest in "new religions," now a decade old, has yet to yield a clear overview of their relation to traditional norms and values, their appeal to specific social groups, and their resonance with broader changes in American culture. Instead, we find ourselves still awash in exotic ethnographic detail, buffeted by membership statistics, or swept away by generalizations on modernity that new religions as an undifferentiated class are supposed to reflect. To clarify our overview of these movements and their ideas, we need to look more closely at the cultural dynamics of conversion to them. Youth of the sixties have joined alternative religious movements of the seventies and eighties basically, I will argue, to make moral sense of their lives.[1] Their conversion may be an intensely

1. For fuller development of this thesis, applied to conservative Christian, Zen Buddhist, and human potential movements, see my *Getting Saved from the Sixties* (Berkeley: University of California Press, 1982).

This selection has been abridged and revised from Steven M. Tipton, "The Moral Logic of Alternative Religions," *Dædalus* 111 (Winter 1982): pp. 185–213.

personal and subjective change of heart, but it is also a change of mind that draws on and transforms the public, objectified resources for moral meaning carried by our culture.

* * *

Understood in ethical terms, the ideas we hold give us a model of and for social reality[2] They tell us what is so and what we ought to do about it. They mirror the world we enter every day, and they point out the path we ought to take through it, so that we can justify self and society only in relation to each other. . . . Interpreted as a shift in moral outlook, the process of conversion begins with problems of right and wrong that an earlier view cannot resolve and a later one can. Such problems are couched in the social situation of those who face them, and their solution turns on changes in that situation.

The conflict of values between mainstream American culture and counterculture during the 1960s framed problems that alternative religious movements of the 1970s and 1980s have mediated and resolved. Whether conservative Christian, neo-Oriental, or psychotherapeutic, these movements are successors to this conflict. In its terms they have acquired their special significance for the sixties youth who make up their core membership. These youths were raised on traditional ethics they came to deny in favor of countercultural values, only to find these, too, impossible to live out. At the end of their youth, and the decade, they converted to religious movements that resolved their moral predicament by recombining elements of its opposing sides into unified ethics that have given new meaning to their experience and new purpose to their lives. Contrasting styles of ethical evaluation have shaped this conflict and its mediation. These styles distinctively characterize the romantic tradition of the counterculture and, as well, the traditions that underpin mainstream culture: biblical religion, classical humanism, and utilitarian individualism.[3]

2. See Clifford Geertz, "Religion as a Cultural System," in his *The Interpretation of Cultures* (New York: Basic Books, 1973) for a classic statement of this view. Max Heirich points to the need for some such interpretation of conversion in "Change of Heart: A Test of Some Widely Held Theories about Conversion," *American Journal of Sociology* 83, 3 (1977): pp. 653–80.
3. This interpretation rests on Robert N. Bellah's argument in "New Religious Consciousness and the Crisis of Modernity," chapter 15 of *The New Religious Conscious-*

Biblical religion traditionally conceives of reality in terms of an absolute objective God who is the Creator and Father of all human beings. God reveals himself to them in sacred scripture and commands them to obey him. Biblical morality embodies an "authoritative" style of ethical evaluation. This means it is oriented toward an authoritative moral source whose will is known by faith, conscience, and scriptural exegesis. The moral question, "What should I do?" is posed by asking, "What does God command and love?" An act is right because divine authority commands it and loves us. It is to be done in obedience and charity, the cardinal virtues of this ethic. (See Table 1 for the styles of ethical evaluation typified here.)

In addition to this revelational aspect, biblical religion includes a rationalist line of development consonant with classical humanism and characterized by a rule-governed or "regular" style of ethical evaluation. It is oriented to rules and principles of right conduct as discerned by dialectical reason. It poses the moral question, "What should I do?" by asking, "What is the relevant rule, virtue, or principle?" An act is right, not solely because of its consequences, but because it conforms in itself to ideals of action and character taken as relevant by reason. It also accords with the regularity of nature and human existence. To do the right act, therefore, is a matter of rationality, seen as naturally lawful, consistent, and generalizable, and as such defining the cardinal virtue of the regular ethic.

Utilitarian individualism begins with the individual person as an actor seeking to satisfy his own wants and interests. He asks first, "What do I want?" and second, "Which act will yield the most of what I want?" "Wants" are taken as given, suggesting notions such as happiness, pleasure, or self-preservation as the good. Good consequences are those that most satisfy wants. Right acts are those that produce the most good consequences, as reckoned by cost-benefit calculation. Thus the chief virtue of the "consequential" style of evaluation employed by utilitarian culture is not rationality

---

ness, C. Y. Glock and R. N. Bellah, eds., (Berkeley: University of California Press, 1976). I have developed its specifically normative dimension, using a taxonomy of styles of ethical evaluation taken from Ralph B. Potter, "The Structure of Certain Christian Responses to the Nuclear Dilemma, 1959–1963" (unpublished Th.D. thesis, Harvard Divinity School, 1965), pp. 363–98.

STYLES OF ETHICAL EVALUATION

	ORIENTED TO	MODE OF KNOWLEDGE	DISCOURSE	RIGHT-MAKING CHARACTERISTIC	VIRTUE
Authoritative	Authority (God)	Faith/ Conscience	What does God command?	Commanded by God	Obedience
Regular	Rules	Reason	What is the relevant rule, principle?	Conforms to rules	Rationality
Consequential	Consequences	Cost/benefit calculation	What do I want? What will most satisfy it?	Produces most good consequences	Efficiency
Expressive	Self and situation	Intuition/ feelings	What's happening?	Expresses self/responds to situations	Sensitivity

Adapted from Ralph Potter, *Nuclear Dilemma* (see Ref. 3).

or obedience, but the efficiency of actors in maximizing the satisfaction of their wants.

* * *

The counterculture of the sixties arose out of the romantic tradition to repudiate these earlier conceptions of reality in America, especially utilitarian individualism. The counterculture begins with the individual, not as an actor efficiently pursuing his own self-interest, but as a personality that experiences, knows, and simply *is*. "The way to do is to be." Neither a logic of following rules nor of maximizing consequences predominates in the counterculture's ethic. What does, is the idea that everyone ought to act in any given situation in a way that fully expresses herself, specifically her inner feelings and experience of the situation. This situational and "expressive" style of evaluation is oriented to the feelings of the agent, those of others around her, and to their present situation, as discerned by empathic intuition. This style shapes an ethic of impulse ("do what you feel") and *self*-expression ("let it all hang out"), on the one hand; on the other, it shapes an ethic of situational appropriateness ("go with the flow; different strokes for different folks"). The moral question, "What should I do?" is posed by asking, "What's happening?" An act is right because it "feels right," most simply; or because it expresses the inner integrity of the agent and responds most appropriately to the situation here and now. The chief countercultural virtue is sensitivity of feeling. "Be here now," this ethic exhorts. "Get in touch with yourself."

* * *

The counterculture challenged utilitarian culture at the most fundamental level. It asked what in life possessed intrinsic value, and to what ends ought we to act. It rejected money, power, and technical knowledge, mainstays of "the good life" of middle-class society, as ends good in themselves. Instead, it identified them as means that did not, after all, enable one to experience what is intrinsically valuable—love, self-awareness, intimacy with others and nature. Utilitarian culture grew away from biblical morality in a modernizing America, but it could not generate autonomous moral rules by itself. This opened space for the counterculture to emerge. Because the counterculture relied on unregulated feelings to realize its values, it could not institutionalize them stably. Further, utilitarian culture fits with the structural conditions of modern society: technological production, bureaucratic organization, and empirical science. This blocked the counterculture's growth and bound its revolutionary impulse to failure. But in the process, utilitarian culture was stripped of moral authority, especially in the eyes of the young. The conflict of values during the 1960s left both sides of the battlefield strewn with ideological wreckage. In this atmosphere of disillusionment, many youths sought out alternative religious and therapeutic movements. Here they found a way both to cope with the instrumental demands of adulthood in conventional society *and* to sustain the counterculture's expressive ideals by reinforcing them with moralities of authority, rules, and utility. Changes in the ethical outlook of sixties youth involved in the human potential movement, specifically in *est*, describe one aspect of this larger transformation. The moral logic of these changes reveal the dynamics of conversion and cultural change as interrelated processes of ethical recombination.

EST AND ETHICS: RULE-EGOISM IN MIDDLE-CLASS CULTURE

Erhard Seminars Training *(est)* describes itself as an "educational corporation" that trains its clients "to transform [their] ability to experience living so that the situations [they] have been trying to change or have been putting up with clear up just in the process of life itself."[4] The standard training program takes over sixty hours spread across four days. A single "trainer" delivers it in a hotel ballroom to groups of two hundred or so persons, mostly urban, middle-class young adults, at a cost of $350 per person. Werner Erhard gave the first *est* training in a friend's borrowed apartment in 1971. Today the *est* organization is a model bureaucracy . . . which coordinates the efforts of some two hundred fifty paid employees and twenty-five thousand volunteers in twenty-nine cities. At a rate peaking above six thousand per month, *est* trained more than three hundred thousand persons through 1981, a quarter of whom are concentrated in California. In the San Francisco Bay area, where *est*

4. From "What is the purpose of the *est* training?," *est* pamphlet #680-3, 13 January 1976.

is based, one out of every nine college-educated young adults has taken the training.[5]

* * *

est mediates the moral conflict between mainstream and counterculture with a consequential ethic. It justifies following conventional rules for the sake of satisfying one's own wants. These are defined in forms integral with self-expression and situational responsiveness. *est* echoes the counterculture in calling "appropriateness" the characteristic of actions that makes them right. But *est*'s idea of acting appropriately rests on the moral logic of utilitarian individualism. Explains a young graduate:

> Acting appropriately means "playing for aliveness" and getting what you want in life. When you act appropriately, your life works. You experience satisfaction and aliveness. . . . The reason why [you should act appropriately] is because it works, not because it's right or wrong.[6]

The appropriate action is the one that yields the most feelings of aliveness to the agent. Like utilitarian culture, *est* holds that acts are not right or wrong in themselves. Acts are right only by virtue of the goodness of their consequences. What is good, according to *est*, are certain feelings the individual experiences: aliveness, satisfaction, and so on. To act rightly, then, one simply "plays for aliveness" by doing whatever produces this feeling.

What sorts of acts produce aliveness? According to *est*, such feelings follow from "having your life work." This in turn results from "realizing your intentions and achieving your goals." By this logic feelings of individual well-being depend on achieving one's goals. They cannot be arrived at simply by "turning on, tuning in, and dropping out." For sixties youth who tried and failed to enact the expressive ethic by such direct means, this consequential refor-

5. *est, The Graduate Review*, February 1978, p. 3; June 1978, p. 2; and personal communication with staff, 1980.

6. These data come from formal taped interviews averaging three hours each with twenty sixties youths who are *est* graduates, done in the San Francisco Bay Area during 1975–78; and informal interviews with thirty or so others done over a year's participant-observation, during which period the writer took the *est* training and two "graduate seminar series," and worked as an *est* volunteer.

mulation of it has great appeal. *est* explains the failure of the counterculture's dropout lifestyle to realize its own ends of self-fulfillment. And it justifies dropping back into middle-class life in order to do so. What must one do to achieve his goals? "Follow the rules and keep your agreements," answers the *est* graduate. Why do this? "To get what you want in life," she replies. The individual follows rules to satisfy his own wants, through achieving his goals and feeling aliveness. *est* justifies following rules and keeping agreements because these practices produce good consequences for the agent, not because they obey God or conform to reason. This constitutes "rule-egoism": compliance with rules is being justified on egoistic grounds.

What are the rules to which *est* refers? Their identification outside the training is unclear. They are "the rules of life." Inside the training, however, comprehensive "ground rules" prescribe schedule, seating, interaction, movement, posture, and ideal attitude in precise and concrete detail. Trainees are told that with respect to the rules, as in every other respect, *est* parallels life. "If you follow the ground rules, you'll get value from the training. If you follow the rules of life, life will work for you." Taking this parallel concretely, the procedural rules that govern *est* as a bureaucratized voluntary association mainly reflect the bureaucratic regulations that govern life in modern society, especially middle-class adult life centered on white-collar work. And indeed it is from this social setting that *est* draws almost all its clients. Eighty-eight percent of them are white, 1.3 percent black. Eighty-eight percent began college, 57 percent finished it. Few *est* graduates are skilled laborers— or technically specialized professionals. They work primarily with other persons, not physical objects or abstractions. Sixties youth, now in their thirties and early forties, comprise 47 percent of all *est* graduates, two and a half times their share of San Francisco's population and four times their share of the nation's.[7]

7. The following data are drawn from Robert Ornstein, et al., *A Self-Report Survey: Preliminary Study of Participants in Erhard Seminars Training* (The *est* Foundation, 1975, pp. 25–27, 34–36, 59); supplemented by reference to Ornstein data sets in File SYS8, 10/11/74, Variables W29–88; and by 20 sixties youths formally interviewed by the writer. Average age data come from *est*'s own records (see *The Graduate Review*, February 1978, p. 3). Occupational data come from Ornstein File SYS8, Variable W88, pp. 76–78.

Rule-egoism in its vintage corporate form advises the organization man to "Go along to get along." *est*'s counsel to "Follow the rules to get what you want in life" implies conventional success as a good, but it makes clear that feelings of aliveness are what is ultimately good.

These individual feelings are the ultimate good which appropriate action yields, and also as the motivational source from which it arises. When a person "comes from aliveness," she always acts appropriately. In advocating this motive, *est* sponsors a facsimile of the counterculture's idea that appropriate action arises from and expresses the individual's true inner self. Hip self-expression squares with the bureaucratic constraints of rule-egoism in light of *est*'s subjectivist epistemology. It interprets social norms as expressing the "intentions" and "choice" of each individual, who is herself seen to be the "total cause" of her experience, including "the rules" of society. The individual has "created" the rules by a process of self-expression and "communication" leading to interpersonal "agreements" from which the rules have evolved. Once each person has intuited her own subjective interests and empathically communicated them to another, then the two are able to make agreements with each other that will serve the self-interest of each and will, therefore, be kept by both.

Here we have reached a moral locale resembling the marketplace of classical economics and the focal situation of social contract theory. Mutually disinterested agents are each seeking to serve their own interests by mutual exchange. But in *est* the approach to this situation has been psychologized in tones echoing the expressive ethic, and the contract itself has been placed chiefly at the level of interpersonal relationships instead of social structure. John Locke and Adam Smith have entered therapy. *est*'s teaching on communication resonates with counterculture ideals of self-expression, interpersonal honesty, and sensitivity as ends good in themselves. In the consequential style of *est*'s ethic they appear, on one hand, as means to making viable agreements with others, in order to achieve one's own goals and feel aliveness. On the other hand, *est* points out that satisfying interpersonal relationships, which may themselves be chosen as goals, require the participant to keep agreements and follow rules. In this latter respect, *est* reinforces expressive values with elements of a regular ethic. As a result, sixties youth experience relationships idealized by the counterculture to be realized reliably for the first time in *est.*

est conceives moral responsibility as each individual acknowledging that he is the total cause of his own experience. The responsible person attributes whatever happens to him to his own ultimate doing instead of blaming others. He introspects his own consciousness to disclose the hidden motives for his difficulties. He "acknowledges" and "experiences out" these ultimate causes, thus allowing them to "disappear" and causing his problems to "clear up just in the process of life itself." The responsibility each person bears toward others is to "assist" each of them in taking responsibility for himself in the abreactive fashion just described. In practice this presupposes fluid interpersonal ties, which in fact obtain for *est*'s clients. Their divorce rate is twice that of San Franciscans and four times that of Americans generally. They live in an urban, white-collar, singles milieu, where decoupling from spouses or lovers and leaving behind co-workers and friends are familiar facts of life. The relative economic security of this milieu, where individual graduates earn comfortable incomes, likewise lends plausibility to the laissez-faire side of *est*'s ethic. In theory *est*'s concept of moral responsibility is finally binocular, because its beginning assumptions are radically individualistic on one side and monistic on the other. *est* posits that each individual is the total cause of his experience, implying that he is totally *and exclusively* responsible for his own situation and its difficulties. But *est* also posits that each individual exists ultimately as a "being" coextensive with all existence, implying that he is responsible for everyone else.

The plausibility of *est*'s ethic depends less on its internal logic than on the experienced power of the training itself in tandem with the social situation of the trainee. Sixties youth involved in *est* typically come from the urban middle class. They saw themselves as members of the counterculture while going to college and for several years afterward, often living during this time in modestly hip, dropout style. Now they have come of age and entered the white-collar work force. Rule-egoism makes sense to these exiles from youth, still seeking self-fulfillment adn hoping for a better world, yet needing to consolidate a career and relationships within the existing order. Follow the rules and work hard to achieve your goals, *est* advises, and then you will feel alive and natural. This formula justifies sixties youth in giving up their utopian expectations of political and personal change, and dropping back into middle-class social and economic life. *est* motivates them to lead this life effectively, with an eye to inner satisfaction as well as external success; and it trains them in the face-to-face fluency and emotional self-management this life requires in a white-collar singles milieu.

Engaging yet detached, *est*'s therapeutic ideal responds adaptively to the social conditions permeating urban bureaucratic life, especially, but not only, for young adults. Largely secularized, college-educated, white-collar singles and divorcees, *est*'s clients embody religious, educational, occupational, and marital characteristics now spreading through our society. Expressive yet utilitarian, *est*'s ideas claim legitimate kinship with recognizable moral traditions long contained in our culture but now strengthening their hold on what we recognize as common sense. *est* presents a powerfully convincing model of and for interpersonal behavior in the urban office, schoolroom, sales conference, and singles bar. The appeal of this model, whatever its merits, suggests how deep and troubling are the questions *est* addresses in contemporary American middle-class culture. *est* appeals, says a psychiatrist-graduate, "because it's so middle class, so all-American—like the Chevrolet."[8] Indeed, it *is* such an ideological vehicle, but one redesigned for a society unsettled in new ways and now picking up freeway speed toward an end that may leave us far from home.

CONVERSION IN CULTURAL CONTEXT

Alternative religious movements have not overturned tradition and replaced it with something entirely new. Rather, they have drawn out strands from traditional moralities and rewoven them into a fabric that ties into American culture as a whole yet differs in pattern from any one of its traditions. The human potential movement recombines the expressive ethic of the counterculture with the consequential ethic of utilitarian individualism, with particular plausibility for the middle middle class. Conservative Christian groups recombine the expressive ethic with the authoritative ethic of revealed biblical religion, with particular plausibility for the lower

8. *The Graduate Review*, June 1977, p. 12.

middle class. Neo-Oriental groups recombine the expressive ethic with the regular ethic of rationalized religion and humanism, with particular plausibility for the upper middle class.

* * *

The stock answers of utilitarian individualism begin to unravel when its adherent asks, "Why don't I feel happy?" This question presupposes, of course, the individual's right to possess happiness, not merely to pursue it, a shift in American expectations nowhere more dramatically visible than between sixties youth and the generation of their parents. Already possessed of much that money can buy, and still unsatisfied, these youths found the ultimate meaning of conventional values and their logic of action undercut by the counterculture. Yet its expressive alternative also proved unable to stand up to their experience . "Money can't buy you love," it is true, but that does not mean that "love is all you need." You also need moral rules to live by, authority to respect, and contracts to keep— even to sustain your love. Alternative religions resolve this predicament . . . By mapping out moralities of loving authority, antinomian rules, and rule-egoism through the middle of a conflicted culture, alternative religions saved sixties youth caught between the devils of self-interest, law-and-order authority, and heartless rules on one side and the deep blue sea of boundless self-expression on the other.

As long as technological production, bureaucratic organization, and a massed urban population remain central to the structure of American society, outright rejections of the instrumental behavior rationalized by utilitarian culture are likely to flourish only within small subcultures or for short periods in the life cycle of their carriers. Otherwise, Americans must respond to the practical demands exerted on adults by the modernized society in which they live. Yet they must also respond to the integrity of meaning exerted by the different moral traditions with which they think. In this double-edged process, members of alternative religious movements carry nonutilitarian perceptions, assumptions, loyalties, and styles of evaluation out into a utilitarian culture, which absorbs these contrary elements even as it dilutes and makes them over. . . . This process of reciprocal cultural change will go on for as long as utilitarian culture cannot justify by itself the dedicated work, cooperative behavior, and distributive justice that its political and social structure requires. It will continue, too, for as long as utilitarian culture cannot symbolize the enchantment the human mind finds in the world around and within itself.[9]

However little direct difference alternative religious movements may make to existing social structures, their public impact cannot be dismissed without gauging the secondary effects of the changes in moral and cultural meaning that they carry. The nature of selfhood and virtue, the individual in relation to the group, (inexhaustible) wants in relation to (limited) needs, rights in relation to duties, the legitimacy of moral authority and rules—redefinition of such ideas occurs at the foundation of social values and eventually makes itself felt in the structure of social arrangements. It does so by relocating the good ends at which social practices and policies aim, and by reshaping the criteria of justice that institutions seek to satisfy. Giving each person his due assumes that we know what a person is, what things are good, and what a person should do to deserve them. When such moral knowledge changes, so does the just arrangement of our institutions. Chances are it will be an unforeseeable while before American society turns into a Christian theocracy, a monastic ecotopia, or one vast encounter group. But the ideological upsurge of conservative Christianity, neo-Oriental and ecological monism, and psychologized individualism through out American culture is already unmistakable. So is the weakening of liberalism, that synthesis of rational religion and humanism with utilitarian views that has long held sway over the moral middle ground in America. This weakening has created a vacuum of meaning these other ideologies are expanding to fill, echoing from the political podium as well as the religious pulpit.

Styles of ethical evaluation by themselves are empty analytical categories. They take on substance only when they are applied in turn to the different layers of moral meaning that make up social life. These include (1) cultural historical patterns of morality like biblical religion, which support (2) the norms of social institutions like the family, and underlie (3) the formal ethics of ideological organizations like *est*, which inform (4) the ethical outlook of per-

9. Cf. Weber, *The Protestant Ethic and the Spirit of Capitalism* (New York: Scribners, 1930), pp. 181–82; also "Science as a Vocation," pp. 155–56 in *From Max Weber* (New York: Oxford University Press, 1958).

sons in a particular place in society at a particular time in their own lives and in history, like middle-class sixties youth. Only when styles of ethical evaluation link the other elements that make up moral understanding—that is, perceptions of facts, loyalties to others, and axial assumptions about the nature of reality—do these analytical categories reveal a living ethic by which persons make particular judgments.[10]

Without considering styles of evaluation, on the other hand, we cannot understand moral behavior nor can we change it, except by coercion or by the manipulation of interests. This is because we *think* our way to moral actions. Circumstances influence our thinking, but they do not do it for us. Recognizing this fact makes it possible to enrich research that neatly correlates social and economic data with discrete opinions on concrete issues, by exposing the interlocking assumptions, arguments, and modes of discourse that hold together these particulars within a cultural matrix. It also makes it possible to honor the commonsense conviction we have of our own moral views—that they come from our understanding, not our circumstances.

JERRY FALWELL

Revival in America

Listen, America! Our nation is on a perilous path in regard to her political, economic, and military positions. If America continues down the path she is traveling, she will one day find that she is no longer a free nation. Our nation's internal problems are direct results of her spiritual condition. America is desperately in need of a divine healing, which can only come if God's people will humble themselves, pray, seek His face, and turn from their wicked ways. It

10. See Ralph Potter, "The Logic of Moral Argument," pp. 93–114 in *Toward a Discipline of Social Ethics*, Paul Deats (ed.) (Boston: Boston University Press, 1972).

Jerry Falwell, "Revival in America," excerpted from Falwell, *Listen, America!* (Garden City, N.Y.: Doubleday, 1980), pp.243–4; 265–6.

is now time that moral Americans awake to the fact that our future depends upon how we stand on moral issues. God has no reason to spare us if we continue to reject Him.

America has been great because her people have been good. We are certainly far from being a perfect society, but our heritage is one of genuine concern for all mankind. It is God Almighty who has made and preserved us as a nation, and the day that we forget that is the day that the United States will become a byword among the nations of the world. We will become nothing more than a memory in a history book, like the many great civilizations that have preceded us. America's only hope for survival is a spiritual awakening that begins in the lives of her individual citizens. It is only in the spiritual rebirth of our nation's citizens that we can have a positive hope in the future. The destiny of America awaits that decision.

We are facing many serious issues at this time. Action must be taken quickly in the areas of politics, economics, and defense. But the most brilliant plans and programs of men will never accomplish enough to save America. The answer to America's continued existence rests with the spiritual condition of her people. When a person allows biblical morality to be the guiding principle of his life, he can have the confidence that "righteousness exalts a nation."

I do not believe that God is finished with America. Yet America has more God-fearing citizens per capita than any other nation on earth. There are millions of Americans who love God, decency, and biblical morality. North America is the last logical base for world evangelization. While it is true that God could use any nation or means possible to spread the gospel to the world, it is also true that we have the churches, the schools, the young people, the media, the money, and the means of spreading the Gospel worldwide in our lifetime. God loves all the world, not just America. However, I am convinced that our freedoms are essential to world evangelism in this latter part of the twentieth century.

I am seeking to rally together the people of this country who still believe in decency, the home, the family, morality, the free-enterprise system, and all the great ideals that are the cornerstone of this nation. Against the growing tide of permissiveness and moral decay that is crushing our society, we must make a sacred commitment to God Almighty to turn this nation around immediately. I know that there are millions of law-abiding, God-fearing Americans who want to do some thing about the moral decline of our country, but when you ask the average person what can be done about revival in America, he will often reply, "I'm just one person. What can I do anyhow?" As long as the average moral American believes that, the political and social liberals in this society will be able to pass their socialistic legislation at will. We are late, but I do not believe that we are too late. It is time to put our lives on the line for this great nation of ours.

Right living must be re-established as an American way of life. We as American citizens must recommit ourselves to the faith of our fathers and to the premises and moral foundations upon which this country was established. Now is the time to begin calling America back to God, back to the Bible, back to morality! We must be willing to live by the moral convictions that we claim to believe. There is no way that we will ever be willing to die for something for which we are not willing to live. The authority of Bible morality must once again be recognized as the legitimate guiding principle of our nation. Our love for our fellow man must ever be grounded in the truth and never be allowed to blind us from the truth that is the basis of our love for our fellow man.

As a pastor and as a parent I am calling my fellow American citizens to unite in a moral crusade for righteousness in our generation. It is time to call America back to her moral roots. It is time to call America back to God. We need a revival of righteous living based on a proper confession of sin and repentance of heart if we are to remain the land of the free and the home of the brave! I am convinced that God is calling millions of Americans in the so-often silent majority to join in the moral majority crusade to turn America around in our lifetime. Won't you begin now to pray with us for revival in America? Let us unite our hearts and lives together for the cause of a new America . . . a moral America in which righteousness will exalt this nation. Only as we do this can we exempt ourselves from one day having to look our children in the eyes and answer this searching question: "Mom and Dad, where were you the day freedom died in America?"

The choice is now ours.

JESSE JACKSON

The Call of Conscience

Tonight we come together bound by our faith in a mighty God, with genuine respect and love for our country, and inheriting the legacy of a great party, the Democratic Party, which is the best hope for redirecting our nation on a more humane, just and peaceful course.

This is not a perfect party. We are not a perfect people. Yet, we are called to a perfect mission: Our mission, to feed the hungry, to clothe the naked, to house the homeless, to teach the illiterate, to provide jobs for the jobless, and to choose the human race over the nuclear race.

We are gathered here this week to nominate a candidate and adopt a platform which will expand, unify, direct and inspire our party and the nation to fulfill this mission.

My constituency is the desperate, the damned, the disinherited, the disrespected, and the despised.

They are restless and seek relief. They've voted in record numbers. They have invested faith, hope and trust that they have in us. The Democratic Party must send them a signal that we care. I pledge my best to not let them down.

There is the call of conscience: redemption, expansion, healing and unity. Leadership must heed the call of conscience: redemption expansion, healing and unity for they are the key to achieving our mission.

Our flag is red, white and blue, but our nation is a rainbow— red, yellow, brown, black and white—and we're all precious in God's sight. America is not like a blanket—one piece of unbroken cloth, the same color, the same texture, the same size. America is more like a quilt—many patches, many pieces, many colors, many sizes, all woven and held together by a common thread.

Jesse L. Jackson, "The Call of Conscience, The Courage of Conviction," Address to the 1984 Democratic Convention, July 17, 1984, excerpted from the *New York Times* (July 18, 1984), p. A18. Reprinted in Jackson *Straight from the Heart* (Philadelphia: Fortress Press, 1987), pp. 3–18.

The white, the Hispanic, the black, the Arab, the Jew, the woman, the native American, the small farmer, the businessperson, the environmentalist, the peace activist, the young, the old, the lesbian, the gay and the disabled make up the American quilt.

Even in our fractured state, all of us count and all of us fit somewhere. We have proven that we can survive without each other. But we have not proven that we can win and progress without each other. We must come together.

From Fannie Lee Hamer in Atlantic City in 1964 to the Rainbow Coalition in San Francisco today, from the Atlantic to the Pacific, we have experienced pain but progress as we ended American apartheid laws, we got public accommodation, we secured voting rights, we obtained open housing, as young people got the right to vote, we lost Malcolm, Martin, Medgar, Bobby, John and Viola.

The team that got us here must be expanded, not abandoned. Twenty years ago, tears welled up in our eyes as the bodies of Schwerner, Goodman and Cheney were dredged from the depths of a river in Mississippi. Twenty years later, our communities black and Jewish, are in anguish, anger and pain.

Feelings have been hurt on both sides. There is a crisis in communications. Confusion is in the air. But we cannot afford to lose our way. We may agree to agree, or agree to disagree on issues, but we must bring back civility to these tensions.

We are co-partners in a long and rich religious history—the Judeo-Christian traditions. Many blacks and Jews have a shared passion for social justice at home and peace abroad. We must seek a revival of the spirit, inspired by a new vision and new possibilities. We must return to higher ground. We are bound by Moses and Jesus, but also connected with Islam and Mohammed.

These three great religions; Judaism, Christianity and Islam, were all born in the revered and holy city of Jerusalem. We are bound by Dr. Martin Luther King, Jr., and Rabbi Abraham Heschel, crying out from their graves for us to reach common ground.

We are bound by shared blood and shared sacrifices. We are much too intelligent; much too bound by our Judeo-Christian heritage; much too victimized by racism, sexism, militarism, and anti-Semitism; much too threatened as historical scapegoats to go on divided one from another. We must turn from finger pointing to clasped hands. We must share our burdens and our joys with each other once again. We must turn to each other and not on each other and choose higher ground.

Jesus said that we should not be judged by the bark we wear but by the fruit that we bear. Jesus said that we must measure greatness by how we treat the least of these.

President Reagan says the nation is in recovery. Those 90,000 corporations that made a profit last year but paid no Federal taxes are recovering. The 37,000 military contractors who have benefited from Reagan's more than doubling of the military budget in peacetime surely they are recovering. The big corporations and rich individuals who received the bulk of a three year, multibillion tax cut from Mr. Reagan are recovering. But no such recovery is under way for the least of these. Rising tides don't lift all boats, particularly those stuck at the bottom.

For the boats stuck at the bottom there's a misery index. This Administration has made life more miserable for the poor. Its attitude has been contemptuous. Its policies and programs have been cruel and unfair to working people.

Our time has come. Our faith, hope and dreams have prevailed. Our time has come. Weeping has endured for nights but that joy cometh in the morning. Our time has come. No grave can hold our body down. Our time has come. No lie can live forever. Our time has come. We must leave the racial battle ground and come to the economic common ground and moral higher ground. America, our time has come. We come from this grace, to amazing grace. Our time has come.

Give me your tired, give me your poor, your huddled masses who learn to breathe free and come November, there will be a change because our time has come. Thank you and God bless you.

H. Richard Niebuhr

The Social Sources of Denominationalism

THE ETHICAL FAILURE OF THE DIVIDED CHURCH

Christendom has often achieved apparent success by ignoring the precepts of its founder. The church, as an organization interested in self-preservation and in the gain of power, has sometimes found the counsel of the Cross quite as inexpedient as have national and economic groups. In dealing with such major social evils as war, slavery, and social inequality, it has discovered convenient ambiguities in the letter of the Gospels which enabled it to violate their spirit and to ally itself with the prestige and power those evils had gained in their corporate organization. In adapting itself to the conditions of a civilization which its founder had bidden it to permeate with the spirit of divine love, it found that it was easier to give to Caesar the things belonging to Caesar if the examination of what might belong to God were not too closely pressed.

This proneness toward compromise which characterizes the whole history of the church, is no more difficult to understand than is the similar and inevitable tendency by which each individual Christian adapts the demands of the gospel to the necessities of existence in the body and in civilized society. It has often been pointed out that no ideal can be incorporated without the loss of some of its ideal character. When liberty gains a constitution, liberty is compromised; when fraternity elects officers, fraternity yields some of the ideal qualities of brotherhood to the necessities of government. And the gospel of Christ is especially subject to this sacrifice of character in the interest of organic embodiment; for the very essence of Christianity lies in the tension which it presupposes

---

H. Richard Niebuhr, excerpted from *The Social Sources of Denominationalism* (New York: Meridien/World Publishing, 1957), pp. 3–6, 21, 22,; 25, 236–8, 278–282, 283–4. Copyright © Henry Holt, 1920, 1957.

or creates between the worlds of nature and of spirit, and in its resolution of that conflict by means of justifying faith. It demands the impossible in conduct and belief; it runs counter to the instinctive life of man and exalts the rationality of the irrational; in a world of relativity it calls for unyielding loyalty to unchangeable absolutes. Clothe its faith in terms of philosophy, whether medieval or modern, and you lose the meaning of its high desires, of its living experience, reducing these to a set of opinions often irrelevant, sometimes contrary, to the original content. Organize its ethics—as organize them you must whenever two or three are gathered in the name of Christ—and the free spirit of forgiving love becomes a new law, requiring interpretation, commentary, and all the machinery of justice—just the sort of impersonal relationship which the gospel denies and combats. Place this society in the world, demanding that it be not of the world, and strenuous as may be its efforts to transcend or to sublimate the mundane life, it will yet be unable to escape all taint of conspiracy and connivance with the worldly interests it despises. Yet, on the other hand, Christian ethics will not permit a world-fleeing asceticism which seeks purity at the cost of service. At the end, if not at the beginning, of every effort to incorporate Christianity there is, therefore, a compromise, and the Christian cannot escape the necessity of seeking the last source of righteousness outside himself and the world in the divine aggression, in a justification that is by faith.

The fact that compromise is inevitable does not make it less an evil. The fault of every concession, of course, is that it is made too soon, before the ultimate resistance "to the blood" has been offered. But compromises are doubly evil when they are unacknowledged, when the emasculation of the Christian ideal remains undiscovered and when, in consequence, men take pride, as in an achievement, in a defeat of the essential gospel. Such unconscious hypocrisy not only bars the way to continued efforts to penetrate the stubborn stuff of life with the ethics of Jesus but is the author of further compromises made all too early. So it produces at last a spurious gospel unaware of its departure from the faith once delivered to the saints.

Denominationalism in the Christian church is such an unacknowledged hypocrisy. It is a compromise, made far too lightly, between Christianity and the world. Yet it often regards itself as a

Christian achievement and glorifies its martyrs as bearers of the Cross. It represents the accommodation of Christianity to the caste-system of human society. It carries over into the organization of the Christian principle of brotherhood the prides and prejudices, the privilege and prestige, as well as the humiliations and abasements, the injustices and inequalities of that specious order of high and low wherein men find the satisfaction of their craving for vain glory. The division of the churches closely follows the division of men into the castes of national, racial, and economic groups. It draws the color line in the church of God; it fosters the misunderstandings, the self-exaltations, the hatreds of jingoistic nationalism by continuing in the body of Christ the spurious differences of provincial loyalties; it seats the rich and poor apart at the table of the Lord, where the fortunate may enjoy the bounty they have provided while the others feed upon the crusts their poverty affords.

* * *

The domination of class and self-preservative church ethics over the ethics of the gospel must be held responsible for much of the moral ineffectiveness of Christianity in the West. Not only or primarily because denominationalism divides and scatters the energies of Christendom, but more because it signalizes that the defeat of the Christian ethics of brotherhood by the ethics of caste is at the source of Christendom's moral weakness. The ethical effectiveness of an individual depends on the integration of his character, on the synthesis of his values and desires into a system dominated by his highest good; the ethical effectiveness of a group is no less dependent on its control by a morale in which all subordinate purposes are organized around a leading ideal. And the churches are ineffective because they lack such a common morale.

* * *

Denominationalism thus represents the moral failure of Christianity. And unless the ethics of brotherhood can gain the victory over this divisiveness within the body of Christ it is useless to expect it to be victorious in the world. But before the church can hope to overcome its fatal division it must learn to recognize and to acknowledge the secular character of its denominationalism.

* * *

Rationalization has been used to defend discrimination rather than to obscure it. The dogma which divides the racial churches is anthropological, not theological, in content. Whether the dogma of white superiority and Negro inferiority has been openly avowed or unconsciously accepted, the white churches have nevertheless taken it for granted and have come to regard it as not incompatible with the remainder of their beliefs. At times, indeed, they have incorporated it in their popular theology and sought to provide a biblical basis for it. More frequently they have received it as a simple dogma of nature, similar to the doctrine of sex. In both cases the assumption of superiority by one group—an assumption which became unquestioned social tradition—has been given the dignity of an impartial natural law and regarded as a self-evident truth. By virtue of the marvellous inconsistency of human reason, it has often been maintained unchallenged alongside of the other self-evident truth that all men are created free and equal and endowed with the same rights to life, liberty, and the pursuit of happiness. Just as the church accepted the doctrine of female inferiority and refused women the right to be ordained or even to participate in its government, so also it accepted the dogma of Negro inferiority and without compunction refused ecclesiastical equality to this race. As it separated men and women in the houses of worship so it segregated and continues to segregate the races. The fact that in Christ there is neither male nor female has, of course, been recognized much more freely in the church than has the fact that in him there can be neither white nor black. Even the truth that in him there is neither bond nor free has been more definitely accepted than the implied doctrine of racial equality and unity. On the whole, however, the ideal of unity and equality has never been recognized in reality until the inferior group, whether women or slaves or a racial group, has asserted that equality and compelled the church to translate its principles into practice.

WAYS TO UNITY

Is there not available some form of the Christian faith which possesses both the compelling ideal that can bring inner unity to the world and courage to undertake the penetration of human society with that ideal despite the difficulties and confusions which tempt to surrender or to flight?

The Christianity of the gospels doubtless contains the required ideal. Its purpose is not the foundation of an ecclesiastical institution or the proclamation of a metaphysical creed, though it seeks the formation of a divine society and presupposes the metaphysics of a Christlike God. Its purpose is the revelation to men of their potential childhood to the Father and their possible brotherhood with each other. That revelation is made not in terms of dogma but of life, above all in the life of Christ. His sonship and his brotherhood, as delineated in the gospel, are not the example which men are asked to follow if they will, but rather the demonstration of that character of ultimate reality which they can ignore only at the cost of their souls. The *summum bonum* which this faith sets before men is nothing less than the eternal harmony of love, in which each individual can realize the full potentiality of an eternal life in self-sacrificing devotion to the Beloved Community of the Father and all the brethren.

* * *

For the proclamation of this Christianity of Christ and the Gospels a church is needed which has transcended the divisions of the world and has adjusted itself not to the local interests and needs of classes, races, or nations but to the common interests of mankind and to the constitution of the unrealized kingdom of God. No denominational Christianity, no matter how broad its scope, suffices for the task. The church which can proclaim this gospel must be one in which no national allegiance will be suffered to infringe upon the unity of an international fellowship. In it the vow of love of enemy and neighbor and the practice of non-resistance will need to take their place beside the confession of faith and the rites. For without complete abstention from nationalist ethics the universal fellowship of this church would inevitably fall apart into nationalist groups at the threat of war or under the influence of jingoistic propaganda. In such a church distinctions between rich and poor will be abrogated by the kind of communism of love which prevailed in the early Jerusalem community. This communism differs as radically from the dictatorship of the proletariat as it does from the dictatorship of capitalism. The principle of harmony and love upon which it alone can be established requires that each contribute to the community according to his ability and receive from it according to his need, not according to some predetermined principles of quantitative equality or of privilege. Furthermore, this church of love will need to bridge the chasm between the races, not only by practising complete fellowship within the house of God but by extending that practice into all the relationships of life. It will need to mediate the differences of culture by supplying equality of opportunity to tutored and untutored alike and by giving each their share in the common task and in the common love.

Only such a church can transcend the divisions of men and by transcending heal them; only such a church can substitute for the self-interest and the machinery of denominationalism the dominant desire for the kingdom and its righteousness and the free activity of familiar fellowship. It requires from its members the sacrifice of privilege and pride and bids each count the other better than himself. It can plant within the nations a fellowship of reconciliation which will resist the animosities nurtured by strife for political and economic values—a fellowship which, doubtless, may often be required to carry crosses of shame and pain when the passions of men have been aroused for conflict.

To describe such a church, it will be objected, is only to describe another sect, which will be added to the denominations and increase the confusion. But the church of fellowship in love need never be a sect. Rather it has always existed as a church within the churches. It is no mere vision born of desire. It is a fellowship with a long history and a record of many victories. It flourished in the primitive church of Jerusalem, where all were one in Christ. It came to appearance in the brotherhood of the early friars under Francis' leadership. It has functioned in every movement of mercy and reconciliation. The sects which it has founded have failed to hold fast to the ideal and have become partisan champions of a provincialized gospel. But though its sects have failed, the fellowship has continued. Again and again it has been the creative center of movements of the spirit which have penetrated the world. The band of disciples, the communities of Jerusalem and Antioch, did not fail when the sect of Jewish Christianity perished. The fellowship of love which had been nurtured among them impressed its ideals upon the ancient world. It did not change the whole world into conformity with its own pattern, to be sure, but it gave its savor, through the mediation of Paul, to the institutions of society so that family life, the relations of masters and slaves, and of the races were at least partially redeemed.

*   *   *

The increase of that fellowship today is the hope of Christendom and of the world. It is the church which can save the churches from the ruin of their secularism and consequent division. It challenges the world to recall its better nature and to find unity and peace in the knowledge of the divine love upon which all stable and just social life must be built.

The road to unity which love requires denominations, nations, classes, and races to take is no easy way. There is no short cut even to the union of the churches. The way to the organic, active peace of brotherhood leads through the hearts of peacemakers who will knit together, with patience and self-sacrifice, the shorn and tangled fibers of human aspirations, faiths, and hopes, who will transcend the fears and dangers of an adventure of trust. The road to unity is the road of repentance. It demands a resolute turning away from all those loyalties to the lesser values of the self, the denomination, and the nation, which deny the inclusiveness of divine love. It requires that Christians learn to look upon their separate establishments and exclusive creeds with contrition rather than with pride. The road to unity is the road of sacrifice which asks of churches as of individuals that they lose their lives in order that they may find the fulfilment of their better selves. But it is also the road to the eternal values of a Kingdom of God that is among us.

PART TEN

THE NATIONAL SOCIETY

As we have seen in the preceding parts of this anthology, the American quest for a genuine civic community emerges as a disturbing, sometimes painful, sometimes glorious memory of struggles for a more just and inclusive society. As we have also seen, this quest has been spurred and guided from the beginning by questions and convictions about the ultimate nature of things and the significance of human life. As a consequence political and social questions have for Americans always been intertwined with religious and moral concerns. Together these strands of thinking and debate have at important moments come together to form great overarching visions of how the nation's life ought to be shaped and the kinds of institutions required to make these visions of a good society effective in history.

In its tenth chapter, *Habits of the Heart* presents this ongoing debate about the shape of the national society as "an uncompleted quest" for "the public good." That chapter traces some of the major differences among some of the important visions of the public good that have attained widespread adherence among Americans in the twentieth century. However, through that discussion, as through the analysis of religious understandings in chapter 9, there runs a nagging question. Is there sufficient coherence in our national culture to permit a comprehensible and fruitful debate about the great issues of public life? While the selections in the following part of this anthology will take on that question directly, the readings in this part lay necessary groundwork by providing a look at the central tension of articulating a pattern of national life that can incorporate diversity within unity, and individual liberty within an order of justice and equality.

The first selection is from James Madison who, with Alexander

Hamilton and John Jay, coauthored *The Federalist Papers.* The republic of the United States of America is the longest-established constitutional government in the world, and the Constitution of 1787, which James Madison first conceived, has proven a remarkably effective founding document capable of adaptations to meet new situations. The essays collected in *The Federalist Papers,* written as pamphlets under the pseudonym "Publius," were a coordinated effort by Madison and his collaborators. Their aim was to persuade public opinion in the original thirteen states toward ratifying the constitutional document hammered out at the Constitutional Convention in Philadelphia. Number 10 is probably the most famous of the papers, and sets out the theory of government that is at the heart of the whole constitutional order.

It is instructive that Madison starts out in the Tenth *Federalist* to argue for his new conception of government by presenting his idea of "federalism" as the solution to the underlying problem besetting the new states. He begins by calling the problem one of instability due to "the violence of faction." Faction he later defines as "a number of citizens, whether amounting to a majority or minority of the whole," who join together in a way adverse to either "the rights of other citizens" or "the permanent and aggregate interests of the community." Both instability and faction are political evils, for Madison, because they work to deflect republican government from its true aims. By a republic, Madison means not the direct democracy of the ancients, but government through councils of popularly elected representatives. But this "modern" conception of representative republic shares with the ancient tradition of republicanism a common aim. In its deliberations, it is the common good rather than selfish interest—or "faction"—that is to rule republican assemblies.

"Faction," then, is the problem that confronts efforts to construct an institutional order that can ensure "the public good," meaning the rights of all citizens as well as the community's "permanent and aggregate interests." But what causes faction? Madison is quite clear that while faction stems in an ultimate sense from "the nature of man," in modern commercial societies it derives from "the various and unequal distribution of property." It is this which gives rise to the various interests, dividing nations into "different classes, actuated by different sentiments and views." Once one accepts, as Madison like much of the Enlightment did, that commerce is a force producing the goods of abundance and progress, the principal task of "modern legislation" becomes "the regulation of these various and interfering interests."

But what is Madison's solution? Few apparently clear texts have given rise to so many conflicting answers! However, if one focuses on Madison's purpose of presenting his national republican system as the solution to the problem of faction, and one bears in mind that Madison uses "republicanism" to mean government by popular representation, then the answer seems to be the following. The proposed federal system of representative government provides a better check on the evils of faction—and so of regulating "the various and interfering interests" generated by the working of commercial society—than any small-scale, direct, or "democratic" system of self-government in the individual states. This is so because in a republic of great size and extent there is a better chance to "enlarge and refine the public views" by "passing them through" a representative body. There is the notion that the elected representatives to this body, because they must each appeal outside their particular local "interests" to be elected, must compete, so to speak, by presenting their claims to advance not the particular, but the public, good. Madison's solution, then, is "a greater probability of a fit choice," a theme which resonates with fellow Virginian Thomas Jefferson's thoughts in the hope that republics better promote real talent and genuine civic virtue than other forms of government.

The succeeding selections give evidence of the accuracy of Madison's diagnosis of the chief problem confronting a society aiming to honor individual freedom and enterprise while striving for the common good. They also show how difficult it has proven to achieve that republican aim under the conditions of twentieth-century industrial society. Like Jefferson, Madison could take for granted that these matters would be approached within a common language and cultural frame of reference, and by gentlemen whose situation and perspective would be much like his own. The two intervening centuries of social and economic, technological and political change have, as we have seen, greatly complicated that eighteenth-century picture, in many ways for the better. Still, the problem of diversity calls for an answer of coherence. How can this be achieved in a way that is faithful to the nation's best ideals and yet adequate to the scale of the twentieth-century life?

John Dewey was America's outstanding public philosopher during the first half of the twentieth century. *Individualism—Old and New* responds to the Madisonian problem by attempting a kind of updated analysis of the causes of incoherence in the workings of modern institutions. For Dewey, writing at the onset of the Great Depression in 1929, modern corporate capitalism, which prides itself on liberating individuality through the efficient management of a growing economy, has in fact produced a nearly opposite effect. "The loyalties which once held individuals, which gave them support, direction, and unity of outlook on life have well-nigh disappeared," to be replaced by an insecure and frantic struggle for a standard of living defined only by reference to individual comfort and competitive superiority to others. The blind economics' mechanism that has spawned these disoriented individuals also undercuts republican government. The winners in the economic competition come to form a powerful "faction," but they are as unable as the less advantaged to provide leadership toward sustaining the moral coherence needed for a truly high quality of life.

William M. Sullivan, philosopher and coauthor of *Habits of the Heart*, continues the spirit of Dewey's diagnosis in the selection from *Reconstructing Public Philosophy* but adapts it to conditions half a century after Dewey wrote. Like Dewey, Sullivan rejects liberal individualism on the grounds that, both as a moral language and as a social vision, it falls short in not acknowledging the scope of modern social interdependence. By contrast, Sullivan argues that democracy today needs a common framework of discourse, a public philosophy that is able to make clear the moral dimension of the complexities of the contemporary economic and technological order which remain unilluminated by liberal individualism and invisible to most citizens. Sullivan looks to a reconstructed civic republicanism, "based upon the common aim of the basic goods of dignity, justice, and community," as a form of socially engaged practical discourse to provide a common language in which to take up the quest for the public good.

The final three selections provide examples of how political leaders have presented visions of the public good to the American public during the last half of the twentieth century. These three speeches provide different kinds of echo and response to Madison's arguments two centuries earlier. Read this way, the speeches help demonstrate both continuity and change in the terms and themes of the national dialogue. President Dwight D. Eisenhower's Farewell Address—a presidential custom initiated by George Washington—addresses the issue of American power in a century dominated by war. Himself a former general, Eisenhower follows Madison in emphasizing "balance between the actions of the moment and the national welfare of the future," and finds the greatest threat to this "good judgment" in the rise of a new faction, the "conjunction of an immense military establishment and a large arms industry . . . the military-industrial complex."

Finally, there are the two speeches of the 1980s, the 1981 inaugural address by Republican President Ronald Reagan, and the Keynote address delivered to the 1984 Democratic National Convention by New York Governor Mario Cuomo. Both explicitly invoke the ideals of the nation's founding and its great figures. But they do so to justify strongly divergent programs for achieving the nation's welfare. From this clash of words and images emerges the complexity, but also the passion and vitality, of a still hotly contested heritage and set of traditions.

James Madison

The Federalist Papers

AMONG the numerous advantages promised by a well-constructed Union, none deserves to be more accurately developed than its tendency to break and control the violence of faction. The friend of popular governments never finds himself so much alarmed for their character and fate as when he contemplates their propensity to this dangerous vice. He will not fail, therefore, to set a due value on any plan which, without violating the principles to which he is attached, provides a proper cure for it. The instability, injustice, and confusion introduced into the public councils have, in truth, been the mortal diseases under which popular governments have everywhere perished, as they continue to be the favorite and fruitful topics from which the adversaries to liberty derive their most specious declamations. The valuable improvements made by the American constitutions on the popular models, both ancient and modern, cannot certainly be too much admired; but it would be an unwarrantable partiality to contend that they have as effectually obviated the danger on this side, as was wished and expected. Complaints are everywhere heard from our most considerate and virtuous citizens, equally the friends of public and private faith and of public and personal liberty, that our governments are too unstable, that the public good is disregarded in the conflicts of rival parties, and that measures are too often decided, not according to the rules of justice and the rights of the minor party, but by the superior force of an interested and overbearing majority. However anxiously we may wish that these complaints had no foundation, the evidence of known facts will not permit us to deny that they are in some degree

James Madison, *The Federalist Papers,* Number 10, (New York: New American Library, 1961), pp. 77–84.

true. It will be found, indeed, on a candid review of our situation, that some of the distresses under which we labor have been erroneously charged on the operation of our governments; but it will be found, at the same time, that other causes will not alone account for many of our heaviest misfortunes; and, particularly, for that prevailing and increasing distrust of public engagements and alarm for private rights which are echoed from one end of the continent to the other. These must be chiefly, if not wholly, effects of the unsteadiness and injustice with which a factious spirit has tainted our public administration.

By a faction I understand a number of citizens, whether amounting to a majority or minority of the whole, who are united and actuated by some common impulse of passion, or of interest, adverse to the rights of other citizens, or to the permanent and aggregate interests of the community.

There are two methods of curing the mischiefs of faction: the one, by removing its causes; the other, by controlling its effects.

There are again two methods of removing the causes of faction: the one, by destroying the liberty which is essential to its existence; the other, by giving to every citizen the same opinions, the same passions, and the same interests.

It could never be more truly said than of the first remedy that it was worse than the disease. Liberty is to faction what air is to fire, an aliment without which it instantly expires. But it could not be a less folly to abolish liberty, which is essential to political life, because it nourishes faction than it would be to wish the annihilation of air, which is essential to animal life, because it imparts to fire its destructive agency.

The second expedient is as impracticable as the first would be unwise. As long as the reason of man continues fallible, and he is at liberty to exercise it, different opinions will be formed. As long as the connection subsists between his reason and his self-love, his opinions and his passions will have a reciprocal influence on each other; and the former will be objects to which the latter will attach themselves. The diversity in the faculties of men, from which the rights of property originate, is not less an insuperable obstacle to a uniformity of interests. The protection of these faculties is the first object of government. From the protection of different and unequal faculties of acquiring property, the possession of different degrees and kinds of property immediately results; and from the influence of these on the sentiments and views of the respective proprietors ensues a division of the society into different interests and parties.

The latent causes of faction are thus sown in the nature of man; and we see them everywhere brought into different degrees of activity, according to the different circumstances of civil society. A zeal for different opinions concerning religion, concerning government, and many other points, as well of speculation as of practice; an attachment to different leaders ambitiously contending for pre-eminence and power; or to persons of other descriptions whose fortunes have been interesting to the human passions, have, in turn, divided mankind into parties, inflamed them with mutual animosity, and rendered them much more disposed to vex and oppress each other than to co-operate for their common good. So strong is this propensity of mankind to fall into mutual animosities that where no substantial occasion presents itself the most frivolous and fanciful distinctions have been sufficient to kindle their unfriendly passions and excite their most violent conflicts. But the most common and durable source of factions has been the various and unequal distribution of property. Those who hold and those who are without property have ever formed distinct interests in society. Those who are creditors, and those who are debtors, fall under a like discrimination. A landed interest, a manufacturing interest, a mercantile interest, a moneyed interest, with many lesser interests, grow up of necessity in civilized nations, and divide them into different classes, actuated by different sentiments and views. The regulation of these various and interfering interests forms the principal task of modern legislation and involves the spirit of party and faction in the necessary and ordinary operations of government.

No man is allowed to be a judge in his own cause, because his interest would certainly bias his judgment, and, not improbably, corrupt his integrity. With equal, nay with greater reason, a body of men are unfit to be both judges and parties at the same time; yet what are many of the most important acts of legislation but so many judicial determinations, not indeed concerning the rights of single persons, but concerning the rights of large bodies of citizens? And what are the different classes of legislators but advocates and parties to the causes which they determine? Is a law proposed concerning private debts? It is a question to which the creditors are parties on one side and the debtors on the other. Justice ought to hold the balance between them. Yet the parties are, and must be, themselves the judges; and the most numerous party, or in other words, the most powerful faction must be expected to prevail. Shall domestic manufacturers be encouraged, and in what degree, by restrictions on foreign manufacturers? are questions which would be differently decided by the landed and the manufacturing classes, and probably by neither with a sole regard to justice and the public good. The apportionment of taxes on the various descriptions of property is an act which seems to require the most exact impartiality; yet there is, perhaps, no legislative act in which greater opportunity and temptation are given to a predominant party to trample on the rules of justice. Every shilling with which they overburden the inferior number is a shilling saved to their own pockets.

It is in vain to say that enlightened statesmen will be able to adjust these clashing interests and render them all subservient to the public good. Enlightened statesmen will not always be at the helm. Nor, in many cases, can such an adjustment be made at all without taking into view indirect and remote considerations, which will rarely prevail over the immediate interest which one party may find in disregarding the rights of another or the good of the whole.

The inference to which we are brought is that the *causes* of faction cannot be removed and that relief is only to be sought in the means of controlling its *effects*.

If a faction consists of less than a majority, relief is supplied by the republican principle, which enables the majority to defeat its sinister views by regular vote. It may clog the administration, it may convulse the society; but it will be unable to execute and mask its violence under the forms of the Constitution. When a majority is included in a faction, the form of popular government, on the other hand, enables it to sacrifice to its ruling passion or interest both the public good and the rights of other citizens. To secure the public good and private rights against the danger of such a faction, and at the same time to preserve the spirit and the form of popular government, is then the great object to which our inquiries are directed. Let me add that it is the great desideratum by which alone this form of government can be rescued from the opprobrium under which it has so long labored and be recommended to the esteem and adoption of mankind.

By what means is this object attainable? Evidently by one of two only. Either the existence of the same passion or interest in a majority at the same time must be prevented, or the majority, having such coexistent passion or interest, must be rendered, by their number and local situation, unable to concert and carry into effect schemes of oppression. If the impulse and the opportunity be suffered to coincide, we well know that neither moral nor religious motives can be relied on as an adequate control. They are not found to be such on the injustice and violence of individuals, and lose their efficacy in proportion to the number combined together, that is, in proportion as their efficacy becomes needful.

From this view of the subject it may be concluded that a pure democracy, by which I mean a society consisting of a small number of citizens, who assemble and administer the government in person, can admit of no cure for the mischiefs of faction. A common passion or interest will, in almost every case, be felt by a majority of the whole; a communication and concert results from the form of government itself; and there is nothing to check the inducements to sacrifice the weaker party or an obnoxious individual. Hence it is that such democracies have ever been spectacles of turbulence and contention; have ever been found incompatible with personal security or the rights of property; and have in general been as short in their lives as they have been violent in their deaths. Theoretic politicians, who have patronized this species of government, have erroneously supposed that by reducing mankind to a perfect equality in their political rights, they would at the same time be perfectly equalized and assimilated in their possessions, their opinions, and their passions.

A republic, by which I mean a government in which the scheme of representation takes place, opens a different prospect and promises the cure for which we are seeking. Let us examine the points in which it varies from pure democracy, and we shall comprehend both the nature of the cure and the efficacy which it must derive from the Union.

The two great points of difference between a democracy and a republic are: first, the delegation of the government, in the latter, to a small number of citizens elected by the rest; secondly, the greater number of citizens and greater sphere of country over which the latter may be extended.

The effect of the first difference is, on the one hand, to refine and enlarge the public views by passing them through the medium of a chosen body of citizens, whose wisdom may best discern the true interest of their country and whose patriotism and love of justice will be least likely to sacrifice it to temporary or partial considerations. Under such a regulation it may well happen that the public voice, pronounced by the representatives of the people, will be more consonant to the public good than if pronounced by the people themselves, convened for the purpose. On the other hand, the effect may be inverted. Men of factious tempers, of local prejudices, or of sinister designs, may, by intrigue, by corruption, or by other means, first obtain the suffrages, and then betray the interests of the people. The question resulting is, whether small or extensive republics are most favorable to the election of proper guardians of the public weal; and it is clearly decided in favor of the latter by two obvious considerations.

In the first place it is to be remarked that however small the republic may be the representatives must be raised to a certain number in order to guard against the cabals of a few; and that however large it may be they must be limited to a certain number in order to guard against the confusion of a multitude. Hence, the number of representatives in the two cases not being in proportion to that of the constituents, and being proportionally greatest in the small republic, it follows that if the proportion of fit characters be not less in the large than in the small republic, the former will present a greater option, and consequently a greater probability of a fit choice.

In the next place, as each representative will be chosen by a greater number of citizens in the large than in the small republic, it will be more difficult for unworthy candidates to practise with success the vicious arts by which elections are too often carried; and the suffrages of the people being more free, will be more likely to center on men who possess the most attractive merit and the most diffusive and established characters.

It must be confessed that in this, as in most other cases, there is a mean, on both sides of which inconveniencies will be found to lie. By enlarging too much the number of electors, you render the representative too little acquainted with all their local circumstances and lesser interests; as by reducing it too much, you render him unduly attached to these, and too little fit to comprehend and pursue great and national objects. The federal Constitution forms a happy combination in this respect; the great and aggregate interests being referred to the national, the local and particular to the State legislatures.

The other point of difference is the greater number of citizens and extent of territory which may be brought within the compass of republican than of democratic government; and it is this circumstance principally which renders factious combinations less to be dreaded in the former than in the latter. The smaller the society, the fewer probably will be the distinct parties and interests composing it; the fewer the distinct parties and interests, the more frequently will a majority be found of the same party; and the smaller the number of individuals composing a majority, and the smaller the compass within which they are placed, the more easily will they concert and execute their plans of oppression. Extend the sphere and you take in a greater variety of parties and interests; you make it less probable that a majority of the whole will have a common motive to invade the rights of other citizens; or if such a common motive exists, it will be more difficult for all who feel it to discover their own strength and to act in unison with each other. Besides other impediments, it may be remarked that, where there is a consciousness of unjust or dishonorable purposes, communication is always checked by distrust in proportion to the number whose concurrence is necessary.

Hence, it clearly appears that the same advantage which a republic has over a democracy in controlling the effects of faction is enjoyed by a large over a small republic—is enjoyed by the Union over the States composing it. Does this advantage consist in the substitution of representatives whose enlightened views and virtuous sentiments render them superior to local prejudices and to schemes of injustice? It will not be denied that the representation of the Union will be most likely to possess these requisite endowments. Does it consist in the greater security afforded by a greater variety of parties, against the event of any one party being able to outnumber and oppress the rest? In an equal degree does the increased variety of parties comprised within the Union increase this security. Does it, in fine, consist in the greater obstacles opposed to the concert and accomplishment of the secret wishes of an unjust and interested majority? Here again the extent of the Union gives it the most palpable advantage.

The influence of factious leaders may kindle a flame within their particular States but will be unable to spread a general conflagration through the other States. A religious sect may degenerate into a political faction in a part of the Confederacy; but the variety of sects dispersed over the entire face of it must secure the national councils against any danger from that source. A rage for paper money, for an abolition of debts, for an equal division of property, or for any other improper or wicked project, will be less apt to pervade the whole body of the Union than a particular member of it, in the same proportion as such a malady is more likely to taint a particular county or district than an entire State.

In the extent and proper structure of the Union, therefore, we behold a republican remedy for the diseases most incident to republican government. And according to the degree of pleasure and pride we feel in being republicans ought to be our zeal in cherishing the spirit and supporting the character of federalists.

JOHN DEWEY

Individualism—Old and New

THE LOST INDIVIDUAL

The development of a civilization that is outwardly corporate—or rapidly becoming so—has been accompanied by a submergence of the individual. Just how far this is true of the individual's opportunities in action, how far initiative and choice in what an individual does are restricted by the economic forces that make for consolidation, I shall not attempt to say. It is arguable that there has been a diminution of the range of decision and activity for the many along with exaggeration of opportunity of personal expression for the

John Dewey, excerpted from *Individualism—Old and New* (New York: Capricorn Books, 1962), pp. 51–58, 68–73.

few. It may be contended that no one class in the past has the power now possessed by an industrial oligarchy. On the other hand, it may be held that this power of the few is, with respect to genuine individuality, specious; that those outwardly in control are in reality as much carried by forces external to themselves as are the many; that in fact these forces impel them into a common mold to such an extent that individuality is suppressed.

What is here meant by "the lost individual" is, however, so irrelevant to this question that it is not necessary to decide between the two views. For by it is meant a moral and intellectual fact which is independent of any manifestation of power in action. The significant thing is that the loyalties which once held individuals, which gave them support, direction, and unity of outlook on life, have well-nigh disappeared. In consequence, individuals are confused and bewildered. It would be difficult to find in history an epoch as lacking in solid and assured objects of belief and approved ends of action as is the present. Stability of individuality is dependent upon stable objects to which allegiance firmly attaches itself. There are, of course, those who are still militantly fundamentalist in religious and social creed. But their very clamor is evidence that the tide is set against them. For the others, traditional objects of loyalty have become hollow or are openly repudiated, and they drift without sure anchorage. Individuals vibrate between a past that is intellectually too empty to give stability and a present that is too diversely crowded and chaotic to afford balance or direction to ideas and emotion.

Assured and integrated individuality is the product of definite social relationships and publicly acknowledged functions. Judged by this standard, even those who seem to be in control, and to carry the expression of their special individual abilities to a high pitch, are submerged. They may be captains of finance and industry, but until there is some consensus of belief as to the meaning of finance and industry in civilization as a whole, they cannot be captains of their own souls—their beliefs and aims. They exercise leadership surreptitiously and, as it were, absentmindedly. They lead, but it is under cover of impersonal and socially undirected economic forces. Their reward is found not in what they do, in their social office and function, but in a deflection of social consequences to private gain. They receive the acclaim and command the envy and admiration of the crowd, but the crowd is also composed of private individuals who are equally lost to a sense of social bearings and uses.

The explanation is found in the fact that while the actions promote corporate and collective results, these results are outside their intent and irrelevant to that reward of satisfaction which comes from a sense of social fulfillment. To themselves and to others, their business is private and its outcome is private profit. No complete satisfaction is possible where such a split exists. Hence the absence of a sense of social value is made up for by an exacerbated acceleration of the activities that increase private advantage and power. One cannot look into the inner consciousness of his fellows; but if there is any general degree of inner contentment on the part of those who form our pecuniary oligarchy, the evidence is sadly lacking. As for the many, they are impelled hither and yon by forces beyond their control.

The most marked trait of present life, economically speaking, is insecurity. It is tragic that millions of men desirous of working should be recurrently out of employment; aside from cyclical depressions there is a standing army at all times who have no regular work. We have not any adequate information as to the number of these persons. But the ignorance even as to numbers is slight compared with our inability to grasp the psychological and moral consequences of the precarious condition in which vast multitudes live. Insecurity cuts deeper and extends more widely than bare unemployment. Fear of loss of work, dread of the oncoming of old age, create anxiety and eat into self-respect in a way that impairs personal dignity. Where fears abound, courageous and robust individuality is undermined. The vast development of technological resources that might bring security in its train has actually brought a new mode of insecurity, as mechanization displaces labor. The mergers and consolidations that mark a corporate age are beginning to bring uncertainty into the economic lives of the higher salaried class, and that tendency is only just in its early stage. Realization that honest and industrious pursuit of a calling or business will not guarantee any stable level of life lessens respect for work and stirs large numbers to take a chance of some adventitious way of getting the wealth that will make security possible: witness the orgies of the stock-market in recent days.

The unrest, impatience, irritation and hurry that are so marked in American life are inevitable accompaniments of a situation in which individuals do not find support and contentment in the fact that they are sustaining and sustained members of a social whole. They are evidence, psychologically, of abnormality, and it is as idle to seek for their explanation within the deliberate intent of individuals as it is futile to think that they can be got rid of by hortatory moral appeal. Only an acute maladjustment between individuals and the social conditions under which they live can account for such widespread pathological phenomena. Feverish love of anything as long as it is a change which is distracting, impatience, unsettlement, nervous discontentment, and desire for excitement, are not native to human nature. They are so abnormal as to demand explanation in some deep-seated cause.

I should explain a seeming hypocrisy on the same ground. We are not consciously insincere in our professions of devotion to ideals of "service"; they mean something. Neither the Rotarian nor the big business enterprise uses the term merely as a cloak for "putting something over" which makes for pecuniary gain. But the lady doth protest too much. The wide currency of such professions testifies to a sense of a social function of business which is expressed in words because it is so lacking in fact, and yet which is felt to be rightfully there. If our external combinations in industrial activity were reflected in organic integrations of the desires, purposes and satisfactions of individuals, the verbal protestations would disappear, because social utility would be a matter of course.

Some persons hold that a genuine mental counterpart of the outward social scheme is actually forming. Our prevailing mentality, our "ideology," is said to be that of the "business mind" which has become so deplorably pervasive. Are not the prevailing standards of value those derived from pecuniary success and economic prosperity? Were the answer unqualifiedly in the affirmative, we should have to admit that our outer civilization is attaining an inner culture which corresponds to it, however much we might disesteem the quality of that culture. The objection that such a condition is impossible, since man cannot live by bread, by material prosperity, alone, is tempting, but it may be said to beg the question. The conclusive answer is that the business mind is not itself unified. It is divided within itself and must remain so as long as the results of industry as the determining force in life are corporate and collective while its animating motives and compensations are so unmitigatedly private. A unified mind, even of the business type, can come into being only when conscious intent and consummation are in harmony with consequences actually effected. This statement expresses conditions so psychologically assured that it may be termed a law of mental integrity. Proof of the existence of the split is found in the fact that while there is much planning of future development with a view to dividends within large business corporations, there is no corresponding coordinated planning of social development.

The growth of corporateness is arbitrarily restricted. Hence it operates to limit individuality, to put burdens on it, to confuse and submerge it. It crowds more out than it incorporates in an ordered and secure life. It has made rural districts stagnant while bringing excess and restless movement to the city. The restriction of corporateness lies in the fact that it remains on the cash level. Men are brought together on the one side by investment in the same joint stock company, and on the other hand by the fact that the machine compels mass production in order that investors may get their profits. The results affect all society in all its phases. But they are as inorganic as the ultimate human motives that operate are private and egoistic. An economic individualism of motives and aims underlies our present corporate mechanisms, and undoes the individual.

* * *

Instances of the flux in which individuals are loosened from the ties that once gave order and support to their lives are glaring. They are indeed so glaring that they blind our eyes to the causes which produce them. Individuals are groping their way through situations which they do not direct and which do not give them direction. The beliefs and ideals that are uppermost in their consciousness are not relevant to the society in which they outwardly act and which constantly reacts upon them. Their conscious ideas and standards are inherited from an age that has passed away; their minds, as far as consciously entertained principles and methods of interpretation are concerned, are at odds with actual conditions. This profound split is the cause of distraction and bewilderment.

Individuals will refind themselves only as their ideas and ideals are brought into harmony with the realities of the age in which they act. The task of attaining this harmony is not an easy one. But it is more negative than it seems. If we could inhibit the principles and standards that are merely traditional, if we could slough off the opinions that have no living relationship to the situations in which we live, the unavowed forces that now work upon us unconsciously but unremittingly would have a chance to build minds after their own pattern, and individuals might, in consequence, find themselves in possession of objects to which imagination and emotion would stably attach themselves.

I do not mean, however, that the process of rebuilding can go on automatically. Discrimination is required in order to detect the beliefs and institutions that dominate merely because of custom and inertia, and in order to discover the moving realities of the present. Intelligence must distinguish, for example, the tendencies of the technology which produce the new corporateness from those inheritances proceeding out of the individualism of an earlier epoch which arrest and divide the operation of the new dynamics. It is difficult for us to conceive of individualism except in terms of stereotypes derived from former centuries. Individualism has been identified with ideas of initiative and invention that are bound up with private and exclusive economic gain. As long as this conception possesses our minds, the ideal of harmonizing our thought and desire with the realities of present social conditions will be interpreted to mean accommodation and surrender. It will even be understood to signify rationalization of the evils of existing society. A stable recovery of individuality waits upon an elimination of the older economic and political individualism, an elimination which will liberate imagination and endeavor for the task of making corporate society contribute to the free culture of its members. Only by economic revision can the sound element in the older individualism—equality of opportunity—be made a reality.

It is the part of wisdom to note the double meaning of such ideas as "acceptance." There is an acceptance that is of the intellect; it signifies facing facts for what they are. There is another acceptance that is of the emotions and will; that involves commitment of desire and effort. So far are the two from being identical that acceptance in the first sense is the precondition of all intelligent refusal of acceptance in the second sense. There is a prophetic aspect to all observation; we can perceive the meaning of what exists only as we forecast the consequences it entails. When a situation is as confused and divided within itself as is the present social estate, choice is implicated *in observation*. As one perceives different tendencies and different possible consequences, preference inevitably goes out to one or the other. Because acknowledgment in thought brings with it intelligent discrimination and choice, it is the first step out of confusion, the first step in forming those objects of significant allegiance out of which stable and efficacious individuality may grow. It might even perform the miracle of rendering conservatism relevant and thoughtful. It certainly is the prerequisite of an anchored liberalism.

WILLIAM M. SULLIVAN

Reconstructing Public Philosophy

The civic republican tradition contains disagreement and ambiguity, but its principles and the direction of its moral aspiration are clear. Civic republicanism has manifested its vitality as its aspiration toward an inclusive community providing dignity and justice for all has encountered the limits of actual institutions. For the tradition, the civic ideals of justice and dignity entail moral equality of all individuals, based on a recognition that all share the same human ends.[1] Human fulfillment takes many forms, but the common attribute is that concern and care for the dignity of self and others which the tradition calls virtue. For the civic republican vision, equality is a fundamental value of political life, but its foundation is not, as for utilitarian liberalism, a studied agnosticism about the nature of a

1. Wilson Carey McWilliams makes this point well, citing Aristotle on the equality of citizens in a *polis,* particularly the importance that their most important desires be equal, that is, that they aspire to the life of citizenship and not tyranny. See Wilson Carey McWilliams, "On Equality as the Moral Foundation of Community," in Robert H. Horwitz, ed., *Moral Foundations of the American Republic* (Charlottesville: University of Virginia Press, 1976), esp. pp. 185–89.

William M. Sullivan, excerpted from *Reconstructing Public Philosophy* (Berkeley and Los Angeles: University of California Press, 1982), pp. 181–84, 208–11.

good life. Rather, it is based upon the common aim of the basic goods of dignity, justice and community through which human beings become equally worthy of respect and concern.

Because of the importance it gives to practical, prudential reasoning, the republican tradition has emphasized ideals of character, models of conduct, and exemplary institutions. As the classical theorists of the tradition taught, the form and the end immanent in a style of life give significance and worth to living. The moral and political discourse of republicanism is built around qualitative language, in particular the qualitative contrast between virtue and corruption. This mode of discourse emphasizes what utilitarian language denies: that qualities are intrinsic to forms of life, that there are important differences of kind among various ways of living, that it distorts and trivializes life to treat all claims to quality as directly comparable on some supposedly neutral and objective scale of satisfaction.

Liberal utilitarianism treats quality as a subjective experience, a satisfaction an individual "has" or "derives" from an exchange with the outside world. Since in this scheme qualitative judgments are entirely subjective and individual, social practices are imagined to be instruments for providing individual satisfactions. For the utilitarian there is no standard of worth except the satisfaction of subjective needs and, since these differ among individuals, there is no hope of assessing the worth of any social practice except by taking the sum of the individual experiences it generates. It is thus consistent for utilitarians to maintain that value judgments are non-rational and cannot be defended on intrinsic grounds. The term *value* already suggests this: it derives from economics, in which discipline utilitarian philosophy has been most completely embodied.

An intrinsic claim of quality, on the other hand, states that an activity is important because there is some prized good which exists within and is not separable from that activity. Life is clearly such a good, and so is friendship and, for civic thinkers, so are justice and civic community. For example, collective deliberation on matters of common concern is good intrinsically, not just instrumentally. As long as the participants can share in the discussion without coercion, it is in the deliberative process itself that the participants come to understand each other and, through a sharing of viewpoints, expand and deepen their sense of worth and efficacy in a way impossible in any private experience.

Satisfactions have meaning for those who experience them; they are not mere sensations. Indeed, satisfaction of individual desires is shaped through the social forms by which individuals orient themselves, whether or not they are conscious of this. The great defect of liberalism is its almost willful blindness to this fact. The limitation of conservative thinking of Edmund Burke's stripe is that it notes only the passive side of the individual's relation to the community. It is thus a perfect mirror-image of liberalism, and it is equally incomplete. The civic tradition sees that individuality grows in a social matrix but also stresses that this process can be cultivated by the participants themselves. Unlike the liberal, the civic thinker realizes he is always within and shaped by a tradition of moral orientation. Yet, unlike the conservative, the civic thinker sees that he has a responsibility to shape this tradition by actively responding to new situations with a style and sensitivity shaped by his *paideia*. The critical difference in understanding that puts the conservative and the liberal on one side and the civic republican on the other is that the latter takes seriously and critically his involvement in the forms of life he shares.

The assumptions undergirding liberal theories of politics, human nature, and social investigation have, as we have seen, given rise to both the liberal and conservative variants of modern political theory. In American political thinking the liberal utilitarian strand has predominated, so that utilitarian assumptions, like the capitalist exchange system which embodies those assumptions, have often distorted articulations of republican movements—or, at least, they have made it difficult for the civic tradition to find its voice. A major step, if not the starting point, in the contemporary effort to reformulate a civic public philosophy in America must be development of a conception of politics that builds from the understanding of life as both shared tradition and responsible, critical initiative. Concretely, this means finding a way to transcend conceptually a purely utilitarian understanding of politics and a way to challenge the domination of social relationships by bureaucratic management and the workings of capitalist economics. The elucidation of this project would be at the same time a recovery of the notion of practical reason.

For civic republican thinkers, political understanding has its basis in the social cultivation of practical prudence. Indeed, civic ideals make sense only in a context in which human beings live more than instrumental lives. This is to say that there is an intrinsic relationship between cognitive understanding and practical involvement, but that relationship is not one in which social location determines awareness in any simple sense. Rather, the insight of the tradition of practical reason discussed in the last chapter is precisely that human beings live within as well as use language and forms of social life, that they can both understand and take up a stance toward their situation and, by so doing, help to organize and structure it. Persons are not simply counters in a systemic map or game, moved from without, but are moral agents in that they can question both themselves and their situations and take responsibility for the stances they adopt. Understanding requires a kind of enactment, and this further entails an ineluctably social and, finally, political dimension.

Insight thus requires a disposition toward a certain kind of ethical relationship toward others, a notion of society as aiming at a consensual and shared realm characterized by reciprocity. This conception implies a political practice opposite to the strategic and instrumental conception. An understanding of practical reason reveals that recovery of the civic republican tradition is actually a process of coming to understand in a new way what is important and possible in our own historical situation. The civic tradition is important for us because it articulates an understanding that the interdependency of the members of a society is a moral and political relationship. The tradition speaks to our predicament of great factual interdependency organized by an economic and administrative ethos which conceals, denies, or suppresses the moral and political nature of those relationships.

Our need is to extend the spirit of republican democratic life into the sphere of the major economic and administrative institutions. And the heritage of the civic tradition is in part responsible for our being able to see the situation this way. Thus developing effective strategies to transform our predicament so as more fully to actualize civic life has the kind of fruitful circularity that characterizes engaged practical reasoning. Any view of our past is already formed by a diagnosis of our present situation; yet, historical inquiry can help correct and deepen our present understanding.

* * *

TOWARD A PUBLIC PHILOSOPHY: ARTICULATING A DEMOCRATIC ECONOMY

A public philosophy develops out of the insight that the quality of personal life is grounded in social relationships, an insight that is embodied in the political art of integrating the various kinds of self-concern into an awareness of mutual interdependency. Despite its discontinuous development, the civic republican tradition has been a major vehicle through which this insight has been transmitted in American experience, and it may once again provide a new articulation of the understanding underlying a self-governing society, as the antagonism of self-interest, fed by inequity, pushes a badly shredded civility to the breaking point.[2] Our best hope for an alternative to authoritarian tyranny is to develop an awareness of our interdependency out of which to forge the movements and institutions which can give new political and social form to our sense of common concern. Public philosophy, like a meaningful public life, must be a continuing process of reappropriation and experiment, of reinvigorating the tradition by creating anew.

Americans of the revolutionary, founding generation were able to envision a public life, however imperfectly, within economic and social conditions that did not seem completely antagonistic to their hopes. They consciously sought, and found, religious and cultural traditions that could buttress and reinforce the social and moral bases of a self-governing society. They feared excessive wealth, excessive poverty, and lack of independence in one's occupation. They thought self-employment to be the best guarantee of the

---

2. Public philosophy in this sense is more than the vector-sum of contests among competing interests. To this extent Walter Lippmann's famous formulation of a public philosophy as a "code of civility" that transcends human choice is correct: see Walter Lippmann, *The Public Philosophy* (Boston: Little, Brown, 1955). However, serious reflection upon the historically rooted nature of all cultural forms makes a univocal articulation of this "code" dubious.

sturdy virtues of citizenship that would then lead to civic cooperation in the local community, particularly when nurtured by the religious and moral ideal of the covenant. These conditions, described so well by Alexis de Tocqueville, persisted throughout much of the nineteenth century.

Our present situation, with its massive concentrations of economic power, great inequality of wealth, and the near-disappearance of the self-employed farmer, merchant, and artisan, seems so far from the social conditions of early republican America as to have no connection with it. But if the guiding purpose of republican society is to create citizens who can then cooperate to produce a democratic culture, it is both realistic and vital to consider how we may gain the same ends under the conditions of the present world political economy.

A renewed citizenship must build upon our still-living traditions of voluntarism and cooperation wherever they may be found, but it cannot take the older forms and resources for granted. Contemporary citizenship requires at once a moral culture and an institutional basis appropriate to the interdependent, occupationally segmented national society we have come to be. And because professionalism and occupational identification have become so crucial to contemporary society and personal identity, a renewed civic culture must be institutionalized in the workplace as well as in the community at large if it is powerfully to influence public mores. Indeed, it is clear that if we are to recover the social and personal commitment to free institutions that is the lifeblood of a democratic society, we must bring a public and democratic ethos into the sphere of economic life. To view economic institutions as private perhaps made sense when most Americans spent their lives on family farms or in family firms, but today, when most American men and a rapidly increasing proportion of American women spend much of their lives in large economic structures that are for most purposes public—except that the profits they make go to an impersonal collection of institutional and individual private stockholders—it becomes imperative to bring the forms of citizenship and of civic association into a more central position in the economic sphere.

The theme of a reconstructed republican spirit must be to subordinate the flows of economic capital, now overwhelmingly collective in their generation, to a process of disposition more equitable and effectively democratic than the present American political economy. Democratizing and realigning economic relationships at national as well as regional levels according to a civic conception of justice means aggressively developing alternatives to the dominance of private capital over public life. Such a transformation, requiring nothing less than a renegotiation of the public covenant against powerful particular interests, will be the long-term test of the viability of the republic. Yet, though immensely difficult, this project also opens the heartening possibility of transforming the nation's international stance toward a more republican sense of equity.

However, if the ethos and mores remain heavily individualistic and competitive, then Americans will continue to define the goals of economic organization in essentially private terms. Conceiving of economic justice as a mere balance of self-interests has often focused reform efforts on obtaining for disadvantaged groups greater relative advantage within an inequitable system; certainly, that has been better than nothing. But, as many contemporary analysts warn, American hegemony in international politics and trade, the economic and technological cornucopia which has been the premise of that method of accommodation, is rapidly running dry.[3] In these conditions, the option of a genuinely cooperative economic democracy becomes a particularly unlikely choice from the basis of self-interested calculation. Thus the interrelation between public institutions and mores has today become particularly salient, which is why Tocqueville's analysis retains its importance.

Our contemporary situation highlights the relevance to both national and international affairs of a civic republican politics that insists on the primacy of interdependency over self-interest. If one key blockage to revitalizing public life is the privatism so deeply embedded in liberal culture, then no new democratic advance and, probably, no more equitable international order will be possible

3. See Lester C. Thurow, *The Zero-Sum Society: Distribution and the Possibilities for Economic Change* (New York: Basic Books, 1980). Thurow notes the high concentration of wealth in the top quintile of the population: the top quintile by *wealth* owns 80 percent of all assets, while these households receive just 44 percent of the national income. In other words, inequality of ownership—and thus control of resources—is far sharper than the more widely discussed inequality of income distribution, despite the alleged "leveling" tendencies of the welfare state (see pp. 167–68).

without widespread expansion of public understanding, not only in the cognitive but in the full practical sense of understanding. Therein lies the importance of renewed civic practice as well as public philosophy.

DWIGHT D. EISENHOWER

Farewell Address

Good evening, my fellow Americans.

First, I should like to express my gratitude to the radio and television networks for the opportunities they have given me over the years to bring reports and messages to our nation. My special thanks go to them for the opportunity of addressing you this evening.

Three days from now, after half a century in the service of our country, I shall lay down the responsibilities of office as, in traditional and solemn ceremony, the authority of the presidency is vested in my successor.

This evening I come to you with a message of leave-taking and farewell and to share a few final thoughts with you, my countrymen.

Like every other citizen, I wish the new president, and all who will labor with him, Godspeed. I pray that the coming years will be blessed with peace and prosperity for all.

Our people expect their president and the Congress to find essential agreement on issues of great moment, the wise resolution of which will better shape the future of the nation.

My own relations with the Congress, which began on a remote and tenuous basis when, long ago, a member of the Senate appointed me to West Point, have since ranged to the intimate during the war and immediate post-war period, and finally to the mutually interdependent during these past eight years.

In this final relationship, Congress and the administration have,

Dwight D. Eisenhower, "Farewell Address," *New York Times,* January 17, 1961.

on most vital issues, cooperated well, to serve the national good rather than mere partisanship, and so have assured that the business of the nation should go forward. So my official relationship with the Congress ends in a feeling, on my part, of gratitude that we have been able to do so much together.

We now stand 10 years past the mid-point of a century that has witnessed four major wars among great nations—three of these involved our own country. Despite these holocausts, America is today the strongest, the most influential and most productive nation in the world. Understandably proud of this pre-eminence, we yet realize that America's leadership and prestige depend, not merely upon our unmatched material progress, but on how we use our power in the interest of world peace and human betterment.

Throughout America's adventure in free government, our basic purposes have been to keep the peace, to foster progress in human achievement and to enhance liberty, dignity and integrity among people and among nations. To strive for less would be unworthy of a free and religious people. Any failure traceable to arrogance, or our lack of comprehension or readiness to sacrifice would inflict upon us grievous hurt both at home and abroad.

Progress toward these noble goals is persistently threatened by the conflict now engulfing the world. It commands our whole attention, absorbs our very being.

We face a hostile ideology—global in scope, atheistic in character, ruthless in purpose and insidious in method. Unhappily, the danger it poses promises to be of indefinite duration.

To meet it successfully there is called for not so much the emotional and transitory sacrifices of crisis, but rather those which enable us to carry forward steadily, surely and without complaint the burdens of a prolonged and complex struggle—with liberty the stake. Only thus shall we remain, despite every provocation, on our charted course toward permanent peace and human betterment.

Crises there will continue to be. In meeting them, whether foreign or domestic, great or small, there is a recurring temptation to feel that some spectacular and costly action could become the miraculous solution to all current difficulties.

A huge increase in newer elements of our defense; development of unrealistic programs to cure every ill in agriculture; a dramatic expansion in basic and applied research—these and many other possibilities, each possibly promising in itself, may be suggested as the only way to the road we wish to travel.

But each proposal must be weighed in the light of a broader consideration: the need to maintain balance in and among national programs—balance between the private and the public economy, balance between cost and hoped for advantage, balance between the clearly necessary and the comfortably desirable; balance between our essential requirements as a nation and the duties imposed by the nation upon the individual; balance between actions of the moment and the national welfare of the future. Good judgment seeks balance and progress; lack of it eventually finds imbalance and frustration.

The record of many decades stands as proof that our people and their government have, in the main, understood these truths and have responded to them well, in the face of stress and threat. But threats, new in kind or degree, constantly arise. I mention two only.

A vital element in keeping the peace is our military establishment. Our arms must be mighty, ready for instant action, so that no potential aggressor may be tempted to risk his own destruction.

Our military organization today bears little relation to that known by any of my predecessors in peacetime, or indeed by the fighting men of World War II or Korea.

Until the latest of our world conflicts, the United States had no armaments industry. American makers of plowshares could, with time and as required, make swords as well. But now we can no longer risk emergency improvisation of national defense; we have been compelled to create a permanent armaments industry of vast proportions.

Added to this, three and a half million men and women are directly engaged in the defense establishment. We annually spend on military security more than the net income of all United States corporations.

This conjunction of an immense military establishment and a large arms industry is new in the American experience. The total influence—economic, political, even spiritual—is felt in every city, every state house, every office of the federal government. We recognize the imperative need for this development. Yet we must not fail to comprehend its grave implications. Our toil, resources and livelihood are all involved; so is the very structure of our society.

In the councils of government, we must guard against the acquisition of unwarranted influence, whether sought or unsought, by the military-industrial complex. The potential for the disastrous rise of misplaced power exists and will persist.

We must never let the weight of this combination endanger our liberties or democratic processes. We should take nothing for granted. Only an alert and knowledgeable citizenry can compel the proper meshing of the huge industrial and military machinery of defense with our peaceful methods and goals, so that security and liberty may prosper together.

Akin to, and largely responsible for the sweeping changes in our industrial-military posture, has been the technological revolution during the recent decades. In this revolution, research has become central; it also becomes more formalized, complex and costly. A steadily increasing share is conducted for, by or at the direction of, the federal government.

The solitary inventor, tinkering in his shop, has been overshadowed by task forces of scientists in laboratories and testing fields. In the same fashion, the free university, historically the fountainhead of free ideas and scientific discovery, has experienced a revolution in the conduct of research. Partly because of the huge costs involved, a government contract becomes virtually a substitute for intellectual curiosity. For every old blackboard there are now hundreds of new electronic computers.

The prospect of domination of the nation's scholars by federal employment, project allocations and the power of money is ever present—and is gravely to be regarded. Yet, in holding scientific research and discovery in respect, as we should, we must also be alert to the equal and opposite danger that public policy could itself become the captive of a scientific-technological elite.

It is the task of statesmanship to mold, to balance and to integrate these and other forces, new and old, within the principles of our democratic system—ever aiming toward the supreme goals of our free society.

Another factor in maintaining balance involves the element of time. As we peer into society's future, we—you and I and our government—must avoid the impulse to live only for today, plundering for our own ease and convenience, the precious resources of tomorrow. We cannot mortgage the material assets of our grandchildren without risking the loss also of their political and spiritual heritage. We want democracy to survive for all generations to come, not to become the insolvent phantom of tomorrow.

Down the long lane of history yet to be written, America knows that this world of ours, ever growing smaller, must avoid becoming a community of dreadful fear and hate and be, instead, a proud confederation of mutual trust and respect.

Such a confederation must be one of equals. The weakest must come to the conference table with the same confidence as do we, protected as we are by our moral, economic and military strength. That table, though scarred by many past frustrations, cannot be abandoned for the certain agony of the battlefield.

Disarmament, with mutual honor and confidence, is a continuing imperative. Together we must learn how to compose differences, not with arms, but with intellect and decent purpose. Because this need is so sharp and apparent, I confess that I lay down my official responsibilities in this field with a definite sense of disappointment.

As one who has witnessed the horror and the lingering sadness of war—as one who knows that another war could utterly destroy civilization which has been so slowly and painfully built over thousands of years—I wish I could say tonight that a lasting peace is in sight.

Happily, I can say that war has been avoided. Steady progress toward our ultimate goal has been made. But, so much remains to be done. As a private citizen, I shall never cease to do what little I can to help the world advance along that road.

So in this, my last good night to you as your president, I thank you for the many opportunities you have given me for public service in war and peace. I trust that in that service you find things worthy.

Dwight D. Eisenhower / 403

As for the rest of it, I know you will find ways to improve performance in the future.

You and I, my fellow citizens, need to be strong in our faith that all nations, under God, will reach the goal of peace with justice. May we be ever unswerving in devotion to principle, confident but humble with power, diligent in pursuit of the nation's great goals.

To all the peoples of the world, I once more give expression to America's prayerful and continuing aspiration:

We pray that peoples of all faiths, all races, all nations, may have their great human needs satisfied; that those now denied opportunity shall come to enjoy it to the full; that all who yearn for freedom may experience, its spiritual blessing; that those who have freedom will understand, also, its heavy responsibilities; that all who are insensitive to the needs of others will learn charity; that the scourges of poverty, disease and ignorance will be made to disappear from the earth and that, in the goodness of time, all peoples will come to live together in a peace guaranteed by the binding force of mutual respect and love.

Now, on Friday noon, I am to become a private citizen. I am proud to do so. I look forward to it.

Thank you, and good night.

RONALD REAGAN

First Inaugural Address

PUTTING AMERICA BACK TO WORK

Thank you, Senator Hatfield, Mr. Chief Justice, Mr. President, Vice President Bush, Vice President Mondale, Senator Baker, Speaker O'Neill, Reverend Moomaw, and my fellow citizens:

To a few of us here today this is a solemn and most momentous

Ronald Reagan, "First Inaugural Address," January 20, 1981, in *Vital Speeches of the Day* 47 (1981), pp. 258–60.

occasion. And, yet, in the history of our nation it is a commonplace occurrence.

The orderly transfer of authority as called for in the Constitution routinely takes place as it has for almost two centuries and few of us stop to think how unique we really are.

In the eyes of many in the world, this every-four-year ceremony we accept as normal is nothing less than a miracle.

Mr. President, I want our fellow citizens to know how much you did to carry on this tradition.

By your gracious cooperation in the transition process you have shown a watching world that we are a united people pledged to maintaining a political system which guarantees individual liberty to a greater degree than any other. And I thank you and your people for all your help in maintaining the continuity which is the bulwark of our republic.

The business of our nation goes forward.

These United States are confronted with an economic affliction of great proportions.

We suffer from the longest and one of the worst sustained inflations in our national history. It distorts our economic decisions, penalizes thrift and crushes the struggling young and the fixed-income elderly alike. It threatens to shatter the lives of millions of our people.

Idle industries have cast workers into unemployment, human misery and personal indignity.

Those who do work are denied a fair return for their labor by a tax system which penalizes successful achievement and keeps us from maintaining full productivity.

But great as our tax burden is, it has not kept pace with public spending. For decades we have piled deficit upon deficit, mortgaging our future and our children's future for the temporary convenience of the present.

To continue this long trend is to guarantee tremendous social, cultural, political and economic upheavals.

You and I, as individuals, can, by borrowing, live beyond our means, but for only a limited period of time. Why then should we think that collectively, as a nation, we are not bound by that same limitation?

We must act today in order to preserve tomorrow. And let there be no misunderstanding—we're going to begin to act beginning today.

The economic ills we suffer have come upon us over several decades.

They will not go away in days, weeks or months, but they will go away. They will go away because we as Americans have the capacity now, as we have had in the past, to do whatever needs to be done to preserve this last and greatest bastion of freedom.

In this present crisis, government is not the solution to our problem; government is the problem.

From time to time we've been tempted to believe that society has become too complex to be managed by self-rule, that government by an elite group is superior to government for, by and of the people.

But if no one among us is capable of governing himself, then who among us has the capacity to govern someone else?

All of us together—in and out of government—must bear the burden. The solutions we seek must be equitable with no one group singled out to pay a higher price.

We hear much of special interest groups. Well, our concern must be for a special interest group that has been too long neglected.

It knows no sectional boundaries, or ethnic and racial divisions and it crosses political party lines. It is made up of men and women who raise our food, patrol our streets, man our mines and factories, teach our children, keep our homes and heal us when we're sick.

Professionals, industrialists, shopkeepers, clerks, cabbies and truck drivers. They are, in short, "We the people." This breed called Americans.

Well, this Administration's objective will be a healthy, vigorous, growing economy that provides equal opportunities for all Americans with no barriers born of bigotry or discrimination.

Putting America back to work means putting all Americans back to work. Ending inflation means freeing all Americans from the terror of runaway living costs.

All must share in the productive work of this "new beginning," and all must share in the bounty of a revived economy.

With the idealism and fair play which are the core of our system and our strength, we can have a strong, prosperous America at peace with itself and the world.

So as we begin, let us take inventory.

We are a nation that has a government—not the other way around. And this makes us special among the nations of the earth.

Our Government has no power except that granted it by the people. It is time to check and reverse the growth of government which shows signs of having grown beyond the consent of the governed.

It is my intention to curb the size and influence of the Federal establishment and to demand recognition of the distinction between the powers granted to the Federal Government and those reserved to the states or to the people.

All of us—all of us need to be reminded that the Federal Government did not create the states; the states created the Federal Government.

Now, so there will be no misunderstanding, it's not my intention to do away with government

It is rather to make it work—work with us, not over us; to stand by our side, not ride on our back. Government can and must provide opportunity, not smother it; foster productivity, not stifle it.

If we look to the answer as to why for so many years we achieved so much, prospered as no other people on earth, it was because here in this land we unleashed the energy and individual genius of man to a greater extent than has ever been done before.

Freedom and the dignity of the individual have been more available and assured here than in any other place on earth. The price for this freedom at times has been high, but we have never been unwilling to pay that price.

It is no coincidence that our present troubles parallel and are proportionate to the intervention and intrusion in our lives that result from unnecessary and excessive growth of Government.

It is time for us to realize that we are too great a nation to limit ourselves to small dreams. We're not, as some would have us believe, doomed to an inevitable decline. I do not believe in a fate that will fall on us no matter what we do. I do believe in a fate that will fall on us if we do nothing.

So, with all the creative energy at our command let us begin an era of national renewal. Let us renew our determination, our courage and our strength. And let us renew our faith and our hope. We have every right to dream heroic dreams.

Those who say that we're in a time when there are no heroes—they just don't know where to look. You can see heroes every day going in and out of factory gates. Others, a handful in number, produce enough food to feed all of us and then the world beyond.

You meet heroes across a counter—and they're on both sides of that counter. There are entrepreneurs with faith in themselves and faith in an idea who create new jobs, new wealth and opportunity.

There are individuals and families whose taxes support the Government and whose voluntary gifts support church, charity, culture, art and education. Their patriotism is quiet but deep. Their values sustain our national life.

Now, I have used the words "they" and "their" in speaking of these heroes. I could say "you" and "your" because I'm addressing the heroes of whom I speak—you, the citizens of this blessed land.

Your dreams, your hopes, your goals are going to be the dreams, the hopes and the goals of this Administration, so help me God.

We shall reflect the compassion that is so much a part of your makeup.

How can we love our country and not love our countrymen? And loving them reach out a hand when they fall, heal them when they're sick and provide opportunity to make them self-sufficient so they will be equal in fact and not just in theory?

Can we solve the problems confronting us? Well the answer is a unequivocal and emphatic yes.

To paraphrase Winston Churchill, I did not take the oath I've just taken with the intention of presiding over the dissolution of the world's strongest economy.

In the days ahead I will propose removing the roadblocks that have slowed our economy and reduced productivity.

Steps will be taken aimed at restoring the balance between the various levels of government. Progress may be slow—measured in inches and feet, not miles—but we will progress.

It is time to reawaken this industrial giant, to get government back within its means and to lighten our punitive tax burden.

And these will be our first priorities, and on these principles there will be no compromise.

On the eve of our struggle for independence a man who might've been one of the greatest among the Founding Fathers, Dr. Joseph Warren, president of the Massachusetts Congress, said to his fellow Americans, "Our country is in danger, but not to be despaired of. On you depend the fortunes of America. You are to decide the important question upon which rest the happiness and the liberty of millions yet unborn. Act worthy of yourselves."

Well, I believe we the Americans of today are ready to act worthy of ourselves, ready to do what must be done to insure happiness and liberty for ourselves, our children and our children's children.

And as we renew ourselves here in our own land we will be seen as having greater strength throughout the world. We will again be the exemplar of freedom and a beacon of hope for those who do not now have freedom.

To those neighbors and allies who share our freedom, we will strengthen our historic ties and assure them of our support and firm commitment.

We will match loyalty with loyalty. We will strive for mutually beneficial relations. We will not use our friendship to impose on their sovereignty, for our own sovereignty is not for sale.

As for the enemies of freedom, those who are potential adversaries, they will be reminded that peace is the highest aspiration of the American people. We will negotiate for it, sacrifice for it; we will not surrender for it—now or ever.

Our forbearance should never be misunderstood. Our reluctance for conflict should not be misjudged as a failure of will.

When action is required to preserve our national security, we will act. We will maintain sufficient strength to prevail if need be, knowing that if we do we have the best chance of never having to use that strength.

Above all we must realize that no arsenal or no weapon in the arsenals of the world is so formidable as the will and moral courage of free men and women.

It is a weapon our adversaries in today's world do not have.

It is a weapon that we as Americans do have.

Let that be understood by those who practice terrorism and prey upon their neighbors.

I am told that tens of thousands of prayer meetings are being held on this day; for that I am deeply grateful. We are a nation under God, and I believe God intended for us to be free. It would be fitting and good, I think, if on each inaugural day in future years it should be declared a day of prayer.

This is the first time in our history that this ceremony has been held, as you've been told, on this West Front of the Capitol.

Standing here, one faces a magnificent vista, opening up on this city's special beauty and history.

At the end of this open mall are those shrines to the giants on whose shoulders we stand.

Directly in front of me, the monument to a monumental man. George Washington, father of our country. A man of humility who came to greatness reluctantly. He led America out of revolutionary victory into infant nationhood.

Off to one side, the stately memorial to Thomas Jefferson. The Declaration of Independence flames with his eloquence.

And then beyond the Reflecting Pool, the dignified columns of the Lincoln Memorial. Whoever would understand in his heart the meaning of America will find it in the life of Abraham Lincoln.

Beyond those moments, monuments to heroism is the Potomac River, and on the far shore the sloping hills of Arlington National Cemetery with its row upon row of simple white markers bearing crosses or Stars of David. They add up to only a tiny fraction of the price that has been paid for our freedom.

Each one of those markers is a monument to the kind of hero I spoke of earlier.

Their lives ended in places called Belleau Wood, the Argonne, Omaha Beach, Salerno and halfway around the world on Guadalcanal, Tarawa, Pork Chop Hill, the Chosin Reservoir, and in a hundred rice paddies and jungles of a place called Vietnam.

Under such a marker lies a young man, Martin Treptow, who left his job in a small town barber shop in 1917 to go to France with the famed Rainbow Division.

There, on the Western front, he was killed trying to carry a message between battalions under heavy artillery fire.

We are told that on his body was found a diary.

On the flyleaf under the heading, "My Pledge," he had written these words:

"America must win this war. Therefore I will work, I will save, I will sacrifice, I will endure, I will fight cheerfully and do my utmost, as if the issue of the whole struggle depended on me alone."

The crisis we are facing today does not require of us the kind of sacrifice that Martin Treptow and so many thousands of others were called upon to make.

It does require, however, our best effort, and our willingness to believe in ourselves and to believe in our capacity to perform great deeds; to believe that together with God's help we can and will resolve the problems which now confront us.

And after all, why shouldn't we believe that? We are Americans. God bless you and thank you. Thank you very much.

MARIO CUOMO

Two Cities

On behalf of the Empire State and the family of New York, I thank you for the great privilege of being allowed to address this convention.

Please allow me to skip the stories and the poetry and the temptation to deal in nice but vague rhetoric.

Let me instead use this valuable opportunity to deal with the questions that should determine this election and that are vital to the American people.

Ten days ago, President Reagan admitted that although some people in this country seemed to be doing well nowadays, others were unhappy, and even worried, about themselves, their families and their futures.

Mario Cuomo, "Two Cities," Keynote Address to the Democratic National Convention, San Francisco, California, July 17, 1984, in *Vital Speeches of the Day*, pp. 646–49.

The President said he didn't understand that fear. He said, "Why, this country is a shining city on a hill."

The President is right. In many ways we are "a shining city on a hill."

But the hard truth is that not everyone is sharing in this city's splendor and glory.

A shining city is perhaps all the President sees from the portico of the White House and the veranda of his ranch, where everyone seems to be doing well.

But there's another part of the city, the part where some people can't pay their mortgages and most young people can't afford one, where students can't afford the education they need and middle-class parents watch the dreams they hold for their children evaporate.

In this part of the city there are more poor than ever, more families in trouble. More and more people who need help but can't find it.

Even worse: There are elderly people who tremble in the basements of the houses there.

There are people who sleep in the city's streets, in the gutter, where the glitter doesn't show.

There are ghettos where thousands of young people, without an education or a job, give their lives away to drug dealers every day.

There is despair, Mr. President, in faces you never see, in the places you never visit in your shining city.

In fact, Mr. President, this nation is more a "Tale of Two Cities" than it is a "Shining City on a Hill."

Maybe if you visited more places, Mr. President, you'd understand.

Maybe if you went to Appalachia where some people still live in sheds and to Lackawanna where thousands of unemployed steel workers wonder why we subsidized foreign steel while we surrender their dignity to unemployment and to welfare checks; maybe if you stepped into a shelter in Chicago and talked with some of the homeless there; maybe, Mr. President, if you asked a woman who'd been denied the help she needs to feed her children because you say we need the money to give a tax break to a millionaire or to build a missile we can't even afford to use—maybe then you'd understand.

Maybe, Mr. President.

But I'm afraid not.

Because, the truth is, this is how we were warned it would be.

President Reagan told us from the beginning that he believed in a kind of social Darwinism. Survival of the fittest. "Government can't do everything," we were told. "So it should settle for taking care of the strong and hope their economic ambition and charity will do the rest. Make the rich richer and what falls from their table will be enough for the middle class and those trying to make it into the middle class."

The Republicans called it trickle-down when Hoover tried it. Now they call it supply side. It is the same shining city for those relative few who are lucky enough to live in its good neighborhoods.

But for the people who are excluded—locked out—all they can do is to stare from a distance at that city's glimmering towers.

It's an old story. As old as our history.

The difference between Democrats and Republicans has always been measured in courage and confidence. The Republicans believe the wagon train will not make it to the frontier unless some of our old, some of our young and some of our weak are left behind by the side of the trail.

The strong will inherit the land!

We Democrats believe that we can make it all the way with the whole family intact.

We have. More than once.

Ever since Franklin Roosevelt lifted himself from his wheelchair to lift this nation from its knees. Wagon train after wagon train. To new frontier of education, housing, peace. The whole family aboard. Constantly reaching out to extend and enlarge that family. Lifting them up into the wagon on the way. Blacks and Hispanics, people of every ethnic group, and Native Americans—all those struggling to build their families claim some small share of America.

For nearly fifty years we carried them to new levels of comfort, security, dignity, even affluence.

Some of us are in this room today only because this nation had that confidence.

It would be wrong to forget that.

So, we are at this convention to remind ourselves where we come from and to claim the future for ourselves and for our children.

Today, our great Democratic Party, which has saved this nation from depression, from fascism, from racism, from corruption, is called upon to do it again—this time to save the nation from confusion and division, most of all from a fear of a nuclear holocaust.

In order to succeed, we must answer our opponent's polished and appealing rhetoric with a more telling reasonableness and rationality.

We must win this case on the merits.

We must get the American public to look past the glitter, beyond the showmanship—to reality, to the hard substance of things. And we will do that not so much with speeches that sound good as with speeches that are good and sound.

Not so much with speeches that bring people to their feet as with speeches that bring people to their senses.

We must make the American people hear our "tale of two cities."

We must convince them that we don't have to settle for two cities, that we can have one city, indivisible, shining for all its people.

We will have no chance to do that if what comes out of this convention, what is heard throughout the campaign, is a babel of arguing voices.

To succeed we will have to surrender small parts of our individual interests, to build a platform we can all stand on, at once, comfortably, proudly singing out the truth for the nation to hear, in chorus, its logic so clear and commanding that no slick commercial, no amount of geniality, no martial music will be able to muffle it.

We democrats must unite so that the entire nation can. Surely the Republicans won't bring the convention together. Their policies divide the nation: into the lucky and the left-out, the royalty and the rabble.

The Republicans are willing to treat that division as victory. They would cut this nation in half, into those temporarily better off and those worse off than before, and call it recovery.

We should not be embarrassed or dismayed if the process of unifying is difficult, even at times wrenching.

Unlike any other party, we embrace men and women of every

color, every creed, every orientation, every economic class. In our family are gathered everyone from the abject poor of Essex County in New York to the enlightened affluent of the gold coasts of both ends of our nation. And in between is the heart of our constituency. The middle class, the people not rich enough to be worry-free but not poor enough to be on welfare, those who work for a living because they have to. White collar and blue collar. Young professionals. Men and women in small business desperate for the capital and contracts they need to prove their worth.

We speak for the minorities who have not yet entered the mainstream.

For ethnics who want to add their culture to the mosaic that is America.

For women indignant that we refuse to etch into our governmental commandments the simple rule "thou shalt not sin against equality," a commandment so obvious it can be spelled in three letters: E.R.A.!

For young people demanding an education and a future.

For senior citizens terrorized by the idea that their only security, their Social Security, is being threatened.

For millions of reasoning people fighting to preserve our environment from greed and stupidity. And fighting to preserve our very existence from a macho intransigence that refuses to make intelligent attempts to discuss the possibility of nuclear holocaust with our enemy. Refusing because they believe we can pile missiles so high that they will pierce the clouds and the sight of them will frighten our enemies into submission.

We're proud of this diversity. Grateful we don't have to manufacture its appearance the way the Republicans will next month in Dallas, by propping up mannequin delegates on the convention floor.

But we pay a price for it.

The different people we represent have many points of view. Sometimes they compete and then we have debates, even arguments. That's what our primaries were.

But now the primaries are over, and it is time to lock arms and move into this campaign together.

If we need any inspiration to make the effort to put aside our small differences, all we need to do is to reflect on the Republican policy of divide and cajole and how it has injured our land since 1980.

The President has asked us to judge him on whether or not he's fulfilled the promises he made four years ago. I accept that. Just consider what he said and what he's done.

Inflation is down since 1980. But not because of the supply-side miracle promised by the President. Inflation was reduced the old-fashioned way, with a recession, the worst since 1932. More than 55,000 bankruptcies. Two years of massive unemployment. Two-hundred-thousand farmers and ranchers forced off the land. More homeless than at any time since the Great Depression. More hungry, more poor—mostly women—and a nearly $200 billion deficit threatening our future.

The President's deficit is a direct and dramatic repudiation of his promise to balance our budget by 1983.

That deficit is the largest in the history of this universe; more than three times larger than the deficit in President Carter's last year.

It is a deficit that, according to the President's own fiscal advisor, could grow as high as $300 billion a year, stretching "as far as the eye can see."

It is a debt so large that as much as one-half of our revenue from the income tax goes to pay the interest on it each year.

It is a mortgage on our children's futures that can only be paid in pain and that could eventually bring this nation to its knees.

Don't take my word for it—I'm a Democrat.

Ask the Republican investment bankers on Wall Street what they think the chances are this recovery will be permanent. If they're not too embarrassed to tell you the truth, they'll say they are appalled and frightened by the President's deficit. Ask them what they think of our economy, now that it has been driven by the distorted value of the dollar back to its colonial condition, exporting agricultural products and importing manufactured ones.

Ask those Republican investment bankers what they expect the interest rate to be a year from now. And ask them what they predict for the inflation rate then.

How important is this question of the deficit?

Think about it: What chance would the Republican candidate

have had in 1980 if he had told the American people that he intended to pay for his so-called economic recovery with bankruptcies, unemployment and the largest Government debt known to humankind? Would American voters have signed the loan certificate for him on Election Day? Of course not! It was an election won with smoke and mirrors, with illusions. It is a recovery made of the same stuff.

And what about foreign policy?

They said they would make us and the whole world safer. They say they have.

By creating the largest defense budget in history, one even they now admit is excessive, and failing to discuss peace with our enemies. By the loss of 279 young Americans in Lebanon in pursuit of a plan and a policy no one can find or describe.

We give monies to Latin American governments that murder nuns, and then lie about it.

We have been less than zealous in our support of the only real friend we have in the Middle East, the one democracy there, our flesh and blood ally, the state of Israel.

Our policy drifts with no real direction, other than an hysterical commitment to an arms race that leads nowhere, if we're lucky. If we're not—could lead us to bankruptcy or war.

Of course we must have a strong defense!

Of course Democrats believe that there are times when we must stand and fight. And we have. Thousands of us have paid for freedom with our lives. But always, when we've been at our best, our purposes were clear.

Now they're not. Now our allies are as confused as our enemies.

Now we have no real commitment to our friends or our ideals, to human rights, to the refuseniks, to Sakharov, to Bishop Tutu and the others struggling for freedom in South Africa.

We have spent more than we can afford. We have pounded our chest and made bold speeches. But we lost 279 young Americans in Lebanon and we are forced to live behind sand bags in Washington.

How can anyone believe that we are stronger, safer or better?

That's the Republican record.

That its disastrous quality is not more fully understood by the American people is attributable, I think, to the President's amiability and the failure by some to separate the salesman from the product.

It's now up to us to make the case to America.

And to remind Americans that if they are not happy with all the President has done so far, they should consider how much worse it will be if he is left to his radical proclivities for another four years unrestrained by the need once again to come before the American people.

If July brings back Anne Gorsuch Burford, what can we expect of December?

Where would another four years take us?

How much larger will the deficit be?

How much deeper the cuts in programs for the struggling middle class and the poor to limit that deficit? How high the interest rates? How much more acid rain killing our forests and fouling our lakes?

What kind of Supreme Court? What kind of court and country will be fashioned by the man who believes in having government mandate people's religion and morality?

The man who believes that trees pollute the environment, that the laws against discrimination go too far. The man who threatens Social Security and Medicaid and help for the disabled.

How high will we pile the missiles?

How much deeper will be the gulf between us and our enemies?

Will we make meaner the spirit of our people?

This election will measure the record of the past four years. But more than that, it will answer the question of what kind of people we want to be.

We Democrats still have a dream. We still believe in this nation's future.

And this is our answer—our credo:

We believe in only the government we need, but we insist on all the government we need.

We believe in a government characterized by fairness and reasonableness, a reasonableness that goes beyond labels, that doesn't distort or promise to do what it knows it can't do.

A government strong enough to use the words "love" and "compassion" and smart enough to convert our noblest aspirations.

We believe in encouraging the talented, but we believe that

while survival of the fittest may be a good working description of the process of evolution, a government of humans should elevate itself to a higher order, one which fills the gaps left by chance or a wisdom we don't understand.

We would rather have laws written by the patron of this great city, the man called the "world's most sincere Democrat," St. Francis of Assisi, than laws written by Darwin.

We believe, as Democrats, that a society as blessed as ours, the most affluent democracy in the world's history, that can spend trillions on instruments of destruction, ought to be able to help the middle class in its struggle, ought to be able to find work for all who can do it, room at the table, shelter for the homeless, care for the elderly and infirm, hope for the destitute.

We proclaim as loudly as we can the utter insanity of nuclear proliferation and the need for a nuclear freeze, if only to affirm the simple truth that peace is better than war because life is better than death.

We believe in firm but fair law and order, in the union movement, in privacy for people, openness by government, civil rights, and human rights.

We believe in a single fundamental idea that describes better than most textbooks and any speech what a proper government should be. The idea of family. Mutuality. The sharing of benefits and burdens for the good of all. Feeling one another's pain. Sharing one another's blessings. Reasonably, honestly, fairly, without respect to race, or sex, or geography or political affiliation.

We believe we must be the family of America, recognizing that at the heart of the matter we are bound one to another, that the problems of a retired school teacher in Duluth are our problems. That the future of the child in Buffalo is our future. The struggle of a disabled man in Boston to survive, to live decently in our struggle. The hunger of a woman in Little Rock, our hunger. The failure anywhere to provide what reasonably we might, to avoid pain, is our failure.

For fifty years we Democrats created a better future for our children, using traditional democratic principles as a fixed beacon, giving us direction and purpose, but constantly innovating, adapting to new realities; Roosevelt's alphabet programs; Truman's NATO and the GI Bill of Rights; Kennedy's intelligent tax incentives and the Alliance for Progress; Johnson's civil rights; Carter's human rights and the nearly miraculous Camp David peace accord.

Democrats did it—and Democrats can do it again.

We can build a future that deals with our deficit.

Remember, fifty years of progress never cost us what the last four years of stagnation have. We can deal with that deficit intelligently, by shared sacrifice, with all parts of the nation's family contributing, building partnerships with the private sector, providing a sound defense without depriving ourselves of what we need to feed our children and care for our people.

We can have a future that provides for all the young of the present by marrying common sense and compassion.

We know we can, because we did it for nearly fifty years before 1980.

We can do it again. If we do not forget. Forget that this entire nation has profited by these progressive principles. That they helped lift up generations to the middle class and higher: gave us a chance to work, to go to college, to raise a family, to own a house, to be secure in our old age and, before that, to reach heights that our own parents would not have dared dream of.

That struggle to live with dignity is the real story of the shining city. It's a story I didn't read in a book, or learn in a classroom. I saw it, and lived it. Like many of you.

I watched a small man with thick calluses on both hands work fifteen and sixteen hours a day. I saw him once literally bleed from the bottoms of his feet, a man who came here uneducated, alone, unable to speak the language, who taught me all I needed to know about faith and hard work by the simple eloquence of his example. I learned about our kind of democracy from my father. I learned about our obligation to each other from him and from my mother. They asked only for a chance to work and to make the world better for their children and to be protected in those moments when they would not be able to protect themselves. This nation and its government did that for them.

And that they were able to build a family and live in dignity and see one of their children go from behind their little grocery store on the other side of the tracks in south Jamaica where he was born, to occupy the highest seat in the greatest state of the greatest nation in the only world we know, is an ineffably beautiful tribute to the democratic process.

And on January 20, 1985, it will happen again. Only on a much grander scale. We will have a new President of the United States, a Democrat born not to the blood of kings but to the blood of immigrants and pioneers.

We will have America's first woman Vice President, the child of immigrants, a New Yorker, opening with one magnificent stroke a whole new frontier for the United States.

It will happen, if we make it happen.

I ask you, ladies and gentlemen, brothers and sisters—for the good of all of us, for the love of this great nation, for the family of America, for the love of God. Please make this nation remember how futures are built.

PART ELEVEN

VISIONS OF THE FUTURE

Reconnecting the broken fragments of our culture requires first of all that we find a language capable of expressing a vision of ourselves as a social whole. One source of such a language is our religious traditions, and the churches constitute an important social context for creatively weaving such a language into a vision of our moral interdependence. An important recent example of this enterprise is the "Economic Justice for All: Catholic Social Teaching and the U.S. Economy" promulgated by the National Conference of Catholic Bishops. The excerpt reproduced here is from the second draft of this document, which was later revised in the light of criticisms from clergy and laity to produce a slightly less controversial final draft. We have reprinted a part of the second rather than the final draft because its sharper formulation of the implications of Catholic social teaching offers a clearer contrast to individualistic visions of American political economy.

The bishops base their reflections about the American economy on a biblical tradition which understands the dignity of the human person as founded in the fact that human beings do not in the end create and fulfill themselves but are created, "in the image and likeness of God," and redeemed by God. This common dependence on God implies a fundamental solidarity among all members of the human community and makes moral life dependent on affirming that solidarity. Given this understanding of human dignity as rooted in community, and of community as founded in a common relationship to a loving God, the bishops find much to criticize in American economic life. As presently structured, economic productivity is primarily driven by competitive acquisitiveness rather than by a concern to contribute to the welfare of others. And one result of this is that all too many persons are left in degrading poverty even as the means to produce enormous wealth multiply. The bishops do not attempt to spell out the technical economic and political arrangements that might be necessary to change this. They recognize that that is beyond their competence as religious educators. But they offer a moral vision that gives reason and rationale for creative efforts to develop such arrangements.

The second selection comes from a critical response to the draft of their pastoral letter that the Catholic bishops circulated for reaction and debate. Called *Toward the Future*, the response was drafted by an independent group of Catholic laity calling itself the Lay Commission on Catholic Social Teaching and the U.S. Economy. This "lay letter" takes issue with much of the criticism the bishops make of the structure and workings of American economic life, arguing that American tradition has as much to teach the body of Catholic social thought as the other way around. In particular, *Toward the Future* emphasizes three aspects of American culture: "the practice of free association," "the habit of cooperation," and "the principle of self-interest rightly understood," themes borrowed from Tocqueville. The center of the controversy with the bishops is the lay letter's claim that in American economic life "the ancient dichotomy between self-interest and the common good has at the very least been diminished. . . . And the practice of virtue is institutionally unimpeded." In direct contrast with the bishops, the lay letter, while surveying areas needing improvement, does not find fundamental moral problems with the workings of the U.S. economy.

Biblical religion is not, of course, the only source of language for expressing and exploring the implications of our wholeness, and the churches are not the only sources for visions of moral community. All of the great classics of our inherited culture have the power to convey to their readers what Helen Vendler, in her 1980 presidential address to the Modern Language Association, calls "that rich web of associations . . . by which they could begin to understand themselves as individuals and as social beings." Meditating on some of these classics within the context of a life devoted to domestic agriculture and with the support of the modern ecology movement, Wendell Berry weaves an eloquent vision of our wholeness in his essay on "The Body and the Earth." For Berry, who is a Kentucky farmer, as well as a famous novelist, poet, and essayist, the work of agriculture is what Alasdair MacIntyre would call a practice, a kind of activity that is good in itself, not good simply as a means to make money or even to put food on the table. A prerequisite to engage in agricultural work in this fashion is to accept a stance of fundamental humility in the face of Creation, a stance which has always been affirmed by the wisest voices of our classical cultural tradition. Farming is a way of affirming one's dependency on nature—one's connectedness with the natural, material world—even as one transforms nature to serve the needs of the human community. Modern industrial civilization leads to a forgetfulness of such dependency, a denial of such connectedness. As a result, its triumphs turn out to be hollow. "If we have built towering cities, we have raised even higher the cloud of megadeath. If people are as grass before God, they are as nothing before their machines."

The awareness of interconnectedness with Creation that Berry recognizes in the performance of agriculture both sustains and is sustained by a complementary awareness of interconnectedness with one's household, and one's wider community. In the ancient story of Odysseus, Berry finds the words to express such interconnectedness. Industrialized agriculture and the culture of industrial society make it difficult not only to express, but to live, such interconnectedness—and difficult to live therefore a humanly meaningful life. By drawing upon some of the literary classics of our cultural tradition Berry is thus able to show us what our modern culture denies to us and why this denial is intolerable. He defines the agenda of a search for a social ecology that, without denying the benefits of modern science and technology, would encompass them within a renewed web of connections among our society, our bodies, and the earth.

NATIONAL CONFERENCE OF CATHOLIC BISHOPS

Pastoral Letter on Catholic Social Teaching and the U.S. Economy

The basis for all that the Church believes about the moral dimensions of economic life is its vision of the transcendent worth—the sacredness—of human beings. *The dignity of the human person, realized in community with others, is the criterion against which all aspects of economic life must be measured.* All human beings, therefore, are ends to be served by the institutions which make up the economy, not means to be exploited for more narrowly defined goals. Human personhood must be respected with a reverence that is religious. When we deal with each other we should do so with the sense of awe that arises in the presence of something holy and sacred. For that is what human beings are: we are created "in the image and likeness of God." Economic life must serve and support this dignity which needs to be realized in relationship and solidarity with others.

These convictions have a biblical and theological basis. They also draw support from a long tradition of philosophical reflection and from the common human experience of contemporary men and women. Throughout its history the Christian community has developed a rich tradition of ethical reflection that has broadened its understanding of the challenge of discipleship in economic life. This tradition testifies to the many ways our Christian forebears have sought to live as disciples and to proclaim the Kingdom of God. Especially since the industrial revolution and the seminal writings of Pope Leo XIII, the Church teaching has evaluated shifting economic and social patterns in the light of God's revelation in Scripture and human history, and has defended the dignity and

National Conference of Catholic Bishops, excerpted from the "Economic Justice For All: Catholic Social Teaching and the U.S. Economy," pp. 10–12, 18, 19, 21–30)

rights of those most adversely affected by these patterns. Drawing on the rich resources of philosophy and empirical analysis, these reflections have led to a deeper understanding of the dignity of the human person, the rights and duties of different groups, and of the nature of communal life. In this task, the Church seeks a dialogue with those in a pluralistic society who, while not sharing our religious vision or heritage, voice a common concern for human dignity and human freedom.

* * *

BIBLICAL PERSPECTIVES

The fundamental conviction of our faith is that human life is fulfilled in the knowledge and love of the living God in communion with others who, as recipients of God's love, are called to love the same God. The Sacred Scriptures offer guidance so that men and women may enter into full communion with God and with each other, and witness to God's saving acts. We discover there a God who is Creator of heaven and earth, and of the human family. Though our first parents reject the God who created them, God does not abandon them, but from Abraham and Sarah forms a people of promise. When this people is enslaved in an alien land, God delivers them and makes a covenant with them in which they are summoned to be faithful to the *torah* or sacred teaching. The focal points of Israel's faith—creation, covenant, and saving history—provide a foundation for reflection on issues of economic and social justice.

Created in God's Image

After the exile, when Israel combined its traditions into a written *torah,* it prefaced its history as a people with the story of the creation of all peoples and of the whole world by the same God who created them as a nation (Gn. 1–11). God is the creator of heaven and earth (Gn. 14:19–22; Is. 40:28; 45:18); creation proclaims God's glory (Ps. 89:5–12) and is "very good" (Gn. 1:31). Fruitful harvests, bountiful flocks, a loving family, are God's blessings on those who heed God's word. Such is the joyful refrain that echoes throughout the Bible. One legacy of this theology of creation is the conviction that no dimension of human life lies beyond God's care and concern. God is present to creation and creative engagement with God's handiwork is itself reverence for God.

At the summit of creation stands the creation of man and woman, made in God's image (Gn. 1:26–27). *As such every human being possesses an inalienable dignity which stamps human existence prior to any division into races or nations and prior to human labor and human achievement (Gn. 4–11).* Men and women are also to share in the creative activity of God. They are to be fruitful, to care for the earth (Gn. 2:15), and to have "dominion" over it (Gn. 1:28), which the Book of Wisdom states is "to govern the world in holiness and justice and to render judgment in integrity of heart" (Wis. 9:3). Creation is a gift; men and women are to be faithful stewards in caring for the earth. They can justly consider that by their labor they are unfolding the Creator's work.

The narratives of Genesis 1–11 also portray the origin of the strife and suffering that mar the world. Though created to enjoy intimacy with God and the fruits of the earth, Adam and Eve disrupted God's design by trying to live independently of God through a denial of their status as creatures. They turned away from God and gave to God's creation the obedience due to God alone. For this reason the prime sin in so much of the biblical tradition is idolatry: service of the creature rather than of the creator (Rom. 1:25), and the attempt to overturn creation by making God in human likeness. The Bible castigates not only the worship of idols, but also manifestations of idolatry such as the quest for unrestrained power and the desire for great wealth (Is. 40:12–20; 44:1–20; Wis. 13:1–14:31; Col. 3:5, "covetousness which is idolatry"). The sin of our first parents had other consequences as well. Alienation from God pits brother against brother (Gn. 4:8–16), in a cycle of war and vengeance (Gn. 5:22–23). Sin and evil abound, and the primeval history culminates with another assault on the heavens, this time ending in a babble of tongues scattered over the face of the earth (Gn. 11:1–9). Sin simultaneously alienates human beings from God and shatters the solidarity of the human community. Yet this reign of sin is not the final word. The primeval history is followed by the call of Abraham, a man of faith, who was to be the bearer of the promise to many nations (Gn. 12:1–4). Throughout the Bible we find this struggle between sin and repentance. God's judgment on evil is followed by God's seeking out a sinful people.

The biblical vision of creation has provided one of the most enduring legacies of Church teaching. To stand before God as creator is to respect God's creation, both the world of nature and of human history. *From the Patristic period to the present, the Church has affirmed that misuse of the world's resources or appropriation of them by a minority of the world's population betrays the gift of creation since "whatever belongs to God belongs to all."*

A People of the Covenant
* * *

Early Christianity saw the poor as an object of God's special love, but it neither canonized material poverty nor accepted deprivation as an inevitable fact of life. Though few early Christians possessed wealth or power (1 Cor. 1:26–28; Jas. 2:5), their communities had well-off members (Acts 16:14, 18:8). Jesus' concern for the poor was continued in different forms in the early Church. The early community at Jerusalem distributes its possessions so that "there was not a needy person among them," and "holds all things in common"—a phrase which suggests not only shared material possessions, but even more basically friendship and mutual concern among all its members (Acts 2:44; 4:32). While recognizing the dangers of wealth, the early Church proposed the proper use of possessions to alleviate need and suffering as the ideal, rather than universal dispossession. Beginning in the first century and throughout the Patristic period Christian communities organized structures to support and sustain the weak and powerless in a society which was often brutally unconcerned about human suffering.

Such perspectives provide a basis for what today is called the "preferential option for the poor." Though in the Gospels and in the New Testament as a whole the offer of salvation is extended to all peoples, Jesus takes the side of those most in need, physically and spiritually. The example of Jesus poses a number of challenges to the contemporary Church. It imposes a prophetic mandate to speak for those who have no one to speak for them, to be a defender of the defenseless, who in biblical terms are the poor. It also demands a compassionate vision which enables the Church to see things from the side of the poor and powerless, and to assess lifestyle, policies, and social institutions in terms of their impact on the poor. It summons the Church also to be an instrument in assisting people to experience the liberating power of God in their own lives, so that they may respond to the Gospel in freedom and in dignity. Finally, and most radically, it calls for an emptying of self, both individually and corporately, that allows the Church to experience the power of God in the midst of poverty and powerlessness.

We live in one of the most affluent cultures in history where many social values are in direct conflict with the Gospel vision. Our contemporary prosperity exists alongside the poverty of many both at home and abroad, and the image of disciples who "left all" to follow Jesus is difficult to reconcile with a contemporary ethos which encourages amassing as much as possible.

* * *

ETHICAL NORMS FOR ECONOMIC LIFE

These biblical and theological themes shape the overall Christian perspective on economic ethics. The Catholic tradition also affirms that this ethical perspective is intelligible to those who do not share Christian religious convictions. Human beings are created in God's image, and their dignity is manifest in the ability to reason and understand, in their freedom to shape their own lives and the life of their communities, and in the capacity for love and friendship. Human understanding and religious belief are complementary, not contradictory. In proposing ethical norms, therefore, we appeal both to Christians and to all in our pluralist society to show that respect and reverence owed to the dignity of every person. Intelligent reflection on the social and economic realities of today are also indispensable in the effort to respond to economic circumstances never envisioned in biblical times. Therefore, we now want to outline an ethical framework that can guide economic life today in ways that are both faithful to the Gospel and shaped by human experience and reason. First are the duties all people have to each other and to the whole community: love of neighbor, the basic requirements of justice, and the special obligation to those who are poor or vulnerable. Corresponding to these duties are the human rights of every person: the obligation to protect the dignity of all demands respect for these rights. Finally these duties and rights suggest several priorities that should guide the economic choices of individuals, communities and the nation as a whole.

The Responsibilities of Social Living

Human life is life in community. Catholic social teaching proposes several complementary perspectives that show how moral obligations and duties in the economic sphere are rooted in this call to community.

LOVE AND SOLIDARITY

The commandments to love God with all one's heart and to love one's neighbor as oneself are the heart and soul of Christian morality. These commands point out the path toward true human fulfillment and happiness. They are not arbitrary restrictions on human freedom. Only active love of God and neighbor makes the fullness of community happen. Christians look forward in hope to a true communion among all persons with each other and with God. The Spirit of Christ labors in history to build up the bonds of solidarity among all persons until that day on which their union is brought to perfection in the Kingdom of God. Indeed, Christian theological reflection on the very reality of God as a trinitarian unity of persons—Father, Son, and Holy Spirit—shows that being a person means being united to other persons in mutual love.

What the Bible and Christian tradition teach, human wisdom confirms. Centuries before Christ the Greeks and Romans spoke of the human person as a "social animal," made for friendship, community and public life. These insights show that human beings cannot grow to full self-realization in isolation, but in interaction with others.

The virtues of citizenship are an expression of Christian love more crucial in today's interdependent world than ever before. These virtues grow out of a lively sense of one's dependence on the commonweal and obligations to it. This civic commitment must also guide the economic institutions of society. In the absence of a vital sense of citizenship among the businesses, corporations, labor unions, and other groups that shape economic life, society as a whole is endangered. Solidarity is another name for this social friendship and civic commitment that make human moral and economic life possible.

The Christian tradition recognizes, of course, that the fullness of love and community will be achieved only when God's work in

Christ comes to completion in the kingdom of God. Within history, knowledge of how to achieve the goal of social unity is limited. Human sin continues to wound the lives of both individuals and larger social bodies. Efforts to achieve social solidarity that do not take into account these limits on knowledge and love may only end by suppressing human freedom and degenerating into oppression. Nevertheless, sober realism should not be confused with resigned or cynical pessimism.

JUSTICE AND PARTICIPATION

The norms of basic justice state the minimum levels of mutual care and respect that all persons and communities owe to each other. Though the rich biblical understanding of the "wholeness" *(shalom)* of a fully just society reaches beyond these levels, the criteria of basic justice establish the minimum standards for all social and economic life. Catholic social teaching, like much philosophical reflection, distinguishes three dimensions of basic justice: commutative justice, social justice, and distributive justice.

Commutative justice calls for fundamental fairness in all agreements and exchanges between individuals or private social groups. It demands respect for the equal human dignity of all persons in economic transactions, contracts, or promises. For example, workers owe their employers diligent work in exchange for their wages. Employers are obligated to treat their employees as persons, paying them fair wages in exchange for the work done and by establishing conditions and patterns of work that are truly human.

Justice also means that the larger social, economic, and political institutions of society have obligations. *Social justice implies that persons have an obligation to be active and productive participants in the life of society and that society has a duty to enable them to participate in this way.* This form of justice can also be called "contributive," for it stresses the duty of all who are able to help create the goods, services, and other nonmaterial or spiritual values necessary for the welfare of the whole community. In the words of Pius XI, "It is of the very essence of social justice to demand from each individual all that is necessary for the common good." Productivity is essential if the community is to have the resources to serve the well-being of all. The meaning of social justice includes a duty to organize economic and social institutions so that people can contribute to society in ways which respect their freedom and the dignity of their labor. Work should enable the working person to become "more a human being," more capable of acting intelligently, freely and in a way that leads to self-realization. Economic conditions which leave large numbers of people unemployed, underemployed, or employed in dehumanizing conditions fail to meet these demands of basic justice.

Distributive justice requires that the allocation of income, wealth, and power in society be evaluated in light of its effects on persons whose basic material needs are unmet. The Second Vatican Council stated: "The right to have a share of earthly goods sufficient for oneself and one's family belongs to everyone. The Fathers and Doctors of the Church held this view, teaching that we are obliged to come to the relief of the poor and to do so not merely out of our superfluous goods." Minimum material resources are an absolute necessity for human life. If persons are to be treated as members of the human community, then the community has an obligation to help fulfill these basic needs unless an absolute scarcity of resources makes this strictly impossible. No such scarcity exists in the United States today.

Work with adequate pay for all who seek it is the primary means to the achievement of basic justice in our society. Discrimination in job opportunities or income levels on the basis of race, sex, or other arbitrary standard can never be justified. It is a scandal that such discrimination continues in the United States today. Where the effects of past discrimination persist today, society has the obligation to take positive steps to overcome the legacy of injustice. Judiciously administered affirmative action programs in education and employment can be important expressions of that drive for solidarity and participation that is at the heart of true justice. Social harm calls for social relief.

Distributive justice also calls for the establishment of a floor of material well-being on which all can stand. This is a duty of the whole of society and it creates particular obligations for those with greater resources. This duty calls into question extreme inequalities of income and consumption when so many lack basic necessities. Catholic social teaching does not maintain that a flat, arithmetical equality of income and wealth is a demand of justice, but it does challenge economic arrangements that leave large numbers of people impoverished. Further, it sees extreme inequality as a threat to the solidarity of the human community, for great disparities lead to deep social divisions and conflict.

This means that all of us must examine our way of living in light of others' needs. Christian faith and the norms of justice impose distinct limits on what we consume and how we view material goods. The great wealth of the United States can easily blind us to the poverty that exists in this nation and the destitution of hundreds of millions of people in other parts of the world. Americans are challenged today as never before to develop the inner freedom to resist the temptation constantly to seek more. Only in this way will the nation avoid what Paul VI called "the most evident form of moral underdevelopment," namely greed.

These duties call not only for individual charitable giving but also for a more systematic approach by businesses, labor unions, and the many other groups that shape economic life—as well as government. The concentration of privilege that exists today results far more from institutional relationships that distribute power and wealth inequitably than from differences in talent or lack of desire to work. These institutional patterns must be examined and revised if we are to meet the demands of basic justice. For example, a system of taxation based on "assessment according to ability to pay" is a prime necessity for the fulfillment of these social obligations.

OVERCOMING MARGINALIZATION AND POWERLESSNESS

These fundamental duties can be summarized this way: *Basic justice demands the establishment of minimum levels of participation in the life of the human community for all persons.* The ultimate injustice is for a person or group to be actively treated or passively abandoned as if they were non-members of the human race. To treat people in this way is effectively to say that they simply do not count as human beings. This can take many forms, all of which can be described as varieties of "marginalization," or exclusion from social life. Exclusion can take a political shape, as when a person or group is denied influence on public decision making through restriction of free speech, through an inordinate concentration of power in the hands of a few, or through outright repression by the state. Marginalization can also take economic forms that are equally harmful. Within the United States, individuals, families, and local communities can fall victim to a downward cycle of poverty generated by economic forces they are powerless to influence. The poor, the disabled, and the unemployed too often are simply left behind. This pattern is even more severe beyond our borders in the least-developed countries. Whole nations are prevented from participating in the international economic order because they lack both the resources to do so and the power to change their disadvantaged position. Many people within the less developed countries are excluded from sharing in the meager resources available in their homelands.

Recent Catholic social thought regards the task of overcoming these patterns of exclusion and powerlessness as a most basic demand of justice. Stated positively, justice demands that social institutions be ordered in a way that guarantees all persons the ability to participate actively in the economic, political, and cultural life of society. The level of participation may legitimately be greater for some persons than for others, but there is a basic level of access that must be made available for all. Such participation is an essential expression of the social nature of human beings and of their communitarian vocation.

Human Rights: The Minimum Conditions for Life
in Community

The basic demands of justice are spelled out in greater detail in the human rights of every person which are affirmed by Catholic social teaching. These fundamental rights are prerequisites for a dignified life in community. The Bible vigorously affirms the sacredness of every person as a creature formed in the image and likeness of God. The biblical emphasis on covenant and community also shows that human dignity can only be realized and protected in solidarity with others. In Catholic social thought, therefore, respect for human rights and a strong sense of both personal and community responsibility are linked, not opposed. Vatican II described the common good as "the sum of those conditions of social life which allow social groups and their individual members relatively thorough and ready access to their own fulfillment." These conditions include the rights to fulfillment of material needs, a guarantee of fundamental freedoms, and the protection of relationships that are essential to participation in the life of society.

The full range of human rights has been systematically outlined by John XXIII in his encyclical *Peace on Earth*. His discussion echoes the United Nations Universal Declaration of Human Rights and implies that internationally accepted human rights agreements are strongly supported by Catholic teaching. A number of these rights are of a specifically economic nature. In the first place stand the rights to life, food, clothing, shelter, rest, and medical care. These are absolutely basic to the protection of human dignity. In order to ensure these basic necessities, all persons have a right to security in the event of sickness, unemployment, and old age. Participation in the life of the community also calls for the protection of the rights to employment, to healthful working conditions, to wages and other benefits sufficient to provide individuals and their families with a standard of living in keeping with human dignity, and to the possibility of property ownership. These fundamental personal rights state the minimum conditions for economic institutions that respect human dignity, social solidarity, and justice. Any denial of these rights harms persons and wounds the human community. Their serious and sustained denial violates individuals and destroys solidarity among persons.

These economic rights are as essential to human dignity as are the political and civil freedoms granted pride of place in the Bill of Rights of the U. S. Constitution. Indeed, protection of these economic minimums is crucial to the growth of freedom within our borders and throughout the world. Nothing will threaten the cause of freedom in the world more surely than the notion that political democracy and economic justice for the poor are incompatible. We believe, therefore, that these economic rights should be granted a status in the cultural and legal traditions of this nation analogous to that held by the civil and political rights to freedom of religion, speech, and assembly.

Securing these economic rights for all will be an arduous task. There are a number of precedents in U.S. history, however, which show that the work has already begun. The country needs a serious dialogue about the appropriate levels of private and public sector involvement that are needed to move forward. There is certainly room for diversity of opinion in the Church and in U.S. society on *how* to protect the human dignity and economic rights of all our

brothers and sisters. In our view, however, there can be no legitimate disagreement on the basic moral objectives.

Moral Priorities for the Nation

*The common good demands justice for all, the protection of the human rights
of all.* Dedication to the common good, therefore, implies special
duties toward those who are economically vulnerable or needy.
Many in the lower middle class in this country are barely getting by
and fear becoming the victims of economic forces over which they
have no control. If the common good is to be truly *common,* greater
economic freedom, power, and security for these vulnerable middle-class members of the community is an important national goal.

*The obligation to provide justice for all means that the poor have the single
most urgent claim on the conscience of the nation.* Poverty can take many
forms, spiritual as well as material. All people face struggles of the
spirit as they ask deep questions about their purpose in life. Many
have serious problems in marriage and family life at some time in
their lives and all of us face the certain reality of sickness and death.
The Gospel of Christ proclaims that God's love is stronger than all
these forms of diminishment. Material deprivation seriously compounds such sufferings of the spirit and heart. To see a loved one
sick is bad enough, but to have no possibility of obtaining health
care is worse. To have family problems, such as the death of a
spouse or a divorce, can be devastating, but to have these lead to
the loss of one's home and even living on the streets is something
no one should have to endure in a country as rich as ours. In
developing countries these human problems are compounded by
extreme material deprivation. This form of human suffering can
also be reduced if our own country, so rich in resources, chooses to
help.

As individuals and as a nation, therefore, we are called to make
a fundamental "option for the poor." The obligation to evaluate
social and economic activity from the viewpoint of the poor and the
powerless arises from the radical command to love one's neighbor
as one's self. Those who are marginalized and whose rights are
denied have privileged claims if society is to provide justice *for all.*
This obligation is deeply rooted in Christian belief. As Paul VI
stated:

In teaching us charity, the gospel instructs us in the preferential respect due the poor and the special situation they have in society: the more fortunate should renounce some of their rights so as to place their goods more generously at the service of others.

John Paul II has described this special obligation to the poor as "a call to have a special openness with the small and the weak, those that suffer and weep, those that are humiliated and left on the margin of society, so as to help them win their dignity as human persons and children of God."

The prime purpose of this special commitment to the poor is to enable them to become active participants in the life of society. It is to enable *all* persons to share in and contribute to the common good. The "option for the poor," therefore, is not an adversarial slogan which pits one group or class against another. Rather it states that the deprivation and powerlessness of the poor wounds the whole community. The extent of their suffering is a measure of how far we are from being a true community of persons.

In summary, the norms of love, basic justice, and human rights imply that personal decisions, social policies, and economic institutions should be governed by several key priorities. These priorities do not specify everything that must be considered in economic decision-making. They do indicate the most fundamental and urgent objectives.

The fulfillment of the basic needs of the poor is of the highest priority. Personal decisions, policies of private and public bodies, and power relationships must all be evaluated by their effects on those who lack the minimum necessities of nutrition, housing, education, and health care. In particular, this principle recognizes that meeting fundamental human needs must come before the fulfillment of desires for luxury consumer goods, for profits not conducive to the common good, and for unnecessary military hardware.

Increasing active participation in economic life by those who are presently excluded or vulnerable is a high social priority. The human dignity of all is realized when people gain the power to work together to improve their lives and to make their contribution to society. Basic justice calls for more than providing help *to* the poor and other vulnerable members of society. It recognizes the priority of policies and programs that enhance economic participation through employment. It challenges privileged economic power in favor of the well-being of all. It points to the need to improve the present situation of those unjustly discriminated against in the past. And it has very important implications for both the domestic and the international distribution of power.

The investment of wealth, talent, and human energy should be specially directed to benefit those who are poor or economically insecure. Achieving a more just economy in the United States and the world depends in part on increasing economic resources and productivity. Different sorts of investment of human and financial resources, however, can have very different outcomes for people even when they have similar rates of productivity. This priority presents a strong moral challenge to policies that put large amounts of talent and capital into the production of luxury consumer goods and military technology while failing to invest sufficiently in education, health, and the basic infrastructure of our society, or in economic sectors that produce urgently needed jobs, goods, and services.

These three priorities are not policies. They are norms which should guide the economic choices of all and shape economic institutions. They can help the United States move forward to fulfill the duties of justice and protect economic rights. They were strongly affirmed as implications of Catholic social teaching by Pope John Paul II during his visit to Canada in 1984: "The needs of the poor take priority over the desires of the rich; the rights of workers over the maximization of profits; the preservation of the environment over uncontrolled industrial expansion; production to meet social needs over production for military purposes." There will undoubtedly be disputes about the concrete applications of these priorities in our complex world. We do not seek to foreclose discussion about them. However, we believe that an effort to move in the direction they indicate is urgently needed.

The economic challenge of today has many parallels with the political challenge that confronted the founders of our nation. In order to create a new form of political democracy they were compelled to develop ways of thinking and political institutions that had never existed before. Their efforts were arduous and their goals imperfectly realized, but they launched an experiment in the protection of civil and political rights that has prospered through the efforts of those who came after them. *We believe the time has come for a similar experiment in securing economic rights: the creation of an order that guarantees the minimum conditions of human dignity in the economic sphere for every person.* By drawing on the resources of the Catholic moral-religious tradition, we hope to make a contribution through this letter to such a new "American Experiment": a new venture to secure economic justice for all.

WORKING FOR GREATER JUSTICE: PERSONS AND INSTITUTIONS

The economy of this nation has been built by the labor of human hands and minds. Its future will be forged by the ways persons direct all this work toward greater justice. The economy is not a machine that operates according to its own inexorable laws, and persons are not mere objects tossed about by economic forces. Pope John Paul II has stated that "human work is a key, probably the essential key, to the whole social question." The Pope's understanding of work includes virtually all forms of productive human activity: agriculture, entrepreneurship, industry, the care of children, the sustaining of family life, politics, medical care, the arts, and scientific research. Through their daily work, persons are the subjects and creators of the economic life of the nation. It is primarily through the way people engage in this ordinary activity throughout their lives that they make their most important contributions to the pursuit of economic justice.

All work has a three-fold moral significance. First, it embodies the distinctive human capacity for self-expression and self-realization. Second, it is the ordinary way for human beings to fulfill their material needs. Finally, work enables people to contribute to the well-being of the larger community. Work is not only for oneself. It is for one's family, for the nation, and indeed for the benefit of the entire human family.

These three moral concerns should be visible in the work of all, no matter what their role in the marketplace: blue collar workers, managers, homemakers, politicians, etc. They should also govern the activities of the many different, overlapping communities and institutions that make up society: families, neighborhoods, small businesses, giant corporations, trade unions, the various levels of government, international organizations, and a host of other human associations including communities of faith. In all their activities these groups should be working in ways that express their distinctive capacities for action, that help meet human needs, and that make true contributions to the common good of the human community. The task of creating a more just U.S. economy is the vocation of all and depends on strengthening the virtues of public service and responsible citizenship in personal and institutional life.

LAY COMMISSION ON CATHOLIC SOCIAL TEACHING AND THE U.S. ECONOMY

Toward the Future

James Madison, architect of the Bill of Rights, once argued that to set such a Bill in writing was unnecessary. The rights of Americans, he argued, are not defended by "parchment barriers," but by the habits and institutions of the American people. Habits and institutions are precisely what Catholic social teaching needs in order to become incarnated in everyday life. Principles do not suffice. Lived practice is necessary. What are some of the distinctively American habits and institutions, especially significant in the economic sphere and transferable to any who would wish to learn them?

There seem to us to be three American habits especially deserving of comment: the practice of free association; the habit of cooperation; and the underlying virtue of both, typically called by Americans "the principle of self-interest rightly understood." There has been no more clear-eyed observer of these qualities in American life than the great French Catholic aristocrat, parliamentarian, and so-

Lay Commission on Catholic Social Teaching and the U.S. Economy, excerpted from *Toward the Future: Catholic Social Thought and the U.S. Economy* (New York: American Catholic Committee, 1984), pp. 17–24.

cial thinker, Alexis de Tocqueville, whose sense of American originality we here trace.

(1) *The Practice of Free Association.* Although European commentators even today often oppose American "individualism" to European "collectivism" and "solidarity," the true identity of the American character is best revealed in its associative instinct. Thus, Tocqueville:

> Americans of all ages, all conditions, and all dispositions, constantly form associations. They have not only commercial and manufacturing companies, in which all take part, but associations of a thousand other kinds,—religious, moral, serious, futile, extensive or restricted, enormous or diminutive. The Americans make associations to give entertainments, to found establishments for education, to build inns, to construct churches, to diffuse books, to send missionaries to the antipodes; and in this manner they found hospitals, prisons, and schools. If it be proposed to advance some truth, or to foster some feeling by the encouragement of a great example, they form a society. Wherever, at the head of some new undertaking, you see the Government in France, or a man of rank in England, in the United States you will be sure to find an association.

These qualities persist in the United States. Through a multitude of private associations, American citizens in 1983 gave $65 billion in charitable assistance. About 55 percent of adult Americans took part in voluntary work and together contributed many millions of person/hours. During 1983, more new businesses were established—601,000—than in any previous year in American history. The vast majority of Americans today work with others. There are currently fifteen million business enterprises in the United States, among 104 million employed civilians. The words which Tocqueville penned in 1832 are still valid:

> . . . I have often admired the extreme skill with which the inhabitants of the United States succeed in proposing a common object to the exertions of a great many men, and in getting them voluntarily to pursue it. . . . Thus the most democratic country on the face of the earth is that in which men have in our time carried to the

highest perfection the art of pursuing in common the object of their common desires, and have applied this new science to the greatest number of purposes. Is this the result of accident?

Tocqueville did not think it an accident. He argued that where privileged classes dominate, or where government dominates, tyranny ensues. Where, by contrast, equality of condition obtains, and government is limited, a new law of social association comes into play. Governments, he thought, should not be the only active powers: associations ought, in democratic nations, to take the place of powerful private individuals and state bureaucracies. Free citizens should voluntarily combine their efforts to act for themselves.

For Tocqueville, "the science of association is the mother of science; the progress of all the rest depends upon the progress it has made." And he added: "Amongst the laws which rule human societies there is one which seems to be more precise and clear than all others. If men are to remain civilized, or to become so, the art of associating together must grow and improve."

Catholic social thought—of which Tocqueville, as a serious layman, was a nineteenth-century exemplar—has strongly supported the principle of association. One finds many passages in Leo XIII, Pius XI, and other popes including Pope John Paul II emphatic in this regard. Yet no people in the world has shown greater practical skill in forming associations, encouraged by the very design of their political economy, than Americans.

We underline here the crucial role of associations in the economy. If an inventor of a new product or a new service wishes quickly to share his invention with the public through the market, such a person naturally forms an association with many others: with lawyers, venture capitalists, managers, workers, distributors, etc. When the state does not command such things, citizens must voluntarily cooperate to do them on their own. The power of association is the great power of a free economy. Through the principle of association, the free economy has proven its immense creativity in human history.

This same principle operates to meet the social needs which lie outside the marketplace. Countless libraries, schools, clinics, orphanages and other "non-profit" associations characterize the U.S. economy. No branch of the Church universal has generated so vast an array of such associations as the American Catholic Church. Indeed, more citizens in the U.S. derive their income from non-profit activities than from employment in the great industrial firms of the *Fortune 500.* Non-profit enterprises are of enormous importance to the welfare of U.S. citizens in every sphere; through education and in other ways, they contribute much to economic dynamism, too. In return, so fruitful is the U.S. "for profit" sector that it supports over 25 percent of the total civilian work force in non-profit activities, including both government and the private sector.

(2) *The Habit of Cooperation.* Much has been written about the free economy as a sphere of "competition." Indeed, it is so. The graveyard of defunct corporations and business enterprises is many times larger than the list of the living. New technologies regularly render industries based upon the old obsolete. The path of a free economy is marked, like that of God's creation itself, with what Schumpeter has called "creative destruction." The old dies, the new, nourished by the old, is constantly being born. Yet this law of competition is often cited polemically, in such fashion as to overlook the far more powerful and fundamental law of cooperation, which lies at the heart of every successful enterprise. Where human beings voluntarily associate themselves in a common task, their success or failure depends to a very large extent upon their capacities for instinctive, regular, and habitual cooperation with one another. An enterprise divided against itself cannot stand.

The Republic itself is witness to this principle. The principle is repeated, again and again, through all the miniature republics which compose it. Again, observing how different in this respect the New World was from the Old, Tocqueville remarked:

> Although private interest directs the greater part of human actions in the United States, as well as elsewhere, it does not regulate them all. I must say that I have often seen Americans make great and real sacrifices to the public welfare; and I have remarked a hundred instances in which they hardly ever failed to lend faithful support to each other. The free institutions which the inhabitants of the United States possess, and the political rights of which they make so much use, remind every citizen, and in a thousand ways, that he lives in society. They every instant impress upon his mind the

notion that it is the duty as well as the interest of men to make themselves useful to their fellow-creatures; and as he sees no particular ground of animosity to them, since he is never either their master or their slave, his heart readily leans to the side of kindness. Men attend to the interests of the public, first by necessity, afterwards by choice: what was intentional becomes an instinct; and by dint of working for the good of one's fellow-citizens, the habit and the taste for serving them is at length acquired.

Those of us with long experience in the business enterprise, large or small, have reason, over and over again, to be grateful for the cooperative habits of all those with whom we work, from the highest to the lowest. Without their mutual teamwork, no enterprise could function. We have also had reason to see how much damage can be done by failures in communication, by breakdowns in voluntary cooperation, by festering discontent, and even by a single unusually disruptive personality in a key position. The system works best by incentives, by the flowering of natural virtues, by candor and open communication, by a sense of dignity and belonging. Good managers and good workers are characteristically team players, caring individuals. Since most human beings, ourselves included, are not saints, we are well aware of daily failings in this regard. Moreover, in the real world, every sort of character must be accommodated. The rule is not sweetness and light, but tolerance of one another's sharp edges, quirks, drives, and manners. Often successful persons, whether "bosses" or workers, are prima donnas, irascible, temperamental, gruff, driving, difficult. Working with one another is not always pleasant, and sometimes those who are the most difficult to work with or under succeed, somehow, in drawing the best out of us, obliging us to perform at higher levels than anyone else ever has. Athletes under a variety of coaches know as much.

The principle, however, is intact: the more an enterprise exemplifies the qualities of a family or a team (families and teams, too, deal with us as we are, not in some idealistic way) the higher premium there is upon cooperation, to the benefit of productivity and the general sense of well-being.

Free institutions, while absorbing all the quirks of human nature, cannot survive a rupture in the spirit of cooperation. For they function, not by coercion, but by freely accepted mutual obligations, owed by one person to another. Lacking these, Americans properly complain, demand reforms in the way things are done, speak of injustice, and, in numbers unprecedented in any other world economy, leave one employment for another.

Every moral principle is made clear by failures and by abuses. Every firm, even the best, sometimes fails the test of the cooperative principle. Beyond doubt, however, Americans seek human satisfaction in their employment, and especially a sense of belonging and mutual cooperation—and they are right to do so. This is the principle by which both non-profit and profit-making enterprises are properly judged in America.

(3) *The Principle of Self-interest Rightly Understood.* In classical philosophy, well known to Tocqueville, many virtues (such as Aristotle's liberality, magnificence, and contemplation) seemed to be most attainable by those of noble station, who did not have to get their hands dirty. Tocqueville grasped clearly that, in the history of virtue, the American spirit had worked a decisive revolution of great importance to the future of the human race.

> I doubt whether men were more virtuous in aristocratic ages than in others; but they were incessantly talking of the beauties of virtue, and its utility was only studied in secret.

By contrast, Tocqueville observed, "the inhabitants of the United States almost always manage to combine their own advantage with that of their fellow citizens." The poor, he noted, were as apt to do so as the rich.

> In the United States hardly anybody talks of the beauty of virtue; but they maintain that virtue is useful, and prove it every day. The American moralists do not profess that men ought to sacrifice themselves for their fellow-creatures *because* it is noble to make such sacrifices; but they boldly aver that such sacrifices are as necessary to him who imposes them upon himself, as to him for whose sake they are made. . . . They therefore do not deny that every man may follow his own interest; but they endeavour to prove that it is the interest of every man to be virtuous.

Americans, too, follow "those disinterested and spontaneous impulses which are natural to man," but, even when they do,

Tocqueville notes, they try to show that both their self-interest and that of others have been served. This is an egalitarian conception of virtue, open to all, of every station. It is admirably conformed to human weaknesses, and yet "checks one personal interest by another," and thus directs the passions toward virtues crucial to the common good. The principle of interest rightly understood "suggests daily small acts of self-denial. By itself it cannot suffice to make a man virtuous, but it disciplines a number of citizens in habits of regularity, temperance, moderation, foresight, self-command; and, if it does not lead men straight to virtue by the will, it gradually draws them in that direction by their habits."

A free political economy does not discourage great acts of heroism and self-sacrifice; far from it. It encourages many to dream very great dreams, spiritual as well as temporal, transcendent as well as secular. But a free society is not constructed upon the belief that humans are angels. The sound daily working of its institutions depends upon the practice of common virtues accessible to all, conformed to common weaknesses, checking the worst excesses, and trying to inspire the common best. Such common virtues, hidden from view, often go unsung.

"Love your neighbor as yourself," the gospels instruct us. In this profound saying, a certain kind of self-love is used as the measure of the love of one's neighbor. In the divine ordering of love, St. Thomas Aquinas wrote, ". . . it is necessary that the affection of man be so inclined through charity that, first and foremost, each one loves God; secondly, that he love himself; and thirdly, that he love his neighbor. And among the fellow-men, he ought to give mutual help to those who are more closely united to him or who are more closely related to him." The American principle of self-interest rightly understood falls far short of the full message of the Gospels. It is appropriate to a commonwealth of sinners. While the Church has an obligation to encourage even heroic virtue, builders of political economy must be modest; hence, Tocqueville makes bold to conclude:

> I am not afraid to say, that the principle of interest rightly understood appears to me the best suited of all philosophical theories to the wants of the men of our time, and that I regard it as their chief

remaining security against themselves. Towards it, therefore, the minds of the moralists of our age should turn.

These days, American elites are often so critical of their own people and culture that some are certain to object: "Association and cooperation may have been visible in Tocqueville's time; today, heartlessness and anonymity prevail." Two sorts of facts tell against this objection.

First, immense progress in civil rights occurred, not in the nineteenth-century, but in our own. Group relations in twentieth-century America certainly meet higher standards of ecumenism, mutual respect, and integrated fellowship than in any previous period. Organizations for social purposes and associations of every sort thrive. It would be difficult, indeed, to show that Americans are less tolerant, less generous, or less cooperative in social action of every kind in the twentieth-century than a century ago.

Secondly, as Walter Lippmann pointed out in *The Great Society*, the new age of industrialization introduced a novel moral principle into economic relations. In prior ages, one part of society could gain only at the expense of others; capital investment and creativity changed the rules. "For the first time in human history," Lippmann wrote, human beings had constructed "a way of producing wealth in which the good fortune of others multiplied their own" and "the golden rule was economically sound." The production of wealth and the abolition of poverty moved in tandem. Poverty could no longer be regarded as the natural state of a majority but as an ever shrinking problem which could be overcome. Lippmann called this new vision "The Good Society":

> Until the division of labor had begun to make men dependent on the free collaboration of other men, the worldly policy was to be predatory. The claims of the spirit were otherworldly. So it was not until the industrial revolution had altered the traditional mode of life that the vista was opened at the end of which men could see the possibility of the Good Society on this earth. At long last the ancient schism between the world and the spirit, between self-interest and disinterestedness, was potentially closed.

Objectively, in the internal design of the system, and subjectively, in the rise of social awareness and compassion, the ancient dichotomy between self-interest and the common good has at the very least been diminished. To produce goods and services that make life better for others serves not only self-interest but the common good. And the perception has grown that it is in the self-interest of the affluent genuinely to help lift up the poor and the needy (but not to keep them in dependency). Self-interest rightly understood does not automatically serve the common good; but neither does it automatically undermine it. In that creative space, the ideal of economic development has attained moral and even religious significance. Its driving force does not depend on extraordinary altruism, but on far more ordinary and statistically more frequent motivations. This is not a weakness; it is a social strength. And the practice of virtue is institutionally unimpeded.

In summary, we believe that the new principles of political economy forged in the American experiment offer rich materials for critical reflection in Catholic social thought. Not by accident has the American political economy been fertile in promoting the practice of association, the habits of cooperation, and the habits of the heart guided by self-interest rightly understood—that self-interest which reaches out to embrace the interests of others, near and far. Religion takes no direct part in the government of society, but in encouraging such habits, as Tocqueville recognized, it is the foremost of the political institutions of the land. The generosity of the American people, praised by popes as early as Pius X and as recent as John Paul II, is not simply an aggregated sum of individual virtue; it is the recurrent fruit of institutions designed to promote social generosity. Where generosity of soul is lacking, Americans quickly feel that something in their common life is amiss. Typically, they bestir themselves to recover their original sources and to seek reform. The sources of these reforms lie in the institutions established by the Founding Fathers, "building wiser than they knew, the Almighty's hand guiding them."

Helen Vendler

Modern Language Association Presidential Address 1980

Even forms and substances are circumfused
By that transparent veil with light divine.
And, through the turnings intricate of verse.
Present themselves as objects recognized.
In flashes, and with glory not their own.
(*The Prelude* v.595–605)

* * *

Our students come to us from secondary chool having read no works of literature in foreign languages and scarcely any works of literature in their own language. The very years, between twelve and eighteen, when they might be reading rapidly, uncritically, rangingly, happily, thoughtlessly, are somehow dissipated without cumulative force. Those who end their education with secondary school have been cheated altogether of their literary inheritance from the Bible to Robert Lowell. It is no wonder that they do not love what we love; we as a culture have not taught them to. With a reformed curriculum beginning in preschool, all children would know about the Prodigal Son and the Minotaur; they would know the stories presumed by our literature, as children reading Lamb's *Tales from Shakespeare* or Hawthorne's *Tanglewood Tales* once knew them. We can surely tell them the tales before they can read Shakespeare or Ovid: there are literary forms appropriate to every age, even the youngest. Nothing is more lonely than to go through life uncompanioned by a sense that others have also gone through it, and have left a record of their experience. Every adult needs to be able to think of Job, or Orpheus, or Circe, or Ruth, or Lear, or Jesus, or the Golden Calf, or the Holy Grail, or Antigone in order to refer private experience to some identifying frame or solacing reflection.

I do not mean, by emphasizing the great tales of our inherited

Helen Vendler, "Presidential Address 1980," *PMLA* 96 (1981): pp. 349–50.

culture, to minimize the local and the ethnic. Literary imagination is incurably local. But it is against the indispensable background of the general literary culture that native authors assert their local imaginations. Our schools cannot afford to neglect either resource. Nor do I mean, by dwelling on the narrative content of literature, to ignore the difference between a retelling like Lamb's *Tales from Shakespeare* and Shakespeare himself. If we give our children the tales, in abridged or adapted form, it is because we hope they will then come to the real thing—the *Nibelungenlied* or the Gospels or Homer—with some sense of intimacy and delighted recognition, rather than with a sense of the unfamiliar and the daunting. And if they know the story in one form, a simple one, and meet it later in another, more complicated form, they are bound to be curious about the differences of linguistic embodiment: and there literary interest, and literary appreciation can begin.

It is not within our power to reform the primary and secondary schools, even if we have a sense of how that reform might begin. We do have it within our power, I believe, to reform ourselves, to make it our own first task to give, especially to our beginning students, that rich web of associations, lodged in the tales of majority and minority culture alike, by which they could begin to understand themselves as individuals and as social beings. We must give them some examples of literature, suited to their level of reading, in which these tales have an indisputably literary embodiment. All freshman English courses, to my mind, should devote at least half their time to the reading of myth, legend, and parable; and beginning language courses should do the same. We owe it to ourselves to teach what we love on our first, decisive encounter with our students and to insist that the freedom to write is based on a freedom of reading. Otherwise we misrepresent ourselves, and we deprive our students. Too often, they go away, disheartened by our implicit or explicit criticism of their speech and writing in English or in a foreign language: and we go away disheartened by our conviction that we have not in that first year engaged their hearts or their minds: and both parties never see each other again. And the public, instead of remembering how often, in later life, they have thought of the parable of the talents, or the loss of Eurydice, or the sacrifice of Isaac, or the patience of Penelope, or the fox and the grapes, or the minister's black veil, remember the humiliations of freshman English or long-lost drills in language laboratories. We owe it to ourselves to show our students, when they first meet us, what we are; we owe their dormant appetites, thwarted for so long in their previous schooling, that deep sustenance that will make them realize that they too, having been taught, love what we love.

WENDELL BERRY

The Unsettling of America

ON THE CLIFF

The question of human limits, of the proper definition and place of human beings within the order of Creation, finally rests upon our attitude toward our biological existence, the life of the body in this world. What value and respect do we give to our bodies? What uses do we have for them? What relation do we see, if any, between body and mind, or body and soul? What connections or responsibilities do we maintain between our bodies and the earth? These are religious questions, obviously, for our bodies are part of the Creation, and they involve us in all the issues of mystery. But the questions are also agricultural, for no matter how urban our life, our bodies live by farming; we come from the earth and return to it, and so we live in agriculture as we live in flesh. While we live our bodies are moving particles of the earth, joined inextricably both to the soil and to the bodies of other living creatures. It is hardly surprising, then, that there should be some profound resemblances between our treatment of our bodies and our treatment of the earth.

That humans are small within the Creation is an ancient perception, represented often enough in art that it must be supposed to have an elemental importance. On one of the painted walls of the Lascaux cave (20,000–15,000 B.C.), surrounded by the exquisitely shaped, shaded, and colored bodies of animals, there is the childish

Wendell Berry, excerpted from "The Body and the Earth," in *The Unsettling of America* (San Francisco: Sierra Club Books, 1977), pp. 97–102, 106–8, 110–12, 123–31.

stick figure of a man, a huntsman who, having cast his spear into the guts of a bison, is now weaponless and vulnerable, poignantly frail, exposed, and incomplete. The message seems essentially that of the voice out of the whirlwind in the Book of Job: the Creation is bounteous and mysterious, and humanity is only a part of it—not its equal, much less its master.

Old Chinese landscape paintings reveal, among towering mountains, the frail outline of a roof or a tiny human figure passing along a road on foot or horseback. These landscapes are almost always populated. There is no implication of a dehumanized interest in nature "for its own sake." What is represented is a world in which humans belong, but which does not belong to humans in any tidy economic sense; the Creation provides a place for humans, but it is greater than humanity and within it even great men are small. Such humility is the consequence of an accurate insight, ecological in its bearing, not a pious deference to "spiritual" value.

Closer to us is a passage from the fourth act of *King Lear,* describing the outlook from one of the Dover cliffs:

> The crows and choughs that wing the midway air
> Show scarce so gross as beetles. Halfway down
> Hangs one that gathers samphire, dreadful trade!
> Methinks he seems no bigger than his head.
> The fishermen that walk upon the beach
> Appear like mice, and yond tall anchoring bark
> Diminished to her cock—her cock, a buoy
> Almost too small for sight.

And this is no mere description of a scenic "view." It is part of a play-within-a-play, a sort of ritual of healing. In it Shakespeare is concerned with the curative power of the perception we are dealing with: by understanding accurately his proper place in Creation, a man may be made whole.

In the lines quoted, Edgar, disguised as a lunatic, a Bedlamite, is speaking to his father, the Earl of Gloucester. Gloucester, having been blinded by the treachery of his false son, Edmund, has despaired and has asked the supposed madman to lead him to the cliff's edge, where he intends to destroy himself. But Edgar's description is from memory: the two are not standing on any such dizzy verge. What we are witnessing is the working out of Edgar's strategy to save his father from false feeling—both the pride, the smug credulity, that led to his suffering and the despair that is its result. These emotions are perceived as madness; Gloucester's blindness is literally the result of the moral blindness of his pride, and it is symbolic of the spiritual blindness of his despair.

Thinking himself on the edge of a cliff, he renounces this world and throws himself down. Though he falls only to the level of his own feet, he is momentarily stunned. Edgar remains with him, but now represents himself as an innocent bystander at the foot of what Gloucester will continue to think is a tall cliff. As the old man recovers his senses, Edgar persuades him that the madman who led him to the cliff's edge was in reality a "fiend." And Gloucester repents his self-destructiveness, which he now recognizes as another kind of pride; a human has no right to destroy what he did not create:

> You ever-gentle gods, take my breath from me.
> Let not my worser spirit tempt me again
> To die before you please.

What Gloucester has passed through, then, is a rite of death and rebirth. In his new awakening he is finally able to recognize his true son. He escapes the unhuman conditions of godly pride and fiendish despair and dies "smilingly" in the truly human estate " 'Twixt two extremes of passion, joy and grief . . ."

Until modern times, we focused a great deal of the best of our thought upon such rituals of return to the human condition. Seeking enlightenment or the Promised Land or the way home, a man would go or be forced to go into the wilderness, measure himself against the Creation, recognize finally his true place within it, and thus be saved both from pride and from despair. Seeing himself as a tiny member of a world he cannot comprehend or master or in any final sense possess, he cannot possibly think of himself as a god. And by the same token, since he shares in, depends upon, and is graced by all of which he is a part, neither can be become a fiend; he cannot descend into the final despair of destructiveness. Returning from the wilderness, he becomes a restorer of order, a preserver. He sees the truth, recognizes his true heir, honors his forebears and his heritage, and gives his blessing to his successors. He embodies the passing of human time, living and dying within the human limits of grief and joy.

ON THE TOWER

Apparently with the rise of industry, we began to romanticize the wilderness—which is to say we began to institutionalize it within the concept of the "scenic." Because of railroads and improved highways, the wilderness was no longer an arduous passage for the traveler, but something to be looked at as grand or beautiful from the high vantages of the roadside. We became viewers of "views." And because we no longer traveled in the wilderness as a matter of course, we forgot that wilderness still circumscribed civilization and persisted in domesticity. We forgot, indeed, that the civilized and the domestic continued to *depend* upon wilderness—that is, upon natural forces within the climate and within the soil that have never in any meaningful sense been controlled or conquered. Modern civilization has been built largely in this forgetfulness.

And as we transformed the wilderness into scenery, we began to feel in the presence of "nature" an awe that was increasingly statistical. We would not become appreciators of the Creation until we had taken its measure. Once we had climbed or driven to the mountain top, we were awed by the view, but it was an awe that we felt compelled to validate or prove by the knowledge of how high we stood and how far we saw. We are invited to "see seven states from atop Lookout Mountain," as if our political boundaries had been drawn in red on the third morning of Creation.

We became less and less capable of sensing ourselves as small within Creation, partly because we thought we could comprehend it statistically, but also because we were becoming creators, ourselves, of a mechanical creation by which we felt ourselves greatly magnified. We built bridges that stood imposingly in titanic settings, towers that stood around us like geologic presences, single machines that could do the work of hundreds of people. Why, after all, should one get excited about a mountain when one can see almost as far from the top of a building, much farther from an airplane, farther still from a space capsule? We have learned to be fascinated by the statistics of magnitude and power. There is apparently no limit in sight, no end, and so it is no wonder that our minds, dizzy with numbers, take refuge in a yearning for infinitudes of energy and materials.

And yet these works that so magnify us also dwarf us, reduce us to insignificance. They magnify us because we are capable of them. They diminish us because, say what we will, once we build beyond a human scale, once we conceive ourselves as Titans or as gods, we are lost in magnitude: we cannot control or limit what we do. The statistics of magnitude call out like Sirens to the statistics of destruction. If we have built towering cities, we have raised even higher the cloud of megadeath. If people are as grass before God, they are as nothing before their machines.

If we are fascinated by the statistics of magnitude, we are no less fascinated by the statistics of our insignificance. We never tire of repeating the commonizing figures of population and population growth. We are entranced to think of ourselves as specks on the pages of our own overwhelming history. I remember that my high-school biology text dealt with the human body by listing its constituent elements, measuring their quantities, and giving their monetary worth—at that time a little less than a dollar. That was a bit of the typical fodder of the modern mind, at once sensational and belittling—no accidental product of the age of Dachau and Hiroshima.

In our time Shakespeare's cliff has become the tower of a bridge—not the scene of a wakening rite of symbolic death and rebirth, but of the real and final death of suicide. Hart Crane wrote its paradigm, as if against his will, in *The Bridge:*

> Out of some subway scuttle, cell or loft
> A bedlamite speeds to thy parapets,
> Tilting there momentarily, shrill shirt ballooning,
> A jest falls from the speechless caravan.

In Shakespeare, the real Bedlamite or madman is the desperate and suicidal Gloucester. The supposed Bedlamite is in reality his true son, and together they enact an eloquent ritual in which Edgar gives his father a vision of Creation. Gloucester abandons himself to this vision, literally casting himself into it, and is renewed; he finds his life by losing it. Gloucester is saved by a renewal of his sense of the world and of his proper place in it. And this is brought about by an enactment that is communal, both in the sense that he is accompanied in it by his son, who for the time being has assumed the disguise of a madman but the role of a priest, and in the sense that it is deeply traditional in its symbols and meanings. In Crane, on the other hand, the Bedlamite is alone, surrounded by speechlessness, cut off within the crowd from any saving or renewing vision. The height, which in Shakespeare is the traditional place of vision, has become in Crane a place of blindness; the bridge, which Crane intended as a unifying symbol, has become the symbol of a final estrangement.

* * *

COMPETITION

By dividing body and soul, we divide both from all else. We thus condemn ourselves to a loneliness for which the only compensation is violence—against other creatures, against the earth, against ourselves. For no matter the distinctions we draw between body and soul, body and earth, ourselves and others—the connections, the dependences, the identities remain. And so we fail to contain or control our violence. It gets loose. Though there are categories of violence, or so we think, there are no categories of victims. Violence against one is ultimately violence against all. The willingness to abuse other bodies is the willingness to abuse one's own. To damage the earth is to damage your children. To despise the ground is to despise its fruit; to despise the fruit is to despise its eaters. The wholeness of health is broken by despite.

If competition is the correct relation of creatures to one another and to the earth, then we must ask why exploitation is not more successful than it is. Why, having lived so long at the expense of other creatures and the earth, are we not healthier and happier than we are? Why does modern society exist under constant threat of the same suffering, deprivation, spite, contempt, and obliteration that it has imposed on other people and other creatures? Why do the health of the body and the health of the earth decline together? And why, in consideration of this decline of our worldly flesh and household, our "sinful earth," are we not healthier in spirit?

It is not necessary to have recourse to statistics to see that the human estate is declining with the estate of nature, and that the corruption of the body is the corruption of the soul. I know that the country is full of "leaders" and experts of various sorts who are using statistics to prove the opposite: that we have more cars, more superhighways, more TV sets, motorboats, prepared foods, etc., than any people ever had before—and are therefore better off than any people ever were before. I can see the burgeoning of this "consumer economy" and can appreciate some of its attractions and comforts. But that economy has an inside and an outside; from the outside there are other things to be seen.

I am writing this in the north-central part of Kentucky on a morning near the end of June. We have had rain for two days, hard rain during the last several hours. From where I sit I can see the Kentucky River swiftening and rising, the water already yellow with mud. I know that inside this city-oriented consumer economy there are many people who will never see this muddy rise and many who will see it without knowing what it means. I know also that there are many who will see it, and know what it means, and not care. If it lasts until the weekend there will be people who will find it as good as clear water for motorboating and waterskiing.

In the past several days I have seen some of the worst eroded corn fields that I have seen in this country in my life. This erosion is occurring on the cash-rented farms of farmers' widows and city farmers, absentee owners, the doctors and businessmen who buy a farm for the tax breaks or to have "a quiet place in the country" for the weekends. It is the direct result of economic and agricultural policy: it might be said to *be* an economic and agricultural policy. The signs of the "agridollar," big-business fantasy of the Butz mentality are all present: the absenteeism, the temporary and shallow interest of the land-renter, the row-cropping of slopes, the lack of rotation, the plowed-out waterways, the rows running up and down the hills. Looked at from the field's edge, this is ruin, criminal folly, moral idiocy. Looked at from Washington, D.C., from inside the "economy," it is called "free enterprise" and "full production."

And around me here, as everywhere else I have been in this country—in Nebraska, Iowa, Indiana, New York, New England, Tennessee—the farmland is in general decline: fields and whole farms abandoned, given up with their scars unmended, washing away under the weeds and bushes; fine land put to row crops year after year, without rest or rotation; buildings and fences going down; good houses standing empty, unpainted, their windows broken.

And it is clear to anyone who looks carefully at any crowd that we are wasting our bodies exactly as we are wasting our land. Our bodies are fat, weak, joyless, sickly, ugly, the virtual prey of the manufacturers of medicine and cosmetics. Our bodies have become marginal: they are growing useless like our "marginal" land because we have less and less use for them. After the games and idle flourishes of modern youth, we use them only as shipping cartons to transport our brains and our few employable muscles back and forth to work.

As for our spirits, they seem more and more to comfort themselves by buying things. No longer in need of the exalted drama of grief and joy, they feed now on little shocks of greed, scandal, and violence.

*   *   *

CONNECTIONS

I do not want to speak of unity misleadingly or too simply. Obvious distinctions can be made between body and soul, one body and other bodies, body and world, etc. But these things that appear to be distinct are nevertheless caught in a network of mutual dependence and influence that is the substantiation of their unity. Body, soul (or mind or spirit), community, and world are all susceptible to each other's influence, and they are all conductors of each other's influence. The body is damaged by the bewilderment of the spirit, and it conducts the influence of that bewilderment into the earth, the earth conducts it into the community, and so on. If a farmer fails to understand what health is, his farm becomes unhealthy; it produces unhealthy food, which damages the health of the community. But this is a network, a spherical network, by which each part is connected to every other part. The farmer is a part of the community, and so it is as impossible to say exactly where the trouble began as to say where it will end. The influences go backward and forward, up and down, round and round, compounding and branching as they go. All that is certain is that an error introduced anywhere in the network ramifies beyond the scope of prediction; consequences occur all over the place, and each consequence breeds further consequences. But it seems unlikely that an error can ramify endlessly. It spreads by way of the connections in the network, but sooner or later it must also begin to break them. We are talking, obviously, about a circulatory system, and a disease of a circulatory system tends first to impair circulation and then to stop it altogether.

Healing, on the other hand, complicates the system by opening and restoring connections among the various parts—in this way restoring the ultimate simplicity of their union. When all the parts of the body are working together, are under each other's influence, we say that it is whole; it is healthy. The same is true of the world, of which our bodies are parts. The parts are healthy insofar as they are joined harmoniously to the whole.

What the specialization of our age suggests, in one example after another, is not only that fragmentation is a disease, but that the diseases of the disconnected parts are similar or analogous to one another. Thus they memorialize their lost unity, their relation persisting in their disconnection. Any severance produces two wounds that are, among other things, the record of how the severed parts once fitted together.

The so-called identity crisis, for instance, is a disease that seems to have become prevalent after the disconnection of body and soul and the other piecemealings of the modern period. One's "identity" is apparently the immaterial part of one's being—also known as psyche, soul, spirit, self, mind, etc. The dividing of this principle from the body and from any particular worldly locality would seem reason enough for a crisis. Treatment, it might be thought, would logically consist in the restoration of these connections: the lost identity would find itself by recognizing physical landmarks, by connecting itself responsibly to practical circumstances; it would learn to stay put in the body to which it belongs and in the place to which preference or history or accident has brought it; it would, in short, find itself in finding its work. But "finding yourself," the pseudo-ritual by which the identity crisis is supposed to be resolved, makes use of no such immediate references. Leaving aside the obvious, and ancient, realities of doubt and self-doubt, as well as the authentic madness that is often the result of cultural disintegration, it seems likely that the identity crisis has become a sort of social myth, a genre of self-indulgence. It can be an excuse for irresponsibility or a fashionable mode of self-dramatization. It is the easiest form of self-flattery—a way to construe procrastination as a virtue—based on the romantic assumption that "who I really am" is better in some fundamental way than the available evidence proves.

The fashionable cure for this condition, if I understand the lore of it correctly, has nothing to do with the assumption of responsibilities or the renewal of connections. The cure is "autonomy," another mythical condition, suggesting that the self can be self-determining and independent without regard for any determining circumstance or any of the obvious dependences. This seems little more than a jargon term for indifference to the opinions and feelings of other people. There is, in practice, no such thing as autonomy. Practically, there is only a distinction between responsible and irresponsible dependence. Inevitably failing this impossible standard of autonomy, the modern self-seeker becomes a tourist of cures, submitting his quest to the guidance of one guru after another. The "cure" thus preserves the disease.

It is not surprising that this strange disease of the spirit—the self's search for the self—should have its counterpart in an anguish of the body. One of the commonplaces of modern experience is dissatisfaction with the body—not as one has allowed it to become, but as it naturally is. The hardship is perhaps greater here because the body, unlike the self, is substantial and cannot be supposed to be inherently better than it was born to be. It can only be thought inherently worse than it *ought* to be. For the appropriate standard for the body—that is, health—has been replaced, not even by another standard, but by very exclusive physical *models*. The concept of "model" here conforms very closely to the model of the scientists and planners: it is an exclusive, narrowly defined ideal which affects destructively whatever it does not include.

Thus our young people are offered the ideal of health only by what they know to be lip service. What they are made to feel forcibly, and to measure themselves by, is the exclusive desirability of a certain physical model. Girls are taught to want to be leggy, slender, large-breasted, curly-haired, unimposingly beautiful. Boys are instructed to be "athletic" in build, tall but not too tall, broad-shouldered, deep-chested, narrow-hipped, square-jawed, straight-nosed, not bald, unimposingly handsome. Both sexes should look what passes for "sexy" in a bathing suit. Neither, above all, should look old.

Though many people, in health, are beautiful, very few resemble these models. The result is widespread suffering that does immeasurable damage both to individual persons and to the society as a whole. The result is another absurd pseudo-ritual, "accepting one's body," which may take years or may be the distraction of a lifetime. Woe to the man who is short or skinny or bald. Woe to the man with a big nose. Woe, above all, to the woman with small breasts or a muscular body or strong features; Homer and Solomon might have thought her beautiful, but she will see her own beauty only by a difficult rebellion. And like the crisis of identity, this crisis of the body brings a helpless dependence on cures. One spends one's life dressing and "making up" to compensate for one's supposed deficiencies. Again, the cure preserves the disease. And the putative healer is the guru of style and beauty aid. The sufferer is by definition a customer.

* * *

HOME LAND AND HOUSE HOLD

What I have been trying to do is to define a pattern of disintegration that is at once cultural and agricultural. I have been groping for connections—that I think are indissoluble, though obscured by modern ambitions—between the spirit and the body, the body and other bodies, the body and the earth. If these connections do necessarily exist, as I believe they do, then it is impossible for material order to exist side by side with spiritual disorder, or vice versa, and impossible for one to thrive long at the expense of the other; it is impossible, ultimately, to preserve ourselves apart from our willingness to preserve other creatures, or to respect and care for ourselves except as we respect and care for other creatures; and, most to the point of this book, it is impossible to care for each other more or differently than we care for the earth.

This last statement becomes obvious enough when it is considered that the earth is what we all have in common, that it is what we are made of and what we live from, and that we therefore cannot damage it without damaging those with whom we share it. But I believe it goes farther and deeper than that. There is an uncanny *resemblance* between our behavior toward each other and our behavior toward the earth. Between our relation to our own sexuality and our relation to the reproductivity of the earth, for instance, the resemblance is plain and strong and apparently inescapable. By some connection that we do not recognize, the willingness to exploit one becomes the willingness to exploit the other. The conditions and the means of exploitation are likewise similar.

The modern failure of marriage that has so estranged the sexes from each other seems analogous to the "social mobility" that has estranged us from our land, and the two are historically parallel. It may even be argued that these two estrangements are very close to being one, both of them having been caused by the disintegration of the household, which was the formal bond between marriage and the earth, between human sexuality and its sources in the sexuality of Creation. The importance of this practical bond has not been often or very openly recognized in our tradition; in modern times it has almost disappeared under the burden of adverse fashion and economics. It is necessary to go far back to find it clearly exemplified.

To my mind, one of the best examples that we have is in Homer's *Odyssey*. Nowhere else that I know are the connections between marriage and household and the earth so fully and so carefully understood.

At the opening of the story Odysseus, after a twenty-year absence, is about to begin the last leg of his homeward journey. The sole survivor of all his company of warriors, having lived through terrible trials and losses, Odysseus is now a castaway on the island of the goddess Kalypso. He is Kalypso's lover but also virtually her prisoner. At night he sleeps with Kalypso in her cave; by day he looks across the sea toward Ithaka, his home, and weeps. Homer does not stint either feeling—the delights of Kalypso's cave, where the lovers "revel and rest softly, side by side," or the grief and longing of exile.

But now Zeus commands Kalypso to allow Odysseus to depart; she comes to tell him that he is free to go. And yet it is a tragic choice that she offers him: he must choose between her and Penélopê, his wife. If he chooses Kalypso, he will be immortal, but remain in exile: if he chooses Penélopê, he will return home at last, but will die in his time like other men:

> *If you could see it all, before you go—*
> *all the adversity you face at sea—*

> you would stay here, and guard this house, and be
> immortal—though you wanted her forever,
> that bride for whom you pine each day.
> Can I be less desirable than she is?
> Less interesting? Less beautiful? Can mortals
> compare with goddesses in grace and form?

And Odysseus answers:

> My quiet Penélopê—how well I know—
> would seem a shade before your majesty,
> death and old age being unknown to you,
> while she must die. Yet, it is true, each day
> I long for home . . .

This is, in effect, a wedding ritual much like our own, in which Odysseus forsakes all others, in renouncing the immortal womanhood of the goddess, and renews his pledge to the mortal terms of his marriage. But unlike our ritual, this one involves an explicit loyalty to a home. Odysseus' far-wandering through the wilderness of the sea is not merely the return of a husband; it is a journey home. And a great deal of the power as well as the moral complexity of *The Odyssey* rises out of the richness of its sense of home.

By the end of Book XXIII, it is clear that the action of the narrative, Odysseus' journey from the cave of Kalypso to the bed of Penélopê, has revealed a structure that is at once geographical and moral. This structure may be graphed as a series of diminishing circles centered on one of the posts of the marriage bed. Odysseus makes his way from the periphery toward that center.

All around, this structure verges on the sea, which is the wilderness, ruled by the forces of nature and by the gods. In spite of the excellence of his ship and crew and his skill in navigation, a man is alien there. Only when he steps ashore does he enter a human order. From the shoreline of his island of Ithaka, Odysseus makes his way across a succession of boundaries, enclosed and enclosing, with the concentricity of a blossom around its pistil, a human pattern resembling a pattern of nature. He comes to his island, to his own lands, to his town, to his household and house, to his bedroom, to his bed.

As he moves toward this center he moves also through a series of recognitions, tests of identity and devotion. By these, his home-coming becomes at the same time a restoration of order. At first, having been for a while uncertain of his whereabouts, he recognizes his homeland by the conformation of the countryside and by a certain olive tree. He then becomes the guest of his swineherd, Eumaios, and tests his loyalty, though Eumaios will not be permitted to recognize his master until the story approaches its crisis. In the house of Eumaios, Odysseus meets and makes himself known to his son, Telémakhos. As he comes, disguised as a beggar, into his own house, he is recognized by Argus, his old hunting dog. That night, as the guest of Penélopê, who does not yet know who he is, he is recognized by his aged nurse, Eurýkleia, who sees a well-remembered scar on his thigh as she is bathing his feet.

He is scorned and abused as a vagabond by the band of suitors who, believing him dead, have been courting his wife, consuming his meat and wine, desecrating his household, and plotting the murder of his son. Penélopê proposes a trial by which the suitors will compete for her: she will become the bride of whichever one can string the bow of her supposedly dead husband and shoot an arrow through the aligned helve-sockets of twelve axe heads. The suitors fail. Odysseus performs the feat easily and is thereby recognized as "the great husband" himself. And then, with the help of the swine-herd, the cowherd, and Telémakhos, he proceeds to trap the suitors and slaughter them all without mercy. To so distinguished a commentator as Richmond Lattimore, their punishment "seems excessive." But granting the acceptability of violent means to a warrior such as Odysseus, this outcome seems to me appropriate to the moral terms of the poem. It is made clear that the punishment is not merely the caprice of a human passion: Odysseus enacts the will of the gods; he is the agent of a divine judgment. The suitors' sin is their utter contempt for the domestic order that the poem affirms. They do not respect or honor the meaning of the household, and in *The Odyssey* this meaning is paramount.

It is therefore the recognition of Odysseus by Penélopê that is the most interesting and the most crucial. By the time Odysseus' vengeance and his purification of the house is complete, Penélopê is the only one in the household who has not acknowledged him. It is only reasonable that she should delay this until she is absolutely certain. After all, she has waited twenty years; it is not to be expected that she would be less than cautious now. Her faith has been equal and more than equal to his, and now she proves his equal also in cunning. She tells Eurýkleia to move their bed outside their bedroom and to make it up for Odysseus there. Odysseus' rage at hearing that identifies him beyond doubt, for she knew that only Odysseus would know—it is their "pact and pledge" and "secret sign"—that the bed could not be moved without destroying it. He built their bedroom with his own hands, and an old olive tree, as he says,

> grew like a pillar on the building plot,
> and I laid out our bedroom round that tree . . .
> . . . I lopped off the silvery leaves and branches,
> hewed and shaped that stump from the roots up
> into a bedpost . . .

She acknowledges him then, and only then does she give herself to his embrace.

> Now from his heart into his eyes the ache
> of longing mounted, and he wept at last,
> his dear wife, clear and faithful in his arms,
> longed for
> as the sunwarmed earth is longed for by a swimmer
> spent in rough water where his ship went down . . .

And so in the renewal of his marriage, the return of Odysseus and the restoration of order are complete. The order of the kingdom is centered on the marriage bed of the king and queen, and that bed is rooted in the earth. The figure last quoted makes explicit at last the long-hinted analogy between Odysseus' fidelity to his wife and his fidelity to his homeland. In Penélopê's welcoming embrace his two fidelities become one.

For Odysseus, then, marriage was not merely a legal bond, nor even merely a sacred bond, between himself and Penélopê. It was part of a complex practical circumstance involving, in addition to husband and wife, their family of both descendants and forebears, their household, their community, and the sources of all these lives in memory and tradition, in the countryside, and in the earth. These things, wedded together in his marriage, he thought of as his home, and it held his love and faith so strongly that sleeping with a goddess could not divert or console him in his exile.

In Odysseus' return, then, we see a complete marriage and a complete fidelity. To reduce marriage, as we have done, to a mere contract of sexual exclusiveness is at once to degrade it and to make it impossible. That is to take away its dignity and its potency of joy, and to make it only a pitiful little duty—not a union, but a division and a solitude.

The Odyssey's understanding of marriage as the vital link which joins the human community and the earth is obviously full of political implication. In this it will remind us of the Confucian principle that "The government of the state is rooted in family order." But *The Odyssey* goes further than the Confucian texts, it seems to me, in its understanding of agricultural value as the foundation of domestic order and peace.

I have considered the poem so far as describing a journey from the non-human order of the sea wilderness to the human order of the cleansed and reunited household. But it is also a journey between two kinds of human value; it moves from the battlefield of Troy to the terraced fields of Ithaka, which, through all the years and great deeds of Odysseus' absence, the peasants have not ceased to farm.

The Odyssey begins in the world of *The Iliad,* a world which, like our own, is war-obsessed, preoccupied with "manly" deeds of exploitation, anger, aggression, pillage, and the disorder, uprootedness, and vagabondage that are their result. At the end of the poem, Odysseus moves away from the values of that world toward the values of domesticity and peace. He restores order to his household by an awesome violence, it is true. But that finished and the house purified, he re-enters his marriage, the bedchamber and the marriage bed rooted in the earth. From there he goes into the fields.

The final recognition scene occurs between Odysseus and his old father, Laërtês:

> *Odysseus found his father in solitude*
> *spading the earth around a young fruit tree.*

> *He wore a tunic, patched and soiled, and leggings—*
> *oxhide patches, bound below his knees*
> *against the brambles . . .*

The point is not stated—the story is moving so evenly now toward its conclusion that it will not trouble to remind us that the man thus dressed is a *king*—but it is clear that Laërtês has survived his son's absence and the consequent grief and disorder *as a peasant*. Although Odysseus jokes about his father's appearance, the appropriateness of what he is doing is never questioned. In a time of disorder he has returned to the care of the earth, the foundation of life and hope. And Odysseus finds him in an act emblematic of the best and most responsible kind of agriculture: an old man caring for a young tree.

But the homecoming of Odysseus is still not complete. During his wanderings, he was instructed by the ghost of the seer Teirêsias to perform what is apparently to be a ritual of atonement. As the poem ends he still has this before him. Carrying an oar on his shoulder, he must walk inland until he comes to a place where men have no knowledge of the sea or ships, where a passerby will mistake his oar for a winnowing fan. There he must "plant" his oar in the ground and make a sacrifice to the sea god, Poseidon. Home again, he must sacrifice to all the gods. Like those people of the Biblical prophecy who will "beat their swords into plowshares, and their spears into pruning hooks" and not "learn war any more," Odysseus will not know rest until he has carried the instrument of his sea wanderings inland and planted it like a tree, until he has seen the symbol of his warrior life as a farming tool. But after his atonement has been made, a gentle death will come to him when he is weary with age, his countrymen around him "in blessed peace."

The Odyssey, then, is in a sense an anti-*Iliad*, posing against the warrior values of the other epic—the glories of battle and foreign adventuring—an affirmation of the values of domesticity and farming. But at the same time *The Odyssey* is too bountiful and wise to set these two kinds of value against each other in any purity or exclusiveness of opposition. Even less does it set into such opposition the two kinds of experience. The point seems to be that these apparently opposed experiences are linked together. The higher value may be given to domesticity, but this cannot be valued or understood alone. Odysseus' fidelity and his homecoming are as moving and instructive as they are precisely because they are the result of *choice*. We know—as Odysseus undoubtedly does also—the extent of his love for Penélopê because he can return to her only by choosing her, at the price of death, over Kalypso. We feel and understand, with Odysseus, the value of Ithaka as a homeland, because bound inextricably to the experience of his return is the memory of his absence, of his long wandering at sea, and even of the excitement of his adventures. The prophecy of the peaceful death that is to come to him is so deeply touching because the poem has so fully realized the experiences of discord and violent death. The farm life of the island seems so sweet and orderly because we know the dark wilderness of natural force and mystery within which they are cleared and lighted.

THE NECESSITY OF WILDNESS

Domestic order is obviously threatened by the margin of wilderness that surrounds it. Marriage may be destroyed by instinctive sexuality; the husband may choose to remain with Kalypso or the wife may run away with godlike Paris. And the forest is always waiting to overrun the fields. These are real possibilities. They must be considered, respected, even feared.

And yet I think that no culture that hopes to endure can afford to destroy them or to set up absolute safeguards against them. Invariably the failure of organized religions, by which they cut themselves off from mystery and therefore from the sacred, lies in the attempt to impose an absolute division between faith and doubt, to make belief perform as knowledge; when they forbid their prophets to go into the wilderness, they lose the possibility of renewal. And the most dangerous tendency in modern society, now rapidly emerging as a scientific-industrial ambition, is the tendency toward encapsulation of human order—the severance, once and for all, of the umbilical cord fastening us to the wilderness or the Creation. The threat is not only in the totalitarian desire for absolute control. It lies in the willingness to ignore an essential paradox: the natural forces that so threaten us are the same forces that preserve and renew us.

An enduring agriculture must never cease to consider and respect and preserve wildness. The farm can exist only within the wilderness of mystery and natural force. And if the farm is to last and remain in health, the wilderness must survive within the farm. That is what agricultural fertility *is:* the survival of natural process in the human order. To learn to preserve the fertility of the farm, Sir Albert Howard wrote, we must study the forest.

Similarly, the instinctive sexuality within which marriage exists must somehow be made to thrive within marriage. To divide one from the other is to degrade both and ultimately to destroy marriage.

Fidelity to human order, then, if it is fully responsible, implies fidelity also to natural order. Fidelity to human order makes devotion possible. Fidelity to natural order preserves the possibility of choice, the possibility of the renewal of devotion. Where there is no possibility of choice, there is no possibility of faith. One who returns home—to one's marriage and household and place in the world—desiring anew what was previously chosen, is neither the world's stranger nor its prisoner, but is at once in place and free.

The relation between these two fidelities, inasmuch as they sometimes appear to contradict one another, cannot help but be complex and tricky. In our present stage of cultural evolution, it cannot help but be baffling as well. And yet it is only the double faith that is adequate to our need. If we are to have a culture as resilient and competent in the face of necessity as it needs to be, then it must somehow involve within itself a ceremonious generosity toward the wilderness of natural force and instinct. The farm must yield a place to the forest, not as a wood lot, or even as a necessary agricultural principle, but as a sacred grove—a place where the Creation is let alone, to serve as instruction, example, refuge; a place for people to go, free of work and presumption, to let themselves alone. And marriage must recognize that it survives because of, as well as in spite of, Kalypso and Paris and the generosity of instinct that they represent. It must give some ceremonially acknowledged place to the sexual energies that now thrive outside all established forms, in the destructive freedom of moral ignorance or disregard. Without these accommodations we will remain divided: some of us will continue to destroy the world for purely human ends, while others, for the sake of nature, will abandon the task of human order.

What forms or revisions of forms may be adequate to this double faith, I do not know. Cultural solutions are organisms, not machines, and they cannot be invented deliberately or imposed by prescription. Perhaps all that one can do is to clarify as well as possible the needs and pressures that bear upon the process of cultural evolution. I am certain, however, that no satisfactory solution can come from considering marriage alone or agriculture alone. These are our basic connections to each other and to the earth, and they tend to relate analogically and to be reciprocally defining: our demands upon the earth are determined by our ways of living with one another: our regard for one another is brought to light in our ways of using the earth. And I am certain that neither can be changed for the better in the experimental, prescriptive ways we have been using. Ways of life change only in living. To live by expert advice is to abandon one's life.

COPYRIGHT ACKNOWLEDGMENTS

About the Editors

ROBERT BELLAH is Elliott Professor of Sociology, University of California, Berkeley, and author of several books, including *The New Religious Consciousness* (with Charles Y. Glock). RICHARD MADSEN is Professor of Sociology, University of California, San Diego, and his most recent book is *Morality and Power in a Chinese Village.* WILLIAM SULLIVAN is Professor of Philosophy, La Salle University, Philadelphia, and the author of *Reconstructing Public Philosophy.* ANN SWIDLER is Associate Professor of Sociology, University of California at Berkeley, and the author of *Organization Without Authority: Dilemmas of Social Control in Free Schools.* STEVEN TIPTON is Associate Professor, Candler School of Theology of Emory University. He is the author of *Getting Saved from the Sixties: Moral Meaning in Conversion and Cultural Change.*